D1447934

CompTIA Server+ Certification

Student Manual

2009 Edition

CompTIA Server+ Certification, 2009 Edition

President, Axzo Press:	Jon Winder
Vice President, Product Development:	Charles G. Blum
Vice President, Operations:	Josh Pincus
Director of Publishing Systems Development:	Dan Quackenbush
Developmental Editors:	Andy LaPage, Tim Poulsen, Judi Kling
Copyeditor:	Catherine Oliver
Keytester:	Cliff Coryea

COPYRIGHT © 2010 Axzo Press. All rights reserved.

No part of this work may be reproduced, transcribed, or used in any form or by any means—graphic, electronic, or mechanical, including photocopying, recording, taping, Web distribution, or information storage and retrieval systems—without the prior written permission of the publisher.

For more information, go to www.axzopress.com.

Trademarks

ILT Series is a trademark of Axzo Press.

Some of the product names and company names used in this book have been used for identification purposes only and may be trademarks or registered trademarks of their respective manufacturers and sellers.

Disclaimers

We reserve the right to revise this publication and make changes from time to time in its content without notice.

The logo of the CompTIA Authorized Quality Curriculum (CAQC) program and the status of this or other training material as "Authorized" under the CompTIA Authorized Quality Curriculum program signifies that, in CompTIA's opinion, such training material covers the content of CompTIA's related certification exam.

The contents of this training material were created for the CompTIA Server+ exam, 2009 Edition (SK0-003), covering CompTIA certification objectives that were current as of March 2010.

ISBN 10: 1-4260-1905-X
ISBN 13: 978-1-4260-1905-0

Printed in the United States of America

4 5 6 7 8 9 10 GL 13 12 11

Contents

Introduction

After reading this introduction, you will know how to:

A Use ILT Series manuals in general.

B Use prerequisites, a target student description, course objectives, and a skills inventory to properly set your expectations for the course.

C Re-key this course after class.

Topic A: About the manual

ILT Series philosophy

Our manuals facilitate your learning by providing structured interaction with the software itself. While we provide text to explain difficult concepts, the hands-on activities are the focus of our courses. By paying close attention as your instructor leads you through these activities, you will learn the skills and concepts effectively.

We believe strongly in the instructor-led class. During class, focus on your instructor. Our manuals are designed and written to facilitate your interaction with your instructor, and not to call attention to manuals themselves.

We believe in the basic approach of setting expectations, delivering instruction, and providing summary and review afterwards. For this reason, lessons begin with objectives and end with summaries. We also provide overall course objectives and a course summary to provide both an introduction to and closure on the entire course.

Manual components

The manuals contain these major components:

- Table of contents
- Introduction
- Units
- Appendices
- Course summary
- Glossary
- Index

Each element is described below.

Table of contents

The table of contents acts as a learning roadmap.

Introduction

The introduction contains information about our training philosophy and our manual components, features, and conventions. It contains target student, prerequisite, objective, and setup information for the specific course.

Units

Units are the largest structural component of the course content. A unit begins with a title page that lists objectives for each major subdivision, or topic, within the unit. Within each topic, conceptual and explanatory information alternates with hands-on activities. Units conclude with a summary comprising one paragraph for each topic, and an independent practice activity that gives you an opportunity to practice the skills you've learned.

The conceptual information takes the form of text paragraphs, exhibits, lists, and tables. The activities are structured in two columns, one telling you what to do, the other providing explanations, descriptions, and graphics.

Appendices

An appendix is similar to a unit in that it contains objectives and conceptual explanations. However, an appendix does not include hands-on activities, a summary, or an independent practice activity.

Course summary

This section provides a text summary of the entire course. It is useful for providing closure at the end of the course. The course summary also indicates the next course in this series, if there is one, and lists additional resources you might find useful as you continue to learn about the software.

Glossary

The glossary provides definitions for all of the key terms used in this course.

Index

The index at the end of this manual makes it easy for you to find information about a particular software component, feature, or concept.

Manual conventions

We've tried to keep the number of elements and the types of formatting to a minimum in the manuals. This aids in clarity and makes the manuals more classically elegant looking. But there are some conventions and icons you should know about.

Item	Description
Italic text	In conceptual text, indicates a new term or feature.
Bold text	In unit summaries, indicates a key term or concept. In an independent practice activity, indicates an explicit item that you select, choose, or type.
`Code font`	Indicates code or syntax.
`Longer strings of ▶ code will look ▶ like this.`	In the hands-on activities, any code that's too long to fit on a single line is divided into segments by one or more continuation characters (▶). This code should be entered as a continuous string of text.
Select **bold item**	In the left column of hands-on activities, bold sans-serif text indicates an explicit item that you select, choose, or type.
Keycaps like (↵ ENTER)	Indicate a key on the keyboard you must press.

Hands-on activities

The hands-on activities are the most important parts of our manuals. They are divided into two primary columns. The "Here's how" column gives short instructions to you about what to do. The "Here's why" column provides explanations, graphics, and clarifications. Here's a sample:

Do it!

A-1: Creating a commission formula

Here's how	Here's why
1 Open Sales	This is an oversimplified sales compensation worksheet. It shows sales totals, commissions, and incentives for five sales reps.
2 Observe the contents of cell F4	F4 ▼ = =E4*C_Rate
	The commission rate formulas use the name "C_Rate" instead of a value for the commission rate.

For these activities, we have provided a collection of data files designed to help you learn each skill in a real-world business context. As you work through the activities, you will modify and update these files. Of course, you might make a mistake and therefore want to re-key the activity starting from scratch. To make it easy to start over, you will rename each data file at the end of the first activity in which the file is modified. Our convention for renaming files is to add the word "My" to the beginning of the file name. In the above activity, for example, a file called "Sales" is being used for the first time. At the end of this activity, you would save the file as "My sales," thus leaving the "Sales" file unchanged. If you make a mistake, you can start over using the original "Sales" file.

In some activities, however, it might not be practical to rename the data file. If you want to retry one of these activities, ask your instructor for a fresh copy of the original data file.

Topic B: Setting your expectations

Properly setting your expectations is essential to your success. This topic will help you do that by providing:

- Prerequisites for this course
- A description of the target student
- A list of the objectives for the course
- A skills assessment for the course

Course prerequisites

Before taking this course, you should be familiar with personal computers and the use of a keyboard and a mouse. Furthermore, this course assumes that you've completed the following courses or have equivalent experience:

- *CompTIA® A+ Certification*

Target student

This course will prepare you for the CompTIA® Server+ certification exam (2009 objectives). It is designed for students seeking foundation-level server administration skills and knowledge. The associated exam is targeted toward individuals with 18–24 months of IT experience. If you meet these descriptions or have earned your A+ certification, you will be well placed for this course.

Course objectives

These overall course objectives will give you an idea about what to expect from the course. It is also possible that they will help you see that this course is not the right one for you. If you think you either lack the prerequisite knowledge or already know most of the subject matter to be covered, you should let your instructor know that you think you are misplaced in the class.

After completing this course, you will know how to:

- Describe server-related form factors, power supplies, and cooling systems.
- Identify various motherboards and CPUs.
- Configure the PC's BIOS and boot the computer.
- Identify various types of memory.
- Describe various troubleshooting methodologies.
- Install expansion cards.
- Install data storage devices.
- Install a network operating system.
- Identify network components and valid network addresses, and troubleshoot basic network connectivity problems.
- Monitor and manage the Windows operating system.
- Document the IT environment, plan and implement change, and manage physical security.
- Prepare for disaster through backups, redundancy, and planning.

How to become CompTIA certified

To achieve CompTIA Server+ certification, you must register for and pass the CompTIA Server+ (2009 Edition) exam.

In order to become CompTIA certified, you must:

1   Select a certification exam provider. For more information, students should visit http://www.comptia.org/certifications/testprep.aspx.

2   Register for and schedule a time to take the CompTIA certification exam(s) at a convenient location.

3   Read and sign the Candidate Agreement, which will be presented at the time of the exam. The complete text of the Candidate Agreement can be found at http://www.comptia.org/certifications/policies/agreement.aspx.

4   Take and pass the CompTIA certification exam(s).

For more information about CompTIA's certifications, such as its industry acceptance, benefits, or program news, students should visit http://www.comptia.org/certifications.aspx.

CompTIA is a not-for-profit information technology (IT) trade association. CompTIA's certifications are designed by subject matter experts from across the IT industry. Each CompTIA certification is vendor-neutral, covers multiple technologies, and requires demonstration of skills and knowledge widely sought after by the IT industry.

To contact CompTIA with any questions or comments, please call (630) 678-8300 or e-mail questions@comptia.org.

Skills inventory

Use the following form to gauge your skill level entering the class. For each skill listed, rate your familiarity from 1 to 5, with five being the most familiar. *This is not a test.* Rather, it is intended to provide you with an idea of where you're starting from at the beginning of class. If you're wholly unfamiliar with all the skills, you might not be ready for the class. If you think you already understand all of the skills, you might need to move on to the next course in the series. In either case, you should let your instructor know as soon as possible.

Skill	1	2	3	4	5
Describing the dimensions associated with rack units (1U, 2U, and so forth)					
Identifying power connectors, power supply characteristics, and suitable power conditions for a server environment					
Selecting appropriate computer, rack, and row cooling solutions					
Identifying electrostatic discharge and following ESD safe practices while working with computer components					
Describing the purpose and features of PC power supplies					
Describing the function and features of CPUs, identifying a CPU, and classifying CPUs according to their specifications					
Describing motherboards, their components, and their form factors					
Accessing the BIOS setup utility, modifying hardware configuration values, and researching BIOS updates					
Explaining the POST and boot processes					
Describing the function of memory and differentiating among various types of memory chips					
Differentiating among the various memory packages					
Describing the primary types of buses, and defining the terms interrupt, IRQ, I/O address, DMA, and base memory address					
Describing the features and functions of the PCI bus					
Defining the common drive interfaces					
Identifying and connecting USB ports, cables, and connectors					
Identifying and connecting FireWire ports, cables, and connectors					
Identifying and connecting multimedia ports					
Describing hard drives, partitions, and file systems					

Skill	1	2	3	4	5
Describing optical data storage and using optical drives and discs					
Using removable drives					
Maintaining hard disks					
Identifying operating system problems					
Examining proper methods for disposing of computer equipment					
Backing up your computer					
Interpreting common hardware-related symptoms and their causes					
Describing troubleshooting models and problem-tracking systems					
Identifying characteristics of various network technologies					
Describing the functions of the protocols in the TCP/IP protocol suite					
Configuring TCP/IP					
Comparing wired network connections					
Describing how various types of addresses are used to identify devices on a network					
Troubleshooting common network-related problems and their causes					
Monitoring system performance					
Managing the operating system via SNMP, WBEM, and WMI					
Describing networking models					
Identifying the basic components of a network					
Explaining server roles					
Exploring the purposes and application of virtualization					
Investigating storage virtualization					
Considering the security implications of virtualization					
Evaluating virtualization best practices					
Exploring Linux distributions					
Installing Linux					

Skill	1	2	3	4	5
Logging onto Debian					
Installing Windows Server 2008					
Configuring computer information					
Configuring Windows Update					
Searching for Windows updates					
Customizing a Windows Server installation					
Discussing malware protection software					
Implementing various server access methods					

Topic C: Re-keying the course

If you have the proper hardware and software, you can re-key this course after class. This section explains what you'll need in order to do so, and how to do it.

Your lab station will need at least one server computer. You will need an additional Linux-compatible computer so you can install Linux during Unit 8 ("Installing a network operating system").

Lab station servers should have:

- A keyboard and a mouse
- At least 1 GHz 32-bit or 1.4 GHz 64-bit processor (2 GHz or faster recommended)
- At least 1 GB RAM (2 GB or greater recommended)
- At least 50 GB hard drive
- A DVD-ROM drive
- SVGA monitor at 1024×768 or higher
- A KVM switch and necessary cabling to complete Activity D-7 ("Implementing server access methods") in Unit 8 ("Installing a network operating system").

Software requirements

You will need the following software:

- Windows Server 2008 Standard
- Debian 5.0 (Lenny); newer versions will probably work, but the Linux installation activity in Unit 8 might not key exactly as written.

Network requirements

The following network components and connectivity are also required for this course:

- Internet access, for the following purposes:
  - Downloading the latest critical updates and service packs from www.windowsupdate.com
  - Completing activities within the units.
  - Downloading the Student Data files from www.axzopress.com (if necessary)
- The lab computer needs to be connected through TCP/IP and must receive IP addressing information from a DHCP server.

Setup instructions to re-key the course

Before you re-key the course, you will need to perform the following steps.

1 Install Windows Server 2008 Standard Edition on your server computer.

   a Select the appropriate language, time and currency, and keyboard or input method for your location.

   b Select Windows Server 2008 Standard Edition (Full Installation).

   c Accept the license terms.

   d Click Custom, and create at least a 40 GB partition.

   e When prompted to change the user's password, click OK. For the Administrator account, enter and confirm a password of **!pass1234**. Press Enter and click OK.

   f If prompted to install drivers, install them now.

2 Use the Initial Configuration Tasks window to configure the following settings.

   a Set the time zone appropriate for your location.

   b Configure networking so the server has dynamic IP addressing information from a DHCP server (including default gateway and DNS server address) and can connect to the Internet. Internet connectivity is required throughout the course.

   c Name the computer **WINSRV01**. Leave the computer in the default workgroup named WORKGROUP. Restart the computer when prompted.

   d Log back on as Administrator with the password !pass1234. In the Initial Configuration Tasks window, select "Do not show this window at logon," and click Close.

3 Open Device Manager and ensure that all devices were installed. Install any additional drivers, if necessary.

4 In Server Manager, in the details pane, click Configure IE ESC. Turn off ESC for both administrators and users. Click OK.

Setting up troubleshooting activities

Some of the units contain a troubleshooting activity. In these activities, you are asked to solve problems related to the material of that unit. Your course instructor was provided directions on strategies for preparing for these troubleshooting activities.

When re-keying this course, you will need to either skip these troubleshooting activities or ask a co-worker or friend to introduce topic-appropriate problems into your computer environment. The following sections provide some ideas.

Unit 5: Troubleshooting methodology

For the Topic C activity entitled "Troubleshooting power supply problems," you can implement one or more of these problems:

- Unplug the computer from the wall outlet.
- Plug the computer into a non-functioning UPS device or surge protector.
- Disconnect the power supply from the motherboard.
- Disconnect the hard disk from the power supply.
- Replace the power supply with a non-functioning power supply.

For the Topic C activity entitled "Troubleshooting problems with system startup," you can implement one or more of these problems:

- Switch the keyboard and mouse cables so that each one is plugged into the other's port.
- Substitute a keyboard with a stuck key or some other defect that would cause the POST to fail.
- Replace the CMOS battery with a dead battery, or simply remove the battery from the motherboard.
- Reset one or more BIOS setup values that would leave the computer unbootable or unusable. For example, change the boot drive order, disable the hard drive controller (if it's the boot device), or configure the on-board video controller to an extremely low-resolution display.
- Install a defective memory module so that the POST fails when it tests memory.
- (Advanced) Flash the BIOS with an incorrect or outdated version.

For the Topic C activity entitled "Troubleshooting memory," you can implement one or more of these problems:

- Replace one or more memory modules with a defective memory module.
- Loosen a module in its socket so that its pins don't make proper connections.
- Reconfigure the BIOS with an incorrect quantity of memory.
- Install the incorrect type of module for the computer—install modules that are too slow, implement parity when the motherboard doesn't, or don't implement parity when the motherboard does, and so forth.
- Install modules of different size or speed within a single bank.
- Remove one of the modules from a bank.

Unit 9: Networking

For the Topic C activity entitled "Troubleshooting network problems," you can implement one or more of these problems:

- Disconnect or loosely connect the network cable on either the NIC end or the hub end of the connection.
- Change the IP address to an invalid address for the network.
- Change the subnet mask to one that is invalid for the network.
- Replace the network cable with a crossover Ethernet cable.
- Replace the network cable with a broken network cable.
- Disable the network card in the system's BIOS.
- Install the wrong driver for the network card.
- Replace the NIC with a non-working NIC.
- Configure the DHCP server to hand out invalid IP addresses, an invalid gateway address, or an invalid DNS server address.
- Disconnect or disable the connection between the classroom network and the Internet.
- Create a local routing table with invalid routing information for the default gateway or a specific host.

CertBlaster software

CertBlaster pre- and post-assessment software is available for this course. To download and install this free software, students should complete the following steps:

1   Go to www.axzopress.com.

2   Under Downloads, click CertBlaster.

3   Click the link for CompTIA Server+ 2009

4   Save the .EXE file to a folder on your hard drive. (**Note:** If you skip this step, the CertBlaster software will not install correctly.)

5   Click Start and choose Run.

6   Click Browse and then navigate to the folder that contains the .EXE file.

7   Select the .EXE file and click Open.

8   Click OK and follow the on-screen instructions. When prompted for the password, enter **c_srv+09**

Unit 1

Deploying the chassis

Unit time: 90 minutes

Complete this unit, and you'll know how to:

A Describe the form and features of typical cases and racks.

B Identify power connectors, power supply characteristics, and the features needed to provide proper power in a server environment.

C Identify and select appropriate cooling systems for standalone and rack-mounted server systems.

Topic A: Form factors

This topic covers the following CompTIA Server+ (2009 Edition) exam objective.

#	Objective
1.2	**Deploy different chassis types and the appropriate components** • Form factor – Space utilization (U size, height, width, depth) • Redundant power • Shutoff switches; chassis intrusion • Power buttons • Reset buttons • Diagnostic LEDs • Expansion bays

Client form factors

Explanation

Computer cases enclose a computer's components. The various classes of computers—clients, servers, notebooks—use different types of cases, though types overlap classes. The following table describes the common form factors for client computer cases.

Form factor	Description
Desktop	Once the most popular form factor, but rare today. The case was designed to lie horizontally on a desk, with the monitor sitting atop it. Floppy and CD drives were mounted horizontally so they would work correctly in a case in this orientation.
Tower	An upright version of the desktop case (it stands vertically, rather than horizontally). It's designed to sit on the floor or on a shelf. Drives and other components are mounted such that they're horizontal in the tower. Dimensions are in the range of 20" tall by 8" wide by 18" deep or larger.
Mid-tower	A smaller version of the tower case. Dimensions are in the range of 18" tall by 8" wide by 18" deep.
Mini-tower	A still smaller version of the tower case. Dimensions are in the range of 16" tall by 8" wide by 16" deep or smaller.
Brick (or cube)	A small case, more cube-shaped than a typical tower case. This case style was introduced many years ago, but is regaining favor among some users and manufacturers. Dimensions are in the range of 8" tall by 12" wide by 8" deep or smaller.
Laptop or notebook	A self-contained portable computer. All of the core hardware components—monitor, keyboard, hard drive—are integrated into the unit. Additional peripherals are connected via expansion ports or installed into mounting bays. A distinction used to be made between laptops and notebooks, with the latter being the smaller form factor.

Server form factors

Many servers use the form factors described in the preceding table: tower and mid-tower form factors, for example, are commonly used by servers. A rack-mounted computer is an example of a server that uses a very different form factor.

Computer racks

A computer rack is a standardized mounting unit for computing devices, such as servers, routers, internetworking devices, fans, and so forth. Standard racks, as defined by the EIA-310 specification, are 19" wide (23" wide racks are used in some telecommunications applications). This measurement is made from the outsides of the two mounting rails, which are 0.625" wide each. This makes for a 17.75" separation between rails, and 18.3" between the centers of the mounting holes.

Exhibit 1-1: A typical computer rack (photo by David Lippincott for Chassis Plans)

The depth of racks varies. Commonly, the distance between the front and back sets of rails is either 31.5 or 39.4 inches. (Some racks don't provide back rails and are described as two-rail racks.) The overall outside dimensions of a rack are larger and vary by manufacturer and style. The extra width or depth provides space for air flow (for cooling) and for chases for running wires and cables. A column of electrical outlets is typically mounted along the inside of the back of the rack.

Rack units

As shown in Exhibit 1-2, mounting holes are provided in groups of three, spaced 0.625" on center, with a space of 0.5" between groups. This arrangement leads to standard *rack units*, which are measures of vertical height. One rack unit (1U) is 1.75", which is the distance between three-hole groups. The common U sizes are shown in the following diagram.

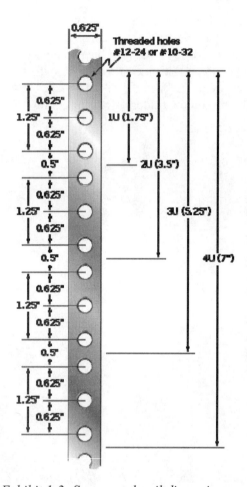

Exhibit 1-2: Server-rack rail dimensions and their correspondence to U size

Server manufacturers normally design their servers to occupy whole-number U spaces. Thus, you will see devices described as 1U, 2U, and so forth. Rarely, you will encounter devices that occupy a fractional size, such as 1.5U. Most servers are 1U or 2U.

Do it!

A-1: Comparing form factors

Questions	Answers
1 What form factor is your PC's case?	
2 If your instructor has cases of other form factors available, compare those with your case	
3 What are the advantages of standardizing the U height?	
4 In your opinion or experience, must rack-mounted devices fill the depth of the rack and mount to the back rails?	

Electrical and static safety

Explanation
Electricity can be dangerous. If you don't follow proper safety precautions, electricity can kill you. Current, not voltage, is what causes the danger. Even a small amount of current passing through your heart can be sufficient to cause ventricular fibrillation or stop your heart entirely. A dangerous level of current is possible even with low voltage sources, such as a 9 V battery.

The 1-10-100 rule

The 1-10-100 rule states that you can feel 1 mA (1 milliamp, or 1/1000 amp) of current through your body; 10 mA is sufficient to make your muscles contract to the point where you can't let go of a power source; and 100 mA is sufficient to stop your heart. This is a rule you should learn and respect.

Safety precautions

You should always follow common-sense safety precautions to avoid electric shock. These precautions include the following:

- Don't touch exposed electrical contacts with any part of your skin.
- Touch only insulated handles and parts of tools, probes, cords, etc.
- Leave covers on equipment unless you need to access their internal components.
- Work one-handed. If you use only one hand, electricity is less likely to flow through your body (specifically, your heart or head) and cause injury or death.
- Never insert anything into a wall outlet other than a power cord.
- Remove jewelry and watches when working around electricity. Rings, watches, and jewelry can cause unintended contact with electrified components. Furthermore, these metallic items can increase the surface area that's in contact with an electrical source and thus lower your body's resistance.
- Keep your hands clean and dry.
- Don't work with electricity in wet surroundings, especially on wet floors.

Static electricity

Static electricity is the buildup of an electrical charge on the surfaces of objects. Static electricity can dissipate harmlessly to ground if a suitable path is provided. Often, static is discharged quickly when objects having different electrical charges are brought into contact or simply near enough to each other.

To feel a static shock, you must experience a discharge of approximately 3000 volts or more. Discharges of more than roughly 8000 volts might generate a visible spark. Walking across a carpet on a dry day can generate a charge of up to 35,000 volts. Yet electronics can be damaged by a 1000-volt discharge or less—a third or less than the minimum discharge you can feel.

To reduce the buildup of static charges and limit the likelihood of sudden discharges, follow these tips:

- Don't shuffle your feet as you walk.

- Increase the humidity in the room or building—static charges can dissipate before growing large if the humidity level is sufficiently high.

- Wear cotton clothing, which is less likely to generate static charges than are many synthetic materials.

- Remove carpeting from computer rooms and from rooms where you service computers.

- Use an air ionization system to build up an opposite, and thus neutralizing, charge in the air.

- Use the tools found in a typical ESD (electrostatic discharge) kit, such as wrist straps and mats, to remain electrically connected to the devices you're servicing. You and the components you're servicing do not need to be connected to ground; in fact, that can be dangerous.

- Equalize charges safely. Unplug the equipment, and then touch a metal portion of its chassis.

To prevent damaging discharge from occurring, you need to be at equal charge potential with the device you're servicing (not at equal charge with ground). Do *not* leave the computer plugged in while servicing it. If there's a fault in the building's wiring system, full wall current could be flowing through the ground wire. You could be injured or killed if you came into contact with the ground.

Do it!

A-2: Opening the computer case while following proper ESD precautions

Here's how	Here's why
1 Disconnect the power cord from the computer	
2 Disconnect any other external cables	For example, network cables.
3 Release the restraining mechanisms—screws, slides, or push-buttons—that secure the side that exposes the internal components If you opened the side covering the underside of the main circuit board, open the other side	
4 Touch the metal frame of the computer and count slowly to three	To discharge any static charges present on your body or on the computer.
5 Remove the front cover	
6 Leave the case open	You'll examine the internal components more in upcoming topics.

Case features

Explanation

Almost every PC case includes a basic complement of buttons and switches. These include power buttons, reset buttons, and power or drive-activity lights. In addition, modern cases sometimes include:

- Chassis intrusion switches
- Diagnostic LEDs
- Redundant power supplies
- Expansion bays

Chassis intrusion switches

Some computers include a switch that is triggered when you open the system case. In some cases, triggering this switch prevents you from booting the PC (so that you cannot boot it with the cover open). In other cases, the switch alerts you that the case has been opened. With such cases, when you attempt to boot the PC later, you get an error and must reset the switch in the BIOS before the computer will boot.

Follow your manufacturer's instructions to reset such switches. Often, unplugging the computer and waiting a few seconds will be sufficient. Sometimes you will also need to remove the CMOS battery (which backs up the BIOS configuration) and wait until your BIOS is cleared. Motherboards that include support for chassis intrusion switches sometimes include jumpers or switches you can use to disable them. Consult your system's documentation.

Diagnostic LEDs

Many computers include diagnostic LEDs. These LEDs light up in colors and patterns to indicate the operational state of the computer. For example, four green LEDs might mean that all is well, while one yellow and three green LEDs might indicate failed memory. The exact color and pattern sequences vary by manufacturer.

Sometimes the diagnostic LEDs are mounted on the motherboard. If they are, you must either open the system case or view the LEDs through a ventilation hole or fan. Usually, however, the LEDs are mounted outside the case.

Redundant power

By some estimates, power-related equipment costs 2% of the price of a computer, yet nearly 30% of computer problems are power related. If such figures are even close to accurate, they argue strongly for spending more on high-quality power-related devices, such as power supplies, UPSs, and proper wiring. One way to improve redundancy, and thus lessen problems, is to use redundant power supplies.

Redundant power supplies are simply multiple power supplies in a single case. Each power supply is capable of providing all of the power that the computer requires. Special circuitry monitors the power output and switches to the backup power supply if the primary one fails.

To take full advantage of such a configuration, you would want to plug each power supply into its own UPS, and plug each UPS into its own electrical circuit. Ultimately, each circuit would be backed up by its own generator. In such a configuration, failure due to a power outage would be nearly unimaginable.

Expansion bays

In basic terms, an expansion bay is a space into which you can mount a disk drive or other add-on device. Such a bay might just be a space with available mounting hardware (brackets or screw holes) into which you add a drive. Or the bay might include power and data connectors, plus slides or rails into which you insert custom drive enclosures.

For example, in the Hewlett-Packard media expansion bay, offered in some HP computers, you can slip standard-size removable drives. The bay provides power and data connectors, along with slides or rails that permit you to insert and remove the drive.

Laptop computers often include a similar media expansion bay. The CD/DVD drive would mount in this slot. You often have the option to remove that optical drive and insert a floppy disk or tape drive with such laptops. Such media expansion bays are proprietary and specific to the manufacturer.

In desktop cases, a bay is often just a place to install a drive. Depending on the case size and style, the bay might be accessible from the outside of the case; you'd use such bays to mount optical drives or tape drives that you need to insert media in and remove media from. Other bays are just internal; you'd use these to mount spare hard drives.

Rack-mounted computers often include bays accessible through the front or top of the case. You might slide out the rack PC, and lift the top of its case to access the bay. Such bays enable you to quickly access and replace failed drives.

Do it!   **A-3:   Examining your system case**

Here's how	Here's why
1 Examine your computer's case. Locate the power switch and the reset switch.	
Are these switches clearly labeled?	
Are there any indicator lights on the front of the case, and if so, are they labeled?	
2 Does your case include diagnostic LEDs? If so, where are they located? Is this a convenient location for a technician?	
3 Does your case include externally accessible expansion bays? If so, are they the media bay type or simply mounting locations for devices?	
4 Does your case provide redundant power supplies?	
5 Does your case include a chassis intrusion switch?	Your case should be open from a previous activity.
6 If your instructor has other computers using a different case style, such as a rack PC, examine that case for these same components	Look for diagnostic LEDs, expansion bays, power supplies, and intrusion switches.

Topic B: Power supplies

This topic covers the following CompTIA Server+ (2009 Edition) exam objectives.

#	Objective

1.2	**Deploy different chassis types and the appropriate components**
	
	• Power
	
	   – Connectors
	
	   – Voltages
	
	   – Phase

1.5	**Differentiate between processor features/types, and given a scenario, select an appropriate processor** • VRMs

Electricity background

Explanation

Electricity is the flow of electrons. A *conductor* is a material that permits the flow of electricity. An *insulator* is a material that inhibits the flow of electricity.

Voltage

Voltage is the force of electricity caused by a difference in charge, or electrical potential, at two locations. This value, measured in volts, is also called the potential or potential difference. The abbreviation for volts is officially an uppercase "V," though a lowercase "v" is commonly used.

Current

Current is a measure of the flow of electrons past a given point—essentially measuring the speed of the electrons through the conductor. It is measured in amps, or amperes. For current to flow, there must be a complete *circuit*, or path, from the source, through any intervening devices, and back to ground. A complete circuit is called *closed;* an incomplete circuit is called *open*.

Alternating and direct current

Current that flows in a single direction at a constant voltage through a circuit is called *direct current (DC)*. Batteries provide this sort of current, and it's the type required by most electronic components.

Current that flows repeatedly back and forth through the circuit at a constantly varying voltage level is called *alternating current (AC)*. A building's electrical service is an AC system, and most household devices require AC to operate.

AC systems complete a full cycle—voltage change from zero, through maximum voltage, minimum voltage, and back to zero—many times a second. In the United States, Canada, and elsewhere, AC operates at 60 cycles per second (60 hertz, or Hz). Europe and other countries use 50 Hz AC electricity.

Phase

In North America, most residential and small-business AC electricity is provided as *single-phase* service over three wires. Such a system uses three conductors to deliver an AC voltage on two conductors that vary in unison (though opposite in polarity), with the third conductor acting as a ground connection.

Either 120 V electricity (between one "hot" conductor and ground) or 240 V electricity (between two "hot" conductors) can be provided in a single service drop. Because of this arrangement, this common service type is sometimes incorrectly called two-phase.

Single-phase electricity is suitable for lighting, for small motors, and when converted to DC, for powering computers and office electronics. It is not efficient for high-power-need devices, such as large motors. For those, power companies can provide three-phase electricity service.

In a *three-phase* system, three conductors are used (sometimes a fourth is included to provide a ground connection). Each of the three conductors is "hot," providing an AC voltage. The peak of the AC signal in one conductor is delayed by 1/3 of a cycle from the next conductor, which is delayed by 1/3 of a cycle from the next conductor. This delay between signal peaks provides for a constant transfer of power over the entire cycle.

Three-phase power is more efficient for motors and other high-draw equipment. You might encounter three-phase electricity on the factory floor or in utility areas of a large commercial building, but not in a typical office setting. It is not compatible with office equipment or computers. Three-phase devices use different plugs and sockets to prevent you from accidentally plugging in a single-phase device.

PC power supplies

A PC power supply, shown in Exhibit 1-3, is the internal component that converts wall voltage (110 V or 220 V) to the various DC voltages used by the computer's other components. Power supplies have a fan to cool their components and sometimes to help cool the other components inside the PC. Typically, a power supply provides some conditioning functions and can maintain DC supplies during very brief drops in and outages of supply voltage.

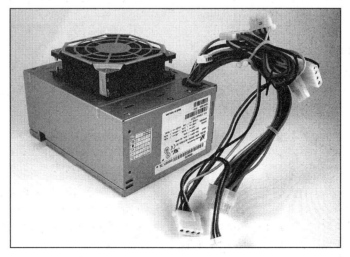

Exhibit 1-3: A PC power supply

Often, you can adjust the power supply to run on either 110 V or 220 V wall voltage. To make this adjustment, with the computer off, you slide a small switch to the appropriate voltage. This switch is normally next to the electrical cord port on the back of the PC, as shown in Exhibit 1-4.

Exhibit 1-4: A voltage selection switch near the electrical cord port

Power supply specifications

Power supplies are rated according to the number of watts of DC power they output. Modern power supplies typically offer at least 300 watts, and often more, to power the PC and its internal components. Older power supplies typically offered 200 watts or less.

The power supply's rating isn't necessarily an indicator of the amount of power that the unit draws from the outlet; a 350 W power supply doesn't necessarily use more electricity than a 200 W model. Power supplies draw only as much power as is needed to supply the internal components. If your system needs less than the power supply's full capability, the power supply draws enough electricity to power the PC, and no more.

The following table lists typical power requirements for common PC components. You can usually find out an exact power requirement from technical specification documents posted on manufacturers' Web sites. It's often not possible, however, to separate memory and CPU power requirements from the motherboard's.

Component	Typical power requirement
Motherboard	30 W, not including the power for the CPU chip and memory. This is for full power mode. Sleeping states use less.
Memory	10 W per 2 GB chip.*
CPU chip	AMD Phenom processors use 65–140 W; AMD Athlon 64 processors use 45–125 W; single-core and dual-core Itanium processors use approximately 100 W; Pentium 4 and Athlon-class processors use 65 or more watts; older CPUs use 50 W or less.
Hard drive	5–15 W. Some manufacturers will print the power requirement right on the drive.
Optical drive	Newer CD or DVD drives can use as little as 5 W. Older optical drives may require 10–20 W.
Floppy drive	5–10 W.
Adapter card	5–30 W. For example, the high-end graphics cards used by professional graphics software developers and computer-aided designers will require more power than a normal graphics card.

* BEHARDWARE.COM determined power consumption in a test system. They measured power consumption at 2 GB and then at 4 GB, because they state that it really isn't possible to load the memory independently of the processor; the difference is an estimate of memory power consumption.

Standard outputs

Most power supplies provide three output voltage levels at various amperage ratings to supply power to the internal components. The following table describes these voltage levels and the typical devices that use them. (More devices draw power at the +12 V level than at any of the other ranges.)

Output	Amperage	Typical devices using this output
+3.3 V	14 A	AGP video cards; motherboards (this output level is not produced by older, AT-class power supplies).
-5 V	0.3 A	ISA bus (AT bus) adapter cards.
+5 V	30 A	Motherboards; CD/DVD drives; hard drives; PCI adapter cards; Pentium III and earlier processors.
+5 V	0.85 A	The "soft power" switch, which maintains the system in a ready-to-start state.
-2 V	1 A	Some older network adapters and serial ports.
+12 V	12 A	CD/DVD drives; hard drives; Pentium 4 and Athlon processors; motherboards.

For newer AMD processors such as the Phenom and Athlon, overall current usage limitation on the power supply doesn't exceed a combined system power output for the +5 V and +3.3 V outputs.

The voltage regulator module (VRM)

The VRM provides the appropriate supply voltage to the processor. If designed according to Intel specifications, a single VRM can supply various voltages to multiple processors installed on the motherboard. The VRM senses the required power needed by a processor by watching for the *VID (voltage ID signal)* sent during the power-on self test.

Power connectors

Standard connectors are used to connect the power supply's output to the various devices. Separate standards exist for the following connectors:

- Drive power connectors
- Motherboard power connectors

Standards for drive power connectors

Hard drives, CD and DVD drives, and floppy drives use power connectors that are standardized in size and shape, as well as in the placement and voltage carried by the wires connected through them. There are three common power connectors: the peripheral, floppy, and serial ATA (SATA) power connectors.

- The peripheral connector is sometimes called a Molex connector, after one of the manufacturers of this style of connector. Peripheral connectors are typically used to connect hard drives and CD or DVD drives to the power supply.
- The floppy connector is a 4-pin Berg connector. The 4-pin Berg connector is smaller than a Molex connector and is used to connect the floppy drive to the computer's power supply unit.
- Serial ATA (SATA) drives use the third type of power connector.

Peripheral, floppy, and serial ATA connectors are shown in Exhibit 1-5 and Exhibit 1-6.

Exhibit 1-5: A peripheral power (Molex) connector, left; and a floppy power (Berg) connector, right

Exhibit 1-6: A serial ATA power connector

Due to their shapes, these connectors can be inserted into drives in only one orientation. They are said to be "keyed," which ensures that you connect the appropriate power input wires to the correct point on the device.

Wire color	Molex pin numbers	Berg pin numbers	SATA pin numbers	Voltage
Yellow	1	4	13, 14, 15	+12 V
Red	4	1 (optional)	7, 8, 9	+5 V
Black	2 and 3	2 (optional) and 3	10, 11, 12	Ground

Standards for motherboard power connectors

The motherboard and its components must get power from the power supply. The motherboard is connected to the power supply with either one or two connectors. Newer, single motherboard connectors are keyed; you can't insert them incorrectly (unless you force-fit them backwards).

The older standard for motherboard power connectors is the two-connector system. These older connectors weren't keyed, so they could be inserted in either direction. Not only could you connect one of the pair to the wrong motherboard connector, but you could also connect the plugs backwards. Such a misconnection sometimes resulted in damage to the motherboard.

A single motherboard power connector is shown in Exhibit 1-7, and dual power connectors are shown in Exhibit 1-8.

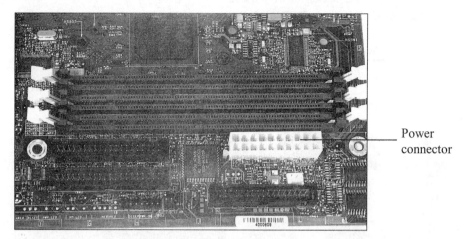

Power connector

Exhibit 1-7: Single motherboard power connector

Exhibit 1-8: Dual power connectors on an older motherboard

The following table lists the wire colors and associated pin numbers for the 20-pin ATX v1.0 single motherboard connector.

Wire color	Pin numbers	DC voltage level
Orange	1, 2, 11	+3.3 V
Red	4, 6, 19, 20	+5 V
Black	3, 5, 7, 13, 15, 16, 17	Ground
Gray	8	+5 V
Purple	9	+5 V
Yellow	10	+12 V
Blue	12	-12 V
Green	14	+5 V (Power_Good signal)
White	18	-5 V

The following table lists the wire colors and associated pin numbers for the 24-pin ATX v2.0 motherboard connector.

Wire color	Pin numbers	DC voltage level
Orange	1, 2, 12	+3.3 V
Red	4, 6, 21, 22, 23	+5 V
Black	3, 5, 7, 15, 17, 18, 19, 24	Ground
Gray	8	Power-Good signal
Purple	9	+5 V
Yellow	10, 11	+12 V
Blue	14	-12 V
Brown	13	+3.3 V
Green	16	PS_ON#, which is an active low signal that turns on all of the main power rails. This signal should be held at +5 V.
No color	20	Reserved

Form factors

The form factor of a power supply refers to its size and shape. The form factor you use must not only fit into the case you use; it must also fit in relation to the motherboard and other components. The names of power-supply form factors match those given to system cases, because together these components form a matched set.

Do it! **B-1:   Examining a power supply and connectors**

Here's how	Here's why
1 Identify the power supply in your computer	
2 Identify your power supply's rating and output voltages	This information is normally listed on a label on the power supply.
3 Locate a peripheral power connector and examine its shape	
4 Locate a floppy-drive power connector and examine its shape	
5 Determine whether your computer has a SATA power connector	The power supplies in newer computers provide these connectors. You can purchase adapters for older power supplies.
6 Locate the motherboard power connector Do you have a single or paired power connector?	
7 With any of the connectors, what is the purpose of the yellow wire? The red wire? The black wire?	

Topic C:　Cooling systems

This topic covers the following CompTIA Server+ (2009 Edition) exam objectives.

#	Objective
1.2	**Deploy different chassis types and the appropriate components** • Cooling 　– Fans 　– Water cooled 　– Passive 　– Active 　– Shroud 　– Ducts 　– Redundant cooling 　– Hot swappable 　– Ventilation
1.5	**Differentiate between processor features/types, and given a scenario, select an appropriate processor** • Heat dissipation (heat sinks, fans, liquid cooling)

CPU cooling

Explanation

CPUs and the other components in a computer are designed to operate within a range of temperatures. Temperatures outside that range can damage components. In particular, too much heat can cause logic errors, in which data within the chips and wires is altered, or cause circuit damage, which can melt components!

The current crop of desktop CPUs (excluding the processor classes defined as energy-efficient or low-power) can draw over 100 watts of power. The CPUs must dissipate the heat from all that power.

Intel specifies that for its Core2 Duo Desktop Processor E4300 processors, the internal temperature of the computer case should not exceed 61.4°C. To maintain that temperature range, PC designers must include the following features to cool the case and the processor itself:

- Fans
- Shrouds
- Heat sinks and cooling fins
- Heat pipes
- Water pumps
- Peltier coolers

Fans and air openings

To maintain allowable temperatures, hardware designers must devise a way to move heat away from the components that generate it. In most situations, this means forcing hot air out of the case to allow cool air to enter.

Older CPUs generated so little heat that a simple fan (typically part of the power supply) and a few openings in the case were all it took to maintain permitted operating temperatures. Modern CPUs (and other components) generate too much heat for such simple thermal management designs.

Modern cases include multiple openings through which air can flow. Some cases include multiple fans, in addition to the power supply fan, to move air. Exhibit 1-9 shows a system case with both power supply and CPU fans.

Exhibit 1-9: A system case with power supply and CPU fans to improve air flow

Heat sinks and cooling fins

Fans aren't sufficient to dissipate the heat from Pentium-class processors. These processors require more high-tech thermal management methods.

The amount of heat that can leave a component is directly proportional to its surface area. Big, hot things cool faster than small, hot things do. Additionally, some materials transfer heat better than others.

A *heat sink* is something that absorbs and transfers heat better than its surroundings. The most common type of heat sink used with CPUs is a set of cooling fins. Fins increase the surface area that can transfer heat away from the CPU. Hardware designers began adding cooling fins to CPUs before the Pentium era—an example is shown in Exhibit 1-10.

Exhibit 1-10: Cooling fins on an older 80486DX2 CPU

The fins are normally connected directly to the die or to an integrated metal plate on the CPU, depending on its packaging design. A thermal compound—basically a glue that transmits heat well—is used between the parts to improve heat flow. You might also hear thermal compound referred to as "thermal grease."

A heat sink (such as a set of cooling fins) relies on convection—warm air rises away from the fins while cooler air flows in from below. At some point, however, heat can't dissipate quickly enough on its own. Thermal engineers can add fans to the cooling fins to forcibly improve convection, as shown in Exhibit 1-11.

Exhibit 1-11: Cooling fins and a fan on a Pentium processor

Shrouds

A shroud is a plastic or metal conduit for cooling air. As shown in Exhibit 1-12, a shroud directs air to or from the fan to the CPU (or other components that need cooling). This helps cool the CPU more than a fan that simply blows air into the system case does. Shrouds and external fans provide better cooling than a CPU-mounted fan like the one shown in Exhibit 1-11.

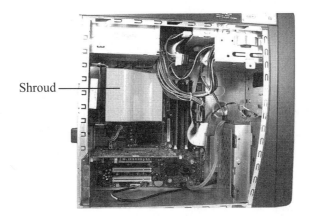

Shroud—

Exhibit 1-12: A shroud directs cooling air to where it is needed most

Heat pipes

Heat sinks, fans, and shrouds can get only so large before they no longer fit in the case or are too heavy for the components to which they're attached. If more heat must be dissipated, designers can turn to other techniques, such as heat pipes.

Heat pipes are small tubes, typically built into cooling fins, that are filled with a small amount of fluid. Heat vaporizes the fluid, which expands and rises to another area of the piping. There, heat is transferred away and condenses, flowing back toward the CPU and heat source.

Exhibit 1-13: Heat pipes and fans from a laptop computer

Even though no pump is involved, heat pipes provide an effective way of moving heat away from the CPU. Additionally, the heat can be moved farther away so that convection can be more effective. Heat pipes also permit smaller and lighter fins.

Water pumps

For systems that generate too much heat for fins and heat pipes to cool, designers can turn to more exotic cooling systems. One such system is a pumped water system. Like heat pipes, tubes carry water past the CPU to pick up heat. The heated water is transported away from the CPU, often outside the computer's case, where the excess heat is removed.

Most water cooling systems use heat exchangers, essentially cooling fins, to radiate away the heat collected in the liquid. Some people have been known to immerse the tubing or exchangers in an ice bath to chill the liquid more, rather than relying on convection with the outside air. Some systems, notably commercial units built into assembled systems, use Peltier devices or refrigeration systems to cool the liquid before it is recirculated.

Peltier coolers

Nearly all of the preceding cooling methods rely on some form of convection. Heat moves from the hot CPU to the cooler surroundings. But what if the surroundings aren't cooler than the inside of the PC's case? Or what if the ambient temperatures aren't cool enough? Factory floors and some other environments can be very hot. Convective cooling devices can't work in those situations.

A Peltier (pronounced "PELT-ee-āy") device is an electronic component that gets colder when a voltage is applied. Peltier coolers for CPUs provide cooling when convective methods won't work. A Peltier device can be connected directly to the CPU or used in conjunction with a water pump. Devices that can drop the temperature of a CPU by 70° C are available.

Do it!

C-1: Examining the cooling systems in your PC

Here's how	Here's why
1 Examine the system case. How many fans does your PC have?	
2 Does your PC have a cooling grille or holes on the side or top? If so, how does the presence of these cooling mechanisms affect where you place a PC in your work area?	
3 You're servicing a computer for a customer who has been complaining of weird system crashes and data loss. The customer's computer is piled high with books and shoved in a cramped space under a desk. It also sits on a thick carpet. What would you suggest?	
4 If necessary, open your PC's case	Make sure to follow proper electrical and ESD safety precautions.
5 Does your CPU have cooling fins? A cooling fan? An "exotic" cooling device, such as a water cooler?	
6 If your instructor has one available, examine a CPU with its cooling fins removed	To see the thermal compound that connects the two components.
7 Of the cooling options listed before this activity, which are active and which are passive?	

Area cooling

Explanation
When cooling the CPU or system case is not sufficient, you must cool the cabinet in which the computers are mounted or the room in which they're located. Cooling options include:

- Room cooling
- Rack cooling
- Row cooling

Before considering cooling options, let's first be clear by what's involved with air conditioning. Computers require greater control of air conditions than simply temperature. You must manage:

- Temperature
- Humidity
- Purity (filtration)

Room cooling

Air-conditioned computer rooms are a common feature of many office buildings. Such rooms provide an ideal environment for heat-sensitive computer equipment. For small installations, simply placing standard servers in an air-conditioned room is all that is needed to provide sufficient cooling.

Larger environments require specialized computer rooms, often built with raised floors and dedicated HVAC (heating, ventilation, and air conditioning) systems. These systems condition the ambient air, but also force conditioned air under the raised floor. Perforated tiles permit the upward flow of cooled air into particular components or racks that need extra cooling.

Room cooling relies on the air conditioning system to circulate enough air to prevent hot spots: the system must pull out enough warm air and push in enough cool air to thoroughly mix the air in the room. High-density computer racks often create more heat than can be sufficiently removed and cooled by a room air conditioning system.

Rack cooling

Rack cooling systems come in two forms. In the first, you place a standard rack in your cooled computer room. Fans are mounted to the top or bottom of the rack to force conditioned air from the room or beneath the floor to flow through the rack. Such units ensure that a known volume of air is blown through the cabinet, rather than relying on convection.

Usually, the rack uses multiple fans in case one fails. Additionally, you can usually swap out fans without shutting off power to the computers and devices mounted in the rack.

In the second form of rack cooling, all of the cooling components are provided within the rack itself. Such cooled racks could be placed in either a cooled computer room or in standard office space. These self-contained units create a conditioned, computer-room environment within the rack.

Self-contained rack cooling units sometimes employ cooling systems based on water (or another liquid). Chilled water circulates through tubing within the rack and picks up heat from the computers mounted there. Then, that liquid passes through what are essentially refrigerator or air conditioner coils to expel the excess heat outside the rack. Air is also drawn in, filtered, and passed by equipment to further expel heat.

These self-contained cooling racks can be used to provide a measure of redundancy. If your room's air conditioning fails, the rack's cooling unit will continue to provide the necessary cooling.

Row cooling

Row cooling is, in some ways, rack cooling extended to an entire row of racks. A dedicated cooling unit is located within the row of racks. This unit circulates cooled and conditioned air to all of the racks in that row. Some such units simply force convection and heat exchange with the computer room's cooled environment. Other types of units use chilled water, circulated among the racks in the row, to actively cool the racks' interiors.

Multiple row chillers provide redundancy in case one unit fails. Many row chillers use multiple fans and redundant refrigeration units, as well as hot-swappable components, to provide reliable cooling.

Do it!

C-2: Evaluating area cooling options

Here's how	Here's why
1 Which area cooling systems are in use at your company?	
2 Have you encountered a situation in which a self-contained cooled rack would be a suitable cooling option? Describe it.	
3 Which is more effective: room, rack, or row cooling?	
4 Why might you need redundant cooling?	
5 Describe a benefit of hot-swappable fans in a rack.	

Unit summary: Deploying the chassis

Topic A   In this topic, you learned that system cases come in a wide variety of sizes and shapes in both standalone server and rack-mounted forms. You identified the characteristics of these **chassis styles** and the common features they can offer.

Topic B   In this topic, you learned that **power supplies** provide conditioned power at appropriate voltages to the components in the server. You learned about the various power supply characteristics, form factors, and features.

Topic C   In this topic, you learned about the various **cooling mechanisms** available to remove the heat generated by servers and related components. You examined cooling in both the standalone and rack-mounted server configurations.

Review questions

1 How tall is a 2U rack mounted device?

    3.5"

2 How wide is a 1U rack-mounted device?

    19"

3 Mounting holes in the rails in a standard computer rack are arranged in groups of _*3*_, with each group spanning a height of *1.75* inches.

4 What is the purpose of a chassis intrusion switch?

    turns screen off when rack is open

5 True or false? Diagnostic LEDs are typically located on the front of a tower PC case.

    False

6 On the front or top of the case, rack-mounted computers often include a(n) *expansion bay* that enables you to quickly swap or add a storage device.

7 True or false? Phase is a characteristic of DC power.

    false

8 PC power supplies are often categorized by the number of *volts* of electrical power they can provide.

9 Which of the following are voltage levels used by typical internal PC components? [Choose all that apply.]

    A 12 V

    B +5 V

    C +3.3 V

    D +2 V

10 What is the purpose of the VRM?

get proper voltage to processor

11 The peripheral power connector, also called the _____ connector, is often used to connect hard drives and CD/DVD drives.   *standard*

12 The yellow wire in a power connector carries ___*12*___ volt DC electricity.

13 Which cooling system relies on small tubes filled with a small amount of fluid?

    A Cooling fins

    (B) Heat pipes

    C Heat sinks

    D Peltier coolers

14 Which cooling system uses an electronic component that gets colder when voltage is applied?

    A Cooling fins

    B Heat pipes

    C Heat sinks

    (D) Peltier coolers

15 True or false? Passive cooling devices rely on convection or conduction to dissipate excess heat.

True

16 The three area cooling options are *room*, *rack* and *row*

17 What is the purpose of a self-contained rack cooling unit?

to keep from affecting the hardware around it

Independent practice activity

1 Using your browser, visit the Web site of a computer and components supplier, such as www.cdw.com or www.newegg.com.

2 Determine a price for a system meeting these specifications:
   - Tower form factor
   - Dual- or quad-core processor
   - SATA hard drive support
   - Built-in Gigabit Ethernet

3 Compare that price to a system meeting the same or similar specifications but in a rack-mount chassis (1U or 2U size).

4 Is there a price premium for the rack-mounted server? If so, speculate why.

5 Visit a site such as www.racksolutions.com, www.kellsystems.com, or www.rackmountsolutions.net to investigate the options available in racks and rack accessories.

6 Visit www.apcc.com and click Products in the main menu. Then click Cooling to view APC's cooling products. Examine the room, row, and rack cooling products this company offers. Examine the product details for at least one of them.

7 If you were designing the cooling needs of a small computer room that would house fewer than six racks, which cooling system would you choose? Why?

8 Close your browser.

Unit 2

Selecting CPUs and motherboards

Unit time: 45 minutes

Complete this unit, and you'll know how to:

A Describe the function and features of CPUs, identify a CPU, and classify CPUs according to their specifications.

B Describe CPU packaging options and related slot and socket technologies.

C Describe motherboards, their components, and form factors.

Topic A: Central processing units

This topic covers the following CompTIA Server+ (2009 Edition) exam objectives.

#	Objective
1.5	**Differentiate between processor features/types, and given a scenario, select an appropriate processor** • Multicore • Multiprocessor • Cache levels • Stepping • Speed • Execute disable (XD) or not execute (NX) • Hyperthreading • VT or AMD-V • AMD vs. Intel (non-compatible CPUs) • Processor architecture (RISC, CISC) • 64 bit vs. 32 bit

Processors

Explanation

The central processing unit (CPU), or processor, is the "brains" of your computer. It's the chip that processes instructions, manipulates data, and controls the interactions of the other circuits in your computer. A CPU is shown in Exhibit 2-1.

Exhibit 2-1: A CPU (a Pentium III)

A CPU has these components:

- A control unit
- One or more execution units
- Registers

Older CPUs and processors, in even modern mini-computers and mainframe computers, were built from multiple chips and components. CPUs contained on a single chip are called *microprocessors*. Almost all CPUs in personal computers are microprocessors.

The control unit

The control unit is responsible for managing the flow of a program. It's the component that retrieves the next instruction to be acted upon or the data to be processed.

Execution units

Execution units are responsible for the processing of instructions and data. Execution units are built from the arithmetic logic unit (ALU) and the floating-point unit (FPU). The ALU calculates and compares numbers. The ALU does most of the work of the processor, but it's best suited to working with operations that act on whole numbers (not fractions).

The FPU is designed specifically to work with real numbers (numbers with fractional components, and very large, very small, or very precise numbers). It's faster and more efficient at performing mathematical manipulations than the ALU is.

Older CPUs didn't include an FPU, though one was sometimes offered as a separate add-on chip called a math co-processor. The Intel 80386 and some 80486 processors, which predate the Pentium line of CPUs, didn't include an FPU. In these older CPUs, the functions of an FPU were performed by the ALU, but at a slower pace.

Cores

A processor can have one or more execution units. A single-core processor has one execution unit. A *core* is an execution unit. A dual-core processor has two execution units, a triple-core processor has three, and a quad-core processor has four.

In a single-core processor, the processor orders, executes, and then selectively stores strings of instructions in its cache (called "registers"; one cache has multiple registers). When the processor needs data outside its cache, it must retrieve the data from RAM through the system bus or from a storage device, such as the hard disk. This process slows down performance to the maximum speed of the bus, memory, or storage device. This speed is slower than the actual speed of the processor itself. The situation is worse when the processor must multitask. When multitasking, the processor switches back and forth between sets of instructions and programs.

In a multi-core processor, each core handles incoming strings of instruction simultaneously. When one core is executing instructions, other cores can be accessing the system bus or executing their own string of instructions. To utilize a multi-core processor, the operating system must be able to recognize multi-threading, and the software must have *simultaneous multi-threading technology (SMT)* written into its code. SMT enables parallel multi-threading, meaning that multi-threaded instructions are delivered to the cores in parallel. Without SMT, the software can recognize only one core.

A multi-core processor is different from a multi-processor system. In a multi-core processor, system resources are shared and all cores reside on the same chip. In a multi-processor system, there are two separate processors, each with its own system resources. All other components being equal, a multi-processor system is faster than a system with a multi-core processor.

Registers

Registers are very small, yet very fast, memory locations for holding instructions or units of data. Registers operate at the same speed as the CPU, whereas normal system memory can be many times slower.

During their operations, CPUs store data and instructions in registers. That information is then transferred back to main system memory. To speed operations, the control unit can "prefetch" instructions and data from system memory and store it in the CPU's registers.

CPUs can have many registers, with groups of registers devoted to a specific purpose (and thus unavailable for other uses). Some modern processors can use registers as needed for the task at hand, rather than being limited by a limited quantity of special-purpose registers.

CPU performance

An instruction is the low-level, hardware-specific command to be acted upon by a processor. It might be something like "SUM 5, 10" to add 5 and 10. Before this instruction can be executed, a previous instruction must have fetched the value 5 from a location in memory and stored it in a register. Another must have fetched 10 from memory. One more instruction is required to write the resulting sum back into a register, from where it is transferred by the control unit to a new memory location.

You can determine the performance of a processor by examining the number of instructions it can perform in a second. With microprocessors, this amount is usually rated in millions of instructions per second (MIPS).

CPUs used to be rated according to their clock speed. In a PC, the clock circuit keeps the CPU and other chips synchronized so that they can work together.

Older CPUs took more than one clock cycle to perform a single instruction. Modern processors perform many instructions in a single cycle. In fact, the clock speed is no longer a good indicator of the performance of a modern CPU. By using the techniques listed in the following table, a modern CPU can perform more than one instruction per clock cycle and even perform multiple instructions at the same time.

Ultimately, many factors control the actual speed (performance) of a CPU. The following table describes some of these factors.

Design	Relation to CPU performance
Addressable RAM	The total amount of memory that's accessible to the processor.
Branch prediction	A technique by which the processor anticipates the code that will be used next and loads that code to try to "get ahead" of the program. When the processor guesses correctly, the program speeds up. Otherwise, performance slows while the correct instruction is retrieved.
Bus, address	The bus (pathway) that connects the processor to main memory. The wider the address bus, the more memory can be accessed. Data isn't transferred over this bus.
Bus, data	The number of bits of data or instructions that can be transferred in a single operation. The larger the data bus, the more data that can be moved and thus the faster the processor can operate.
Bus, internal	The bus that determines how many bits of information the processor can work with at once. If the internal bus is smaller than the data bus, data and instructions must be manipulated in parts. For example, a processor with a 32-bit internal bus and a 64-bit data bus must deal with data in two halves.
Cache	High-speed memory contained within or directly coupled to the processor. Accessing data from cache is considerably faster than accessing it from main memory. Processors use levels 1, 2, and 3 caching, where Level 1 cache is the fastest and most closely coupled to the processor, Level 2 less so, and Level 3 even less (yet still much faster than normal system memory). Processors save instructions, the data to be processed, and the results in the caches.
Clock speed	The number of cycles per second of the computer's synchronization clock, measured in hertz (Hz), millions of cycles per second (megahertz or MHz), or billions of cycles per second (gigahertz or GHz). A modern processor performs more than one instruction during every clock cycle. Older processors performed one or fewer. Normally, a clock speed rating refers to the internal or core speed of the processor, rather than to the actual speed of the computer's synchronizing clock chip.
Clock multiplier	Measures the ratio of internal bus speed to external bus speed in a CPU. For example, consider a system with a 133 MHz clock speed and a CPU with a 10x clock multiplier. Internally, the CPU's bus runs at 1.33 GHz (1,333 MHz) while externally its bus runs at the system's clock speed (133 MHz).
Dual Independent Bus (DIB)	A processor architecture that includes two buses: one to the main system memory, and another to the Level 2 cache. The processor can access both buses simultaneously for improved performance.
Front-side bus speed	The speed at which the processor interacts with the rest of the system. A processor's internal core speed can be many times higher than its front-side bus speed (see clock multiplier). If the core speed is too much higher than the front-side bus speed, the processor can sit idle, waiting for data to be moved in or out and made available for processing.
Hyperthreading	An Intel technology that enables a single processor to execute two streams of instructions at the same time, as if it were two processors.
Multimedia extensions (MMX)	An expanded set of instructions supported by a processor that provides multimedia-specific functions. Without MMX, a programmer might have to implement multiple low-level commands to perform a multimedia operation. With MMX, the same function would involve a single instruction.
Multiprocessing	The use of more than one processor within a system to speed program execution. Operating systems and applications need to be written to support multiprocessing, or no speed benefits are realized.

Design	Relation to CPU performance
Out-of-order completion	A technique by which instructions can be executed out of order when order isn't important and the processor determines a more efficient sequence.
Overclocking	Running the CPU at a higher speed than it was rated to run at. Overclocking increases performance, but also increases the potential for errors. Also, more heat is generated by an overclocked CPU.
Pipelining	The overlapping of the steps involved in processing instructions. Instructions are normally fetched, decoded, and executed, and the results are written out to memory. Modern processors overlap these steps to speed overall execution. While one instruction is being executed, another is being decoded, and a third is being fetched.
Register renaming	A technique by which modern processors can rename registers so that instructions can access their own set of registers and not interfere with other instructions. When multiple instructions are running at the same time, there's a chance that two will attempt to read or write to the same register simultaneously. Register renaming prevents this.
RISC vs. CISC	Reduced Instruction Set Computer (RISC) vs. Complex Instruction Set Computer (CISC). RISC is a CPU design philosophy that holds that performance will be improved if the features of the CPU are reduced, forcing advanced features to be provided through software. CISC holds the opposite: hardware is generally faster, so a more complex CPU will outperform a reduced-instruction-set CPU. RISC CPUs include the PowerPC, Alpha, and ARM architectures. CISC CPUs includes the x86 family from Intel and AMD. In general, CISC has won in the marketplace, though that's not necessarily an endorsement that CISC is somehow better than RISC.
Single Instruction Multiple Data (SIMD)	A technique by which a single instruction can be applied to more than one piece of data. For example, with SIMD, five numbers might be moved into the processor along with the single command to add them up in one operation. The next operation would carry out that instruction. Without SIMD, the numbers would be added together one by one in a longer sequence of instructions.
Speculative execution	A technique by which a processor executes an instruction in the expectation that the result is needed. This technique can improve performance when the program branches, as in an "if this condition is met, do that operation" situation. The processor can begin performing the operation before the condition is fully evaluated, in the expectation that it will be met.
Superpipelining	An improvement over pipelining. Superpipelining uses a larger number of shorter stages and support for a higher clock rate to improve performance.
Superscalar	A technique that enables a processor to execute more than one instruction in a single clock cycle.
Throttling	A technique by which the speed of the processor is scaled back so that it uses less power and creates less heat. Throttling reduces performance. It's most useful with portable computers, for which low power consumption and low heat production are critical design factors.

Support for multiple processors

Some computers come with two processors. However, in order to take advantage of the increased performance gained with two processors, the operating system and applications you run must include symmetric multiprocessing code. Windows Server, Windows 2000 Professional, Windows XP Professional, and Windows Vista Business, Ultimate, and Enterprise include symmetric multiprocessing code. Windows XP Home and Media Center Editions and Windows Vista Home and Home Premium don't. You can get the Linux operating system in symmetric multiprocessing versions.

Virtualization support

Virtualization is a technology through which one or more simulated computers run within a physical computer. The physical computer is called the *host*, and its operating system is the host OS. The simulated computers are called *virtual machines (VMs)*, and their operating systems are called guest OSs.

Virtualization offers a range of benefits and is a suitable solution largely because many user and system functions typically consume far less than the full power of a modern computer. For example, if a user's activities on her PC use just 30% of the computer's capabilities, 70% is being wasted. Through virtualization, potentially three VMs could be run on a single system at this level of utilization, giving similar performance levels.

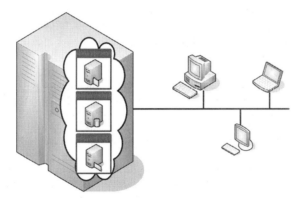

Exhibit 2-2: Multiple VMs on a single physical host

Early virtualization products required modifications to the guest OS, particularly hardware drivers. Some modern CPUs include virtualization support features that enable the host to run unmodified guest operating systems. Intel's Virtualization Technology (VT or VT-x, which stands for Virtualization Technology for x86) and AMD's AMD-V (the V stands for virtualization) are the primary examples of CPU virtualization features.

Intel VT and AMD-V are not compatible, though they provide essentially the same features. Current host OS options typically support both of these virtualization technologies. Citrix XenServer and Microsoft's Hyper-V are examples of host operating systems (or operating system components) that take advantage of CPU virtualization features and enable virtualization.

At the time of this writing, you could visit *http://en.wikipedia.org/wiki/ X86_virtualization#Hardware_support* to obtain a partial list of Intel and AMD processors offering hardware virtualization support. Check the manufacturer's specification sheets for authoritative information before selecting a CPU for your system.

Memory protection

Another feature of modern CPUs is generically called *no execute*, or *NX*. This feature enables the CPU to mark a section of memory as non-executable: any code stored within that area of memory will not be run. NX is called *Execute Disable* (XD) by Intel and *Enhanced Virus Protection* by AMD.

In theory at least, executable program code is supposed to be stored separately from data in memory. This separation is supposed to prevent malicious program code, embedded within data, from running on your computer. In practice, this segregation has not been strictly enforced, leading to *buffer overflow attacks*, in which virus writers overfill an area of data storage, eventually placing executable code within your computer's memory. Then they execute that code to take control of your PC.

NX on the Intel platform was first provided through software, starting with enhancements added to Windows XP Service Pack 2. Since then, CPU makers have added NX support directly to the CPUs. By placing this support into hardware, they make it more difficult for virus authors to circumvent the no-execute protections than if the feature were provided through software.

AMD was the first manufacturer to add NX support to its CPUs, beginning with the Athlon 64 and Opteron processors. Intel followed, adding support to Pentium CPUs based on the Prescott core. In general, all current processors from AMD, Intel, and VIA support the NX technology.

CPU versioning

Each CPU maker uses its own version numbering scheme, making it difficult to keep track of and compare processors across lines. However, in general, all of the manufacturers divide their CPUs in this fashion:

- Brand
- Model number
- Stepping

Brand

A brand, or family, of CPUs is the name you see advertised, such as Intel® Core™2 Duo or AMD Phenom™. Each of these families comprise many specific models of CPUs, each with varying characteristics and capabilities.

Model number

The model number describes a specific line of CPUs within a family. For example, the P7000 model number describes a set of CPUs within the Core2 family by Intel. Model numbers can be more specific. For example, P7350 and P7370 are CPU lines within the larger P7000 line of Intel CPUs.

Higher model numbers generally imply better performance, though not all specifications might be better. For example, a higher-numbered CPU might have a faster front-side bus but a lesser Level 2 cache than a lower-numbered CPU.

Model numbers might begin with a letter prefix or end with a letter suffix. For example, the Intel E8500 and Q9550S are processors in the Intel Core2 family. Each manufacturer assigns its own meaning to these letters. See the manufacturers' Web sites for complete details.

Stepping

The *stepping* is a version indicator within a processor line. Steppings are combinations of letters and numbers, such as A0. A change in the number, such as to A1, indicates a minor design change. A change in the letter indicates a more substantial change, such as changes in cache size, power consumption modes, and so forth.

CPU makers rarely print the stepping on the CPU. Instead, they print an sSpec number. For example, you would see SLAEB printed on the CPU for the M0 stepping of the Core2 Duo T5470 CPU.

It's important to note that a higher stepping value does not automatically mean improved performance or features. A higher stepping number might indicate a CPU with reduced cache size, for example, meant to reduce production (and thus retail) costs. It might also indicate a change made in the processor design to fix a bug or make manufacturing easier.

Do it!

A-1:   Identifying CPUs

Here's how	Here's why
1 Disconnect the power cord from the computer	
2 Disconnect any other external cables	For example, network cables.
3 Release the restraining mechanisms—screws, slides, or push-buttons—that secure the side that exposes the internal components	
4 Touch the metal frame of the computer and count slowly to three	To discharge any static charges present on your body or on the computer.
5 Remove the cover	So you can view the motherboard and processor.
6 Locate your CPU	Modern CPUs typically have a set of cooling fins glued to them, covering all markings. This will prevent you from identifying the CPU or its specifications.

7 If the CPU's label is visible, record the manufacturer and model of the CPU

Your instructor might be able provide you with this information if it is not visible on the CPU.

Manufacturer: _____

Brand (family): _____

Model number: _____

Stepping or sSpec: _____

8 Close your system case and assemble your PC

9 Boot your PC

Log on as **Administrator** with a password of **!pass1234**

10 Open your browser and visit **http://en.wikipedia.org/wiki/►X86_virtualization#Hardware_support**

11 Is your CPU listed among those supporting AMD-V or Intel VT-x support?

If your CPU is not listed, visit the Intel or AMD Web site, as appropriate. Using the published specifications on the site, determine if your CPU supports virtualization features.

Intel: www.intel.com

AMD: www.amd.com

Determine if your CPU supports the NX (no execute) feature.

12 Visit **www.digital-daily.com/cpu**

13 Compare one of the AMD processors with one of the Intel processors; which do you think is the more powerful CPU, and why?

14 Which processors do you or your company use?

Topic B: Packaging and slots

This topic covers the following CompTIA Server+ (2009 Edition) exam objective.

#	Objective
1.5	**Differentiate between processor features/types, and given a scenario, select an appropriate processor** • Vendor slot types

CPU packaging

Explanation

Any type of microchip is made up of microscopic wires, transistors, and other components. This plain chip is called the *die*. To be useful, it must be connected to the rest of the circuitry of the computer. Due to the size differences between the wires on the die and the circuit boards in the computer, the die can't be connected directly to the circuit board.

Instead, the die is built into a package. A package is a case made from plastic, ceramic, glass, metal, or some other material, plus the wires and connectors that bridge the microscopic connections on the die with the external circuitry. A package might also include support function chips, memory, and cooling-related components.

Exhibit 2-3: A PDIP (plastic dual inline package) memory chip

Older package types, such as the PDIP pictured in Exhibit 2-3, used connectors that were large compared to the die. Newer packages use ever smaller connectors, packing more connections into a smaller area. The pin grid array (PGA) package, shown in Exhibit 2-4, includes many more connections in an area not much larger than the die.

Exhibit 2-4: The underside of an 80486DX2 CPU, showing the pins of its pin grid array package

Even though newer packages use smaller connectors, overall package size has grown as functionality has grown. Newer packages include support chips, cache memory, and features that enhance the cooling of the processor. One such larger package is shown in Exhibit 2-5.

Exhibit 2-5: The Single Edge Contact Cartridge package

CPU packages

The following table lists some current and historical CPU packages used in desktop computers. Manufacturers can vary these with updated lines, so be sure to check the technical specifications for your particular CPU on the manufacturer's Web site.

Package	Full name	Description	Processors
PDIP	Plastic dual inline package	The die is encased in plastic (or another material). Large, flat, metal pins are inserted into a socket that's soldered to the motherboard.	8080, 8086, 8088
PGA	Pin grid array	Rows of pins extend from the bottom of the package. A nickel-plated copper slug sits atop the die to improve thermal conductivity. The pins are arranged so that the chip can be inserted in just one way.	80286 (68 pins), 80386 (132 pins), 80486 (168), and Xeon (603 pins)
CPGA	Ceramic pin grid array	A package that uses a ceramic substrate with pins arranged in a pin grid array.	AMD Socket A Athlons and the Duron
SPGA	Staggered pin grid array	Similar to PGA, but pins are staggered to fit more pins in a given area.	Pentium, Pentium MMX, and Pentium Pro with 387 pins
PPGA	Plastic pin grid array	An updated version of the SPGA package.	Pentium Pro, early Celeron processors, and Pentium III with 370 pins
FC-PGA	Flip chip pin grid array	Similar to PGA, but the die is exposed on top. This design enhances heat transfer and cooling options.	Pentium III and Celeron with 370 pins; the 423-pin version is used with Pentium 4 processors

Package	Full name	Description	Processors
FC-PGA2	Flip chip pin grid array 2	Similar to FC-PGA, but with an integrated heat sink, which is connected to the die during manufacturing.	Pentium III and Celeron with 370 pins; the 478-pin version is used with Pentium 4 processors; the 469-pin version is used with AMD Athlon Thunderbird processors
OOI	OLGA On Interpreter	The die is mounted face down for better cooling, as with the FC-PGA package, but uses a different pin arrangement.	423-pin Pentium 4
OPGA	Organic pin grid array	The silicon die is attached to an organic plastic plate (fiberglass), which is pierced by an array of pins to make the connections to the socket. This package is cheaper, thinner, and lighter than the ceramic package. It also reduces electrical impedance.	AMD Athlon XP
SECC	Single Edge Contact Cartridge	Rather than mounting horizontally, this package mounts the CPU vertically on the motherboard. Rather than pins, this package uses an edge connector similar to an adapter card's. The die is covered with a metal case. A metal thermal plate mounted to the back of the cartridge acts as a heat sink.	Pentium II processors with 242 contacts, and Pentium II Xeon and Pentium III Xeon processors with 330 contacts
SECC2	Single Edge Contact Cartridge 2	Similar to SECC, but without the thermal plate.	Later versions of the Pentium II and Pentium III processor with 242 contacts; AMD Athlon K7
SEP	Single Edge Processor	Similar to SECC, but without the metal case.	Early Celeron processors with 242 contacts
FCBGA	Flip chip ball grid array	Similar to FC-PGA, but uses balls rather than pins for contacts. The balls can't be bent as the pins can.	Xeon, plus many support chips in current Pentium-class computers
LGA	Land grid array	Has small raised contacts instead of pins. The corresponding socket has pins that meet the contacts. This is a very high-density package.	Celeron D, Pentium 4, Pentium 4 D, Pentium Extreme Edition, Core2 Duo, Core2 Extreme

Sockets and slots

The processor packages listed in the preceding table must be inserted into a socket or slot on the motherboard. The following table lists common desktop computer sockets and slots. (As with packages, manufacturers can vary sockets and slots with updated lines, so check the technical specifications for your CPU on the manufacturer's Web site.) A desktop processor and its associated socket are shown in Exhibit 2-6.

Type	Supports these packages	Processors	Notes
Slot A	AMD's Card Module package	AMD Athlon	This wasn't a popular design and didn't last long on the market.
Socket A (also called Socket 462)	SPGA with 462 pins	AMD Athlon and Duron	Eleven holes in this socket were plugged to ensure that packages were installed correctly.
Socket 5	PGA, SPGA with 320 pins	Pentium	
Socket 7	PGA, SPGA with 321 pins, and PGA, SPGA, and FC-PGA with 296 pins	AMD K5 and K6, Cyrix 6x86, Pentium, and Pentium MMX	First socket to support dual voltage inputs, which support the various core and I/O voltages introduced with the Pentium MMX processors. Socket 7 has one more holes than Socket 5 but isn't electrically connected. It simply prevents a new CPU from being plugged into a Socket 5 socket.
Socket 8	387-pin PGA, SPGA, and FC-PGA	Pentium Pro	A short-lived socket design used primarily with the Pentium Pro.
Socket 423	423-pin SPGA and FC-PGA, OOI	Pentium 4	A short-lived socket design used for early Pentium 4 processors.
Socket 478	FC-PGA2	Celeron, Pentium 4, Pentium D, and Pentium Extreme Edition	The current general-purpose socket for Pentium-class processors.
Socket 370	SPGA and PPGA with 370 pins	Celeron, Celeron II, Pentium III	Similar to the Socket 7 design, with six staggered rows of pins rather than five.
Slot 1	SECC, SECC2, SEP with 242 contacts	Pentium II, early Celeron, and Pentium III	Edge connector slot developed specifically for the SECC, SECC2, and SEP packages.
Slot 2	SECC, SECC2, SEP with 330 contacts	Pentium II and Xeon	Similar to Slot 1, but the CPU can communicate with the Level 2 cache at full CPU speed, rather than at the half-speed supported through Slot 1.
LGA775 (also called Socket T)	LGA	Celeron D, Pentium 4, Pentium D, Pentium Extreme Edition, Core2 Duo, and Core2 Duo Extreme	Designed to work specifically with the new high-density LGA package. This is Intel's current high-end socket.

Exhibit 2-6: A Pentium with an MMX CPU atop its associated Socket 7 socket

Do it!

B-1:   Identifying your CPU's socket and package type

Here's how	Here's why
1 Shut down and unplug your PC	If necessary.
2 If necessary, open your system case	Make sure to follow proper electrical safety and ESD precautions.
3 Examine your CPU, and record the socket and package type	Package: _____ Socket: _____
4 Identify the chipset chip on your motherboard	It's typically a very large chip placed near the CPU socket.

Topic C: Motherboards

This topic covers the following CompTIA Server+ (2009 Edition) exam objectives.

#	Objective
1.1	**Differentiate between system board types, features, components, and their purposes**
	• Dip switches / jumpers
	• Processor (single and multi)
	• Onboard components
	– NICs – HID
	– Video – Serial
	– Audio – Parallel
	– USB
	• Riser card / backplane
1.5	**Differentiate between processor features/types, and given a scenario, select an appropriate processor**
	• VRMs

Motherboards

Explanation

The motherboard is the main circuit board in a personal computer. It's made up of various components, including the CPU and other electronic devices, wires, and adapter sockets into which additional circuit boards and devices can be attached. Exhibit 2-7 shows a motherboard with some of its primary components labeled.

Exhibit 2-7: A motherboard

The following table describes the functions of various motherboard components.

Component	Function
CPU	The chip that processes instructions, manipulates data, and controls the interactions of the other circuits in the computer. Some servers and high-powered computers support multiple processors on a single motherboard.
Expansion slots	Slots into which you can plug additional circuit boards to expand the capabilities of the computer.
Graphics adapter slot	A slot into which you can plug a graphics adapter card, which produces the output displayed on your monitor.
Hard drive interface connectors	Slots into which you can plug cables to connect hard drives, CD drives, and DVD drives to the system.
Floppy drive interface connector	A slot into which you can plug the cable to connect a floppy drive to the system.
Power connector	The connector to which you connect the output of the power supply to provide electrical power to the motherboard. Older systems have a pair of slots rather than a single connector.
Memory slots	Slots into which you insert memory modules to add system memory to the PC.
PS/2 mouse and keyboard ports	Ports into which you can plug PS/2-style keyboard and mouse cables.
USB port	One or more ports into which you can plug cables to connect USB devices to the PC.
HID port	Human Interface Device port; a port to which you connect input/output devices, such as keyboards, mice, and joysticks. Most often, simply a USB port.
IEEE 1394/FireWire port	One or more ports into which you can plug cables to connect FireWire devices to the PC.
Serial port	One or more ports into which you can plug cables to connect serial devices, such as modems or mice, to the PC.
Parallel port	One or more ports into which you can plug cables to connect parallel devices, such as printers, to the PC.
Battery	A battery to provide power for maintaining system configuration information while the PC is turned off or disconnected from the outlet.
Network interface	Network interface circuitry built into the motherboard to enable connections to a network without using an add-on adapter card.
Video connector	Video circuitry built into the motherboard, which provides a video connector on the back of the system case.
Voltage regulator module	A module that provides the appropriate supply voltage to the processor. If it's designed according to Intel specifications, a single VRM can supply various voltages to multiple processors installed on the motherboard. The VRM senses the required power needed by a processor by watching for the VID (voltage ID signal) sent during the power-on self test.

The motherboard is sometimes called the *system board* or *main board*. However, the latter term is typically used to describe the main circuit board in non-PC devices, such as alarm systems, televisions, and so forth.

Daughter boards

A daughter board is a circuit board that connects to a circuit board (sometimes, though not normally, a motherboard) to provide or assist with its functions. Daughter boards are often used with video cards to add more video-processing capabilities.

Riser cards

As shown in Exhibit 2-8, a riser card is a circuit board that connects to a motherboard. Unlike a daughter board, the purpose of a riser card is to provide additional expansion slots or sockets. Riser cards are most often used with special, small motherboards designed for small cases. Riser cards attach to a backplane, which is a set of connectors in parallel served by a single bus.

Exhibit 2-8: An NLX-style motherboard (top) with its associated riser card, containing the system's expansion slots (bottom)

Form factor

The form factor of a motherboard is its size and shape. In addition, the form factor determines the power supply and case that can be used with a motherboard, along with the general physical layout of the components on the motherboard. Of course, motherboards must fit into cases, which means that screw holes or retaining-clip locations must match between motherboards and cases. Standard dimensions and mounting layouts help ensure that components work together.

The following table lists the common PC motherboard form factors. Other form factors are available. Be sure to check the manufacturer's specification documents for your PC when choosing a replacement motherboard.

Form factor	Dimensions (inches)	Notes
XT	8.5 by 11	Obsolete, used with IBM XT-class computers.
AT	12 by 11–13	Obsolete, used with IBM AT-class computers.
Baby-AT	8.5 by 10–13	A smaller version of the AT form factor.
ATX	9.6 by 12	Standard created by Intel in 1996 and still one of the most popular form factors.
Mini-ATX	8.2 by 11.2	
Micro-ATX	9.6 by 9.6	Released in 1996. Offered fewer slots than the ATX form, so a smaller power supply could be used in PCs with this motherboard design.
LPX	9 by 11–13	Designed for slimline PCs.
Mini-LPX	8–9 by 10–11	Designed for slimline PCs.
NLX	8–9 by 10–13.6	Standard created by Intel in 1999; this form factor requires a riser card for add-on adapters.
FlexATX	9.6 by 9.6	
Mini-ITX	6.7 by 6.7	Standard created by VIA Technologies in 2003.
Nano-ITX	4.7 by 4.7	Standard created by VIA Technologies in 2004.
BTX	10.5 by 12.8	Standard created by Intel in 2004. Intel plans for this to be the standard motherboard form factor for the future.
MicroBTX	10.4 by 10.5	A variation of the BTX form factor. Its different dimensions notwithstanding, the MicroBTX shares the electrical and component design with the BTX form factor.
PicoBTX	8.0 by 10.5	A smaller variation of the BTX standard.

Do it!

C-1: Examining motherboard components and form factors

Here's how	Here's why
1 If necessary, open your computer's case	Make sure to follow proper electrical and ESD safety precautions.
2 Examine your motherboard	
What form factor is your motherboard?	
3 If your instructor has motherboards with other form factors, compare their size and component layout with your motherboard	
4 Identify each of the following items on your motherboard:	CPU and its socket
	Memory slots
	Bus (expansion) slots
	I/O ports (serial, parallel, mouse, and keyboard)
	Integrated drive controller slots, if applicable
	USB and FireWire ports, if applicable
	Integrated video port, if applicable
5 Close your system case and assemble your PC	
6 Boot your PC	
Log on to Windows Server 2008 as **Administrator** with a password of **!pass1234**	
7 Open your browser and visit **www.motherboards.org**	
8 On the left, under Compare Prices, click **Motherboards**	
9 Examine the list of motherboards available for sale	
10 What's the most popular motherboard form factor for sale?	

Unit summary: Selecting CPUs and motherboards

Topic A   In this topic, you learned that **CPUs** are the **chips** that process instructions, manipulate data, and control the interaction of other PC components. You examined the characteristics of popular CPUs, as well as the features that determine a CPU's performance characteristics.

Topic B   In this topic, you examined the various CPU **packages** and the corresponding **slots** and **sockets** into which they're inserted.

Topic C   In this topic, you learned that the **motherboard** is the primary circuit board in a personal computer. You also learned that motherboards come in specific sizes and shapes that describe their **form factor**.

Review questions

1 Which of the following is not a component of a CPU?

A Bus architecture

B Control unit

C Execution unit

D Register

2 The math co-processor was the predecessor of which CPU component?

A ACL

B Core

C FPU

D Register

3 A single-core processor has one of what component?

A Control unit

B Execution unit

C FPU

D Register

4 _RAM_____ are very small, very fast, memory locations for holding instructions or units of data.

5 Which type of bus connects the processor to the main memory?

   A Address bus

   B Data bus

   C Internal bus

   D Generic bus

6 Which processor caching level is the fastest for accessing data?

   A Level 1

   B Level 2

   C Level 3

   D All are equal

7 Which of the following performance features can overheat the processor?

   A Multiprocessing

   B Overclocking

   C Pipelining

   D Superpipelining

   E Throttling

8 True or false? Current processors have both L1 and L2 caches.

   True

9 The plain chip called a "die" is built into a(n) ___bus___ so that it can connect to the rest of the circuitry in the computer.

10 Which socket type is similar to the Socket 7 design, but with six staggered rows of pins instead of five?

   A Socket 8

   B Socket 370

   C Socket 423

   D Socket 478

11 A(n) __riser__ card is a circuit board that connects to a motherboard to provide additional expansion slots or sockets.

Independent practice activity

In this activity, you'll practice identifying appropriate CPU and motherboard requirements for a PC.

1 Given a budget of $1000, use the www.motherboards.org Web site to plan the highest-capability PC that you could purchase. Focus on CPU and motherboard performance and form factor. Make sure your PC could support a sufficient number of add-on devices, such as hard drives and CD/DVD drives.

Record the specifications of the system you'd purchase here:

CPU (type, model, speed): _____

Motherboard (make and model): _____

Form factor and drive bay capacity: _____

2 If available, examine the motherboard and CPU of a computer in your room, other than your lab station computer. Record the following information about this computer:

CPU (type, model, speed): _____

CPU socket type: _____

Motherboard (make and model): _____

Form factor: _____

Ports (serial, parallel, and so forth): _____

Integrated peripherals: _____

Unit 3

Managing the BIOS

Unit time: 60 minutes

Complete this unit, and you'll know how to:

A Access the BIOS setup utility, change hardware configuration values, and research BIOS updates.

B Explain the POST and boot processes.

Topic A: The BIOS and CMOS

This topic covers the following CompTIA Server+ (2009 Edition) exam objectives.

#	Objective
1.1	**Differentiate between system board types, features, components, and their purposes**
	• Dip switches / jumpers
	• BIOS
1.7	**Install, update, and configure appropriate firmware**
	• Driver / hardware compatibility
	• Follow manufacturer instructions and documentation
	• Implications of a failed firmware upgrade (redundant BIOS)

Firmware

Explanation

Firmware straddles a gray area between hardware and software. *Firmware* is software written permanently or semi-permanently on a computer chip. Firmware is used to control electronic devices, such as remote controls, calculators, and digital cameras. In a computer, firmware is implemented using the BIOS and CMOS.

The BIOS

The *BIOS* (Basic Input/Output System) is the computer's firmware—a set of software instructions stored on a chip on the motherboard. The BIOS instructions enable basic computer functions, such as getting input from the keyboard and mouse, serial ports, and so on. Without the BIOS, your computer would be a useless collection of wires and electronic components.

AMD (Advanced Micro Devices), AMI (American Megatrends Inc.), Award, MR BIOS (Microid Research Inc.), and Phoenix are some common BIOS manufacturers. A motherboard manufacturer selects a BIOS and integrates it into the design.

Shadowing

At startup, many computers copy the contents of the BIOS into standard memory to improve performance. This technique is called *shadowing* because the contents in memory are like a shadow of those on the BIOS chip.

CMOS

CMOS (complementary metal oxide semiconductor) is actually a type of computer chip. This type of chip can maintain information without a supply of power. The most common use of CMOS chips is to store BIOS configuration data. The term "CMOS" is frequently used to refer to the storage location of the BIOS configuration information, rather than the chip technology. A battery, typically on the motherboard as shown in Exhibit 3-1, provides power to the CMOS chip so that its contents are maintained when the computer is turned off or unplugged.

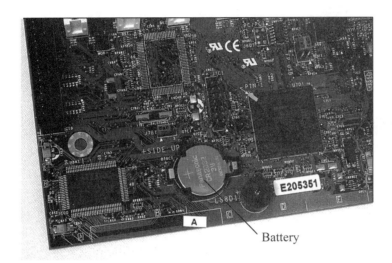

Exhibit 3-1: A CMOS battery

CMOS configuration

To configure the values stored in CMOS, you use a system setup utility provided by your computer's manufacturer (or by the BIOS maker). This utility is often built into the BIOS itself. Sometimes the utility is stored on a special hidden portion of your hard disk (on a separate partition) or an optical disc.

CMOS utility access

BIOS manufacturers provide various ways to access the system setup utility. The following table describes a few of the more common methods. The alternative key combinations represent the methods you use with various computer models from these vendors (rather than alternative options for a single model). Consult your system's documentation to determine the exact procedure you need to follow.

Maker	Key combination	When to press the keys
ALR	F2 or Ctrl+Alt+Esc	During text mode portion of boot.
AMD	F1	During text mode portion of boot.
AMI	Delete	During text mode portion of boot.
Award	Delete or Ctrl+Alt+Esc	During text mode portion of boot.
Compaq	F10	During text mode (black background, white text) portions of boot process, when the underline cursor jumps to the upper-right corner of the screen.*
Dell	F1, Delete, or Ctrl+Alt+Enter (on some systems, you must press the Reset button twice)	During text mode portion of boot.
Gateway	F1	During text mode portion of boot.
HP	F1	During text mode portion of boot.
IBM	Insert or F1 (early ThinkPads used Ctrl+Alt+Insert)	During text mode portion of boot. (This method works only if the PC is configured with a reference partition. Otherwise, you need to use the system setup disk.)
Phoenix	F1, Ctrl+Alt+Esc, Ctrl+Alt+S, or Ctrl+Alt+Insert	During text mode portion of boot.
Toshiba	F1 or Escape	During text mode portion of boot.

* Compaq provides a setup disk, used to access the CMOS in their systems, and a diagnostics disk, used to perform system tests and inspect system-level information. When Compaq configures their systems, they load images of these disks on the hard drive in a 4 MB non-DOS partition. Press F10 to access this partition at boot. If the non-DOS partition has been deleted, you need to boot the computer by using the setup disk to access the CMOS utility.

At the time of this writing, a more comprehensive list of CMOS access key combinations was available here: *http://murfsgarage.cybertechhelp.com/cmossetup.htm*.

Configuring BIOS settings

Setting BIOS configuration values is normally a "set and forget" operation. On most systems, you won't need to configure anything; the settings from the manufacturer have been configured to meet the needs of the system. However, you might need to configure the BIOS when you set up the computer for the first time or when you add new hardware. Other than that, you typically don't need to change the BIOS configuration.

Typical BIOS configuration settings include:

- **Date and time** — Set the system date and time.
- **CPU options** — Specify the type of CPU installed in the system, and configure speed and voltage settings.
- **Optical drive options** — Specify which drives (CD and DVD), and in which order, the system should boot from. You can also typically enable, disable, and configure optical drive options.
- **Floppy drive options** — Specify which floppy drives, and in which order, the system should attempt to boot from. You can also typically enable, disable, and configure floppy drive options.
- **Hard drive options** — Specify the hard drive's type, size, and geometry, and enable or disable on-board hard drive controllers.
- **Serial port options** — Set configuration options, such as device addresses and communication modes.
- **Parallel port options** — Specify whether to enable unidirectional or bidirectional printing, and configure ECP (Extended Capabilities Parallel port) and EPP (Enhanced Parallel Port) settings.
- **Integrated devices** — Enable or disable integrated devices, such as video adapter or network adapter functionality.
- **Plug and Play** — Enable or disable hardware support for Plug and Play features.
- **Power management options** — Specify whether to enable hardware-based power management features. Typically, you must choose a set of supported power management standards, such as APM (Advanced Power Management) or ACPI (Advanced Configuration and Power Interface), as well as "wake up" options, such as whether to wake up the computer when the modem rings.
- **Virus detection** — Enable or disable hardware-based virus detection.
- **Boot password** — Enable or disable hardware-based passwords, and set the password.

To configure the BIOS:

1   If necessary, shut down the PC.
2   From a powered-off state, boot the PC.
3   At the appropriate time in the boot sequence, press the key combination that opens the BIOS setup utility on the system.
4   Follow the on-screen prompts or menu system to configure your system.
5   Follow the on-screen prompts or menu system to save the new configuration data in CMOS memory.

Do it!

A-1: Changing your PC's BIOS settings

Here's how	Here's why
1 If necessary, shut down your PC	Don't put the computer in hibernation or sleep mode. You must turn it all the way off.
2 Turn on the computer	
3 At the appropriate time in the boot sequence, press the key combination that opens the BIOS setup utility on your system	
4 Follow the on-screen instructions or use the menus to set the date and time	If they're already correctly set, set them back an hour or so and then reset them to the current time.
5 Explore your computer system's setup utility	To determine its capabilities. Each BIOS manufacturer provides similar setup options.
6 Exit and save your configuration changes	Your system automatically restarts when you're done.

BIOS updates

Explanation

The BIOS is provided in a form of a memory chip that doesn't lose its contents when the power is turned off. The BIOS can be implemented either in ROM (read-only memory) or flash memory (a type of electronically reprogrammable memory chip).

- ROM-based BIOS is programmed at the factory. You can't change this kind of BIOS without replacing the chip itself.
- Using a special program provided by the computer (or BIOS) manufacturer, you can update a flash-memory-based BIOS without changing the BIOS chip. This action is often called "flashing the BIOS."

Usually, the BIOS version that ships with your PC is all you ever need. However, you might need to upgrade your BIOS in the following situations:

- There are device problems or other bugs that your PC manufacturer identifies as being caused by BIOS problems.
- There are device problems that you can attribute to no other cause than the BIOS. Additionally, you have exhausted all other troubleshooting avenues in trying to fix the problems.
- You need to use new hardware options that, while supported by your motherboard, aren't supported by the BIOS.

BIOS update sources

Usually, you should look to your PC's manufacturer if you need information about your BIOS or are looking for updates or fixes. Typically, the computer manufacturer provides links to BIOS updates and flashing utilities. The BIOS manufacturers provide the BIOS to PC manufacturers in an incomplete state. The PC manufacturers make final modifications to tailor the BIOS to their exact hardware. This tailored BIOS is what's shipped to you in your new PC. For this reason, BIOS updates must come from your PC's manufacturer, not from the original equipment manufacturers.

Determining the BIOS version

You can find the version of the BIOS installed in your system by using the Windows System Information tool. To determine the version of BIOS installed in a Windows 2000 Professional, Windows XP, or Windows Vista system:

1   Click Start and choose All Programs (or Programs), Accessories, System Tools, System Information.

2   Record the value listed in the BIOS Version/Date field. As shown in Exhibit 3-2, this field lists BIOS version data, which you can use to determine if a newer version is available on your PC maker's Web site.

3   If it's present, record the value listed in the SMBIOS field. The SMBIOS is used by PC inventorying programs to collect data about your computer. SMBIOS updates are usually included with BIOS updates. Not all PCs include the SMBIOS.

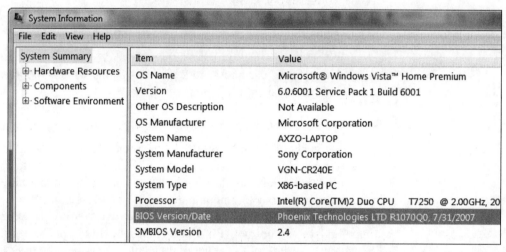

Exhibit 3-2: The System Information utility displays the BIOS version

Flashing the BIOS

To update the BIOS in your system:

1 Use the System Information tool to determine your current BIOS version.

2 Visit your PC manufacturer's Web site and navigate to its support pages to locate the BIOS update files.

3 Compare the version number and release date with the information reported by the System Information tool to determine if a new BIOS version is available.

4 Download the installation file for the new BIOS version. Make sure you choose the version that matches your PC model.

5 If it's not part of the BIOS installation file, download the appropriate BIOS flashing utility from your PC manufacturer's Web site. Make sure you choose the version that matches your PC model and operating system.

6 Close all open applications.

7 Open the flashing utility and follow the instructions it provides to update your BIOS.

8 Restart your PC when prompted.

BIOS update failures

BIOS updates can fail, and when they do, you can be left with an unbootable and useless computer. Follow these guidelines to minimize the risks of a failed update:

- Don't update your BIOS unless you must. Usually, the BIOS version that shipped with your PC is sufficient for the entire operating life of the computer.

- Never turn off your computer during a BIOS update, and make sure the power doesn't go off during an update (connect the PC to a UPS). Don't press Ctrl+Alt+Del during the operation.

- Make sure you use the correct BIOS flash utility. The utility is specific to your brand of computer, model, BIOS chip, and operating system. Contact your PC's manufacturer or visit its Web site to obtain the correct flash utility.

- Follow the flash utility's instructions exactly. Make sure you run the utility under the correct operating system—flash utilities are typically compatible with a single version of Windows (or other operating system).

- Most flash utilities offer the option of backing up your old BIOS before updating it. Perform this backup. You might be able to use it to recover if the update fails.

Recovering from a failed BIOS update

You have a few basic options for recovering from a failed BIOS update:

- Use the BIOS backup created by the flash utility to try to restore the previous version.

- Many modern BIOSs include a small area that's never overwritten during an upgrade. This "boot block" section has sufficient support to boot your PC from a floppy disk. You need to provide a floppy disk containing the correct BIOS and flash utility. The contents of this floppy vary depending on your BIOS's manufacturer. No video is displayed during this operation. After the PC has booted from this floppy and copied the correct BIOS over the corrupt version, you reboot your PC.

- Some Intel motherboards have a flash-recovery jumper switch. (See Exhibit 3-3 for an illustration of DIP switches and jumper switches.) You set this jumper switch to the recovery position, insert the system upgrade floppy disk into the drive, and boot your PC. The system boots from the disk and copies the original BIOS over the corrupted BIOS. No video is displayed during this operation. When the drive light on your floppy drive goes off, the procedure is done. Reset the recovery jumper to its normal position and reboot your PC again.

- Many modern motherboards feature a redundant BIOS chip. This chip maintains a copy of the original BIOS version, as shipped with your motherboard when it was new. BIOS upgrades are applied by default to the primary chip, leaving the redundant chip untouched. If the upgrade fails, you can use a DIP switch or jumper, or perhaps a boot-time keystroke, to start your PC using the redundant BIOS. Some manufacturers provide utilities for upgrading the redundant BIOS, which might be necessary if serious bugs are discovered in it.

- If the preceding methods don't work for you, you might need to get a new BIOS chip from your motherboard or PC's manufacturer. You need to replace the damaged BIOS chip with the new one.

Exhibit 3-3: DIP switches (left) and jumpers are two means for setting hardware options

Do it!

A-2:   Researching BIOS updates for your PC

Here's how	Here's why
1 Boot your computer	If necessary.
2 Log on to Windows Server 2008 as **Administrator** with a password of **!pass1234**	
3 Click **Start** and choose **All Programs**, **Accessories**, **System Tools**, **System Information**	To open the System Information utility.
4 Determine your current BIOS (and SMBIOS if present) version, and record those details here:	Manufacturer: Version: Date:
Close System Information	
5 Visit the support Web site for your PC's manufacturer	
6 Determine the latest version of the BIOS for your make and model of PC	
Is there a newer BIOS version available for your PC?	
7 Read the manufacturer's information about the BIOS update	
Should you update?	
8 Close your Web browser	

Bad CMOS batteries

Explanation   Configuration data is stored in the CMOS. This chip retains its data when the PC is off, thanks to a battery connected to your motherboard. In older PCs, the battery was soldered in place and wasn't replaceable. Nowadays, the battery is inserted into a socket and held in place with retaining clips.

Do it!   ## A-3:   Replacing the CMOS battery

Here's how	Here's why
1 Shut down your PC and unplug it from the electrical outlet	
2 Following electrical and ESD safety precautions, open the case	
3 Locate the CMOS battery on the motherboard	
4 Remove or release the retaining clip, and slide the battery out of its holder	
5 Install the new battery, securing it with the retaining clips	
6 Close the system case	
7 Restart the computer	
8 If necessary, use the BIOS setup utility to set the correct date, time, and device options	These values were probably lost when you removed the battery.

Topic B: The POST and boot processes

This topic covers the following CompTIA Server+ (2009 Edition) exam objectives.

#	Objective
1.1	**Differentiate between system board types, features, components, and their purposes** • BIOS
1.7	**Install, update, and configure appropriate firmware** • Driver / hardware compatibility
6.2	**Given a scenario, effectively troubleshoot hardware problems, selecting the appropriate tools and methods** • Common problems – Failed POST – Memory failure – Onboard component failure – Processor failure – Incorrect boot sequence • Causes of common problems – Incompatible or incorrect BIOS

The power-on self test

Explanation

When you turn on your computer, a program contained in the BIOS performs a series of basic checks to make sure the system components are in proper working order. This set of checks is called the *power-on self test (POST)*.

The POST isn't a complex or comprehensive test. There are four basic parts, which are carried out in this order:

1 The BIOS tests the core hardware, including itself, the processor, CMOS, the input/output system, and so forth. Any errors detected at this stage are reported as a series of beeps (see the "Beep codes" section that follows).

2 The BIOS tests the video subsystem. This test includes checking the memory dedicated to video operations, checking the video processing circuitry, and checking the video configuration (that it's valid and not corrupted).

3 The BIOS identifies itself, including its version, manufacturer, and date.

4 The BIOS tests main system memory. Some BIOS versions display a running count of how much memory has been tested. Others are "silent" unless an error is found.

Beep codes

Before the video system is initialized, the BIOS has no way to display errors on your screen. Thus, errors detected early in the POST test must be reported as one or more beeps played through the internal PC speaker.

The exact beep codes vary by BIOS manufacturer. The following table lists a few of the more common beep tones. For a more complete reference, visit *www.computerhope.com/beep.htm*.

Beeps	Description
1 short beep	Typically indicates that no problems were found. Some systems sound two short beeps to indicate that all is well.
3 long beeps	A keyboard error.
8 short beeps	Video adapter memory problems.
9 short beeps	A BIOS problem.
1 long and 3 short beeps	A memory error.

Numeric codes

When the POST has finished its core hardware tests, the system begins to initialize other devices, including the video display circuitry. Once the video is initialized, any further error codes can be displayed on the monitor.

The exact numeric codes and their meanings vary by manufacturer. You should visit your vendor's Web site to get the list of codes for your specific hardware. For example, for a comprehensive list of numeric codes for IBM-brand PCs, visit *www-307.ibm.com/pc/support/site.wss/document.do?lndocid=MIGR-4BAHK2*.

The following table lists a few IBM-specific numeric error codes you might encounter. Manufacturers other than IBM use similar numbers.

Code	Description
151	Real-time clock failure.
161	Bad CMOS battery.
162	Configuration mismatch: the configuration data stored in the CMOS doesn't match the actual hardware in your PC.
164	Memory size mismatch: your PC has more or less memory than the amount the CMOS says your system has.
201 or any 20#	Memory failure.
1762	Hard drive configuration error.

Logo screens

Some BIOS manufacturers hide the display of BIOS and POST messages. Instead, they display their logo or another graphic. Typically, you can show the POST messages and hide the logo by pressing the Tab key when the logo is displayed.

Do it!

B-1: Observing the POST process

Here's how	Here's why
1 If necessary, shut down your PC	Make sure you turn it all the way off.
2 While holding down (SHIFT), turn on your PC	Holding down a key like this should simulate a keyboard failure.
3 Are any beep codes played?	You might hear the normal one or two "system OK" beeps, followed by your BIOS manufacturer's code for a keyboard failure.
4 Are any numeric codes displayed?	Your BIOS manufacturer's code for a keyboard failure is likely shown on your monitor. Depending on the BIOS, perhaps just the beep code is played.
5 If the option is presented, press (F1)	To bypass the error and continue booting. Your PC might continue booting without interaction or might boot after you release the Shift key.
If the option isn't presented, shut off your PC and turn it on again	To boot normally.
6 If necessary, press (TAB) to hide the logo screen	
7 Observe any POST messages as your system boots	Your PC might display memory test results and other POST information as it boots.

The boot process

Explanation
The POST process covered previously is just one of the steps that a computer performs when starting up. The following steps detail the hardware portions of the boot process.

1 You turn on the power.

2 The timer chip begins sending continual reset signals to the CPU to prevent it from booting the PC.

3 The power supply performs internal checks. When that's done and power output levels have stabilized, it sends the Power_Good signal to the CPU.

4 With the arrival of the Power_Good signal, the timer stops sending reset signals to the CPU, thereby permitting it to begin the boot process.

5 The CPU loads the BIOS and then searches for devices that have BIOS extensions to load. Video adapters are the best example of devices that would require a BIOS extension.

6 The BIOS checks whether this is a cold or warm boot. Cold boots happen when you boot the PC from a powered-off state or when you press the hardware reset button on the front of the system case. Warm boots happen when you click Start, choose Shutdown, and click Restart. (With older versions of Windows and with DOS, you could perform a warm boot by pressing Ctrl+Alt+Delete.)

7 If this is a cold boot, the BIOS performs the POST procedure.

8 The BIOS reads the CMOS configuration data and configures devices.

9 Plug and Play devices are detected and configured.

10 The BIOS determines which drive to boot from by checking the CMOS configuration data.

11 The BIOS reads the master boot record (MBR) from the boot drive. This record provides the information necessary for the boot process to proceed from this point onward. If the MBR can't be located, the CMOS displays an error message, such as "Non-system disk or disk error."

12 The MBR contains the code for passing control of the boot process to the operating system. The OS takes over and completes the boot process.

Boot devices

The boot device is the drive that the computer uses to load an operating system during the boot process. In current computers, a boot device can be many different types of drives, such as:

- An internal hard disk
- An internal optical drive (CD or DVD drive)
- A USB drive (flash drive, or external hard disk or optical drive)
- A network drive, using a network interface card that supports the Preboot eXecution Environment (PXE)

Examples of older boot devices include:

- Floppy disk drives
- SCSI devices
- Zip drives

You add, remove, and change the order of boot devices in the computer's BIOS, as shown in Exhibit 3-4.

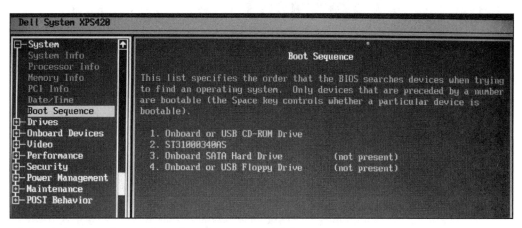

Exhibit 3-4: Boot devices listed in the system BIOS

Do it!

B-2:   Checking the boot order

Here's how	Here's why
1 If necessary, shut down your PC	Don't put the computer in hibernation or sleep mode. You must turn it all the way off.
2 Turn on the computer	
3 At the appropriate time in the boot sequence, press the key combination that opens the BIOS setup utility on your system	
4 Identify the boot devices included in your PC's boot sequence	
5 Identify the order of devices in the boot sequence	
6 Exit the BIOS utility	

Unit summary: Managing the BIOS

Topic A

In this topic, you learned that the **BIOS** is a set of programs that control the most basic hardware interactions within a PC. The BIOS is stored on a chip that isn't erased when you turn off the power. Hardware configuration data used by the BIOS is stored in **CMOS**. CMOS data is retained when the power is off, thanks to a battery installed on the motherboard. You learned how to access and use the **BIOS setup utility** to change the CMOS configuration data. You learned that, with modern PCs, you can **flash the BIOS** to update it. You also learned that a failed BIOS update can render a PC unusable, and you looked at the ways you can recover from a failed BIOS update attempt.

Topic B

In this topic, you learned that the BIOS tests a computer's hardware at boot time by following the **POST** process. You learned about various **beep** and **numeric error codes** that might be reported during the POST if the BIOS detects a hardware failure. You also learned how to determine the order of boot devices in your computer.

Review questions

1 True or false? The BIOS and CMOS are the same thing.

False

2 The battery shown in the following graphic is used to provide power to what component?

timing

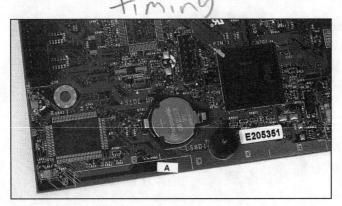

A BIOS

B CMOS

C Firmware

D RAM

3 True or false? The same key combination will get you access to the system utility on all personal computers, except laptops.

false

4 True or false? Power management is controlled through operating system features only.

false

5 Which of the following is not a reason to update your system BIOS?

   A Your system has device problems or other bugs that your PC manufacturer identifies as being caused by BIOS problems.

   B Your system has device problems that you can attribute to no other cause than the BIOS.

   C Your PC manufacturer has sent out a technical document notifying you of an update.

   D You need to use new hardware options that, while supported by your motherboard, aren't supported by your BIOS.

6 True or false? If the system stops responding during a BIOS update, you can use the Ctrl+Alt+Del key combination to recover.

true

7 The clock on your computer reads January 1, 1970. What is the likely cause?

   A Your system BIOS needs updating.

   B When the operating system was installed, the correct date was never set.

   C The CMOS battery needs replacing.

   D A BIOS update failed.

8 Which of the following is not a step in the POST process?

   A BIOS identification

   B Core hardware test

   C Main system memory test

   D Master boot record being read from the boot drive

   E Video subsystem test

9 True or false? The boot processes for a cold boot and a warm boot are exactly the same.

false

10 True or false? To boot the computer, your boot device must be an internal hard disk, internal optical drive, internal floppy drive, or USB flash drive.

true

Independent practice activity

In this activity, you'll practice support tasks related to the computer system's BIOS and CMOS.

1 If your computer has a floppy drive, configure the CMOS data to disable it. Attempt to boot from a floppy disk. Enable the floppy drive.

2 Change the boot order so that your PC attempts to start from disks in this order: CD-ROM drive, hard drive, floppy drive (if present).

3 Test your work by inserting a bootable CD in the CD-ROM drive and a bootable floppy disk in the floppy drive. Your computer should boot from the CD even though your hard disk is bootable and a bootable floppy is in its drive.

4 Shut down your computer and disconnect the mouse. Boot your PC. Does your computer report any beep or numeric error codes? If so, which codes? If not, why not?

5 Attach the mouse and shut down your PC. Disconnect the keyboard and plug it into the mouse port, connecting the mouse to the keyboard port. Boot your PC. Does your computer report any beep or numeric error codes? If so, which codes? If not, why not?

6 Shut down your PC and connect the keyboard and mouse to the correct ports. Boot your PC.

Unit 4

Selecting memory

Unit time: 60 minutes

Complete this unit, and you'll know how to:

A Describe the function of memory and differentiate among various types of memory chips.

B Differentiate among the various memory packages.

Topic A: Memory

This topic covers the following CompTIA Server+ (2009 Edition) exam objectives.

#	Objective

1.3	**Differentiate between memory features/types, and given a scenario, select an appropriate processor**
	
	• Memory pairing
	• ECC vs. non ECC
	• Registered vs. non-registered
	• Types
	  – DDR – SDRAM
	  – DDR2 – DIMM
	  – Fully buffered – DDR3
	• Memory compatibility
	  – Speed – Timing
	  – CAS latency – Pins
	  – Size – Vendor-specific memory
	• On board vs. riser card

Computer memory systems

Explanation

Memory, commonly called RAM (random access memory), is the hardware component that stores data as the CPU works with it. RAM is implemented as computer chips occasionally soldered to the circuit board, but more often attached to a specialized socket.

Memory is different from storage devices, such as hard drives, floppy drives, and optical discs. Storage refers to the locations where data—including your applications—is held in the long term. Data in storage remains there when your computer is turned off.

An analogy for RAM

You can compare RAM and storage with the papers you work with at your desk. You keep important papers in the file drawer, and you pull them out and put them on your desktop to work with them. The file drawer is like the hard disk in your computer; it's where you store your data (papers) when you're not working on them. The desktop is the working area and is analogous to RAM.

In reality, the analogy is strained because the computer can "borrow" an area of your hard disk to use as if it were memory. A *page file* temporarily stores active data that doesn't fit in the RAM installed on your computer. However, the computer can't work with the data in the page file. It must first read the data back into real RAM, while writing some other data to the page file.

Additionally, some types of chips don't lose their contents when power is removed. For example, CompactFlash cards—commonly used with digital cameras—are simply computer chips in a convenient package. Yet a CF card is storage, not memory, because you use it for the long-term storage of data (most often photos, but you can store other types of files, too).

The importance of RAM

Having sufficient RAM in your system is critical for the following reasons:

- **Performance** — Having more RAM almost always leads to improved computer performance. When you have insufficient RAM, the CPU must work harder shuffling data between RAM and the page file.

- **Software support** — Many applications require a minimum amount of RAM. Having less RAM than specified can prevent you from running these applications. Or if they do run on your system, they perform so badly as to be unpleasant to use.

Poor-quality or defective RAM is a major source of system crashes. One bad memory storage location out of the millions of such locations in your RAM chips can bring your system down. Your computer tests the RAM during the POST, but that test isn't exhaustive and problem chips can slip through.

Additionally, the type of RAM your system uses, as well as the maximum amount of RAM supported by your motherboard, has a direct effect on your system's upgradeability. Make sure to buy a system that will support your future RAM needs, as well as those of your current applications.

Measuring memory

The actual storage locations on a memory chip are called *cells*. Each cell stores a single bit of data. A bit is a 0 or 1, representing an on/off or yes/no binary state.

The data you work with and the programs you run are made up of millions and billions of individual bits of data. Describing such large units is confusing and inconvenient. Instead, computer professionals use various units of memory storage to describe memory and storage amounts.

Basic memory units

The following table lists the most basic units of memory storage.

Name	Number of bits	Number of values that can be stored in this much memory
Bit	1	2 (a zero or one, equivalent to 2^1)
Nibble	4	16 (2^4)
Byte	8	256 (2^8)
Word	Depends on the processor. With a 32-bit CPU, a word is 32 bits. On a 64-bit CPU, a word is 64 bits.	Varies, but a 32-bit word offers 4,294,967,296 possible values (2^{32})

Larger units

Saying a computer has 2,147,483,648 bits of RAM is more confusing and less convenient than saying it has 256 MB of RAM. The common units of memory are listed in the following table.

Name	Abbreviation	Number of bytes
Byte	B	1 byte, which equals 8 bits
Kilobyte	KB	1024 bytes, or 2^{10} bytes
Megabyte	MB	1024 KB or 1,048,576 bytes
Gigabyte	GB	1024 MB or 1,073,741,824 bytes
Terabyte	TB	1024 GB or 1,099,511,627,776 bytes

Memory types

Memory can be classified in various ways:

- Volatile vs. non-volatile
- Static vs. dynamic
- Asynchronous vs. synchronous

Volatile and non-volatile memory

Volatile memory loses its contents when power isn't present. Non-volatile memory doesn't lose its contents when power is removed. The following table lists the various types of common memory, categorized as volatile or non-volatile.

Type	Volatile or non-volatile	Description
RAM	Volatile	The working memory for a computer. Because RAM is volatile memory, its contents are lost when power is removed, even for a very brief period.
CMOS	Volatile	The storage location for BIOS configuration data. CMOS requires a battery to retain its information. Without the battery, CMOS loses its contents. Thus, despite what many sources say, it's volatile memory.
ROM	Non-volatile	Read-only memory. ROM is used to store the BIOS and other programs and data that must be preserved when the computer is unplugged. ROM must be programmed at the factory.
PROM	Non-volatile	Programmable read-only memory. PROM must be programmed at the factory and can be programmed only once.
EPROM	Non-volatile	Erasable programmable read-only memory. You erase the contents of an EPROM chip by exposing its glass window to ultraviolet light. Then you can program the chip by using a device called a *PROM burner*.
EEPROM	Non-volatile	Electronically erasable programmable read-only memory. You can erase and program the contents of an EEPROM chip by using a burner or special circuitry within your computer.

Type	Volatile or non-volatile	Description
Flash	Non-volatile	(Similar to EEPROMs.) Chips that don't lose their memory when power is removed and can be burned using burners or circuitry within your computer. The primary difference is that flash memory is written block by block, rather than byte by byte as is done with EEPROMs.

Dynamic and static memory

Some types of RAM lose their contents quickly, even when power is present. Devices that use this type of memory must continually refresh the contents of the chips, or data is lost.

Such memory is called *dynamic RAM*, or DRAM. DRAM must be refreshed hundreds of times per second. Circuits using DRAM must include the components necessary to refresh its contents, adding complexity to the overall system. Due to the design of DRAM circuitry, simply reading its contents is sufficient to refresh it.

In contrast, *static RAM*, or SRAM, doesn't need to be refreshed. Due to the way these chips are built, this memory holds its contents until power is removed. Therefore, circuits using SRAM are simpler, because refresh components aren't required. SRAM chips can be read more quickly than DRAM chips can.

Main system memory is implemented with DRAM. Cache memory and CMOS memory are most often implemented with SRAM.

DRAM chips are as much as four times smaller than SRAM chips per unit of storage. DRAM circuitry is simpler, making DRAM considerably cheaper than SRAM to manufacture. The refresh circuitry is simple and inexpensive to implement, too.

Thus, DRAM is much cheaper to use than SRAM when large amounts of memory are needed, such as for main system memory. SRAM is considerably faster, which makes it well suited to the smaller level 2 and level 3 cache memories that typically use it.

Asynchronous and synchronous memory

Asynchronous DRAM (ADRAM) isn't synchronized to the system clock. Regardless of the clock's speed, asynchronous DRAM takes the same amount of time to access and return data from a memory cell.

In contrast, synchronous DRAM (SDRAM) is tied to the system clock. Modern SDRAM returns data from a memory cell in a single cycle of the system clock. (Older SDRAM required multiple clock cycles per access.)

SDRAM is faster than asynchronous DRAM and keeps pace with the rest of the computer better. For this reason, most modern computers use SDRAM for system memory. The SDRAM you install must be capable of operating at your system's bus speed.

Memory access

To access the data in a particular memory cell, the CPU must have the address of that cell. Although memory cells could be arranged in one long line, giving each cell an individual sequential address, such a design would lead to slow, large chips. Instead, chip designers arrange cells into rows and columns, much like the cells in a spreadsheet. To read the data of any cell, the CPU needs both row and column addresses.

The exact way that CPUs address memory, along with many other factors, leads to a confusing array of abbreviations describing memory types. The following table compares the types of RAM found in older and current computers. The technologies are listed in approximate increasing order of performance.

Abbreviation	RAM type	Description
DRAM	Dynamic RAM	Older technology, not used in modern computers. The CPU sends the row address and then sends the column address to access a cell. The CPU must repeat this process for every cell.
FPM	Fast Page Mode	The CPU sends a row address, followed by a column address. If the CPU needs more cells from the same row, it can send just the column address.
VRAM	Video RAM	A modified version of FPM. VRAM has two ports; one port can be read to refresh the image on the screen, while the other can be used to generate the next image to be displayed.
EDO	Extended Data Out	Works essentially like FPM, except that a new cell access request can begin before a previous request has finished.
BEDO	Burst Extended Data Out	Adds pipelining technology to EDO to improve performance. This technology never caught on.
ADRAM	Asynchronous DRAM	Is not synchronized to the system clock. Regardless of the clock's speed, asynchronous DRAM takes the same amount of time to access and return data from a memory cell.
SDRAM	Synchronous DRAM	Is synchronized with the system clock to improve performance. Internal interleaving enables overlapped accesses, as with EDO and BEDO.
DRDRAM	Direct Rambus DRAM	(Formerly called just RDRAM for Rambus DRAM.) Uses a 16-bit data bus running at up to 800 MHz, transferring data on both the rise and fall of the clock signal.
DDR	Double Data Rate	Doubles the transfer rate by transferring data on both the rise and fall of the clock signal (compared to SDRAM, which transfers on just the rise). Its data transfer range is 200–400 MHz, based on a 100–200 MHz I/O clock. DDR memory modules transfer data on a bus that is 64 data bits wide.
DDR2	Double Data Rate 2	Transfers data at a rate of 400–1066 MHz, using a 200–533 MHz I/O clock on both the rise and fall of the clock signal. DDR2 modules transfer data on a bus that is 64 data bits wide.
DDR3	Double Data Rate 3	Transfers data at a rate of 800–1600 MHz, using both the rise and fall of a 400–800 MHz I/O clock signal. DDR3 memory modules transfer data on a bus that is 64 data bits wide. DDR3 allows for chip capacities of 512 MB to 8 GB, enabling a maximum memory module size of 16 GB.

Access time

It takes a certain amount of time to access the data in memory, regardless of type or technology. Of course, some memory types are faster and some are slower.

All memory suffers from a delay between when an address (of the data being requested) arrives on the bus and when the memory is ready to return that data. This delay, called the *CAS latency*, is due to the time it takes the memory controller on board the memory module to read and decode the address. After initial latency, a certain time passes before the data is retrieved and put onto the bus so that the CPU can use it.

Access time is the overall amount of time between when a request is made and when the data is available on the bus. In modern RAM, this time is very short, sometimes as little as a few nanoseconds. A nanosecond is a billionth of a second.

Memory speed

Although RAM speeds are often measured in nanoseconds (ns), you're more likely to see modern RAM rated by megahertz (MHz). A hertz is a cycle per second, so a megahertz is a million cycles per second. The net result is that the MHz rating of RAM is simply 1 divided by its speed in nanoseconds; alternatively, you can divide 1 by the MHz rating to determine the speed in nanoseconds.

Overall speed

While you might see a module rated at 10 ns and another rated at 20 ns, you shouldn't conclude that the 10 ns module is twice as fast. DRAM ratings don't include the initial latency required for address decoding. Furthermore, DRAM is tied to the system clock. The actual speed at which your memory operates is controlled by your system's bus speed, which is determined by your motherboard's chipset and clock speed.

For example, you must consider not only the memory speed rating but also the overall timing. For each memory request, there will be an initial *CAS latency delay*—a delay during the memory transfer—and if not all of the data is transmitted during those clock cycles, there will be additional latency during each subsequent transfer.

In reality, the speed rating of a memory module represents a maximum speed at which it can operate. When choosing memory, you must select memory with a low enough CAS latency and a high enough speed so that it's fast enough to keep up with the rest of your system.

Bandwidth

Bandwidth, or the amount of data that can be transferred to or from memory per second, is perhaps even more important than a raw speed rating. Overall bandwidth is determined by the speed of the RAM itself, plus the chip's memory technology design. For example, an SDRAM module operating at 100 MHz has a lower bandwidth than a 100 MHz DDR module does.

Speed ratings

How can you know whether a memory module will be able to keep up with your system? Memory and motherboard manufacturers have created a speed notation standard you can use to choose the correct memory.

The following table lists the common PC memory types, along with their technologies, single-channel-mode bandwidths, and speed ratings.

Memory type	Technology	Bandwidth	I/O bus clock speed	Memory clock speed
PC100	SDRAM	0.8 GB/sec.	100 MHz	100 MHz
PC133	SDRAM	1 GB/sec.	133 MHz	133 MHz
PC1600	DDR-200	1.6 GB/sec.	100 MHz	100 MHz
PC2100	DDR-266	2.1 GB/sec.	133 MHz	133 MHz
PC2700	DDR-333	2.7 GB/sec.	166 MHz	166 MHz
PC3200	DDR-400	3.2 GB/sec.	200 MHz	200 MHz
PC2-3200	DDR2-400	3.2 GB/sec.	200 MHz	100 MHz
PC2-4200	DDR2-533	4.2 GB/sec.	266 MHz	133 MHz
PC2-5300	DDR2-667	5.3 GB/sec.	333 MHz	166 MHz
PC2-6400	DDR2-800	6.4 GB/sec.	400 MHz	200 MHz
PC2-8500	DDR2-1066	8.5 GB/sec.	533 MHz	266 MHz
PC3-6400	DDR3-800	6.4 GB/sec.	400 MHz	100 MHz
PC3-8500	DDR3-1066	8.5 GB/sec.	533 MHz	133 MHz
PC3-10600	DDR3-1333	10.6 GB/sec.	667 MHz	166 MHz
PC3-12800	DDR3-1600	12.8 GB/sec.	800 MHz	200 MHz

Consult your PC's owner's manual to determine which type of memory the PC can support. Then purchase that type of memory. Often, a system supports faster memory (a type with a higher rating) than its minimum required type. For example, if your system requires PC2100 memory, you can probably install PC2700 memory without a problem. However, if the system requires PC2700, you can't install PC2100 memory. Make sure to consult your owner's manual before installing any type of memory.

Buffered or registered memory

Registered memory, also called *buffered memory*, contains a register located between the memory cells and the computer's memory controller. This register temporarily holds, or buffers, memory during transfers. This arrangement places a smaller electrical load on the memory controller, enabling the computer to better handle a large number of memory modules. Buffered memory improves stability. However, because the memory is held in the register for a clock cycle, performance is slowed ever so slightly.

Server computers sometimes support or require buffered memory. You cannot install buffered memory in a system that does not support it. Consult your system's documentation to determine if you can or should use registered memory. Registered memory is typically more expensive than non-registered memory.

Banking requirements

You physically install memory modules into slots on the motherboard, and those slots are arranged into groups called *banks*. Depending on your computer's design, a bank might include one, two, or four slots, which are usually color-coded on the motherboard. When you install new memory, you must fill every slot in a bank. For example, if your computer uses two-slot banks, then you must install memory modules in pairs. Many modern computers and laptops use single-slot banks. With this type of bank, you have to install only one module.

With many motherboards, you must use the same type and speed of memory in every slot in a bank. In a few situations, you must use the same type and speed of memory in every memory slot in the computer, even in different banks. In most computers, you simply leave empty any extra slots. However, in computers that use DRDRAM (Rambus memory), you must fill extra slots with a *continuity module*, which is a small circuit board designed to complete the electrical circuit but not add RAM to the system.

Dual-channel architecture is a technology that doubles data throughput from the memory to the memory controller by using two 64-bit data channels, giving you a 128-bit data path. Dual-channel architecture requires both a dual-channel-capable motherboard and two or more DDR, DDR2, or DDR3 memory modules. You install the memory modules into banks. Each memory module accesses the memory controller through a separate path, thus increasing bandwidth. Although using identical memory modules is not required, it's recommended for best compatibility in dual-channel operations.

Do it!

A-1:   Identifying memory characteristics

Questions and answers

1 You want to install the fastest memory you can in your system. Should you install DDR2 or DDR3 memory?

2 What does the number in a PC rating, such as PC2100, tell you about that memory?

3 Which of these memory types are volatile memory? (Choose all that apply.)

   A   RAM

   B   Flash

   C   EEPROM

   D   CMOS

4 Which of these memory types is synchronous memory?

   A   SDRAM

   B   SRAM

   C   EEPROM

   D   CMOS

5 One gigabyte is how many bytes?

6 When you're selecting memory, which is the most critical factor to consider: CAS latency, speed, bandwidth, or memory access type?

7 Should you use registered (buffered) memory in your computer?

Topic B: Memory packaging

This topic covers the following CompTIA Server+ (2009 Edition) exam objectives.

#	Objective
1.3	**Differentiate between memory features/types, and given a scenario, select an appropriate processor** • ECC vs. non-ECC • Types – DDR – DIMM – DDR2 – DDR3 • Memory compatibility – Size – Pins – Vendor-specific memory • On board vs. riser card

Packaging

Explanation

In the very early days of PC computing, you purchased individual DRAM chips and installed them into sockets on your motherboard, as shown in Exhibit 4-1. Such systems typically supported a maximum of 1 MB of memory.

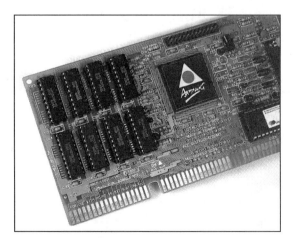

Exhibit 4-1: Individual memory chips installed on an early video card

That era passed with the release of the IBM AT computer. Since that time, DRAM chips have been factory-installed on small circuit boards, called packages. You install the package, more commonly called a module, into a slot in the computer.

Exhibit 4-2: A single inline memory module (SIMM), showing its DRAM chips

Modules are easier to handle and work with than are individual chips. Modules are smaller and support much higher memory densities.

As shown in Exhibit 4-2, a memory module has metal pins, or contacts, along its bottom edge. When inserted into the appropriate motherboard socket, these pins complete the electrical connections between the computer's circuitry and the memory module's circuits.

In some computers, you install the memory module into a riser card and then install the riser card into a special slot on the motherboard. This arrangement typically allows you to fit more modules into a small case or into a space crowded by other components. Some rack-mounted computers, slim-case PCs, and Macintosh systems use a riser card arrangement. Electronically, these riser cards are analogous to an extension cord in that they do little other than extend the wires and connectors to a more convenient orientation. Thus, there is usually no performance impact from installing memory into a riser card versus onto the motherboard.

Single- and double-sided modules

Early memory packages featured DRAM chips on just one side. Manufacturers quickly learned how to double the amount of memory in a given area by installing DRAM on both sides of the module.

In double-sided modules, what appears to be a single row of pins at the bottom is actually two rows. The pins on the front side of the module aren't connected to those on the back side.

Number of DRAM chips

Early module types had eight DRAM chips, one to store each bit in a byte of data. Think back to the addressing schemes described earlier; while each DRAM chip can store multiple rows of data, it stores just one column's worth of data. Thus, eight chips were required to store the eight bits of a byte that spanned a single row of data.

Thanks to ever-shrinking fabrication technologies, the number of chips on a module no longer corresponds to the amount of data being stored. A module might have two, four, or some other number of chips, yet still hold massive quantities of data.

Package types

The following table lists the most common memory package (module) types. The memory package type you use must match the memory slots on the motherboard. Two common examples of PC memory modules are shown in Exhibit 4-3 and Exhibit 4-4.

Package	Pins	Used in	Description
SIMM	30	386-class desktops, early Macintosh computers	Single inline memory module. A notch on one end ensures that you insert this module in the correct orientation. About 3.5" long by 5/8" high.
SIMM	72	486 and early Pentium desktops	One notch in the middle and another notch at one end ensure that you insert this module in the correct orientation. About 4.25" by 1".
DIMM	100	Printers	Dual inline memory module. Has 50 pins on the front and 50 pins on the back. Two notches, one centered and the other off-center, ensure correct installation. About 3.5" by 1.25".
DIMM	168	Pentium and Athlon systems	Has 84 pins on the front and 84 pins on the back. Two notches, one centered and the other off-center, ensure correct installation. About 5.25" by 1".
DIMM	184	DDR SDRAM in desktops	Has 92 pins in front and 92 pins in back. Two notches, one centered and the other off-center, ensure correct installation. About 5.25" by 1".
DIMM	240	DDR2 SDRAM in desktops	Supports 64-bit memory and processors. Has 120 front pins and 120 back pins. Two notches, one centered and the other off-center, ensure correct installation. About 5.25" by 1.18".
DIMM	240	DDR3 SDRAM in desktops	Uses the JEDEC standard fly-by technology, in which signals are routed to each component in serial-like fashion, and times to memory devices are skewed. Compare this to DDR2 technology, in which the signals are routed to arrive at the same time for all of the memory components on the DIMM. Fly-by technology improves signal integrity, but requires additional complexity for the controller. Has 120 front pins and 120 back pins. About 5.25" by 1.18" (heights can vary).
RIMM	184	Intel Pentium III Xeon and Pentium 4 systems	Used with RDRAM chips and trademarked by Rambus. Has 184 edge connector pads with 1 mm pad spacing. RIMM is sometimes incorrectly used as an acronym for "Rambus inline memory module."

Package	Pins	Used in	Description
MICRODIMM	144	Subnotebook computers	Micro dual inline memory module. Has 72 front pins and 72 back pins. A single notch at one end ensures correct installation. About 1.545" by 1".
SODIMM	144	Laptop and notebook computers	Small outline dual inline memory module. Has 72 front pins and 72 back pins. A single off-center notch ensures correct installation. About 2.625" by 1".
SODIMM	200	DDR memory for laptops and notebooks	Has 100 front pins and 100 back pins. A single off-center notch ensures correct installation. About 2.625" by 1". DDR SODIMMs use PC2100, PC2700, and PC3200 SDRAM.
SODIMM	200	DDR2 memory for laptops and notebooks	Has 100 front pins and 100 back pins. A single off-center notch ensures correct installation. About 2.625" by 1". DDR2 SODIMMs use PC2-4200 SDRAM.
SODIMM	204	DDR3 memory for laptops and notebooks	Has 102 front pins and 102 back pins. About 2.6" by 1.75" (heights can vary slightly).

Exhibit 4-3: A PC2100 SODIMM package from a laptop

Exhibit 4-4: A 168-pin DIMM package from a desktop computer

Memory error recovery

Memory errors occur, perhaps more frequently than any of us wants to know. However, there are technologies that enable computer components to detect and even recover from memory errors. These technologies are parity and error correcting code (ECC).

Parity

Parity is a scheme that enables the detection of an error. Consider a memory module that stores eight bits of data in eight chips. If the data in one chip goes bad, the entire byte becomes corrupt. However, designers can add a ninth chip to store a parity bit.

This parity bit is set to zero if the sum of all the other bits is an even number, or set to one if the sum of the bits is odd. To detect whether the bit in one chip has gone bad, the computer recalculates parity after reading the data and comparing the result to the value in the parity bit.

Unfortunately, with this simple scheme, your computer can't tell which of the eight bits in the byte was corrupted. It just knows that one of the bits has been changed.

Exhibit 4-5 shows two early SIMMs. One chip, from a Macintosh, had just eight DRAM chips and didn't support parity. The other chip, from a PC, had nine chips and supported parity.

Exhibit 4-5: Two early SIMMs, one with parity support and one without

ECC

Error correcting code (ECC) permits your computer not only to detect that an error has occurred, but also to correct that error. As with parity, when the computer reads the data from the module, it recalculates the ECC value and compares it to the value on the module. If the values match, no errors have occurred. If they don't, then by using other calculations on the ECC value, the computer can determine what was changed and what its original value was.

Use of parity and ECC in current computers

Early PCs used parity memory, while early Macintosh computers didn't. PC aficionados of the day claimed that as a reason for the PC's superiority, but you could say that the Macintosh was simply ahead of the curve. Modern computers of both platforms rarely use parity or ECC memory.

In a move to save money, hardware designers have eliminated parity and ECC support from most modern desktop and laptop computers. Designers hope that memory errors won't occur that frequently. To a lesser extent, memory errors can be detected with software rather than hardware.

It's cheaper to make a non-parity or non-ECC memory module than one with those features. The difference is probably close to 11%, because designers can use one fewer out of nine chips by not storing that parity bit or ECC code.

Server-class computers often do include ECC or parity. Take care when purchasing memory modules for a computer. You must use modules that either support, or don't support, parity or ECC, as dictated by your system's design.

Do it!

B-1: Comparing RAM packaging

Here's how	Here's why
1 Identify the memory modules supplied by your instructor. For each, note its type, the number of pins, and whether it's for a notebook or desktop computer	
2 You want to add more RAM to a computer you own. What's the first step you should take?	
3 With the instructor, your lab partner, or another student in class, debate the pros and cons of using ECC memory in your computer	

Unit summary: Selecting memory

Topic A

In this topic, you learned that **RAM** is the hardware component that stores active data and applications. You learned about the various units, such as MB and GB, which are used to describe the quantity of RAM installed in a PC. You also learned about the various **characteristics of memory**, such as whether it's volatile or non-volatile and synchronous or asynchronous, as well as the technology by which it's accessed.

Topic B

In this topic, you learned that chips are bundled into packages called **modules**. You learned about the various memory module types, including SIMMs, DIMMs, and SODIMMs. You also learned that **errors in memory** can be detected and even corrected through parity or ECC.

Review questions

1 The actual storage locations on a memory chip are called what?

A Bits

B Cells

C RAM

D Word

2 Which memory unit's size depends on the processor?

A Bit

B Byte

C Nibble

D Word

3 What type of memory loses its contents when power isn't present?

A Asynchronous

B Dynamic

C Non-volatile

D Static

E Synchronous

F Volatile

4 Which of the following memory types are non-volatile? [Choose all that apply.]

A CMOS

B EPROM

C EEPROM

D Flash

E PROM

F RAM

G ROM

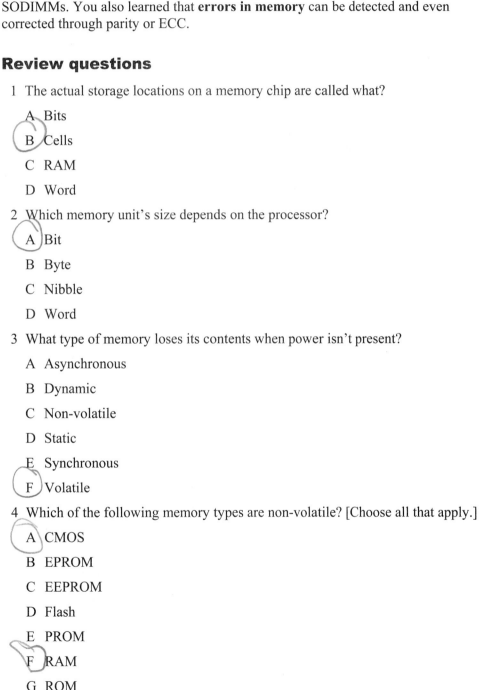

5 What type of RAM loses its contents quickly, even when power is present?

  A DRAM

  B Flash

  C RAM

  D SRAM

6 Which type of memory is tied to the system clock?

  A Asynchronous

  B Dynamic

  C Non-volatile

  D Static

  E Synchronous

  F Volatile

7 Which of the following is defined as "the amount of data that can be transferred to or from memory per second"?

  A Access time

  B Bandwidth

  C Memory speed

  D Overall speed

8 Individual memory chips installed on the motherboard were replaced with memory _Cluster_.

9 Which of the following memory packages are used in laptop or notebook computers? [Choose all that apply.]

  A 144-pin MICRODIMM

  B 168-pin DIMM

  C 184-pin RIMM

  D 200-pin SODIMM

  E 240-pin DIMM

10 True or false? Parity permits a computer not only to detect that an error has occurred, but also to correct that error. _True_

11 True or false? The number of chips on a memory module corresponds to the quantity of data being stored by the package. _false_

Independent practice activity

In this activity, you'll practice identifying correct memory upgrade modules for a PC.

1 Open the Control Panel, and then open System and Maintenance, and System.

2 How much RAM is installed on your computer?

3 Using your computer manufacturer's support Web site or computer's user manual, determine the type of memory modules that your computer supports. Make sure to consider both physical characteristics (size, shape, number of pins, riser card vs. on-board installation, and so forth) as well as performance characteristics (memory access design, CAS latency, timing, speed, and so forth).

4 Using your Web browser, determine the cost to replace 2 GB of RAM for your computer.

Unit 5

Troubleshooting methodology

Unit time: 120 minutes

Complete this unit, and you'll know how to:

A Explain troubleshooting theory and methodology.

B Identify the functions of troubleshooting tools.

C Troubleshoot hardware problems.

Topic A: Troubleshooting models

This topic covers the following CompTIA Server+ (2009 Edition) exam objective.

#	Objective
6.1	**Explain troubleshooting theory and methodologies**

- Identify the problem and determine the scope
  - Question user/stakeholders and identify user changes to the server / environment
  - Collect additional documentation / logs
  - If possible, replicate the problem as appropriate
  - If possible, perform backups before making changes
- Establish a theory of probable cause (question the obvious)
  - Determine whether there is a common element of symptom causing multiple problems
- Test the theory to determine cause
  - Once theory is confirmed, determine next steps to resolve problem
  - If theory is not confirmed, re-establish new theory or escalate
- Establish a plan of action to resolve the problem and notify impacted users
- Implement the solution or escalate as appropriate
  - Make one change at a time and test/confirm that the change has resolved the problem
  - If the problem is not resolved, reverse the change if appropriate and implement new change
- Verify full system functionality and if applicable implement preventative measures
- Root cause analysis
- Document findings, actions, and outcomes throughout the process

The troubleshooting process

Explanation

Troubleshooting is the process of determining the cause of, and ultimately the solution to, a problem. By applying a logical, consistent method to the troubleshooting process, you make your job easier and shorten the time it takes to discover the root of a problem.

There are several popular troubleshooting models to choose from. All models incorporate basic troubleshooting theory. The stages of basic troubleshooting theory are described in the following table.

Stage	Description
Back up data	If the changes you plan to make might make the data on the system inaccessible, back up data before making any changes.
Divide and analyze	Assess the problem systematically. If it's a large or widespread problem, divide it into smaller components to be analyzed individually.
Verify	Verify all aspects of the problem. Be sure not to overlook the obvious problems. Determine whether the problem is something simple. Remember never to make assumptions.
Research	Research ideas about possible solutions to the problem. Establish priorities for resolving the problem.
Document	Document your findings. These include the actions you take and their outcomes, both for the solutions that worked and for those that didn't work.
Inform	Throughout the process, keep affected users and stakeholders informed and aware of actions taken to resolve the problem.

CompTIA's Server+ troubleshooting model

The CompTIA Server+ troubleshooting model has you work through stages to apply basic diagnostic procedures and troubleshooting techniques. CompTIA recommends working through the stages described in the following table.

Stage	Description
Identify the problem	Identify the problem by questioning server users and determining if the IT staff made any changes in the server and its environment. Review log files or other documentation created when the system was changed. Try to replicate the problem, and record any error, warning, or information messages, as well as symptoms of the problem you observe. Perform a backup before making any changes on the system.
Establish a theory of probable cause	Analyze the problem, including potential causes, so you can establish a theory of probable cause. You can then make an initial determination of whether the problem is software- and/or hardware-related. If there are multiple problems, determine if there is a common element among them.
Test the theory to determine the actual cause	Test the theory to determine the actual cause. Test components related to the problem. This process includes inspecting components for obvious things, such as connections and power being connected and turned on, proper hardware and/or software configurations, and indications of conflicts or problems in operating system utilities and logs. Also, consult vendor documentation for descriptions of status lights and other indicators.
	Once you've confirmed your theory, determine the next steps you should take to resolve the problem. If you can't confirm your theory, re-evaluate to establish a new theory or escalate the problem to specialists.
Create a plan of action	Create a plan to resolve the problem and implement the solution. You might need to include other IT professionals, such as your company's network technician, to get assistance in implementing the resolution. If there are users or IT staff who will be affected by the system changes you make, or who will be without services for a period of time, you should notify them of the steps you will be taking to resolve the problem. It's helpful to give them an estimate of the completion time.
Implement the solution	Carry out the steps in your action plan. Be sure to make one change at time, recording as you go, so that if the solution does not resolve the problem, you can revert the system to its original state and implement a new plan of action.
Verify the results	Verify the results, and if necessary, take additional steps to correct the problem. Additional steps might include consulting with other professionals or the vendor, using alternative resources, and reviewing equipment manuals. Once you've established full system functionality, you need to implement applicable preventive measures to prevent the problem from reoccurring.
Root cause analysis	After you have established that the symptoms of the problem are no longer occurring, you need to analyze whether you've resolved the root cause of the problem or just made symptoms disappear temporarily.
Document resolution	Document the actions you took to correct the problem, as well as the outcomes of those actions.

CompTIA's Network+ troubleshooting model

CompTIA recommends a troubleshooting model for network technicians. You can follow this process for computer repair as well. The process consists of eight stages, described in the following table.

Stage	Description
Identify the exact issue	Ask the customer open-ended questions to determine the precise nature of the problem.
Re-create the problem	Have the customer repeat the action or demonstrate the problem. As an alternative, you can follow the steps to re-create the problem.
Isolate the cause	Eliminate factors that are obviously not part of the problem. Then, starting with the most likely cause of the problem, begin to identify the cause.
Formulate a correction	Determine one or more solutions to the cause that you've identified.
Implement the correction	If implementing the correction doesn't solve the customer's problem, undo any changes you made. Then, working with the next most likely cause, formulate a correction and implement it.
Test the solution	Make sure that your solution actually fixed the problem. Verify that the user agrees that you've fixed his or her problem and that the solution hasn't caused other problems.
Document the problem and solution	Create a detailed record of the problem and eventual solution. You'll be able to use this documentation in future troubleshooting situations.
Provide feedback	Based on your assessment of the customer's interest and technical understanding, describe to him or her the exact cause of and solution to the problem.

Novell's troubleshooting model

Novell, the maker of the Open Enterprise Server network operating system, publishes a troubleshooting model for network technicians. You can apply this model to troubleshooting PC hardware problems. This model has six steps, described in the following table.

Step	Description
Try some quick, obvious fixes	Some obvious fixes might include making sure the computer or peripheral is plugged in and turned on, the user is performing the procedure correctly, and so forth.
Gather basic information	Determine the exact symptoms of the problem. Determine whether the system worked correctly before, and if so, what has changed. Check to see if other users are having the same problem.
Develop a plan	Use the information you've gathered to determine a plan for isolating and correcting the problem. Prioritize possible solutions and begin with the most likely solution. Document your plan for future reference.
Execute your plan	Follow the plan you've developed. Make one change at a time, testing after each change. If it doesn't solve the problem, undo your changes before attempting a new solution. Document your changes so that you can either undo them or repeat them in the future with similar problems.
Verify user satisfaction	The problem isn't truly solved until the customer is satisfied. Make sure the customer agrees that your solution actually fixed the problem.
Document the problem and solution	Record the exact symptoms and solution to the problem. Formulate a plan to prevent future, similar problems.

The ASID troubleshooting model

The ASID troubleshooting model offers a four-stage process you can apply to many types of problems. Its stages are:

1 **A**cquire — Acquire information about the problem.
2 **S**implify — Remove any non-critical components.
3 **I**mplement — Identify and implement potential solutions, one at a time.
4 **D**ocument — Document the problem and its resolution.

In the Acquire stage, you collect information about the problem. During this stage, you:

- Elicit symptoms of the problem from the user.
- Have the user repeat the activity that caused the problem to reproduce the error for you.
- Document the exact steps that caused the problem.
- Identify any recent changes in the computer and its configuration.
- Document any error codes reported by the system.
- Check Event Viewer for any recorded problems.
- Place Dr. Watson in the Startup group to log any future occurrences of the problem.

In the Simplify stage, you remove any non-critical components, such as unnecessary peripherals, shut down unnecessary running programs, disconnect from the Internet or network, and so forth. If the problem goes away, its cause lies with one of the components you removed. If not, then you have simplified the system, which makes troubleshooting easier.

In the Implement stage, you identify and implement potential solutions one at a time. Check reference materials for potential solutions. Resources might include:

- User and installation manuals and product documentation
- Internet and Web resources, such as manufacturers' Web sites and users' forums
- Training materials

Make sure to document any changes you make on the system. If a particular change doesn't fix the problem, undo your change and try another solution.

The Document stage occurs throughout the other stages and finishes after you have a resolution to the problem. During the previous stages, you documented:

- The error symptoms
- The components you removed from the computer
- The potential solutions you tried and whether they were successful

At the end of this process, you must fully document the resolution for later reference. It's just as important to record any significant or obvious potential solutions that turned out not to solve the problem so that you can avoid dead ends in the future.

Do it!   ## A-1: Discussing troubleshooting methods

Questions and answers

1 Which troubleshooting model is best, and which is worst? Why?

2 Hector reports that his computer doesn't work. Using either CompTIA model, describe the first step you would take to fix his problem.

3 Isabelle calls you to say she can't print from Microsoft Word but can print fine from other applications. She has a complex system with a scanner, two printers, a fax device, and dual monitors. Following the ASID method, what would your first steps be?

4 What documentation should you record after you've found the solution to Hector's and Isabelle's problems?

5 A user calls the Help desk because her Windows XP Professional computer has unexpectedly shut down and is now displaying a blue screen with a white STOP error. What should you do first in the ASID troubleshooting method?

Gathering information from a user

Explanation

When you're troubleshooting a problem, you need to gather information from the user regarding the situation that needs to be resolved. No matter which troubleshooting method you use, or if your company has its own set of steps to use in resolving problems, you need to gather information from the user. You also need a method for capturing this information. The method can be as simple as using a clipboard with a paper and pencil, or more complex, such as using a portable computing device or a networked application.

You should identify and capture information relating to:

- The customer's environment
- Symptoms and error codes
- Circumstances in which the problem occurred

The customer's environment

You should retrieve information about the customer's environment, including where the user is located and what platform is being used. With today's mobile workforce, you can't assume that just because Josephine is a regular caller from Building 340, that's where she's calling you from today. She might be traveling, might be working from home, or might have moved to another office in the latest company reorganization.

"Platform" includes information about the hardware and the operating system. If the user is using a Macintosh notebook computer and you're assuming she's using an Intel-based Windows Vista desktop system, neither of you is likely to be very successful in resolving the problem.

Symptoms and error codes

Always ask users what they have observed about the problem. Sometimes all users know is that they can't print a document. Other times, they might have received an error message or code. Ask if the printing problem happens in all applications or in just a particular application. For example, if users can print successfully from their word processing application but can't print the report from the mainframe that they connect to from their PC, then you can identify a possible configuration problem or a network problem with the mainframe connection.

The situation when the problem occurred

Knowing under what circumstances a problem occurs can also be a big help in resolving a problem. If the problem occurs only when the user has two particular applications open or when the user's system is connected to the remote server via modem, then those are clues that there are conflicts between the two items. There might be a hardware conflict or some other configuration problem.

It's also useful to know which applications were open when the problem first occurred, whether any new hardware or software was recently installed, and any other information about what was happening at the time. Users might be reluctant to tell you everything, especially if they were playing a game or using software such as instant messaging or music-file-sharing applications, which might be unauthorized for use in the company.

Identifying hardware or software problems

Sometimes it's easy to point fingers and say "It's a hardware problem" (or a software problem) without fully examining the problem. Configuration has become much easier with the use of USB ports for most connections. Often, it can be tricky to determine whether the hardware has developed intermittent problems or whether there's a configuration problem with its device drivers. Other times, the problem might lie with the application that makes use of the hardware, or the cable connecting the hardware to the computer.

You can use the information you gathered from the user as a starting point for pinpointing the source of the problem. Based on this information, you can begin to analyze the problem and hypothesize about whether the likely cause of the problem is hardware- or software-based.

The documentation, the Web site for the hardware or software, and the settings on the computer are all essential sources to check when you're determining whether the problem is a hardware or software issue. You can be sure it's hardware-related if error codes or messages are displayed before the end of the POST (power-on self test). No software or drivers are loaded before the PC boot process begins—that is, after the POST.

If the POST finishes with no issues, the problem could be due to a configuration problem or to failed hardware. If new hardware was just added to the system, check that it was properly set up and configured. If new software was installed, check whether this was the problem.

Do it!

A-2: Developing a hypothesis about a problem's cause

Questions and answers

1 You've have been called to troubleshoot a printer problem in your company's Finance department. How should you begin investigating the problem?

2 What information would lead you to hypothesize that it's a hardware problem (a problem at the printer)?

3 What information would lead you to hypothesize that it's a software problem (a problem at the user's computer)?

Information resources

Explanation When you're troubleshooting, you can use several kinds of resources to research problems and solutions. Let's take a look at some of the resources you should consider when resolving problems.

Documentation

Documentation is the key to successful troubleshooting. Such documentation takes two forms: that which is provided by others and that which you create.

You'll find product manuals, manufacturer Web sites, and technology-related knowledge bases to be invaluable sources of information. You should consult these references early in the troubleshooting process to determine if you're dealing with a known problem that has a previously published solution.

Problems that you must solve are often specific to your customer's combination of hardware and software, as well as specific to how the person uses his system. Your notes are the best reference for future problems because they apply specifically to your customer's environment

When you're determining the best documentation solution for your needs, consider the factors described in the following table.

Factor	Description
Paper or software	Decide which is best for your needs: a paper-based or software-based record of problems and solutions. Paper logs are well suited for one- or two-person troubleshooting teams. You probably need to use software solutions for larger or distributed troubleshooting teams. If you use a software-based system, you must consider how to maintain the information and make it available during a computer outage or after a disaster.
Organization scheme	How you organize your log information determines how you can find the data later. If you're using software, it determines which scheme or schemes you must use. If you're using paper, you could organize your notes by hardware component, by software application, by problem symptom, by user or department, by location, or some other scheme.
Level of detail	Only you and your troubleshooting team can determine how much information to record. If you don't record enough detail about the problem and its solution, the documentation will be useless for solving future similar problems.

Forums

Forums are online discussion groups. They enable various people to gather at a central location online to discuss common interests in an open format. Members of the forum can exchange information and ideas.

A generic forum might be created to discuss general network issues. A forum often contains information on problems and solutions. When you have a problem, you can visit the forum and see if anyone else had a similar problem and found a resolution. These postings are not usually verified by a vendor or manufacturer as providing the best solution to a problem; they are just what worked for a particular person. An example is the Web site at *msfn.org*; it's a site dedicated to Windows operating systems and desktop applications, but it's not a Microsoft-affiliated site.

Vendor-sponsored forums do have experts on staff to review the postings. They can also help members by gathering information about the problem and guiding them through the troubleshooting process. Most vendors then post a summary of the problem and step-by-step instructions for resolving it. An example is *forums.microsoft.com*, which is a Web site dedicated to Microsoft products and technologies.

Other sources

Other resources that you should consult include trade magazines and Web sites, fellow employees, newsgroups, vendor group meetings, and independent consultants. Being open to using a variety of sources to resolve your problem gives you more flexibility in finding a solution as quickly as possible.

Keeping up-to-date on your knowledge through reading trade magazines and attending trade shows and vendor group meetings can help you keep abreast of potential problems. Even if you haven't yet encountered a problem being described in the article or meeting, if it should arise, you will know what to do about it.

Your fellow employees can be a great source of information, especially if you are new to the group. You might have worked for several years in a support capacity at one company, but a new company might have a whole different set of common problems that could be easily resolved if only you knew where to look and what to do. Even on an established team of support technicians, multiple people looking at the problem can bring their own experience to the table, and one team member might see something that another person missed.

If you can't find the solution in a timely manner, you should contact the vendor for specific help. A vendor can usually guide you through the steps to resolve the problem. Another option to consider is hiring an independent consultant who's an expert in the area in which you are experiencing the problem. Consultants often have vast experience in their areas of expertise and can help you find the solution quickly.

Do it!   ## A-3: Identifying documentation and information resources

Questions and answers

1 If the users you are supporting have a recurrent problem, which is the best source to use in resolving the problem?

2 Discuss the potential drawbacks of using a generic forum for answers to your problems.

3 Using a variety of sources, find the best solution to the problem assigned by your instructor.

Microsoft Help and Support

When you're having a problem with software or hardware on a computer running a Microsoft operating system, an excellent troubleshooting reference is Microsoft's Help and Support Web site. This site contains problem and solution references for the Microsoft server operating systems you'll be supporting, such as Windows Server 2000, Windows Server 2003, and Windows Server 2008. You'll also find support information on server applications, such as Microsoft Exchange Server, Microsoft SQL Server, and others. Sometimes the Web site provides a hyperlink to an FTP site, where you can download patches and new releases.

A component of the Help and Support Center is the Microsoft Knowledge Base, which explains many Microsoft error messages. You can enter the specific message in the Search box and retrieve a description of the error's cause and a solution for resolving the problem.

To search the Microsoft Knowledge Base for a specific error:

1 Using Internet Explorer or another Web browser, go to *support.microsoft.com*.

2 Under "Get help with…," click Error messages.

3 Begin typing the error code or phrase for the search.

4 Select the desired error from the list of search results.

5 Click an article to read it. Exhibit 5-1 shows an example of the components of a Microsoft Knowledge Base article. You'd expand each section to read its contents.

You can print articles or save them on your hard disk for later reference.

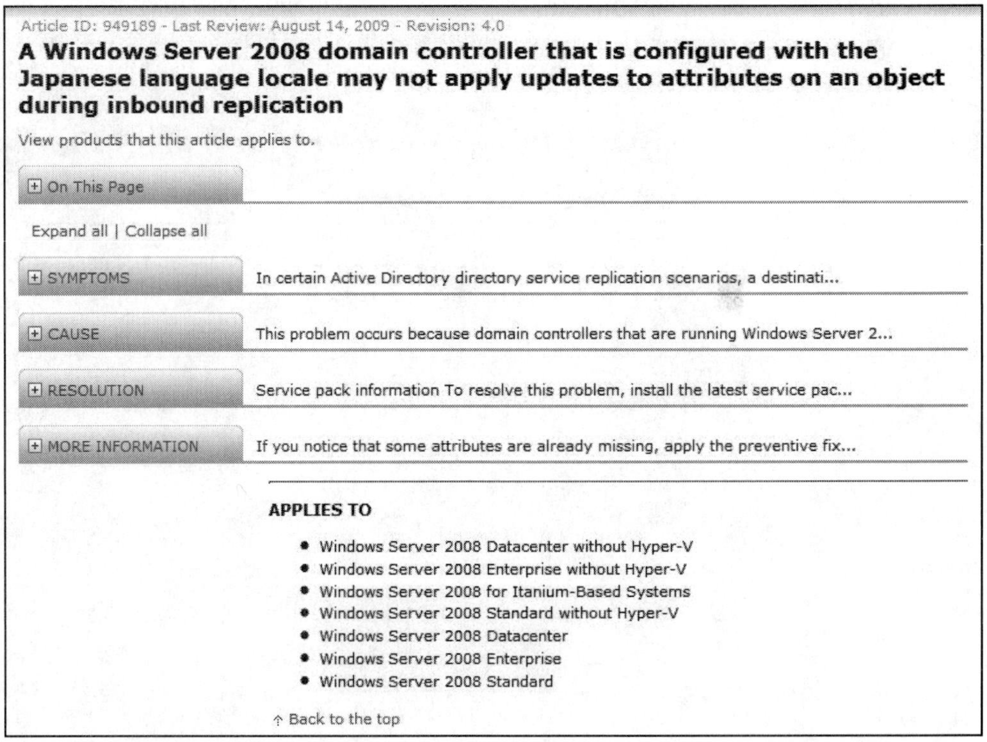

Exhibit 5-1: Components of a Microsoft Knowledge Base article

Do it!

A-4:   Using Microsoft Help and Support to research an error code

Here's how	Here's why
1 You've created a delegation for a reverse lookup zone in DNS Manager on your Windows Server 2008 server. When you refresh the view, the delegation doesn't appear in the list. Where would you go to research the cause of this problem?	
2 If necessary, turn on the power to your computer	
3 Log in as **Administrator** with a password of **!pass1234**	This is an administrative user account that was created during class setup.
4 Open Internet Explorer	
5 Research and determine the cause and resolution of this problem. (You can use the Advanced Search feature to narrow your results to Windows Server 2008.)	

Problem and resolution tracking

Explanation
It's important to maintain information about the problems you need to resolve and the resolutions to those problems. You must keep track of all open issues so you and your support technician teammates don't let customers slip through the cracks. Having a record of past resolutions can help you when you encounter similar problems in the future.

Tracking options

The options for tracking problems and resolutions are nearly endless. They range from something as simple as a pen-and-paper-based system in a three-ring binder, to an off-the-shelf problem tracking and resolution database, to a custom-built application. Your choice depends on the size of the user base you're supporting and the needs of the organization.

Whichever system you use, you should maintain a backup copy in a secure location so that if something happens to the original, you have access to the copy. A system on a server could be unavailable due to server problems, network problems, or computer workstation problems. Any system could be unavailable due to a fire or natural disaster.

Important information you should consider tracking in your system includes:

- User name and location
- Operating system
- Hardware platform
- Date the call was received
- Date the user was visited
- Amount of time spent on the problem
- Date the problem was resolved
- Detailed description of the problem
- Detailed description of steps taken to resolve the problem
- Summary of problem (using keywords or a one-line summary)
- Summary of resolution (using keywords or a one-line summary)

Help desk software

Many vendors offer software for managing problem-tracking and help desk functions. Companies like IBM, Computer Associates, and others offer large-scale commercial problem-tracking applications.

Many smaller companies offer similar packages aimed at smaller companies' needs or targeted vertical markets. For example, you can find applications designed specifically to support the tracking needs of Web site hosting companies or software developers.

Visit *www.helpdesk.com/software-helpdesk.htm* for a long list of help desk software publishers and their Web sites. More information, particularly on the smaller vendor products, is available at *http://linas.org/linux/pm.html*.

Do it!

A-5:   Tracking problems and resolutions

Here's how

1 Use Internet Explorer to search the Web for a problem-tracking system

2 List the features in the solution you found.

3 Are there any features you'd like that aren't included in this solution?

4 Would your company be more likely to develop its own database to track problems or to purchase some type of problem-tracking system? Would it be very basic, or be an integrated solution with modules for tracking assets as well as problems? Explain your reasons.

5 Close your Web browser

Topic B: Troubleshooting toolkits

This topic covers the following CompTIA Server+ (2009 Edition) exam objective.

#	Objective
6.2	**Given a scenario, effectively troubleshoot hardware problems, selecting the appropriate tools and methods** • Hardware tools – Power supply tester (multimeter) – System board tester – Compressed air – ESD equipment

The troubleshooting toolkit

Explanation

Support technicians need tools that perform a wide variety of functions. Repair toolkits are available for amateurs and for professionals. These specialty hardware toolkits contain versions of the tools appropriate for working with computer and network components. You can also assemble your own basic repair toolkit with the following items:

- **A variety of screwdrivers** — You should have large and small versions of flat-blade, Phillips, and Torx screwdrivers.
- **Nut drivers** — Used to remove and replace hex-head nuts. As with screwdrivers, you should have a variety of sizes in your toolkit.
- **Small and large needle-nose pliers** — Useful for grasping objects.
- **Tweezers** — Also used for grasping objects.
- **Three-pronged "grabber"** — Used to pick up screws or other objects in areas too small to get your fingers into.
- **A small flashlight** — A small penlight or a light that can be clamped to the computer case can prove quite useful.
- **Small containers** — Useful for holding screws and small components that are easily lost.
- **Compressed air** — Useful for blowing dust and debris off of electronic components that can't be cleaned with water or other liquid cleaning solutions. Be aware that the propellant is not air, but a hydrofluorocarbon, which is a health risk if inhaled.
- **Antistatic sprays** — Useful if your clothes are likely to generate static.
- **Antistatic bags** — Used to protect components that are sensitive to static electricity.

⚠️ Never lay a component on the outside of an antistatic bag. The bag is designed to collect static charges on the outside of it, so if you place a component on the bag, the collected static charges might discharge onto the component.

- **Grounding wrist straps and antistatic mats** — Used to protect the equipment from any static you might be carrying on your body. You use these tools to prevent the buildup of charge differentials and to equalize them safely. An antistatic wrist strap, pictured in Exhibit 5-2, is a common antistatic device.

⚠ A grounding wrist strap should never be worn when you're working on the interior of a monitor, but in all other situations, this is a highly recommended ESD protection tool.

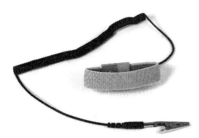

Exhibit 5-2: An antistatic wrist strap

When troubleshooting various hardware components, you can use the specialty tools listed in the following table.

Tool	Used to...
Multimeter	Test equipment with readings of ohms, amps, and volts. Comparing the readings with the appropriate values for a component helps you determine if there's a problem with the component. Multimeters are available in digital and analog models. • Digital multimeters, as shown in Exhibit 5-3, output discrete numeric values on an LED or LCD display. • Analog multimeters, the older type, display their output with a needle and dial.
System board tester	Test a computer that isn't booting to the operating system, displays a blank screen, or has a POST or boot problem that isn't displaying an error code or producing audible beep errors. This device is a circuit board with on-board diagnostic capabilities that you plug into an expansion slot in your computer.
Temperature monitor	Monitor temperature in various environments, especially in rooms containing networking devices. High temperatures can damage some network devices, including servers. Monitors can be configured to warn you when the temperature has exceeded a specific limit, so you can take corrective action.
Voltage event recorder	Measure electrical properties to determine whether there's an adequate power supply and what the quality of that power supply is.

Exhibit 5-3: A digital multimeter

You can use the tools in the following table when working with and troubleshooting network connections. Most often, these tools will be used by a network technician, but it's helpful for all IT support personnel to be familiar with the function of each tool.

Tool	Used to...
Butt set	Test and verify telephone lines.
Cable stripper	Remove the outer insulation from network cables and expose the wires inside them. Usually, this tool also includes wire cutters for cutting the cable or wire.
Certifier	Test and verify network cable speeds by sending data packets across the network. You can use certifiers to verify that network segments are operating at optimal levels.
Crimper	Crimp a connector onto a network cable. It comes in varieties for RJ-11, RJ-45, and coaxial cable.
Optical time-domain reflectometer (OTDR)	Locate faults in optical fiber.
Punchdown tool	Connect wires to a punchdown block.
Snips	Cut or trim cables.
Time-domain reflectometer (TDR)	Locate problems in metallic wires, such as coaxial cable and twisted-pair network cables.

The software toolkit

Most people think of hardware tools when you speak of assembling a toolkit for a network technician. However, there are several software tools you'll need for a complete troubleshooting toolkit, especially when you're troubleshooting clients and servers and their network connections.

Tool	Description
Disk containing common drivers	If your company has standardized a specific set of equipment with common drivers, having a disk with you can make it easy to install the drivers quickly if you have to remove them to fix a problem or if they become corrupted. Many companies place the files on a central server location, but if you can't access the server due to the problem you're trying to fix, having the drivers on the server won't do you any good.
Antivirus software	You should include a boot disk from which you can boot a system that has been infected with a boot virus. Norton and McAfee are examples of companies that make antivirus software you can use to create such a disk. Follow the manufacturer's directions to clean the virus from the system. Sometimes you need to boot from the antivirus software CD or DVD when you need to clean a system, so configure CMOS to be able to boot from CD or DVD.
Boot disk	A bootable floppy disk, CD, or DVD is useful if you can no longer boot from the hard drive. This CD, DVD, or floppy disk should contain basic commands that enable you to perform simple tasks.
Operating system CD or DVD	Having a copy of the operating system CD or DVD enables you to get to the CAB files that you might need when installing or repairing some piece of hardware. It's also useful if you need to boot from the CD or DVD, or if files or drivers have been corrupted and need to be replaced.
Documentation about common problems	If you encounter a set of common problems and need documentation on how to fix them, a CD or flash drive with that information can prove valuable. If the documentation is in a searchable format, then you can easily find the information you need to fix a problem you've encountered in the past.

Web sites for the manufacturers of the equipment you support should be included somewhere in your toolkit. A bookmark list, a paper list, or a document containing the URLs is useful. Being able to access the support sites directly is beneficial when you need to get updated drivers or look for solutions to problems. Another useful site is *drivers.com*. You can download drivers for many components, including some from companies no longer in operation.

A CD or DVD binder is useful for carrying these tools with you. CD or DVD binders come in a variety of sizes. You can also copy the files to a USB flash drive instead of to a CD or DVD if you prefer.

Do it!

B-1:   Identifying common toolkit components

Here's how	Here's why
1 Open a Web browser and go to a search site	You'll examine the components of a hardware technician's toolkit.
2 Search for **computer maintenance toolkit**	
3 Compare your results with those of other students	Options range from small kits with a few tools for a modest price, to comprehensive kits for a facility specializing in hardware repairs.
4 Which tools would you include in your toolkit for your job?	
5 What specialty tools would you add to your toolkit?	
6 On the Web, search for a motherboard tester What types are available?	
7 When would you use a temperature monitor?	
8 What software tools would you include in your troubleshooting kit?	
9 Search for diagnostic software. What are some examples you find?	
10 In addition to the software mentioned in the text, are there any other tools you would include?	
11 Close your Web browser	

Topic C: Troubleshooting system components

This topic covers the following CompTIA Server+ (2009 Edition) exam objectives.

#	Objective
1.7	**Install, update, and configure appropriate firmware** • Driver / hardware compatibility • Implications of a failed firmware upgrade (redundant BIOS) • Follow manufacturer's instructions and documentation
6.2	**Given a scenario, effectively troubleshoot hardware problems, selecting the appropriate tools and methods** • Common problems – Failed POST – Incorrect boot sequence – Overheating – Operating system not found – Memory failure – Drive failure – Onboard component failure – Power supply failure – Processor failure – I/O failure • Causes of common problems – Third-party components or incompatible components – Mismatched components – Incompatible or incorrect BIOS – Backplane failure – Cooling failure
6.3	**Given a scenario, effectively troubleshoot software problems, selecting the appropriate tools and methods** • Common problems – Memory leak – Runaway process – BSOD / stop – Service failure – OS boot failure – Hangs; no shut down – Driver issues • Causes of common problems – Malware – Corrupted files – Unauthorized software – Virtual memory (misconfigured, corrupt)
6.5	**Given a scenario, effectively troubleshoot storage problems, selecting the appropriate tools and methods** • Common problems – OS not found • Causes of common problems – Media failure – Misconfiguration – Drive failure – Improper disk partition – Controller failure – Bad sectors – Loose connectors – Backplane failure

Troubleshooting power supplies

Explanation Power supply failures and electrical service outages can cause a variety of problems. As a PC technician, you should be familiar with the most common symptoms, probable causes, and suggested "first try" solutions for power supply problems.

You might encounter problems not listed in the following table, but it provides a few scenarios to consider when you're troubleshooting.

Symptom	Probable cause	Suggested solution
Computer fails to boot when powered on, but boots after you press Ctrl+Alt+Del	Power_Good signal from the power supply isn't present, is at the wrong voltage, or is being sent at the wrong time.	Replace the power supply with a better-engineered model.
Computer intermittently stops working or reboots	Electrical service supply is causing problems, such as brownouts or blackouts.	Add a UPS or contact an electrician to check your building's wiring. Confirm that UPSs, surge protectors, or generators are working correctly.
There are not enough power connectors for all the devices you want to install in the computer	Power supply is undersized for your needs. Less expensive power supplies sometimes come with just a few connectors.	Replace the power supply if it's undersized. If it's rated to handle your selection of devices, use a Y-adapter to split the connectors and make more available.
Computer fails to boot at all, with no lights or beeps; fans don't start	Computer is not plugged in. "Hard" power switch is turned off. Power supply has failed. Outlet or power cord is bad. No electrical service due to blackout or other outage. Power switch has failed.	Make sure the computer is plugged in. Use a multimeter to test the power source and cords. Make sure the 110/220 V switch on the power supply is set appropriately.
Computer fails to boot, but fans start	Power connector to motherboard is not hooked up. Computer component other than the power supply has failed.	Confirm internal power connections. Troubleshoot to discover other failed devices.

The Power_Good signal

Insufficient power or a disrupted and noisy electrical connection could damage the power supply or the PC's internal components. Modern power supplies provide some monitoring of the quality of the electrical signal. Specifically, they test the voltage levels of the power and send a signal to the motherboard indicating whether the power is sufficiently good.

The Power_Good signal (also called the Power Good, PowerGood, Power_OK, or PWR_OK signal) is a +5 V voltage that is supplied over a specific wire in the connector that sends power from the power supply to the motherboard. If the signal isn't sent because the electrical power is insufficient, the computer won't boot.

Sometimes a system doesn't boot when you press its power button, but finishes booting after you press Ctrl+Alt+Del. This situation indicates a problem with the Power_Good signal and is a sign of a poorly designed power supply. The Power_Good signal might not be arriving when the motherboard expects it, or it might not be at the proper voltage. You can replace the power supply to fix this problem.

Do it!

C-1: Troubleshooting power supply problems

Questions and answers

1 The customer reports that pressing the power button does nothing, and the computer fails to start. You press the button and indeed, nothing happens. What's the first thing you should check? What else might you check?

2 You're working on a computer that beeps and shows drive activity when you press the power button. The monitor's power light comes on, but no image is displayed. You try a different monitor and it works just fine. Do these conditions indicate a problem with the PC's power supply?

3 Your computer shuts itself down shortly after you boot it. You've had power-related problems in the past and have even installed a UPS with software monitoring functions. Because of the past problems, you suspect a power problem. What should you investigate?

4 One or more power supply problems have been introduced into your lab computer. Troubleshoot these problems to determine their causes.

5 Correct the problems you have found in your PC to return it to a working state. Solving one problem might reveal the presence of another problem. Troubleshoot and fix all problems that arise.

6 Document the problem(s) you find:

7 Document the steps you take to fix the problem(s):

Motherboard and CPU failures

Explanation

Motherboards and CPUs can fail for various reasons. One of the most common causes of failure is a large electric spike, such as that caused by a nearby lightning strike. Often, a motherboard or CPU failure shows up in one of two ways: a complete system failure occurs (nothing happens when you turn the computer on); or unusual problems occur, perhaps sporadically. It's important to note that CPUs rarely fail. If the CPU does fail, it is most commonly a result of an electrical problem such as a power surge, a brownout, or a liquid spill which causes a short in the CPU's circuitry. Distinguishing between a failed CPU and a failed motherboard is difficult. Both failures will present many of the same symptoms.

As a PC technician, you should be familiar with the most common symptoms, probable causes, and suggested "first try" solutions for motherboard- and CPU-related problems. You might encounter problems not listed in the following table, but it will give you a few scenarios to consider when troubleshooting motherboard and CPU problems.

Symptom	Probable cause	Suggested solution
The system fails to boot.	Power problems are the most likely cause. If those aren't the cause, a motherboard component could have failed.	Replace the motherboard.
A burning or foul odor or smoke comes out of the case.	Components, including the CPU, are overheated or burning.	Unplug the computer immediately and try to identify the failed component. If it can be replaced, do so. Otherwise, try replacing the motherboard.
	Cooling system failure.	Replace the cooling system.
The computer shuts down at random times.	CPU cooling system failure.	Replace the CPU fan.
Fans come on and power lights indicate that power is present, but the system fails to boot.	Power-control circuitry on the motherboard could have failed.	Replace the motherboard.
Video display problems occur on a system with an integrated display adapter.	Video circuitry has failed.	Replace the motherboard. In some computers, you can disable the on-board video circuitry and then install a separate video adapter.
There's no power to the unit; power lights are not illuminated.	CPU has failed. Backplane has failed or is not seated correctly.	First try reseating the backplane. Replace the CPU or backplane.
Intermittent problems occur that can't be traced to the failure of another component.	Motherboard might be faulty.	Replace the motherboard.
One or more of the following occurs with increasing frequency: intermittent stop errors (Blue Screen of Death, or BSOD); memory errors; system not responding to input; spontaneous reboots.	Motherboard is failing.	Replace the motherboard.

For a motherboard and CPU troubleshooting flow chart, see
www.fonerbooks.com/cpu_ram.htm.

Do it!

C-2:   Troubleshooting motherboard and CPU problems

Questions and answers

1   You are troubleshooting a computer. When it boots, you hear a slow, single beep, but nothing appears on screen. The power light on the monitor is amber. The computer won't begin the POST. What do you suspect is the problem?

2   What should you try first to solve this problem?

3   You are troubleshooting a computer that's unstable (it hangs, gets BSODs and memory errors, spontaneously reboots, etc.). The user states that the symptoms have gotten more frequent. What do you suspect is the problem?

BIOS-related problems and causes

Explanation   As a PC technician, you should be familiar with the most common symptoms, probable causes, and suggested "first try" solutions for BIOS-related problems. You might encounter problems not listed in the following table, but it provides some scenarios to consider when you're troubleshooting problems.

Symptom	Probable cause	Suggested solution
Devices misidentified	BIOS is configured incorrectly.	Use the BIOS setup utility to reconfigure device options in the BIOS.
Wrong memory size reported during POST or available after booting	BIOS is configured incorrectly.	Use the BIOS setup utility to configure the correct memory size.
Hard drive inaccessible	Geometry parameters are set incorrectly in the BIOS (older hard drives). The hard drive might be disabled in the BIOS (newer hard drives).	Use the BIOS setup utility to reconfigure the hard drive settings.
System won't boot from hard drive	Boot drive order is incorrect. Hard drive configuration data in CMOS doesn't match the hard drive's actual geometry. The hard drive is disabled in CMOS.	Use the BIOS setup utility to reconfigure device options in the BIOS.
System boots from the wrong device	BIOS boot order is set incorrectly, or the drive isn't bootable.	Use the BIOS setup utility to configure the boot order. If that doesn't solve the problem, the device isn't bootable; see a hard-drive troubleshooting reference.
Date and time are incorrect or reset after the computer is turned off	Most likely, the CMOS battery is dead and needs replacing. However, the BIOS date could be set wrong.	Try resetting the correct date and time in the BIOS; then shut down and unplug the computer. Wait five minutes or so, and then plug in and start the computer. If the date is still incorrect, replace the CMOS battery.

POST-related problems and causes

The following table lists some common *power-on self test* (POST)–related symptoms that you might encounter, along with probable causes and solutions.

Symptom	Probable cause	Suggested solution
There's no video; instead, the computer emits eight short beeps.	Failed memory on the video adapter. If the system uses integrated video circuitry, this error could also indicate a failure of main system memory.	Replace the memory modules on the video adapter. If that's not possible, swap the video adapter with a known working adapter. If you have an integrated video adapter, try replacing the main system memory modules.
The system emits three long beeps.	A keyboard error: a key is stuck, or the keyboard is plugged into the mouse port.	Attach a different keyboard and try booting again. Confirm that the keyboard and mouse are plugged into the correct ports.

Symptom	Probable cause	Suggested solution
The system emits one long and three short beeps.	A memory problem.	Replace the main system memory modules.
POST code 162 is displayed.	Configuration data stored in CMOS doesn't match the PC's actual hardware.	Run the BIOS setup utility to confirm the proper configuration values.
POST code 164 is displayed.	PC has more or less memory than the amount listed in the CMOS settings.	You can often press a key (your screen tells you which one) to automatically update the CMOS with the correct amount of memory and continue booting. If that's not an option, run the BIOS setup utility to configure the correct value.

CMOS-related problems and causes

The following table lists some common CMOS-related symptoms you might encounter, along with probable causes and solutions.

Symptom	Probable cause	Suggested solution
Error message "Non-system disk or disk error"	The BIOS can't find the master boot record on the boot drive.	You might have specified the wrong drive as the boot drive in the CMOS settings. Use the setup utility to confirm and reconfigure, if necessary. Or your boot drive might not be bootable (it doesn't have the files needed to boot the system).
Error message "Display type mismatch"	The video settings in the CMOS don't match the monitor attached to the system.	Connect the correct type of monitor.
Error message "Memory size mismatch"	The amount of memory listed in the CMOS settings is different from the amount actually installed in the system.	Run the BIOS setup utility to correct the information.
Error message "CMOS checksum failure"	The BIOS has detected a memory problem in the CMOS. This could be a sign that the CMOS chip has failed. More likely, it means that the CMOS battery is dead.	Try replacing the CMOS battery. If that doesn't correct the problem, the CMOS chip is probably bad. This isn't typically a replaceable component. You probably need a new motherboard to correct the error.
	There's a boot block virus.	Replace the motherboard. Use boot-block virus removal or repair software to recover the boot block.

Computer startup problems

There are operating-system problems you'll need to troubleshoot that manifest themselves as symptoms during computer startup. These errors can be grouped into three categories:

- **Boot errors** — The computer system doesn't boot successfully.
- **Operating system startup errors** — The computer system boots successfully, but reports an error message when loading the operating system.
- **Operating system load errors** — The computer boots successfully, but the operating system interface doesn't load properly.

Boot errors

To resolve boot errors, you need access to your computer's system BIOS or CMOS, a boot disk, and disk-based utilities. You can follow the troubleshooting techniques described in the following table to identify and resolve boot errors.

Boot error	Cause	Resolution
Invalid boot or non-system disk error	A floppy or CD-ROM that isn't bootable is in a bootable drive.	Check that there isn't a disk in the floppy or CD-ROM drive.
	The system BIOS or CMOS isn't configured properly to boot to the hard disk.	Verify that system BIOS or CMOS boot-order settings are correct.
	The hard disk drive doesn't have the Windows boot files on it.	Depending on the OS, boot from your emergency repair disk, your Windows installation CD-ROM, or your restore CD.
	The hard disk drive isn't connected properly.	If the computer was moved recently or if the hard drive was just installed, check that the hard disk is properly connected to the computer.
	The hard disk is bad.	If the previous solutions fail to resolve the problem, the hard disk drive might be bad and might need to be replaced.
Inaccessible boot device	The system BIOS or CMOS isn't configured properly to boot to the hard disk.	Verify that system BIOS or CMOS boot-order settings are correct.
	The hard disk drive isn't connected properly.	If the computer was moved recently or if the hard drive was just installed, check that the hard disk is properly connected to the computer.
	The motherboard was recently changed, or you moved the Windows system disk to a computer with a different motherboard.	Reinstall Windows to fix the Registry entries and drivers for the mass storage controller hardware. You might be able to use a Microsoft generic driver until you can find the proper driver.
	The hard disk is bad.	If the previous solutions fail to resolve the problem, the hard disk drive might be bad and might need to be replaced.
	Mismatched components	After a new installation, components might not be compatible with other system resources. Swap out newly installed components with components that meet system specifications.

Boot error	Cause	Resolution
NTLDR is missing or Couldn't find NTLDR	A floppy or CD-ROM that isn't bootable is in a bootable drive.	Check that there isn't a disk in the floppy or CD-ROM drive.
	The system BIOS or CMOS isn't configured properly to boot to the hard disk.	Verify that system BIOS or CMOS boot-order settings are correct.
	The boot.ini file is configured incorrectly.	View the contents of boot.ini. Edit, if necessary.
	The Ntldr file is missing or corrupt.	Copy the Ntldr file from the Windows installation CD-ROM, a Windows boot disk, or another computer. If other Windows files are missing or corrupt, you might have to reinstall the operating system to resolve the problem.
	The hard disk drive isn't connected properly.	If the computer was moved recently or if the hard drive was just installed, check that the hard disk is properly connected to the computer.
	There's a corrupt boot sector or MBR.	There might be a virus. Use your virus removal software.
	You're trying to upgrade from FAT32 to a Windows version that doesn't support FAT32.	Boot into the previous version of the operating system, back up data, and complete a fresh installation of the new operating system.
	The hard disk is bad.	If the previous solutions fail to resolve the problem, the hard disk drive might be bad and might need to be replaced.
Bad or missing Command interpreter	A floppy or CD-ROM that isn't bootable is in a bootable drive.	Check that there isn't a disk in the floppy or CD-ROM drive.
	The system BIOS or CMOS isn't configured properly to boot to the hard disk.	Verify that system BIOS or CMOS boot-order settings are correct.
	The command.com, msdos.sys, io.sys, or drvspace file was deleted, was renamed, or has become corrupt.	Boot the computer by using a boot disk. Replace the missing or corrupt file.
	The hard disk is bad.	If the previous solutions fail to resolve the problem, the hard disk drive might be bad and might need to be replaced.

Startup errors

To identify and resolve startup errors, you can use troubleshooting techniques described in the following table.

Startup message	Cause	Resolution
Error in CONFIG.SYS line ##	There's a problem with the specified line in the config.sys file.	View the specified line in config.sys. Look for typing errors or calls to files that don't exist. Edit as necessary to resolve the problem.
Himem.sys not loaded	The himem.sys file is missing or corrupt.	Copy a new version of himem.sys to the hard disk. Verify that the reference to himem.sys is correct in config.sys. You must place the reference before any drivers that use extended memory. The syntax is: `DEVICE=[drive:][path]HIMEM.SYS`
	There's a problem with physical memory.	If the above solution fails to solve the problem, then physical memory might be bad and needs to be replaced. Himem.sys runs a check on RAM and can't do so if a RAM chip is bad.
Missing or corrupt Himem.sys	The himem.sys file is missing or corrupt.	Copy a new version of himem.sys to the hard disk. Verify that the reference to himem.sys is correct in config.sys.
	There's a problem with physical memory.	If the above solution fails to solve the problem, your physical memory might be bad and needs to be replaced. Himem.sys runs a check on RAM and can't do so if a RAM chip is bad.
Device/service has failed to start	Windows is trying to load a device or service that won't load properly.	Check the Event Viewer logs to determine which device or service failed to load. Check the installation or configuration of the device (by using Device Manager) or service (by using the Services MMC). Reinstall the device or service if necessary.

Operating system load errors

Common operating system load errors and troubleshooting techniques are listed in the following table.

Error	Cause	Resolution
Failure to start GUI	Explorer.exe is missing or corrupt.	Copy Explorer.exe from the Windows installation CD-ROM, a Windows boot disk, or another computer. If other Windows files are missing or corrupt, you might have to reinstall the operating system to resolve the problem.
Windows Protection Error—illegal operation	An application asks the operating system to process an operation that the OS doesn't recognize.	Illegal-operation messages typically have an error code or something else you can use to research the exact cause and resolution of the specific error.
	Outdated device drivers need to be updated.	If the device driver is being loaded by the operating system at startup, try to boot into Safe Mode and roll back or update the driver.

Error	Cause	Resolution
		If the illegal operation causes a GPF, you might need to reboot the computer.
		An incorrect or corrupt device driver can also cause an auto-restart error, in which the computer reboots automatically when it tries to load the driver. Once you identify the driver causing the problem, you'll need to replace it.
User-modified settings cause improper operation at startup	The user has changed a system setting that causes the computer to hang at startup.	If available, boot using one of the Startup modes to reverse the changes. On Windows XP computers, roll back to a System Restore point.
Application install, start, or load failure	An attempt is made to install or start an application that isn't compatible with the operating system.	Research the application to see if a patch is available that allows it to run on your operating system. You might need to upgrade the application to one in which its coding functions according to the application rules of your operating system.

Do it!

C-3: Troubleshooting problems with system startup

Here's how

1 One or more BIOS- and POST-related problems have been introduced into your lab computer. Troubleshoot these problems to determine their causes.

2 Correct the problems you've found in your PC to return it to a working state. Solving one problem might reveal the presence of another problem. Troubleshoot and fix all problems that arise.

3 Document the problem(s) you find:

4 Document the steps you take to fix the problem(s):

5 When you boot your server, Windows Server 2008 won't start, and the screen displays the message, "Invalid boot or non-system disk error." What's the first thing you should check?

6 If your first solution doesn't resolve the problem, what are other possible causes of the "Invalid boot or non-system disk error" message?

Diagnosing memory problems

Explanation

The memory-testing actions performed by the BIOS during the POST are relatively simple and not very accurate. Many memory problems aren't detected by the BIOS. To test memory fully, you should use a dedicated memory-testing utility.

Memory-testing utilities

Memory-testing utilities typically perform hundreds, if not thousands, of read and write operations in every memory location. In addition, the utilities write more than one type of value to every byte of memory to test various types of possible failures. Complete testing cycles with these utilities can take many hours, or even days, depending on the speed of the computer and the amount of RAM installed.

The following are some popular memory-testing utilities.

Utility	License	URL
Memtest86	Free, open source	www.memtest86.com
Memtest86+	Updated version of Memtest86	www.memtest.org
Microsoft Windows Memory Diagnostic	Free, unsupported, commercial	http://oca.microsoft.com/en/windiag.asp
DocMemory Diagnostic	Free, unsupported, commercial	www.docmemory.com
M2K MemScope	Free, commercial	www.micro2000.co.uk/products/ microscope/ MemScope_Free_Memory_Tester.htm

Memtest86

Memtest86 is perhaps the most popular free memory-testing utility available. It's released under the Gnu Public License (GPL). It can test any Intel x86 computer, regardless of operating system.

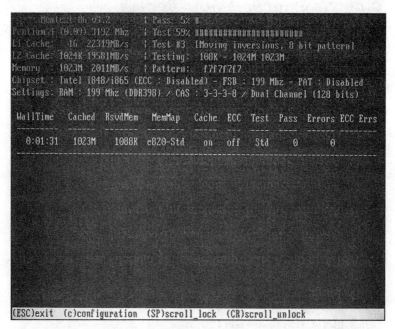

Exhibit 5-4: The Memtest86 screen, showing the default test in progress

As with nearly all such utilities, you must create a bootable floppy disk or CD that contains this utility and support files. Then you boot from that disk rather than running the utility from within Windows.

Windows Server 2008 has a built-in memory-testing utility. Here's how to use it:

1   Open the Control Panel. Click System and Maintenance, and then Administrative Tools, and double-click Memory Diagnostics Tool.

2   Click "Restart now and check for problems."

3   Wait for Windows to restart automatically.

Do it!

C-4: Testing memory

Here's how	Here's why
1 Click **Start** and choose **Control Panel**	
2 Click **Administrative Tools**	
3 Double-click **Memory Diagnostics Tool**	
4 Click **Restart now and check for problems**	
5 Observe the memory test messages	The utility shows you the test pass that is running and the percentage of overall testing that is complete. Pressing the F1 key gives you access to memory test options.
6 Log on to Windows Server 2008 as **Administrator** with a password of **!pass1234**	
7 Observe the notification bar	Windows should report that no errors were found.

Memory leaks

Explanation

A memory leak occurs when an application or driver is done using the memory that it was assigned by the operating system, but fails to release the memory to other processes. Leaks are usually caused by improper coding in the application and can be fixed only by the application's designers. Many times, the memory leak builds slowly over time and doesn't produce noticeable symptoms. A large-scale memory leak can cause your system to report that it is running low on, or has run out of, memory. If the memory leak is in the kernel, the operating system itself can fail.

You can monitor memory to determine if a particular application is causing a memory leak on your system. Two utilities in Windows Server 2008 that can help you identify a memory problem are the Performance tab in Task Manager and the Performance Monitor tool in Reliability and Performance.

Task Manager

You can use the Performance tab in Task Manager to monitor your computer's performance, using the most common indicators. The Performance tab is shown in Exhibit 5-5. The indicators are described in the following table.

Indicator	Description
CPU Usage	Shows the percentage of time the processor is working. If your computer is running slowly, this graph displays a higher percentage.
CPU Usage History	Shows how busy the CPU has been over time. The value selected for Update Speed (on the View menu) determines how often this graph is updated. You can set updates to occur twice per second (High), once every two seconds (Normal), once every four seconds (Low), or not at all (Paused). You can press F5 to update a paused graph. On multiprocessor or multi-core systems, there's one graph per processor or core. On Pentiums with a quad-core processor, Task Manager shows four graphs.
Memory (Windows Server 2008)	Shows, in megabytes, how much physical memory is being used at the current moment.
PF Usage (Windows Server 2000 and 2003)	Shows the amount of the page file's capacity being used by the computer. If this graph shows that the page file's usage is near the maximum, you should increase the page file's size.
Physical Memory Usage History (Windows Server 2008)	Shows how much physical memory has been used over the past few minutes.
Page File Usage History (Windows Server 2000 and 2003)	Shows the percentage of the page file's size used over time. The value selected for Update Speed (on the View menu) determines how often this graph is updated.

Indicator	Description
System (Windows Server 2008) *or* Totals (Windows Server 2000 and 2003)	Shows the dynamic totals for the number of handles, threads, and processes running. A *handle* is a unique object identifier used by a process. A *thread* is an object or process running within a larger process or program. In Windows Server 2008, this section also shows *up time* (the amount of time that has passed since the computer was started) and the size of the page file on the hard disk.
Physical Memory	Shows the total amount of physical memory installed on your computer. "Free" in Windows Server 2008 is the amount of free memory available. "Cached" shows the amount of current physical memory being used to map pages of open files.
Commit Charge (Windows Server 2000 and 2003)	Shows the amount of memory allocated to programs and the operating system. This number includes virtual memory, so the value listed under Peak might exceed the actual physical memory installed. The Total value is the same as in the Page File Usage History graph.
Kernel Memory	Shows the amount of memory being used by the operating system kernel and device drivers. "Paged" is memory that can be copied to the page file to free up physical memory for the operating system to use. "Nonpaged" is memory that won't be paged out.
Summary data	(Along the bottom of the tab.) Shows the current number of processes, the current CPU usage percentage, and the current amount of physical or commit-charge memory being used, compared to the maximum available. In Windows Server 2008, this value is shown as a percentage.

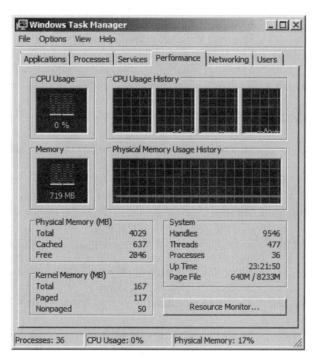

Exhibit 5-5: The Performance tab of Task Manager, on a Windows Server 2008 computer with a quad-core processor

Performance Monitor

By collecting data with the appropriate Performance Monitor memory counters, such as the Process object counters, Pool Paged Bytes, and Pool Nonpaged Bytes, you can determine whether the memory leak is being caused by an application or a kernel-mode driver.

To identify memory leaks in Windows Server 2008:

1   Open Performance Monitor. (Click Start and choose Control Panel, System and Maintenance, and Administrative Tools. Double-click Reliability and Performance.)

2   In the navigation pane, select Performance Monitor.

3   Click the Add button (the + button).

4   From the "Select counters from computer" list, select the computer whose memory you want to monitor. This can be the local computer or a remote computer on which you have administrative rights.

5   In the Available counters box, expand Process.

6   Select Handle Count; then press and hold Ctrl while selecting Private Bytes.

7   In the "Instances of selected object" list, select the application you believe is causing the memory leak, or select <all instances> if you want to monitor all running applications.

8   Click Add.

9   Click OK and observe the graph.

You will see two graph lines: one for memory (private bytes), and one for handle count. Work with your application. In Performance Monitor, you'll see the present status of memory usage and open handles for the application process. If either of the counter values increases continuously without stabilizing, this indicates that there are memory or handle leaks in the application.

Do it!

C-5: Monitoring memory in Performance Monitor

Here's how	Here's why
1 Open Internet Explorer	You'll monitor the memory used by this application.
2 Open **Administrative Tools**	Open the Control Panel, then click Administrative tools
Double-click **Reliability and Performance**	
3 In the navigation pane, select **Performance Monitor**	By default, Performance Monitor shows the percentage of processor time being used.
4 Click ✚	To open the Add Counters dialog box.
5 Observe the "Select counters from computer" list	You are monitoring the local computer. You could browse to select a remote computer.
6 Select **Handle Count**	In the Process category.
Press and hold (CTRL) while selecting **Private Bytes**	To select two individual counters.
7 In the "Instances of selected object" box, select **iexplore**	
Click **Add**	
Click OK	To close the Add Counters dialog box.
8 Double-click each counter and change the scale to the following: Handle Count: **0.01** Private Bytes: **0.000001**	To make the lines easier to see on the graph.
9 In Internet Explorer, navigate to a few sites	
Return to the Performance Monitor graph and observe the data	The Private Bytes value should increase due to the activity and then stabilize. Handle Count should do the same.
10 Close Internet Explorer and then observe the Performance Monitor graph	Private Bytes are released and not shown on the graph anymore. Handle Count decreases as the application releases those as well.
11 Close Reliability and Performance Monitor	
12 Close the Control Panel	

Troubleshooting memory

As a PC technician, you should be familiar with the most common symptoms, probable causes, and suggested "first try" solutions for memory-related problems. You might encounter problems not listed in the following table, but it provides a few scenarios to consider when you're troubleshooting memory-related problems.

Symptom	Probable cause	Suggested solution
201 BIOS error code at boot time	Bad memory location.	Test memory with a RAM-testing utility to determine which portion of memory has failed. Using the output from that program, determine which module has failed, and replace it.
Parity error message	Bad memory (in a system with parity memory).	Test memory with a RAM-testing utility to determine which portion of memory has failed. Using the output from that program, determine which module has failed, and replace it.
Computer randomly freezes, hangs, or crashes	Bad or failing memory chip; bad power supply; inconstant wall voltage.	Test memory with a RAM-testing utility to determine if memory is the cause of these symptoms. Replace modules, if appropriate.
	Using memory that's too slow for the system; mixing memory of different speeds.	Confirm that the proper type of memory is installed, according to manufacturer's specifications.
	Not enough memory to handle applications.	Check the amount of memory in the system. Verify that it's sufficient to cover the OS and multiple applications running at once.
Wrong amount of memory reported by the BIOS	Failed memory module; less memory installed than you thought; modules not installed properly according to PC's banking requirements.	Test memory. Confirm proper BIOS configuration settings. Make sure you've installed as much memory as you think you have. Make sure you've installed memory modules according to the PC's banking requirements, such as installing equal-size DIMMs in pairs.
Windows reports General Protection Fault, Page Fault, or Exception errors	Poorly written applications (most common with Windows 9x); bad memory.	Check the application vendor's Web site for updates or patches. Test memory with a RAM-testing utility.
Random crashes, corrupted data, strange application behavior	Virus infection (more likely); bad memory.	Scan your PC for viruses. If none are found, test memory with a RAM-testing utility.
Receive one of two error messages: • System has recovered from a serious error • DRIVER_IRQL_ NOT_LESS_OR_ EQUAL	One or more faulty RAM modules; RAM modules not compatible with chip set on motherboard. Page file used by Virtual Memory Manager may be damaged.	Make sure the memory modules in the computer are compatible with the chip set on the motherboard. Set virtual memory to "No paging file." Reboot. Reset the virtual memory page file to "System managed size." Reboot.

Symptom	Probable cause	Suggested solution
Windows reports "Your system is low on virtual memory"	Maximum amount of real plus virtual memory supported on the system has been used.	Verify that virtual memory is set to "System managed size." Eliminate non-essential programs. Add RAM to the system.
	Runaway or orphaned process (UNIX)	Use the man and ps commands to find and then terminate the process.

Do it!

C-6:   Troubleshooting memory

Here's how

1 One or more memory-related problems have been introduced into your lab computer. Troubleshoot these problems to determine their cause(s).

2 Correct the problems you've found in your PC to return it to a working state. Solving one problem might reveal the presence of another one. Troubleshoot and fix all problems that arise.

3 Document the problem(s) you find:

4 Document the steps you take to fix the problem(s):

Unit summary: Troubleshooting methodology

Topic A
In this topic, you learned that there are various methods you can use to troubleshoot problems. You examined **four models**: the CompTIA Server+, CompTIA Network+, Novell, and ASID troubleshooting models. You also learned that **problem and resolution tracking** is important to long-term success. Tracking problems and resolutions helps you make sure that all problems get resolved and saves you time in the future when you encounter similar problems.

Topic B
In this topic, you learned about the **hardware** and **software tools** in a typical technician's toolkit. You examined specialty tools for diagnosing and repairing network connection problems and server component problems. You identified the function of each tool and its use in troubleshooting.

Topic C
In this topic, you learned about the common symptoms, causes, and resolutions of problems with the following **system components**: power supplies, motherboards, CPUs, and memory. You looked at the common symptoms, causes and resolutions of problems with the BIOS and CMOS. You also learned how to diagnose and resolve problems with **system startup**, including boot errors, startup errors, and operating system load errors. You then learned how to test and monitor **memory**.

Review questions

1 Which troubleshooting model's first step, "Trying quick, obvious fixes," differs from that of the other models?

A CompTIA A+

B CompTIA Network+

C Novell

D ASID

2 Match each stage of the CompTIA A+ troubleshooting model on the left with its correct order on the right.

Stage	Order
1. Test the theory to determine the actual cause	A. First stage
2. Document the resolution	B. Second stage
3. Establish a theory of probable cause	C. Third stage
4. Verify the results	D. Fourth stage
5. Identify the problem	E. Fifth stage
6. Create a plan of action	F. Sixth stage
7. Implement solution	G. Fifth stage
8. Root cause analysis	H. Sixth stage

3 ASID, in the ASID troubleshooting model, stands for which of the following?

   A Assign, Simplify, Implement, Document

   B *(circled)* Acquire, Simplify, Implement, Document

   C Acquire, Segment, Implement, Document

   D Assign, Segment, Implement, Document

   E Assign, Simplify, Identify, Document

   F Action, Simplify, Identify, Document

4 True or false? All troubleshooting models presented in this unit include a stage in which you document the problem and its resolution.

true

5 Which of the following types of information is not important to identify and capture when you're first presented with a problem?

   A The customer's environment

   B Circumstances in which the problem occurred

   C *(circled)* Knowledge base articles relating to the problem

   D Symptoms and error codes

6 List at least three things you should document after resolving a problem.

the problem

how it occured

how to fix

7 True or false? Intermittent computer problems are typically the most difficult to troubleshoot. *true*

8 An error code is displayed before the end of the POST. Is the problem hardware- or software-related?

   A *(circled)* Hardware

   B Software

9 A paper-based problem-tracking system would be appropriate for what size organization?

   A Very small

   B *(circled)* Small

   C Medium

   D Large

10 What is the name of the Web site containing problem and solution references for Windows Server 2008?

  A Microsoft Answers

  B Microsoft Frequently Asked Questions

  C Microsoft Help and Support

  D Microsoft Windows Support Center

11 True or false? It's useful if the problem-tracking software is integrated with other systems, such as asset tracking.

true

12 Why shouldn't you lay a component on the outside of an antistatic bag?

vulnerable to esd

13 Which tool tests equipment with readings of ohms, amps, and volts?

voltmeter

14 Which tool measures electrical properties to determine whether there's an adequate power supply and what the quality of that power supply is?

voltmeter

15 What do you use an optical time-domain reflectometer (OTDR) for?

to test fiber

16 What might be the cause of intermittent stop errors (the Blue Screen of Death), memory errors, spontaneous reboots, or a system not responding to input, with one or more of these symptoms occurring with increasing frequency?

17 What's a memory leak?

when an app fails to release memory when closed

18 What Windows Server 2008 utilities can you use to detect a memory leak?

task manager

Independent practice activity

In this activity, you'll identify and resolve a problem with one or more of the following:

- Power supply
- Motherboard
- CPU
- BIOS
- POST
- CMOS
- Startup
- Memory

You'll also download, install, and use problem-tracking software.

1 Your instructor has introduced a problem with one of the components listed above. If you are following the Server+ troubleshooting model, what should your first step be to solve this problem?

2 Establish a theory of probable cause.

3 Test the theory to determine the actual cause.

4 Create a plan of action.

5 Implement your solution.

6 Verify the results.

7 Analyze the root cause of the problem.

8 Download a problem-tracking program from the Internet.

9 Install the program.

10 Enter the information to begin tracking the problem you resolved.

Unit 6

Installing expansion cards

Unit time: 100 minutes

Complete this unit, and you'll know how to:

A Describe the primary types of buses and the features and functions of the PCI family of buses.

B Define the common drive interfaces and install a drive adapter.

C Describe multimedia expansion adapters and install an expansion card.

D Troubleshoot expansion card problems.

Topic A: Buses

This topic covers the following CompTIA Server+ (2009 Edition) exam objective.

#	Objective
1.1	**Differentiate between system board types, features, components, and their purpose.**
	• Bus types and bus speeds
	• Expansion slots
	– PCI
	– PCIe
	– PCIx
	– ISA

Computer buses

Explanation

In computer lingo, a *bus* is a communication pathway. A PC has multiple buses to enable communication between the various components of the PC. A bus is defined by various characteristics, including how many bits it can transmit at one time, which signaling techniques are used across it, and how fast data can be transferred.

Bus types

A typical PC has the following types of buses:

- **Address** — The bus that transmits memory addresses between the CPU and RAM.
- **Data** — The bus that transfers data between the CPU and RAM.
- **Expansion** — The bus to which add-on adapter cards are connected in order to enhance the functionality of the PC.
- **Video** — The bus that transmits display information between the CPU and the video circuitry.

In this unit, you'll focus primarily on expansion and video buses.

The address and data buses

Address and data buses enable the basic operations of the CPU and its interactions with memory. You generally don't have to be concerned with these buses, though their characteristics affect the overall performance of your system.

The expansion bus

The *expansion bus* is the communications pathway over which non-core components of your computer interact with the CPU, memory, and other core components. For example, data sent to and from your computer's hard drive travels over the expansion bus.

By installing new adapter cards into slots that connect to the expansion bus, you can add new hardware to a PC. For example, your desktop computer might not have come with a wireless network card for connecting to the network through your wireless router. You can purchase a wireless network adapter card and plug it into the expansion bus to add this capability to your computer.

Many expansion bus standards have been used over the years, but the PCI (Peripheral Component Interconnect) bus, shown in Exhibit 6-1, is the predominant one. Others, such as the ISA, EISA, Micro Channel, and PC bus, are rarely found today, unless you're working on an older computer.

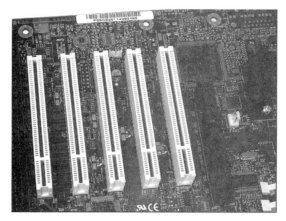

Exhibit 6-1: The slots for the PCI expansion bus

The video bus

The video adapter is the component that generates the signals sent to your monitor. This component can be built into your motherboard or can be an adapter card added to your system later. Depending on the technology used, a video adapter can communicate over the expansion bus or the video bus.

Video generation requires an enormous amount of data to be transmitted in the PC in very short intervals. The demands of graphical operating systems, 3D game graphics, high-resolution digital photos, and digital video can strain the capabilities of the expansion bus.

For this reason, computer designers have developed specialized video buses, sometimes called graphics buses. Video buses, such as the VESA and AGP buses, are well suited to transmitting video data at high speeds. Video adapters in most modern computers are connected through video buses, rather than through expansion buses. The slot for an AGP video bus is shown in Exhibit 6-2.

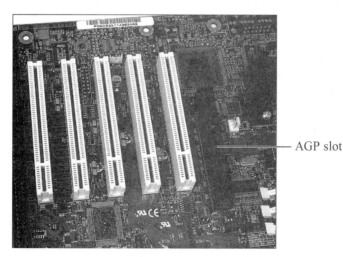

— AGP slot

Exhibit 6-2: The slot for an AGP video bus

The riser bus

A *riser* is a circuit board that connects to a motherboard to provide additional expansion slots or sockets. PC manufacturers use riser buses to bring the basic wiring and control of a function, such as LAN connection or audio support, to a motherboard without using the PCI interface. Using riser buses decreases the cost of including the function.

There are three main riser standards:

- **Advanced Communication Riser (ACR)** — The latest riser version. It can be used to provide modem, LAN, xDSL, and audio support. The ACR standard is backwards-compatible with AMR.

- **Audio/Modem Riser (AMR)** — Can be used to provide both audio and modem support. An MR slot provides modem support; an AMR slot provides both audio and modem support.

- **Communication and Networking Riser (CNR)** — Can be used to provide audio, modem, and LAN interfaces. This standard doesn't support an expansion slot, but uses an OEM built-in board, including the motherboard CNR connector.

Do it!

A-1: Examining buses

Here's how	Here's why
1 Shut down your PC and unplug it from the outlet	
2 Following proper ESD and electrical safety precautions, open your PC	
3 Using Exhibit 6-1 and Exhibit 6-2 as references, identify the expansion and video buses in your PC	
4 Are there connectors for the address or data buses? Why or why not?	
5 Identify one or more devices that connect to your computer through the expansion bus	
6 Close your PC, plug it in, and start it	
Log on	

System interaction

Hardware and adapter cards must work together to access memory and CPU resources. They must do so in an orderly manner so that they don't conflict with each other. To avoid conflicts, hardware must perform the following functions:

- Gain the attention of the CPU.
- Access shared memory locations.
- Extend the system BIOS.
- Transfer data across the bus.

Interrupts

The CPU does the processing (or most of it) in a computer system. Devices must gain the attention of the CPU in order to get it to do their work. The CPU is often busy doing other work, so devices get its attention by sending an interrupt.

An *interrupt* is a signal that a device sends to the CPU to get its attention. For example, whenever you press a key on your keyboard, the keyboard controller sends an interrupt to the CPU. The processor stops whatever it was doing, reads which key was pressed, and passes that key's code to the active application. From there, the CPU might return to what it was doing before or transfer control to another application, depending on the priority of the tasks that need its attention.

Polling

Without interrupts, a CPU would have to poll each device, round-robin fashion, to see if attention was needed. It would ask a device, "Do you need something?" After receiving a response, it would move on to the next device. Polling is an inefficient use of CPU time and is almost never implemented.

Although interrupts might seem inefficient, a modern processor is easily capable of processing tens of millions of instructions every second. Even when you're running multiple applications and typing madly away, the CPU spends the vast majority of its time doing nothing more than just waiting for the next task.

IRQs

Computers rely on interrupts to provide an orderly way of gaining the attention of the CPU. Not every interruption carries the same priority. Furthermore, the CPU must have a way to determine which device interrupted it. These needs are met through IRQs, or interrupt request lines.

Every device that uses interrupts is assigned an IRQ. IRQs are numerical addresses that, in most cases, are uniquely assigned to devices. The original IBM PC and XT-class computers supported IRQ numbers 0–8. AT-class and newer computers support IRQs 0–15.

Rather than redesigning the interrupt controller to directly support the expanded IRQs, which would have made it incompatible with existing operating systems, designers pulled a little trick. The new IRQs, 9–15, are cascaded to IRQ 2. When a device sends an interrupt over IRQ 10, for example, that IRQ is routed through IRQ 2. In this way, an OS that supports only the original IRQ set still receives the interrupt. Additionally, because modern computers have many more devices than older computers do, this architecture has seen further extensions in the way the hardware and operating system address interrupts.

When multiple devices send their interrupts to the CPU at the same time, Windows processes the device request with the lowest IRQ value first. The following table lists the default IRQ assignments for standard hardware devices. As you can see, no devices use IRQ 2, so it can be used to cascade the higher IRQs.

IRQ	Priority	Common use
0	1	System timer
1	2	Keyboard
2	n/a	Cascade of IRQs 9–15
3	10	COM2
4	11	COM1
5	12	Sound cards or LPT2
6	13	Floppy disk controller
7	14	LPT1
8	15	Real-time clock
9	3	Various
10	4	Various
11	5	Various
12	6	PS/2 mouse
13	7	Floating point unit or math coprocessor
14	8	Primary IDE (hard drive) channel
15	9	Secondary IDE (hard drive) channel

Modern operating systems calculate and assign IRQs for you. With Windows, the technique is called Plug and Play (PnP). Of course, the adapters you use must support PnP. With such support, every time you start Windows, it determines which IRQs are available, which devices need IRQs assigned, and what IRQs each device can support. Then, Windows dynamically assigns IRQs to all devices you've installed.

Device Manager

As shown in Exhibit 6-3, you can use the Windows Device Manager to determine which IRQs have been assigned to the various devices in your computer. Should you need to, you can even manually assign IRQs, overriding the default assignments made by the PnP system. PnP takes into account any IRQs that you've manually assigned when it determines which IRQs are available.

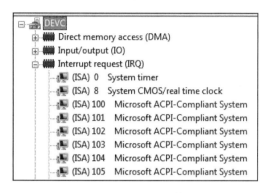

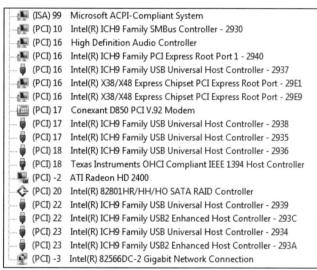

Exhibit 6-3: Device Manager's typical IRQ assignments

To open Device Manager in Windows Server 2008:

1   Click Start.
2   Right-click Computer and choose Manage.
3   Expand Diagnostics.
4   Select Device Manager.
5   Choose View, Resources by type.
6   In the details pane, expand Interrupt request (IRQ).

Do it!

A-2:   Examining IRQ assignments

Here's how	Here's why
1 Click **Start** and right-click **Computer**	
Choose **Manage**	To open Server Manager.
2 In the navigation pane, expand **Diagnostics**	
3 In the navigation pane, select **Device Manager**	
4 Choose **View**, **Resources by type**	To display the list of system resources.
5 Collapse all categories in the list	If necessary.

6 Expand **Interrupt request (IRQ)**	⊞ 📠 Input/output (IO)
	⊟ 📠 Interrupt request (IRQ)
	    💻 (ISA) 0 System timer
	    💻 (ISA) 8 System CMOS/real time clock
	    💻 (ISA) 100 Microsoft ACPI-Compliant System
	    💻 (ISA) 101 Microsoft ACPI-Compliant System
	    💻 (ISA) 102 Microsoft ACPI-Compliant System
	    💻 (ISA) 103 Microsoft ACPI-Compliant System
	    💻 (ISA) 104 Microsoft ACPI-Compliant System
	    💻 (ISA) 105 Microsoft ACPI-Compliant System
	
	To display the list of IRQ assignments determined by PnP when you started your computer.

7 Collapse **Interrupt request (IRQ)**	

I/O addresses

Explanation

Once a device has the attention of the CPU, it often needs to transfer data to main memory. The device does so by sharing a section of main memory with the CPU. The CPU reads input from and writes output to this region of shared memory to transfer data between main memory and the device.

As with interrupts, devices must work together to avoid using the other devices' input-output memory ranges. To ensure this, either you or PnP must configure a range of I/O addresses assigned to each device in your computer.

As shown in Exhibit 6-4, such I/O addresses are designated with hexadecimal numbers, which represent the addresses of the beginning and ending of a range of shared system memory. In general, devices are assigned between 4 and 32 bytes of input-output memory, though some devices get more or less than that.

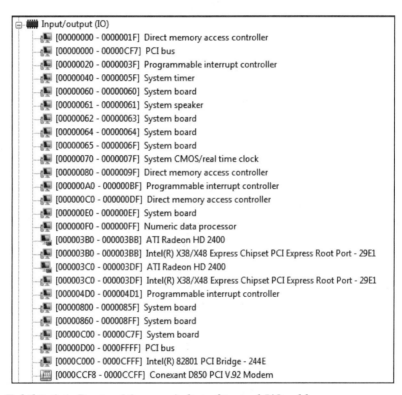

Exhibit 6-4: Device Manager's list of typical I/O addresses

Do it!

A-3: Viewing your computer's I/O address assignments

Here's how	Here's why
1 In Device Manager, expand **Input/output (I/O)**	To display the I/O address assignments on your computer.
2 Examine the assignments	Some items are assigned more than one I/O address.
3 Collapse **Input/output (I/O)**	

Direct memory access (DMA)

Explanation

In the input/output scheme described so far, the CPU must be involved in every data transfer with every device. While the CPU is certainly powerful, this involvement with every data transfer can negatively affect performance. To improve performance, designers created the *direct memory access (DMA) controller*, which is essentially another processor chip to handle data transfers between devices and main memory. DMA frees the CPU to perform other tasks.

The DMA controller communicates with each device over a dedicated channel. Each device must have its own channel with the DMA controller. As with the other resources, you or PnP must configure the DMA channel assigned to every device.

DMA has largely been replaced by newer techniques, such as bus mastering. For this reason, DMA is generally used by core devices, such as the floppy disk controller, whose designs haven't changed significantly over time.

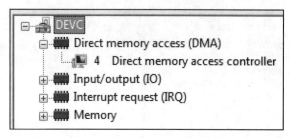

Exhibit 6-5: Device Manager's list of typical DMA channel assignments

Do it!

A-4: Viewing your computer's DMA channel assignments

Here's how	Here's why
1 Expand **Direct memory access (DMA)**	To display the DMA channel assignments on your PC.
2 What types of devices are using DMA channels on your PC?	
3 Collapse **Direct memory access (DMA)**	

Base memory addresses

Explanation

Some devices extend the system BIOS with new routines or new versions of existing routines. Display adapters are the most common type of device to do this, but IDE and SCSI adapters also use BIOS extensions. These devices include their BIOS extensions in a chip on their adapter card.

The system BIOS must locate and load these BIOS extensions. This means that the adapter BIOS must be "mapped" to memory locations where the system BIOS can find it. You, or PnP, must configure the base memory address range of the device's BIOS. By configuring this value, you provide a way for the operating system to access the system routines contained on these devices.

As with the other resources, each device that requires a base memory address assignment needs its own unique assignment. PnP ensures that conflicting address ranges aren't assigned to devices in your computer. Exhibit 6-6 shows a list of base memory address assignments in Device Manager.

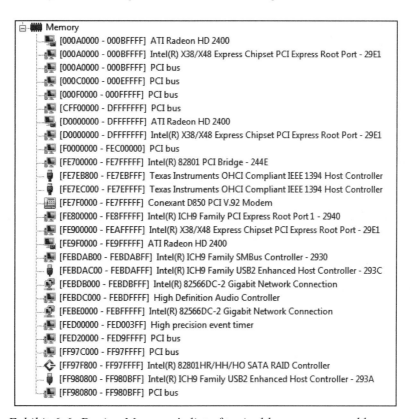

Exhibit 6-6: Device Manager's list of typical base memory address assignments

Do it!

A-5: Viewing your computer's base memory address assignments

Here's how	Here's why
1 Expand **Memory**	To display the base memory address assignments on your PC
2 What device seems to be using the most memory within the base memory address space?	
3 Close Server Manager	

Historical bus types

Explanation
The Peripheral Component Interconnect (PCI) bus is currently the most popular expansion bus used with Windows-based personal computers. Various buses were used before the development of the PCI standard. These include the following:

- PC/XT bus
- PC/AT bus
- Industry Standard Architecture (ISA) bus
- Extended ISA (EISA) bus
- Micro Channel Architecture (MCA) bus

The PC/XT bus

The 8-bit PC bus was the expansion bus used by the original IBM PC and its successor, the IBM XT. In fact, it's sometimes called the PC/XT bus. This bus used a clock speed of 4.77 MHz and a maximum data transfer rate of 1.6 megabits per second (Mbps) or 0.4 megabytes per second (MBps).

The PC/XT bus supported IRQs 0–8, but of those, generally only IRQ 2 was available. Additionally, it supported four DMA channels, but only DMA channel 3 was unused in such systems. This lack of resource support limited the options for expanding PC/XT-bus systems. You had to configure PC/XT bus adapters by using DIP switches or jumper blocks.

As shown in Exhibit 6-7, PC/XT bus adapters featured a single-edge connector. Cards were large, as were the components on them.

Exhibit 6-7: A PC/XT bus adapter card

The PC/AT and ISA buses

With the development of its AT computer, IBM extended the capabilities of the PC/XT bus. In its original form, this bus was known simply as the AT bus. As IBM-clone computers using AT bus technology became more prevalent, the IBM-specific AT bus became known as the ISA bus, where "ISA" stands for "Industry Standard Architecture." This bus is generally called either the ISA or PC/AT bus as a result.

The ISA bus was a 16-bit bus, expanding both the data and memory address lines, compared to the PC/XT bus. As a result, more memory could be accessed in AT-class systems and adapters.

The clock speed was increased to 8 MHz. Thanks to that change and other optimizations, the data transfer rate of the ISA bus improved dramatically, compared to the PC/XT bus, to 8 MBps.

Exhibit 6-8: An ISA adapter card

ISA slot——

Exhibit 6-9: An ISA expansion bus slot

Peripheral Component Interconnect (PCI)

The PCI standard was developed by Intel Corporation and introduced in 1992. The current crop of PCI adapters and expansion slots generally implement the PCI 2.0 specification, released in 1993.

The PCI specification supports bus speeds of either 33 MHz or 66 MHz. It also supports both a 32-bit and a 64-bit bus design, though the 32-bit version is much more popular. With a 32-bit implementation at 33 MHz, the PCI bus supports a peak transfer rate of 133 MBps. In a 64-bit implementation at 66 MHz, the PCI bus supports a peak transfer rate of 533 MBps. A PCI card is shown in Exhibit 6-10.

Exhibit 6-10: A PCI card

PCI slots are, by convention, always white. ISA and other slots are typically black, although they're sometimes white, too. PCI slots are shorter (in length) and taller than ISA slots. PCI slots are shown in Exhibit 6-11.

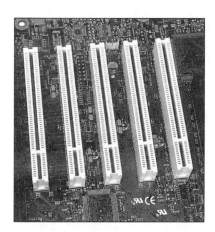

Exhibit 6-11: PCI slots

Multifunction cards and maximum devices

The PCI specification supports multifunction cards, in which a single adapter provides the functions of more than one expansion device. The specification permits up to eight functions on a single card. Additionally, it permits up to five slots and cards per system. So, in theory, through multifunction cards, you could add the equivalent of up to 40 expansion devices to your PC.

PCIx

In 1998, Compaq, HP (which were then separate companies), and IBM worked together to develop the PCI Extended specification. The *PCIx*, or PCI-X, bus was designed to provide the higher bandwidth and speed demanded by servers. The PCIx bus was a 64-bit parallel bus capable of maximum data transfer speeds of 1064 MBps. It followed the same general electrical design characteristics of the PCI bus on which it was based. PCIx was backward compatible with PCI, meaning that you could plug a PCI card into a PCIx slot (though not vice versa).

The specification had a few shortcomings. Like all parallel buses, the PCIx system required more electrical connections (traces), and signals on each of those lines had to arrive at essentially the same time at the destination component. This requirement added design complexity and cost to systems supporting PCIx. Additionally, the PCIx bus ran at the speed of the slowest device on the bus.

PCIe

The *PCI Express* (PCIe or PCI-E) specification was designed to replace both PCI and PCIx in systems that demand the highest bus speeds. PCIe uses serial communication instead of parallel. Unlike both PCI and PCIx, the PCIe bus is a full-duplex channel. This means that devices on the bus can send and receive simultaneously, rather than waiting for the other side to finish communicating.

A connection between a PCIe device and the system is known as a *link*. Each link uses a dedicated, bidirectional, serial, point-to-point connection called a *lane*. Each lane can simultaneously transfer 250 MBps of data in each direction. A link can use more than one lane at a time, but all links must support at least a single-lane connection. This connection is referred to as a "x1" (pronounced "by-one") link. PCIe supports x1, x2, x4, x8, x12, x16, and x32 bus widths.

PCIe is not backward compatible with either PCI or PCIx. It was designed to replace both of those older bus types. PCIe cards physically fit into slots designed for their lane configuration or higher (up-plugging), but not into slots designed for lower lane configurations (down-plugging).

Most modern laptop computers use a version of the PCIe bus. This bus goes by the name Mini PCI Express, Mini PCIe, or Mini PCI-E.

Do it!   ## A-6: Examining the PCI bus

Here's how	Here's why
1 Following all electrical and ESD safety precautions, shut down your PC and open the case	
2 Locate a PCI, PCIx, or PCIe slot	
How many PCI expansion slots does your computer contain?	
How many of the PCI expansion slots are in use? How many are available?	
3 Does your computer contain expansion slots other than PCI?	
Identify them	
4 Leave the cover removed for the next activity	

Topic B: Drive adapters

This topic covers the following CompTIA Server+ (2009 Edition) exam objectives.

#	Objective

1.1	**Differentiate between system board types, features, components, and their purpose.**
	
	• Bus types and bus speeds
	• Storage connectors
	  – SCSI
	  – SATA
	  – IDE
	  – Floppy

1.6	**Given a scenario, install appropriate expansion cards into a server while taking fault tolerance into consideration**
	
	• HBAs
	• Storage controller (SCSI, SATA, RAID)
	  – SCSI low voltage / high voltage (LVD/HVD)
	  – SCSI IDs
	  – Cables and connectors
	  – Active vs. passive termination

Controllers and interfaces

Explanation

In the realm of disk drives, a *controller* is the adapter board that plugs into your PC's expansion slot. An *interface* is the communications standard that defines how data flows to and from the disk drive.

In current practice, an interface is implemented as a circuit board attached to the top (or bottom, depending on how you want to look at it) of the drive unit, as shown in Exhibit 6-12. With older drive technologies, the interface was implemented with circuitry on the controller rather than on the drive. Thus, you sometimes encounter the term "interface" referring to that circuit board. Given that such a circuit board implements the logic and functions of the interface specification, that use of the term makes a certain amount of sense.

Exhibit 6-12: A hard disk drive showing its drive interface board

PC drive interfaces

The following table lists various interfaces that have been developed for PCs. All are in common use now.

Interface	Introduced	Description
SCSI	Early 1980s	The Small Computer Systems Interface (SCSI) is a parallel system bus, in some ways like an expansion bus. Many devices can be connected through a SCSI interface, but drives, particularly optical drives, are the most common devices to use it.
IDE	Mid-1980s and standardized by ANSI in 1994	The Integrated Drive Electronics (IDE) interface is officially known as, and sometimes called, the AT Attachment or ATA interface. This is currently the most popular drive interface for Windows-based PCs.
IEEE 1394 (FireWire, i.Link)	Mid-1990s, standardized in 1995	FireWire was developed by Apple Computer Corp. and later standardized by the IEEE to provide a high-speed serial device interface. Many components, in addition to drives, can be attached through a FireWire interface.
USB 1.1 and USB 2.0	Mid-1990s	USB is a high-speed serial device interface. Many components, in addition to drives, can be attached through a USB interface. USB 2.0 offers speed and expandability improvements over 1.1. Note: The spec for USB 3.0 has been finalized, and devices and USB 3.0 ports on desktops and laptops are starting to roll out.

IDE/ATA

The most popular PC drive interface is the Integrated Drive Electronics (IDE) standard. Officially, this interface is called the AT Attachment (ATA) interface. Most newer drives and controllers that implement this interface use that term rather than IDE.

ATA has undergone many revisions since its first release. It can be divided into two groups: Parallel ATA (PATA) and Serial ATA (SATA). As of 2009, SATA has just about replaced PATA in consumer PCs. PATA continues to be used in CompactFlash storage applications. The following table describes various incarnations of the ATA interface.

Standard	Transfer rate	Description	Speed enhancements
ATA	3.3–8.3 MBps	The first ATA standard. Supported only hard drives.	Programmed Input Output (PIO) modes 0, 1, and 2; single- and multi-word DMA.
Enhanced IDE, Fast ATA, Fast ATA-2	13.3-16.6 MBps	Proprietary extensions to the ATA specification developed by companies such as Western Digital, Seagate, and Quantum.	
ATA-2	11.1–16.6 MBps	The ANSI standardized version of EIDE/Fast ATA. It supported power saving and security features.	PIO modes 3 and 4, plus two multi-word DMA modes. Allowed 32-bit data transfers and block mode transfers.
ATA-3	Up to 16.6 MBps	Improved the reliability of high-speed data transfers compared to ATA-2. Introduced the Self-Monitoring Analysis and Reporting Technology (SMART) for monitoring drive health.	None.
ATAPI	No transfer rate specified in the standard	AT Attachment Packet Interface—an extension of the ATA specifications to support tape and CD-ROM drives.	None.
ATA/ ATAPI-4	16.7–33 MBps	An enhancement of the ATAPI and ATA-3 specifications. It added data integrity checks (CRC checking) and the new drive control commands, and it removed obsolete commands.	UltraDMA modes 0, 1, and 2, and an improved 80-conductor cable specification. UltraDMA mode 2 offered the best performance, and drives supporting it are often called UltraDMA/33 drives, reflecting their 33 MBps transfer rates.
ATA/ ATAPI-5	Up to 66.7 MBps	A further enhancement to the ATA specification that offered speed enhancements, command cleanup, and functions to detect whether the 80-conductor cable was in use.	UltraDMA modes 3 and 4; mandatory use of 80-conductor cable for UltraDMA mode 4. Drives running in UltraDMA mode 4 are most often called UltraDMA/66 drives.
ATA/ ATAPI-6	Up to 100 MBps	Further enhancements to offer increased throughput and support for extremely large hard drives.	UltraDMA mode 5. Drives implementing this mode are often called UltraDMA/100 drives.

Standard	Transfer rate	Description	Speed enhancements
ATA/ ATAPI-7	Up to 133 MBps	Yet another enhancement to offer increased throughput.	UltraDMA mode 6, with drives being called UltraDMA/133 drives.
SATA or S-ATA	150–300 MBps	Serial ATA—a serial bus implementation of an ATA-style interface.	Many enhancements, including a dual cable arrangement and dedicated connections to each device.
eSATA	300 MBps	External SATA—a version of SATA designed for connecting external SATA devices.	Competes against FireWire and USB interfaces. It's faster, but has a shorter maximum cable length: 2 meters. FireWire 800 has a transfer rate of 98 MBps. USB 2.0 has a rate of 60 MBps.

Speed improvement techniques

In the original ATA schemes, the CPU was involved with every data transfer through a scheme called *programmed input/output (PIO)*. Five PIO schemes were developed, with each new level improving performance through various techniques. These schemes are listed in the following table.

PIO mode	Transfer rate
0	3.3 MBps
1	5.2 MBps
2	8.3 MBps
3	11.1 MBps
4	16.7 MBps

Later, designers came up with direct memory access (DMA) schemes, which removed the need for the CPU to be involved with every transfer. The six DMA schemes provided the performance levels listed in the following table.

DMA mode	Transfer rate
Single-word 0	2.1 MBps
Single-word 1	4.2 MBps
Single-word 2	8.3 MBps
Multi-word 0	4.2 MBps
Multi-word 1	13.3 MBps
Multi-word 2	16.7 MBps

Later improvements of the DMA schemes became known as UltraDMA (sometimes called UDMA). Currently, there are seven UltraDMA modes, which provide the performance levels listed in the following table.

UltraDMA mode	Transfer rate
0	16.7 MBps
1	25 MBps
2	33.3 MBps
3	44.4 MBps
4	66.7 MBps
5	100 MBps
6	133 MBps

Cables and connectors

The following exhibits show ATA motherboard connectors, ATA drive cables, and SATA connectors.

Exhibit 6-13: ATA motherboard connectors

Exhibit 6-14: A standard ATA drive cable

Exhibit 6-15: A high-speed 80-pin ATA drive cable for a drive with a 3.5" form factor

PATA uses different cables and connectors for 3.5" (desktop-size) and 2.5" (notebook-size) drives. To connect a 2.5" drive to a desktop system, you typically must use an adapter. It plugs into the smaller drive connector and provides a socket into which you plug the larger cable.

Exhibit 6-16: SATA data cables

SATA uses the same cable for both 2.5" and 3.5" drives, so you don't need to use an adapter to connect either drive to a system. You might need to use mounting brackets or rails to secure a smaller drive into a bay designed for a 3.5" drive.

Drive capacities

The original hard drive specifications limited capacities to 504 MB. This was due to limitations on the physical parameters of various hard drive components, namely the number of read/write heads, the number of tracks on the disk, and the number of sectors (sections) in each track. Memory and other programming space must be set aside for each. The standards that led to this limit were developed when MS-DOS was the primary operating system and memory was limited to 1 MB.

At that time, a 500 MB limit seemed beyond foreseeable needs. However, the need for storage space quickly outgrew this limit. Another limit was reached later when drive capacities pushed beyond the 137 GB maximum capacity supported by the ATA specification itself.

To increase the maximum supported drive size, the various ATA enhancements used a variety of techniques:

- **LBA** — Logical block addressing increased the size limit to 8.4 GB through the use of sector translation. Basically, the interface made the drive appear to have a different physical arrangement that bypassed limits that its actual geometry would impose.

- **ECHS** — ECHS (Extended Cylinder-Head-Sector) is another version of LBA-style sector translation that supports up to 8.4 GB disks.

- **Interrupt 13h extensions** — Limits in the BIOS routines limited drive capacities to 8.4 GB. Moving beyond this limit required BIOS changes. The interrupt 13h extensions changed the way the BIOS accessed disk drives. Changing the BIOS in this way required changes in both the BIOS firmware and the operating system. Since Windows 95, operating systems have supported the interrupt 13h BIOS extensions. Interrupt 13 extensions permit drives of up to 128 GB.

- **ATA limits** — Design limits in the ATA specification limited drives to 137 GB. Newer versions of the ATA specification (after ATA-6) remove this limit.

- **Large LBA** — The most recent capacity enhancements were made possible by the ATA-6 interface standard. It increased the number of bits used for sector addressing to 48, leading to a maximum capacity of 144 petabytes (144,000,000 GB!). This technique is often called "large logical block addressing."

Drive identification

The ATA specification, except for the SATA extension, supports two drives per controller. One drive must be designated as the master, or primary, disk. The other is called the slave. You must configure or connect drives to support this arrangement, or communications between the drives won't work.

With older drives, you had to set a jumper or DIP switch to specify its role: master, slave, or the only drive in the system. Furthermore, you had to connect the drives to the correct location on the cable, as shown in Exhibit 6-17.

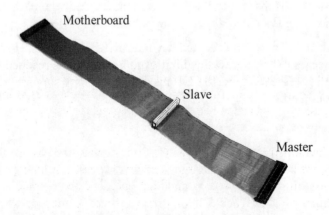

Exhibit 6-17: A PATA cable for a 3.5"-form-factor drive, showing where to connect the master and slave drives

Newer drives detect where they're connected on the cable and configure themselves automatically. This feature is called *cable-select*. Both the motherboard and the drives must support cable-select. If they don't, you have to configure the drives manually.

Primary and secondary channels

On motherboards offering PATA controllers, most include two built-in controllers. These are designated as the primary and secondary channels. You should connect your primary hard drive as the master device on the primary channel. Additional drives can be connected to the slave and secondary channels.

Exhibit 6-18: Primary and secondary PATA connectors on the motherboard

The Advanced Host Controller Interface

The SATA specification provides for two operating modes: IDE emulation and AHCI (Advanced Host Controller Interface). The IDE emulation mode provides backward compatibility to systems, such as Windows XP, that do not support the faster and more capable ACHI mode. AHCI mode offers better performance and support for features such as hot-plugging (connecting or disconnecting devices without shutting down the system).

Windows Vista, Windows 7, and Windows Server 2008, along with Linux versions based on kernel version 2.6.19 and newer, support ACHI. You might need to install new drivers to enable this mode, which is sometimes called "RAID mode" in the BIOS configuration.

SCSI

The Small Computer Systems Interface (SCSI) is a bus interface and is, in many ways, more like an expansion bus than like a drive adapter technology. SCSI, which is pronounced "scuzzy," supports all sorts of data storage devices, printers, scanners, and video devices. SCSI has even been used as the basis for very-high-performance computer networks.

SCSI was developed in the early 1980s but not standardized by ANSI until 1986. Since that time, the technology has undergone many changes. It remains a popular drive interface for workstations, servers, and high-end desktop computers. It's also commonly used with higher-end scanners and digitizing devices. Until recently, SCSI was also very popular with drives used with Macintosh computers.

Standard	Bus width (bits)	Bandwidth	Maximum cable length	Maximum number of devices
SCSI	8 bits	5 MBps	6 meters	8
Fast SCSI	8 bits	10 MBps	1.5–3 m	8
Fast Wide SCSI	16 bits	20 MBps	1.5–3 m	16
Ultra SCSI	8 bits	20 MBps	1.5–3 m	5–8
Ultra Wide SCSI	16 bits	40 MBps	1.5–3 m	5–8
Ultra2/LVD	8 bits	40 MBps	12 m	8
Ultra2 Wide	16 bits	80 MBps	12 m	16
Ultra3	16 bits	160 MBps	12 m	16
Ultra-320	16 bits	320 MBps	12 m	16
Ultra-640	16 bits	640 MBps	12 m	16
Serial-attached SCSI (SAS)	1 bit	300 MBps	8 m	128 device ports, supporting up to 16,384 devices

Device IDs

Every SCSI device, including the *host bus adapter (HBA)*, must be assigned a unique ID number. SCSI IDs begin at 0 and count upward, with higher IDs having a higher priority on the SCSI bus. The HBA is normally assigned the highest SCSI ID. For example, with a SCSI Ultra-320 system, the HBA would be assigned ID 15.

You must assign unique IDs to devices. It's not uncommon when implementing SCSI devices to have ID conflicts that prevent devices from working.

Termination

You must add terminating resistors to each end of the SCSI bus. These terminators are basically electrical resistors that absorb signals that reach the end of the bus. Without them, signals could reflect back onto the bus, leading to a confusing mix of actual and reflected signals.

Typically, the HBA includes removable resistors. Modern devices have switch-selectable termination built in: if you need a device to provide termination, then you switch on its terminators. Otherwise, you can leave its terminators turned off.

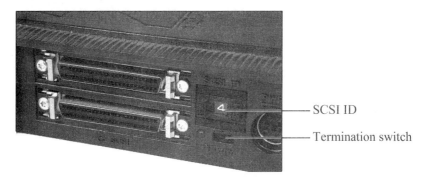

Exhibit 6-19: An external SCSI drive with a SCSI ID selector and a termination slide-switch

SCSI terminators are supposed to add electrical impedance equal to the impedance of the cable. *Passive terminators* are simply resistors that dampen reflected signals through non-electronic means. They come close to matching the impedance in most situations. In demanding applications, however, you should use an active terminator. An *active terminator* is an electronic component that dynamically tunes itself to exactly match the impedance of the cable. Active termination is most often used with the newer, higher-performing types of SCSI.

Differential SCSI

In the original SCSI specification, electronic signals are referenced compared to a common ground. In other words, whether a signal is or isn't present on a particular wire is determined based on its voltage difference as compared to a common ground signal.

This single-ended (SE) scheme works well with lower data transfer rates and short cables. With the introduction of Ultra SCSI, engineers developed differential SCSI, which worked better with longer cables and higher data rates. In *differential SCSI*, later renamed *High Voltage Differential (HVD)*, data lines are paired. The signal on one line is the electrical opposite of that on the other. In this way, the presence of a signal is determined by examining the difference between the voltage levels on these two lines.

In the Ultra2 SCSI specification, designers refined the HVD scheme, reducing the voltage from ±5 V to ±3.3 V, and Low Voltage Differential (LVD) was born. According to Seagate, the terms Ultra2 SCSI and LVD can be used interchangeably.

iSCSI

The Internet SCSI standard, called *iSCSI*, implements SCSI commands and protocols across an Ethernet network. The purpose of iSCSI is to provide location-independent storage. In theory, if you're using iSCSI, your external storage device could be located anywhere in the world as long as you could maintain TCP/IP connectivity over that distance. In practice, iSCSI is used to implement *storage area networks* (SANs).

A SAN is typically implemented as one or more devices within a data center and connected to the network's backbone. A SAN provides bulk storage services that can be allocated as needed to one or more servers. Often, you can dynamically reassign storage allocation, giving a server access to more or less storage as needed.

The iSCSI standard is defined by various RFCs, including RFC 3720. See *http://tools.ietf.org/html/rfc3720* for information on that specification.

SCSI cables and connectors

The SCSI family of standards has existed for more than 30 years, and over that time, many different cable and connector types have been used for SCSI links. The earliest implementations used parallel-port-type DB25 connectors. Exhibit 6-19 shows a newer 50-pin high-density SCSI connector on the back of an external drive. Exhibit 6-20 shows various SCSI connectors for external devices.

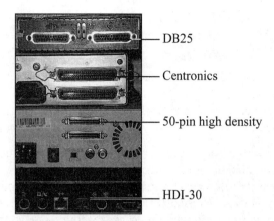

Exhibit 6-20: Various SCSI connectors

External devices typically use round, multiconductor cable, which looks something like a fat network cable. Internal SCSI devices typically use a ribbon cable. SCSI can be implemented over fiber optic cabling, which would use fiber-specific connectors. iSCSI uses your IP networking cable and connectors.

USB

You can connect storage devices to the USB bus. However, many common USB drives are actually ATA drives with an integrated USB interface adapter. While this is certainly a convenient way to attach an external ATA drive to your PC, it's not the same as connecting a drive directly to the USB interface.

True USB drives are feasible, yet uncommon. The interface circuitry of the USB drive would be connected directly to the USB bus without any sort of ATA controller involved. The typical thumb drive or memory card reader is such a drive. Circuitry in these devices translates directly from the memory card's electrical interface to the USB bus.

The USB 1.1 specification limited data transfer to 12 Mbps (megabits per second). The USB 2.0 specification increases that limit to 480 Mbps. The USB 3.0 specification will have a maximum transfer speed of 5.0 Gbps. It is anticipated that USB 3.0 devices will be available for consumers in 2010.

USB supports hot swapping, meaning that you can plug in or unplug devices without powering down the PC. It's also dynamically self-configuring in that all you typically need to do to begin using a USB device is to plug it in.

IEEE 1394

FireWire is the name given to the device interface specification developed by Apple Computer Corp. Apple trademarked the name and charges a licensing fee to use it. Therefore, most manufacturers use its IEEE standard number (IEEE 1394) rather than this name. Sony named its implementation of this technology i.Link. All these names refer to the same technology.

IEEE 1394 is a serial interface technology based on the Serial SCSI standard. It's a general-purpose interface that's widely implemented in video cameras, but less commonly used with other devices.

IEEE 1394 supports up to 400 Mbps throughput, a bit less than USB 2.0. However, IEEE 1394 has an advantage over USB for some applications. You can connect multiple devices to either interface, but with IEEE 1394, a device can be granted dedicated access to the interface for a period of time. Thus, timing-critical data transfers are better supported by IEEE 1394.

Take video transfer as an example. Video that's transferring from a camera or coming in through a digitizing system arrives at a steady rate of a certain number of video frames per second. Not only must an interface keep up with the overall data transfer volume, but it must also keep up precisely with the frame-by-frame rate so that frames of video aren't lost (or don't arrive late). IEEE 1394 can guarantee time-critical access to the interface and, thus, in theory, supports video better than USB 2.0 does.

IEEE 1394 supports hot swapping and is dynamically self-configuring. To use an IEEE 1394 device, all you typically need to do is plug it in.

In July of 2008, IEEE approved two new standards: FireWire S1600, with a data transfer rate of 1.6 Gbps; and FireWire S3200, with a data transfer rate of 3.932 Gbps. These two standards are designed to compete with the new USB 3.0 standard. FireWire S1600 and S3200 devices use the same 9-circuit beta connectors as FireWire 800 and are backward compatible with FireWire 400 and FireWire 800.

The FireWire S800T standard, released in July of 2007, uses a new port configuration— an 800 Mbps connection over RJ-45 connectors with Category 5e cable.

Floppy drives and controllers

A floppy disk is a removable data storage medium composed of a thin, typically brown, plastic disk contained within a stiff or rigid plastic case. Floppy disks are also called floppies or diskettes. A floppy disk drive (FDD) is the PC component that reads or writes data to floppies. Floppy disks were the original storage medium for PCs. By today's standards, they hold a miniscule amount of data and are very slow to access. Many modern computers do not include a floppy drive.

Exhibit 6-21: A 5.25" floppy disk (left) and a 3.5" floppy disk (right)

In early PCs, the floppy drive controller was a separate component. For at least the past decade, floppy drive controllers have been almost universally built into the motherboard. Thus, you will probably never be called upon to install a floppy drive controller.

Many motherboards still contain a built-in controller even if a floppy drive is not provided with the computer. You might need to enable or configure the system resources it uses. You would do so with the BIOS setup utility. The typical resources used by the floppy controller are listed in the following table.

System resource	Typical value
IRQ	6
I/O address range	0x03F0–0x03F7
DMA channel	2

Floppy drive controllers typically support up to two floppy drives, which are assigned drive letters A and B.

Floppy drive cables

The typical cable you use to connect a floppy drive is a 34-pin ribbon cable with either three or five connectors. One connector is meant to be connected to the drive controller (typically on the motherboard), and the others are for connecting to the floppy drives.

The 5.25" drives use a larger, pinch-type connector, whereas 3.5" drives use a smaller pin-socket-style connector. Because you can connect only two floppy drives to a controller, you can use either the 5.25" or 3.5" connector for each of the drives, but not both.

Where you connect the drive on the cable determines whether the drive is assigned drive letter A or B. Floppy cables have a twisted section, and the drive plugged into the connectors beyond the twist are assigned drive letter A by the BIOS. A typical floppy cable is shown in Exhibit 6-22.

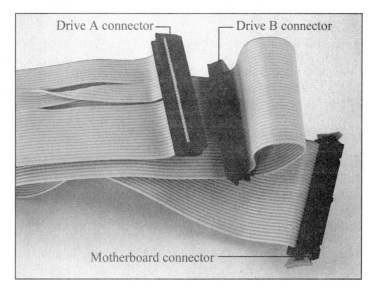

Exhibit 6-22: A floppy cable with connectors

Floppy controller connectors

The typical floppy controller connector is a 34-pin male connector soldered to the motherboard. Such a connector is shown in Exhibit 6-23.

Exhibit 6-23: A floppy controller connector on a motherboard

Do it!

B-1: Distinguishing among drive controllers

Here's how	Here's why
1 If necessary, shut down and power off your computer	
Following all electrical safety and ESD precautions, open your PC's case	
2 Determine whether your PC supports ATA drives	Locate the ATA connectors on the motherboard.
3 Determine whether your PC supports SATA drives	Look for the SATA data and power connectors on the motherboard.
4 Determine whether your PC supports SCSI drives	Look for the SCSI data and power connectors on the motherboard.
If your computer supports SCSI, what type of internal and external connectors does it support?	
5 Determine whether your PC supports USB drives	The interface circuitry of the USB drive is connected directly to the USB bus without any sort of ATA controller involved. This type of internal drive connection is uncommon.
6 Determine whether your PC supports floppy drives	
7 Examine the selection of drives and adapters provided by your instructor. For each one, determine its interface type. Then rank them in increasing order of performance.	

Card installation

Explanation

To install expansion cards, you must know how to handle them safely and how to configure them.

Safe handling

Expansion cards are sensitive to ESD. You should always follow ESD precautions when working with these cards or any device that must be installed inside a PC's chassis. As usual, follow these guidelines when handling expansion cards:

- Unplug your computer before opening it.
- Ground yourself to the chassis before touching internal components.
- Keep expansion cards inside static-protective bags or packaging until you're ready to install them.
- Handle cards by their edges or slot cover plate. Don't touch board components, traces, or edge-connector pins.

Drivers

A *driver* is a form of software that interacts with hardware to enable that device's functionality. It's the responsibility of a driver, for example, to read the data received over the network via a network interface card. Every expansion device or adapter card in your PC requires a driver. (Basically, any device not controlled by the BIOS requires a driver.)

Some drivers are supplied with the operating system. For example, the drivers that are needed to enable on-board serial or parallel ports are supplied with the operating system. Other devices require drivers supplied by the device manufacturers.

Often, device manufacturers will supply their drivers to Microsoft, which includes the drivers in the set of files that constitute the operating system or makes them available on the Windows Update Web site. For Linux systems, many drivers are written by the Linux distribution's authors so the drivers can be included with the rest of the Linux files. If a hardware vendor supports Linux, it's typically in the form of programmers' tools designed to help someone write a driver. There are various versions of Linux, each with its own driver designs.

Installation

In general, you will follow these steps to install an expansion card in your PC:

1 If you're not using a Plug-n-Play (PnP)–compatible expansion card or operating system (for example, some versions of Linux or older Windows versions), determine the available system resources (IRQs, I/O addresses, and so forth). Configure the DIP switches or jumpers on the card, as necessary, to assign it available system resources.

If you're using a PnP-compatible card and operating system, the vendor might direct you to run an installation utility before installing the device. This installation program puts the necessary drivers in a location where the operating system can find them once you're done installing the device. If appropriate, run that setup program now.

2 Unless you are using a computer with an expansion bus that supports hot-plug capabilities, shut down your PC, unplug it, remove peripheral cables, and open the case.

3 Locate an empty and available expansion slot of the correct type. Remove the slot cover for that slot. Slot covers are generally either screwed in place or held by spring-clips.

4 If necessary, temporarily move or remove wires or other expansion cards that are in the way so that you can access the slot.

5 If you need to connect wire assemblies to the expansion board—not to its back slot cover plate, but to the board itself—connect that end of the wire assembly before installing the card. In this way, you can easily reach the connector and be sure that you're installing the wire assembly in its correct orientation. Connect the other end after you have installed the card.

6 Begin inserting the end of the edge connector furthest from the slot cover; then gently push the card into place in the slot. This technique will help you line up the connector correctly. Inserting the card at an angle like this is usually easier than pushing it straight into the slot.

7 Fix the card in place with screws or clips, as appropriate to your case design.

8 Connect any wiring assemblies, including those you temporarily removed to install this card.

9 Close the case, connect peripherals, and start the system.

10 Depending on your operating system, OS version, and adapter card technology, configure the card. If you're using PnP-compatible components, PnP will handle this for you.

11 If necessary, install required drivers. If you have to install drivers yourself, you will most likely need to configure them to use the same hardware resources you configured the card to use.

When you're done, some devices and operating system versions will also require you to restart the computer. This step fully loads the drivers and configures the operating system to support the new device.

Do it!

B-2: Considering the steps to install an expansion card

Questions	Answers
1 Does your computer support hot-plugging, or must you shut it down to install an expansion card? How can you tell?	
2 Examine the expansion slots in your computer. Are there covers that must be removed before you can install an expansion card?	
3 Are there wires or other assemblies that would be in the way?	
4 Why should you unplug your computer before opening it?	

Topic C: Multimedia expansion devices

This topic covers the following CompTIA Server+ (2009 Edition) exam objectives.

#	Objective
1.1	**Differentiate between system board types, features, components, and their purpose** • Bus types and bus speeds • Expansion slots – PCI – PCIe – AGP
1.6	**Given a scenario, install appropriate expansion cards into a server while taking fault tolerance into consideration** • Manufacturer specific – Fax cards – PBX cards – Camera cards – VoIP • Video • Audio • Port expansion cards – USB – FireWire – Serial – Parallel

Video adapters

Explanation

Video adapters convert computer data to the signals required to produce the images that you see on your screen. In the early generations of PCs, video adapters created just text output, and often monochrome output at that. Nowadays, video adapters create the signals necessary to display full-color and full-motion images and video.

Due to the enormous amount of information that must be manipulated by the adapter to produce these signals, modern video adapters are almost computers in their own right. They often feature a specialized processor chip and lots of on-board memory. For end-user computers, the video adapter is perhaps the component most responsible for the overall performance of the PC. Video performance is less critical for servers.

Display characteristics

Even though video performance is not a critical consideration for most servers, you must still understand and account for the basic characteristics of video output. These are described in the following table.

Item	Description
Pixel	An image to be displayed, whether it's text or a picture, is divided by the display adapter into a series of dots called pixels (adapted from "picture elements"). Officially, a pixel is the smallest addressable unit of a picture.
Resolution	A monitor's resolution is the number of pixels across and down that an adapter can create.
Refresh rate	The rate at which the image is painted is called the *refresh rate*. With some early video display standards, the full image couldn't be refreshed entirely in a single pass. These systems used *interlacing*, in which the odd lines of the image were painted during one pass of the beam and the even lines were painted during a second pass.
Pixel depth	The number of shades that each red, green, and blue video component can be set to is determined by the pixel depth, or the number of bits per pixel devoted to each shade.

Video display standards

Video display standards describe levels of support for the display characteristics described in the preceding table. Technically, the standards describe the electronic and software features needed to support a particular set of display characteristics. Additionally, these standards cover physical characteristics, such as the connector type.

Early display standards include VGA (Video Graphics Array) and SuperVGA, officially standardized under the VESA BIOS Extensions (VBE) specification. Newer standards include DVI and HDMI.

You must select a video adapter and monitor that support a common video display standard and the display characteristics you need. For example, for a server, you probably don't need more than SuperVGA-level support of 1024x768 resolution with full-color display.

Video buses

You can install video adapters into a standard expansion bus, such as a PCI slot. However, video-specific buses often provide better system performance. Although you don't necessarily need high-performance video for a server, you don't want the server to get bogged down in processing display output when it could be servicing client requests.

Typically, you install a video expansion card using one of the following bus standards:

- VLB (VESA Local Bus)
- AGP (Accelerated Graphics Port)
- PCI or PCIe

Integrated (on-board) video adapters are typically implemented through the AGP bus.

VESA Local Bus

The VESA local bus, also called the VL-bus or just VLB, was developed in 1992 by the Video Electronics Standards Association. At this point, VLB is of interest only in a historical context. VLB was implemented on many 80486-based systems but fell out of favor by the time the Pentium processor was released.

Exhibit 6-24: A VLB video adapter

AGP

Intel developed the AGP (Accelerated Graphics Port) video bus standard in 1997 to improve video bus performance. AGP's release coincided with the release of the Pentium II chipsets from Intel. Since this initial release, newer AGP standards have been released. These include:

- AGP 1.0, AGP 2.0, and AGP 3.0
- 64-bit AGP
- Ultra-AGP
- AGP Pro
- Ultra-AGPII

Originally, one of AGP's biggest performance improvements was its ability to access and use main system memory. Accessing data in main system memory rather than first transferring the data to the adapter improved rendering speed. Intel called this feature *Direct Memory Execute (DIME)*, and for some operations, it offered as much as a tenfold performance improvement, compared to video adapters that couldn't access main memory in this way.

To save money, reduce power consumption, and reduce heat generation, many laptop and low-end desktop AGP components don't contain any on-board memory. Instead, main system memory is used exclusively for video operations. This setup reduces the amount of main system memory available for normal operations. When you're choosing a computer to use as a server, make sure that the video adapter provides its own on-board memory to ensure that all of the installed system memory is available for normal system operations.

Exhibit 6-25: An AGP adapter (note the hook beside the edge connectors)

AGP slots are typically brown, but sometimes maroon or another dark color. Modern video adapters require active cooling (fans) and thus more space than other adapters. For this reason, an AGP slot is typically well separated from other bus slots.

Exhibit 6-26: An AGP slot

PCI and PCIe video

PCI slot–based video adapters are slower than AGP or PCIe adapters. The PCI-based adapters have to share the PCI bus with all of the other PCI-based devices in the system. However, these adapters work well for implementing a two-monitor system if you are using two separate video cards. If your motherboard doesn't have an AGP or PCIe slot, this setup is your only option for upgrading the video on your system.

PCI Express (PCIe) cards are designed to replace AGP video cards in new systems. Motherboards that support PCIe video cards became available in 2004. A 16x PCIe video card has a 4 GBps bandwidth in each direction. You can theoretically achieve 8 GBps capacity with data moving upstream and downstream at the same time because this is a dual-line technology. The high transfer speeds make this technology an ideal solution for multimedia applications, such as gaming, photography, and videography. This card fits into a 164-pin slot on motherboards equipped with PCIe. A 16x PCIe video card is shown in Exhibit 6-27.

Exhibit 6-27: A PCIe video card

Connectors

The typical VGA or SuperVGA connector is a 15-pin DIN connector, as shown in Exhibit 6-28.

Exhibit 6-28: A 15-pin VGA or SuperVGA connector

The typical VGA or SuperVGA socket is shown in Exhibit 6-29.

Exhibit 6-29: A VGA/SuperVGA socket

Typically, both CRT (television style) and flat-panel (LCD) monitors support the VGA-style 15-pin connector. Many flat-panel monitors also support *digital video interface* (DVI) connections. As shown in Exhibit 6-30, there are various DVI implementations, each using a different connector. You will need to match your video adapter and monitor so that both use the same DVI standard.

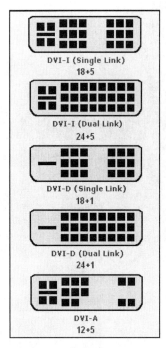

Exhibit 6-30: DVI connection types

HDMI

Like DVI-D, *HDMI (High-Definition Multimedia Interface)* delivers video signals in a digital format without analog conversion, using the *TMDS (Transition Minimized Differential Signaling) protocol*. DVI-D and HDMI are similar in terms of image quality, but HDMI can deliver up to eight channels of audio in addition to video. HDMI also supports higher resolutions than DVI-D does, including some resolutions not yet available commercially. HDMI uses a different type of connector than does DVI-D.

There are two types of HDMI connectors: Type A, which has 19 pins, and Type B, which has 29 pins. The Type B connector is bigger than Type A and allows the use of dual-link configuration. Dual-link configuration doubles the maximum transfer rate, from 165 MHz with Type A to 330 MHz with Type B.

HDMI is fully compatible with DVI-D and DVI-I. DVI-D, DVI-I, and both HDMI connectors use the same encoding scheme, so a DVI-D or DVI-I source can be connected to an HDMI monitor (or vice versa) with a DVI/HDMI cable, and without a converter box. One end of the cable is HDMI, and the other end is DVI-D or DVI-D. HDMI isn't compatible with DVI-A.

Exhibit 6-31: An HDMI Type A port

Do it!

C-1:   Identifying video adapter types

Here's how	Here's why
1 If necessary, shut down your PC and open its case	Follow electrical and ESD safety precautions.
2 Examine the adapter cards in your computer	
Which cards can you use to attach a monitor?	
3 What type of bus is each card connected to?	
For each video card in your computer, does it support analog, digital, or both?	
4 Examine each of the video adapter cards provided by your instructor	
Identify the type of each card	
For each card, does it support analog, digital, or both?	

Sound and your PC

Explanation
Before the introduction of the sound card, PCs could produce simple beeps and clicks through an on-board speaker. Such a speaker is still included in nearly every PC, but it has never been capable of producing music, computerized voices, and other tones.

You won't typically need concert-hall-quality sound support in your server. In fact, you might not need anything more than the on-board speaker for system alerts and warnings. However, management software might use alarm sounds or other audible means to alert you to certain events and conditions. Installing a sound adapter and speakers will better support such audible alarms.

If you need upgraded sound support, you will need to install a sound card in an expansion slot. That card will provide connectors for audio output and input.

Exhibit 6-32: A sound card

Sound card connectors

Sound cards typically feature connectors for speakers, microphones, line-input or line-output devices, and game adapters (joysticks). Some sound cards include connectors for MIDI devices, or have a game adapter port that also supports MIDI device input. The function of each connector is typically labeled with a small icon. Exhibit 6-33 shows some of these connectors and their functions.

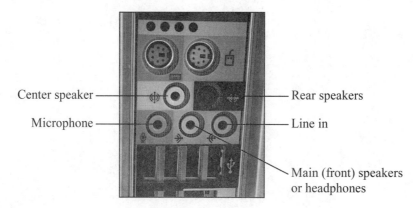

Exhibit 6-33: Standard sound card connectors

Port expansion cards

Your server might not have all of the peripheral ports you need. You can install an expansion card that adds port support. Such port expansion cards might add USB, FireWire, serial, or parallel ports to your PC. Multifunction cards provide more than one of those ports on a single expansion card.

Exhibit 6-34: A PCIe expansion card offering a single RS-232 (serial) port

Do it!

C-2: Examining sound and port expansion adapters

Here's how	Here's why
1 Identify the sound card in your computer	If applicable. Sound functionality might be implemented on the motherboard or as an expansion card.
What type of bus is your sound card connected to?	
2 Identify the connectors included on your sound card	
3 Does your computer use a port expansion card to provide peripheral ports?	
Speculate on the advantages and disadvantages of using port expansion cards.	

Manufacturer-specific adapters

Explanation

When you need specialized functionality, such as shared network faxing services, you might need to turn to proprietary expansion devices. These devices fill a specific niche need and are not typically standardized in the way that commonly used capabilities, such as video or networking, are. The advantage of a proprietary expansion device is of course that you get the functionality you need. The disadvantage is that you can be locked into a single vendor's implementation and be forced to work with that vendor for upgrades, service, and support.

Some commonly used proprietary devices include:

- Fax cards
- PBX cards
- VoIP systems
- Camera cards

Fax cards

A fax card adds the capabilities to send facsimile transmissions from your computer. Some fax cards enable you to connect to a telephone line (or lines) to send traditional faxes. Other fax cards send your fax transmissions over the Internet via protocols such as T.38 (Fax over IP) or T.37 (iFax, which sends your fax as an e-mail attachment).

Fax cards typically include software that supports multi-user access. Functions such as queuing, device sharing, statistics gathering, and reporting are typically provided by the software.

PBX cards

PBX cards enable your server to provide central telephone services for your company. A PBX card would typically provide ports to which you would connect incoming telephone trunk lines and internal telephone extension lines. Using accompanying software on your server, you could manage such features as voice mail, call hold, music on hold, and call forwarding.

VoIP systems

PBX cards enable a server to interact with traditional PSTN (public switched telephone network) phone lines. *Voice over IP*, or VoIP, provides calling capability via an IP network without requiring connections to the PSTN.

Calls originating within your VoIP system are routed over your IP-based network. Outbound calls might be directed over the Internet to a remote VoIP system. Or if your system is connected to the PSTN, calls can be directed to "normal" telephones. Incoming calls from either the Internet or PSTN are digitized, if necessary, and routed to the appropriate IP-based phones.

Some VoIP systems are standalone devices. Others are provided as a combination of hardware (expansion cards) and software. As with PBX cards, the VoIP adapter would include connectors for interconnecting with the PSTN and your IP network. The software would support call management as well as the typical calling features, such as call hold, voice mail, music on hold, and so forth.

Camera cards

Your first thought with a camera card might involve connecting your digital camera to download your family photos.

However, such cards can also be used in a server environment. Camera cards enable you to capture incoming video or to output video. For example, you might use a camera capture card in your server to support centrally managed security-camera monitoring. Outgoing video applications could include producing video output for digital signs, closed-circuit TV systems, or entertainment-video distribution.

Equipment considerations

As with any expansion adapter, you will need to select a manufacturer-specific specialty card that matches an available bus slot in your server and includes software that works with your operating system. Of course, you will need to select a card that provides the features and functions you require. But more important, you should carefully investigate the vendors offering such cards to be sure they can provide the level of service and support your company requires.

Do it!

C-3: Considering manufacturer-specific expansion cards

Here's how	Here's why
1 List some of the criteria you should consider when selecting a manufacturer-specific expansion card.	
2 Name at least one disadvantage of using a manufacturer-specific expansion adapter.	
3 Examine the manufacturer-specific expansion adapters provided by your instructor	
What bus types do they support? What connectors do they provide?	

Topic D: Troubleshooting expansion cards

This topic covers the following CompTIA Server+ (2009 Edition) exam objectives.

#	Objective
1.4	**Explain the importance of a Hardware Compatibility List (HCL)** • Vendor standards for hardware • Expansion cards compatibility

6.2	**Given a scenario, effectively troubleshoot hardware problems, selecting the appropriate tools and methods**
	• Common problems
	  – Onboard component failure
	  – Expansion card failure
	  – Drive failure

6.5	**Given a scenario, effectively troubleshoot storage problems, selecting the appropriate tools and methods**
	• Causes of common problems
	  – Controller failure
	  – HBA failure
	  – Improper termination

Troubleshooting

Explanation

As a server technician, you might be responsible for initial troubleshooting when problems arise. At other companies, you might be required to call on a dedicated hardware technician to troubleshoot problems. However, even in this latter case, it will pay to be familiar with the most common symptoms, probable causes, and suggested "first try" solutions for expansion card problems.

The following tables list problems, probable causes, and suggested solutions for the following types of expansion cards:

- Drive controllers
- Video adapters
- Sound cards
- Internal modems

The following table describes drive controller–related problems you might encounter.

Symptom	Probable cause	Suggested solution
IDE drive is not recognized.	Power or IDE interface cable not connected; interface cable connected incorrectly; master/slave/cable-select setting misconfigured.	Check the power connection. Confirm that the keyed IDE cable connector has been installed correctly. If it's not keyed, make sure the cable is plugged in so that pin 1 on the cable (normally identified with a red stripe) lines up with hole 1 on the motherboard connector. Check the master/slave/cable-select jumper. Make sure the master drive is connected to the correct cable connector, along with the slave drive and the motherboard connection.
SCSI drive is not recognized.	SCSI ID set incorrectly; power cable not connected; termination not set correctly; passive or active terminator used when the other kind is required.	Confirm that there are no SCSI ID conflicts. Check cable connections. Confirm termination switches or install terminator packs, if necessary. Make sure you're using the correct terminator type for your adapter card and devices.
System with IDE drive won't boot, with or without BIOS error message.	Power or IDE interface cable not connected; interface cable connected incorrectly; master/slave/cable-select setting misconfigured.	Check the power connection. Confirm that the keyed IDE cable connector has been installed correctly. If it's not keyed, make sure the cable is plugged in, so that pin 1 on the cable (normally identified with a red stripe) lines up with hole 1 on the motherboard connector. Check the master/slave/cable-select jumper. Make sure the master drive is connected to the correct cable connector, along with the slave drive and the motherboard connection.
System with SCSI drive won't boot, with or without BIOS error message.	SCSI ID set incorrectly; power cable not connected; termination not set correctly; passive or active terminator used when the other kind is required.	Confirm that there are no SCSI ID conflicts. Check cable connections. Confirm termination switches or install terminator packs if necessary. Make sure you're using the correct terminator type for your adapter card and devices.
IDE drive is inaccessible or performs badly.	Master/slave/cable-select setting misconfigured; 40-pin rather than 80-pin cable installed.	Check the master/slave/cable-select jumper. Make sure the master drive is connected to the correct cable connector, along with the slave drive and the motherboard connection. Confirm that the correct type of cable is installed.
Full size of drive is not available.	Adapter card and system BIOS might not support correct extensions to enable very large drives.	Confirm that you really have the size drive you think you have. Check your computer manufacturer's site for BIOS updates. Install the drive maker's specialized software for accessing very large drives. Install an add-on drive adapter with up-to-date BIOS extension support.

The following table describes video adapter–related problems you might encounter.

Symptom	Probable cause	Suggested solution
No video at all	Monitor is turned off or disconnected; video card failed; cable is bad; wrong video mode is used.	Make sure the monitor is connected and turned on. Attach another monitor that's capable of very high resolution modes. If video is displayed, configure a lower resolution mode and then reattach the original monitor. Check for bent or broken pins in the video connector. Replace the video card.
Video scrolls, flips, wavers, is too large, doubles up lines, and so forth	Video card is set to a refresh rate or resolution mode that the monitor can't support.	Either replace the monitor with a better one, or reconfigure the driver to use a lower resolution mode or lower refresh rate.
Video flickers	Refresh rate is too low.	Configure the driver to use a higher refresh rate.
Video is blurry	Monitor is failing.	Replace the monitor.
Image artifacts are displayed across the screen	Software is at fault, either driver software or your application.	Update the video card drivers. Check for application updates.
System freezes during a video change, such as an image scrolling or changing	Video driver could be at fault.	Update the video card drivers.

The following table describes sound card–related problems you might encounter.

Symptom	Probable cause	Suggested solution
No sound	External speakers not connected or turned off; Windows configured to operate silently.	Connect the speakers or turn them on. Confirm the sound configuration in the Control Panel.
Sound is very low	Volume on speakers set too low; audio output levels set too low or muted.	Turn up the volume knob on the speakers. Click the speaker icon in the system tray and slide the volume slider up. You might need to uncheck Mute.
Sound is distorted	Volume set too high for speakers; bad driver.	Turn down the volume knob on the speakers. Click the speaker icon in the system tray and slide the volume slider down. Update the audio card drivers.
No audio captured	Microphone not connected; bad microphone; audio input levels set too low or muted.	Right-click the speaker icon in the system tray and choose Open Volume Controls. Under Line In, slide the volume slider up. Uncheck Mute if necessary.
No audio from CD	CD audio volume set too low or muted; CD audio cable not connected to sound card.	Right-click the speaker icon in the system tray and choose Open Volume Controls. Under CD Audio, slide the volume slider up. You might need to uncheck Mute. Open the PC and confirm that the sound cable from your CD drive is connected to the sound card, and connected properly.

The following table describes modem-related problems you might encounter.

Symptom	Probable cause	Suggested solution
Modem picks up line and dials, but doesn't connect	Not dialing correct number; remote modem disconnected.	Confirm that you're dialing the correct number (try dialing it with a telephone to confirm that you get modem tones from the remote end). Confirm that the remote modem is online and accepting calls.
Modem reports no dial tone detected	Phone line not connected; bad phone line; phone cord connected to wrong port on modem.	Confirm that the modem is correctly connected to the phone jack. Connect a phone to the modem line and pick up the handset. If there's no dial tone, contact your telephone company or technician to troubleshoot the line problem.
Connection drops frequently	Noisy phone line.	Connect a phone to the modem line, pick up the handset, and press a single number. If the line isn't silent, contact your telephone company or technician to troubleshoot the line noise.
Modem connects, but only at low speeds	Noisy phone line; remote modem supports only lower speeds.	Connect a phone to the modem line, pick up the handset, and press a single number. If the line isn't silent, contact your telephone company or technician to troubleshoot the line noise. Confirm that the remote modem supports high-speed connections.
Modem doesn't work at all	Modem has failed; drivers not installed.	Try installing another modem. Confirm that the required modem drivers are installed.
Configuration-related error messages	COM port conflicts; system resource conflicts.	Use Device Manager to confirm that the COM port used by the modem is available and not assigned to another device. Confirm or resolve resource conflicts (IRQs, I/O channels).

NIC indicator lights

Most networking devices have status indicator lights that you can observe to see if the devices are working. Typically, the lights are green if the device is sending or receiving data properly.

Many NICs have indicator lights that flash when data is being sent or received. Some NICs have another light to indicate that there's a working connection to the network. If these lights aren't illuminating, you should check the configuration of the card to see if that's the problem. You can do so through Device Manager.

The network card should appear in Device Manager without any error or warning icons. In Exhibit 6-35, the LAN network card is reported as functioning, but the wireless adapter is reported as disabled.

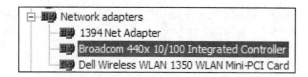

Exhibit 6-35: Device Manager displaying the status of NICs

The General tab of the NIC's Properties dialog also displays the device's status. As shown in Exhibit 6-36, it should display, "This device is working properly."

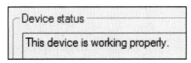

Exhibit 6-36: NIC status

Do it!

D-1:   Interpreting hardware symptoms and their causes

Questions and answers

1 Your computer seems to boot: It makes various beeps, and the fans and lights come on, but nothing is displayed on the monitor. You have already replaced the monitor with one you know to be working. Could this be a sign of a motherboard failure, and if so, how?

2 A user has attached a new monitor to his computer, but calls to complain that the new monitor flickers. What's the probable cause?

Hardware compatibility

Explanation

When selecting an expansion card to install into your computer, you should make sure that the device is on your operating system's hardware compatibility list (HCL). Such lists catalog hardware known to be compatible with certain operating systems.

HCLs can be vendor developed or a collaborative project maintained by users. With vendor-maintained lists (such as Microsoft's Windows HCL), hardware makers pay the operating system's authors to test and approve the expansion hardware and associated driver software. In exchange, they receive permission to use a "tested and compatible" seal of approval.

OS vendors typically define a set of requirements and standards that devices must meet in order to receive approval and be added to the list. As you would expect, such standards require the device to function properly, without errors and without conflicting with other devices in reasonable situations. However, OS vendors also frequently require payment or other compensation from a hardware maker before a device will be added to the HCL.

Each operating system has its own HCL, if such a list is available. You can visit your OS vendor's Web site to view the HCL. Wikipedia maintains a list of links to the HCLs for popular operating systems here: *http://en.wikipedia.org/wiki/Hardware_compatibility_list*.

Do it!

D-2: Examining hardware compatibility lists

Here's how	Here's why
1 Close your computer's case and reattach all cables and peripherals	If you have already reassembled your PC from earlier activities, skip to step 2.
Start your PC	
Log on	
2 Using your browser, visit **http://en.wikipedia.org/wiki/Hardware_compatibility_list**	
3 Follow the various links to locate the HCL for Windows Server 2008	At the time of this writing, you will end up visiting the Windows Server Catalog Web site.
View networking devices compatible with Windows Server	Hundreds of devices have been tested and found compatible.
4 Do you routinely check the HCL before selecting and installing new hardware? Why or why not?	
5 Close your browser	

Data Collector Sets

Explanation

A *Data Collector Set* (DCS) is a mechanism that logs a computer's performance for review at a later time. This later time could be immediately after you run the DCS or several hours, days, or weeks later. The set takes a snapshot of a computer's performance over a given length of time by collecting three types of data:

- Performance counters
- Event trace data (used for debugging and performance tuning)
- System configuration information from the Registry

Windows Vista, Windows Server 2008, and Windows 7 all support Data Collector Sets and the associated reports. Each of these operating systems provides various built-in DCSs. Additional DCSs might be defined when you install system software or hardware.

The Windows Server 2008 built-in Data Collector Sets are described in the following table.

Built-in DCS	Duration	Used to troubleshoot...
LAN Diagnostics	Indefinite	Networking errors and performance
System Diagnostics	1 minute	System errors that are affecting reliability
System Performance	1 minute	Slow system performance

To start a Data Collector Set:

1 Open Server Manager.

2 In Reliability and Performance, expand Data Collector Sets, and expand System.

3 Right-click the Data Collector Set you want to run and choose Start. (To see which system objects the Data Collector Set examines, select it and view the objects in the details pane.) A small green arrow appears on the DCS in the tree pane to indicate that the DCS is running.

4 If it's necessary to stop the Data Collector Set, right-click it and choose Stop. Otherwise, you know the Data Collector Set is done when the small green arrow disappears.

Do it!

D-3: Running a Data Collector Set

Here's how	Here's why
1 Click **Start**, right-click **Computer**, and choose **Manage**	To open Server Manager.
2 In the navigation pane, expand **Diagnostics**	
3 In the navigation pane, expand **Reliability and Performance**	
Expand Data Collector Sets	
Expand **System**	To display the predefined DCSs.
4 Right-click **System Diagnostics** and choose **Start**	To start the DCS.
Right-click **System Diagnostics** and choose **Stop**	To stop the DCS.

Viewing Data Collector Set reports

Explanation

Data Collector Set reports are stored in the Reports node under Reliability and Performance in the tree pane, as shown in Exhibit 6-37. You can drill down in the tree pane and select a report to see its contents in the details pane.

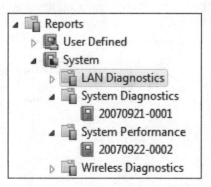

Exhibit 6-37: Data Collector Set reports

To quickly view a report for a Data Collector Set you've just run, right-click the set and choose Latest Report. It will select the latest report in the tree pane, and display the data in the details pane.

D-4:   Viewing a Data Collector Set report

Here's how	Here's why
1 Right-click **System Diagnostics** and choose **Latest Report**	To display the report you just created.
2 Observe the report details	

20090928-0001

System Diagnostics Report

Computer: SERVERPLUS
Collected: Monday, September 28, 2009 11:47:13 AM
Duration: 8 Seconds

Diagnostic Results

Warnings

Warning

Symptom: ⚠ C: has less than 15% free or less than 5120 MB disk space
Cause: The main system disk is low on space.
Details: C: has 4137 MB of free disk space. There is 34% free.
Resolution: 1 Verify disk space is low by viewing the drive in using "Compute

3 Scroll down through the sections of the report	Data collected by the DCS is organized into various sections that describe a particular aspect of your computer.
4 Under Basic System Checks, expand **Hardware Device and Driver Checks**	This system notes the hardware components tested and lists the failure count for each one.
5 Scroll down and expand **Hardware Configuration**	
Expand **System**	To view details of the system hardware checks performed by the DCS. You should see subsections for your disk drives and IRQs.
6 Expand **Devices**	(Still under the Hardware Configuration heading.) This section lists details of the device-level checks performed by the DCS.
7 Close Server Manager	

Unit summary: Installing expansion cards

Topic A

In this topic, you learned that a **bus** is a communication pathway. You can add **adapters** for hard drives, modems, and networks through the **expansion bus**. You learned that your computer's hardware communicates by using interrupts, IRQ lines, I/O addresses, DMA channels, and base memory addresses. You learned that the **PCI** bus, a 32-bit or 64-bit standard, is currently the most popular expansion bus. It supports PnP and **shared system resources** and is considerably faster than previous bus technologies. Multiple functions can be implemented on a single PCI card.

Topic B

In this topic, you learned that **drive controllers** are the adapter boards that plug into a PC's expansion slot and that the **interface** is the communications standard between the controller and the hard drive. You learned about the various **interface standards**, including IDE/ATA, SCSI, USB, and IEEE 1394. You also learned that you must configure IDE/ATA drives to designate one as **master** and one as **slave**. With SCSI drives, you learned that each drive must have a unique **SCSI ID**.

Topic C

In this topic, you learned that **video bus standards** are designed to offer improved throughput to improve video display performance. AGP enables Direct Memory Execution, 32-bit data transfers, and pumped bus speeds. You also learned that you can use PCI and PCIe buses to add a video adapter to your system. You then learned about display standards, including VGA, DVI, and HDMI. Next, you learned about **sound cards** and their functions in desktop and server computers. Finally, you examined **manufacturer-specific cards** and the issues associated with selecting and installing proprietary adapters.

Topic D

In this topic, you identified common symptoms of **hardware-related problems**. You examined probable causes of those symptoms and identified possible resolutions to the problems.

Review questions

1 Typically, the PCI bus is a(n) 16 -bit bus.

2 True or false? Lower-numbered IRQs have a higher priority.

   true

3 With the PCI specification, a single adapter can provide up to how many functions?

   A One

   B Two

   C Four

   D Eight

4 PCIe uses 64 bit communication.

5 PCIe is a(n) multi -line technology.

6 Which PC drive interface is a parallel system bus?

  A IEEE 1394

  B SATA

  C SCSI

  D USB

7 Which of the following is currently the most popular drive interface for Windows-based PCs?

  A IDE

  B IEEE 1394

  C SCSI

  D USB 2.0

8 Which drive interface is officially called the "AT Attachment" or "ATA" interface?

  A IDE

  B IEEE 1394

  C SCSI

  D USB 2.0

9 The following graphic is a photo of which type of drive interface cables?

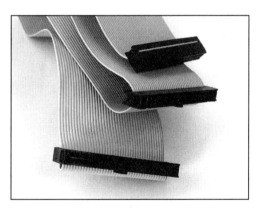

  A High-speed ATA

  B SATA

  C SCSI

  D Standard ATA

10 Which of the following SCSI standards has the highest bandwidth?

  A Fast SCSI

  B Fast-Wide SCSI

  C Ultra2 Wide/LVD

  D Ultra SCSI

11 True or false? SCSI devices with a lower SCSI ID have a higher priority on the SCSI bus.

true

12 True or false? True USB drives, which connect directly to the USB bus without any sort of ATA controller involved, are very common in today's PCs.

true

13 True or false? You can designate a master IDE drive on both the primary and secondary channels.

false

14 The rate at which an image is painted on screen is called which of the following?

   A Interlacing

   B Pixel depth

   C Refresh rate

   D Resolution

15 The number of pixels across and down that an adapter can create is called a monitor's what?

   A Interlacing

   B Pixel depth

   C Refresh rate

   D Resolution

16 Which DVI connection types support both digital and analog signals? [Choose all that apply.]

   A DVI-D single link

   B DVI-D dual link

   C DVI-I single link

   D DVI-I dual link

17 Which type of video port is shown in the following graphic?

   A DVI-A

   B DVI-D

   C DVI-I

   D HDMI

   E VGA/SVGA

18 Most networking devices have status indicator lights that you can observe to see if the devices are working. Typically, the lights are _green_ if the device is sending and receiving data properly.

19 Which DCS would you run to determine if there are system or hardware problems? [Choose all that apply.]

 A System Performance

 B System Diagnostics

 C LAN Diagnostics

 D Reliability and Performance

Independent practice activity

In this activity, you'll install one or more expansion cards and confirm that each one is working as intended. Your instructor will provide you with an expansion card, along with any required software or components.

1 Obtain an expansion card, associated software, and any required adapters or components from your instructor.

2 Examine the expansion card to determine its bus type and the ports and connectors it provides.

3 Read the manufacturer's installation instructions. You might need to insert the device's CD or DVD and read those instructions from an electronic file.

4 If instructed to install driver software before installing the hardware, do so now.

5 Shut down your server and open the system case, following electrical and ESD safety precautions. If your computer and bus support hot-plugging, follow the computer maker's instructions to open the expansion bay.

6 Install the expansion card into an appropriate expansion bus slot. Make any necessary internal connections.

7 Start your server and log on.

8 If you did not install the driver software before installing the hardware, install that software now.

9 Following the manufacturer's instructions, configure the device and confirm that it is working properly.

10 If directed by your instructor, remove the expansion adapter and its software.

Unit 7

Installing data storage devices

Unit time: 90 minutes

Complete this unit, and you'll know how to:

A Install and configure data storage devices.

B Select the appropriate RAID technology.

C Troubleshoot data storage problems.

Topic A: Installing storage devices

This topic covers the following CompTIA Server+ (2009 Edition) exam objectives.

#	Objective
1.1	**Differentiate between system board types, features, components, and their purpose**
	• Storage connectors
	– SCSI – IDE
	– SATA – Floppy
1.2	**Deploy different chassis types and appropriate components**
	• Power
	– Connectors
	• Expansion bays
3.3	**Install and configure different internal storage technologies**
	• Hot swappable vs. non-hot swappable
	• SCSI, Ultra SCSI, Ultra320 (termination), LUNs
	• SAS, SATA
	• Tape
	• Optical
	– DVD – CD-R
	– DVD-R – CD-RW
	– CD-ROM – Blu-Ray
	• Flash
	• Floppy (USB)
	• Controller (firmware levels)
	• Hard drive (firmware, JBOD)
3.4	**Summarize the purpose of external storage technologies**
	• Network attached storage
	• Storage area network
	• Tape library
	• WORM
	• Optical jukebox
	• Transport media
	– iSCSI – SCSI
	– SATA – Fiber Channel
	– SAS

Physical installation of internal hard drives

Explanation

Physically installing a disk drive into a PC involves a few steps, which you must perform in the following order:

1 If appropriate, set jumpers or switches on the drive to enable drive identification.
2 Install the drive into the PC chassis or expansion bay.
3 If you're installing a SCSI drive, you might need to configure bus termination. The bus must be terminated on both ends. It cannot have extra termination installed in the middle of the chain. You might need to set switches or jumpers, or install or remove terminator blocks to set termination.
4 Connect data and control cables from the drive controller to the drive.
5 Connect the power cable from the PC's power supply to the drive.

For most traditional-style PC cases, you must shut down the PC and open its case (observing electrical safety precautions) before you begin these steps. For rack-mounted PCs and hardware-based disk array systems, you might need only to open a hot-plug bay cover; you might not need to shut down the server.

After you have physically installed the drive, you will need to perform additional steps to make it available to the operating system.

ATA drive identification

With IDE/ATA drives, you can install one or two drives per channel. One drive must be designated as the master, or primary disk. The other is called the slave. With older drives, you set a jumper or DIP switch to specify its role: master, slave, or the only drive in the system. With newer drives, you can set the switch to the cable-select position, and the drive detects where it is connected on the cable. Its position defines its role, as shown in Exhibit 7-1.

Exhibit 7-1: An ATA cable showing where to connect the master and slave drives

SCSI drive identification

You must assign a unique SCSI device ID number to every device, including the host bus adapter, on the SCSI bus. SCSI IDs begin at 0 and count upward, with higher IDs having a higher priority on the SCSI bus.

Most newer SCSI devices include switches that you can use to set the device's SCSI ID. Older devices provided a block of jumpers that you used to set the SCSI ID. Exhibit 7-2 shows a typical switch that you'd use to assign SCSI IDs.

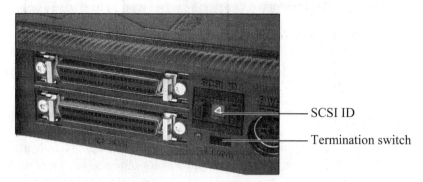

SCSI ID

Termination switch

Exhibit 7-2: A switch for assigning the SCSI ID

Chassis installation

You can usually use any available bay for a hard drive. However, one or more smaller, drive-sized bays are typically available for this precise purpose. Make sure you install the drive in a location that the data and power cables can reach.

Most modern drives work equally well mounted horizontally or vertically. Unlike older drives, there's typically no harm in mounting a drive one way and then mounting it in a different orientation later.

As always, when you open a PC's case, make sure to follow all electrical and ESD safety precautions. Usually, you should shut down the computer and unplug it from the outlet. Do not bump or jar the drives; they are very sensitive to shocks and you can damage them easily.

Data cable connections

Most drive cables are *keyed;* that is, their connectors are molded in such a way that you can insert them only the correct way into the connector socket. If you're using an older non-keyed cable, wire 1 in the cable will be marked with a red stripe. Pin 1 on the socket will be labeled with a number or a small triangle pointing at the pin. You need to line up the cable so that pin 1 goes into socket 1.

With IDE/ATA drives, make sure you connect the drive to the correct connector. As shown in Exhibit 7-1, specific connectors correspond to the master and slave designations for the drives. This consideration does not apply to SCSI, SATA, USB, or other types of drives.

Make sure you terminate each end of the SCSI bus. Typically, the HBA includes removable resistors. Modern devices have switch-selectable termination built in: if you need a device to provide termination, you switch on its terminators. Otherwise, you can leave its terminators turned off.

Power cable connections

Most IDE/ATA and SCSI drives use the large peripheral power connector. This connector has triangular corners so that you can be sure to insert it into the socket correctly. SATA drives use a specialized power connector that looks very different from the peripheral power connector. It is also keyed so that you're sure to connect it properly.

Do it! ## A-1: Physically installing a hard drive

Here's how	Here's why
1 If necessary, shut down your PC and unplug it from the outlet	You will install an additional hard drive in your system.
2 Following all electrical and ESD precautions, open your PC's case	
3 Set the jumpers or switches, as appropriate to specify the drive identification	You'll need to set the master, slave, single-drive, or cable-select designation for an IDE drive, or set the SCSI ID for a SCSI drive.
4 Locate an available drive bay and install the drive	
5 Install the data ribbon cable	Make sure to install the cable in the correct orientation, and connect the drive to the correct connector on the cable.
6 Install the power cable	
7 Close the PC's case	
8 Do not turn on your computer	You have physically installed the drive, but you must prepare it for use with the operating system.

Hard drive preparation

Explanation Once you have physically installed a hard drive, you must prepare it for use by the operating system. With hard drives, the following steps must be performed separately:

- Partition the drive.
- Format the drive.

Partitions and file systems

Partitions divide the full capacity of a drive into smaller, logical portions that are individually usable and configurable. For example, you could divide a 5 GB drive into two 2.5 GB logical drives, commonly called *volumes*.

In addition, partitions define the type of *file system* (often written as "filesystem") that will be used on the hard drive. The file system defines how data is stored on the drive. It also includes the tables and structures that describe where files are stored on the volume and define the size of the various volumes on the computer.

Popular hard-drive file systems for Windows computers include NTFS (the Windows NT File System) and FAT32. The older 16-bit FAT, or file allocation table, file system is not used on hard drives anymore. The virtual FAT (VFAT) system introduced with Windows 95 is still used on some removable media, such as USB drives and camera memory cards.

The following table describes the various file systems.

File system	Primarily used in	Description
FAT	MS-DOS, Windows 9x	This file system, particularly in its virtual FAT (VFAT) incarnation, is still supported by most operating systems, including Windows and Linux. However, these systems cannot use VFAT for their primary disks. In fact, VFAT is rarely used except for smaller removable media, such as CompactFlash cards.
FAT32	Windows 9x, Windows XP	FAT32 removed file size limits and improved performance over FAT. It is still used on older systems and for removable media (camera cards). For the most part, it has been replaced by NTFS.
NTFS	Windows XP, Windows Vista, Windows 7, Windows Server	Introduced with Windows NT, the Windows NT File System adds support for security, very large volumes, and fault tolerance. Microsoft continues to enhance this file system.
ext3, ext4	Linux	The "extended file system" is a Linux-specific journaling file system. The current version is ext4, though ext3 is still widely used. *Journaling file systems* log changes before actually writing them to disk, making these file systems less likely to become corrupted during a system crash.
HFS+	Macintosh OS X	The Mac OS Extended file system, known as HFS+ (Hierarchical File System Plus), is a journaled file system. It is similar to, but incompatible with, the ext3/4 file system. HFS+ preserves the data and resource fork constructs introduced in earlier Macintosh file systems. The resource fork stores a custom icon, license information, and metadata. The data fork stores the file's contents.

The master boot record (MBR)

The first sector on the bootable hard disk is called the *master boot record* (MBR). This sector serves the same purpose as the boot sector on a floppy disk. The MBR, which is sometimes called the *master boot block* or *partition table*, contains partition information and other information used by the computer after the POST has finished.

Primary and extended partitions

Windows-based operating systems make a distinction between primary and extended partitions; other operating systems do not. *Primary partitions* are those partitions that are directly accessed by the operating system as volumes. In DOS and Windows 9.x, you can create a single primary partition on each hard drive. In Windows NT Workstation, Windows 2000 Professional, and all versions of Windows XP and Windows Vista, you can create four primary partitions per drive. Most of the partitions you create are primary partitions.

You can also create extended partitions. Each extended partition contains one or more logical drives, which are what the operating system accesses for file storage. With all of the PC operating systems, you can create a single extended partition, which can contain up to 23 logical drives. In general, you won't create extended partitions unless you need multiple volumes so your system can boot to both DOS/Windows 9x and Windows NT/2000/XP/Vista.

It's important to note that Microsoft changed the partitioning scheme for Windows Vista to accommodate expanded drive sizes. It places the starting and ending points for partitions in different locations on the hard disk than it did in previous versions of Windows. That makes the new partitioning scheme incompatible with the scheme used in previous versions of Windows. If you need to create a multiboot computer, you should create all of your partitions by using Windows Vista, not a previous version of Windows or a third-party utility.

Linux and Mac OS X don't distinguish between primary and extended partitions.

Partitioning utilities

In DOS and Windows 9x systems, you use the MS-DOS `fdisk` command to partition a hard drive. In Windows 2000 Professional, Windows XP, and Windows Vista, you can use the Disk Management component of the Computer Management console. From the Start menu, choose Administrative Tools, Computer Management; then, in the left pane, select Disk Management. (In Windows Vista, click All Programs to access the Administrative Tools menu.) You can use this console, shown in Exhibit 7-3, to partition and format new disk drives, as well as to manage partition types.

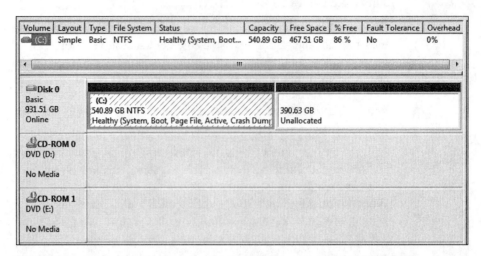

Exhibit 7-3: Disk partitions as shown in Disk Management in Windows

In Linux, you can use distribution-specific utilities or command-line tools. Or you can use a platform-independent tool. A popular partitioning tool is GParted, the GNOME Partition Editor, shown in Exhibit 7-4. You can use GParted to manage Windows and Linux partitions. In fact, GParted is distributed as a bootable CD so that you can use it to manage partitions without actually running Linux.

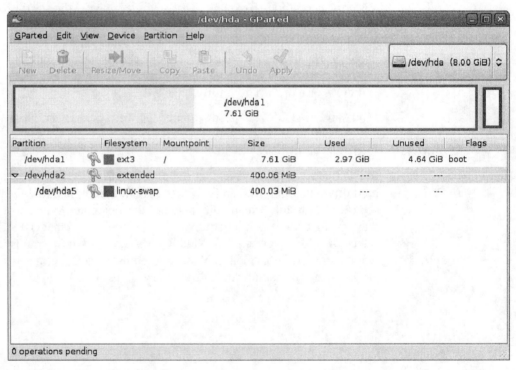

Exhibit 7-4: The GParted utility in Debian Linux

Linux partitions

At minimum, most Linux distributions require two distinct partitions, which can be on the same physical hard drive or separate drives:

- **The root partition** — Stores the operating system, application, and data files.
- **The swap partition** — Stores virtual memory data, similar to the pagefile.sys file on Windows computers.

You can create additional partitions. For example, you could create a volume for just your data files. Doing so would making backing up your data files a bit easier—you would simply back up that entire volume.

Formatting

After creating a partition, you must format a drive to make it ready for the operating system. Formatting creates (or resets) the tables that record file names and physical locations of a file's data.

The directory tree

Most PC operating systems use the paradigm of a directory tree to organize files. In this scheme, a disk contains one or more folders, also called directories. Each folder can contain files and additional folders (subfolders). These folders are arranged in a family-tree-like hierarchy collectively called the directory tree. The root directory is the highest-level folder on the disk; it's the starting point for the directory tree. The root directory can contain files and folders.

In the Windows world, each device has its own directory tree and root directory. Thus, each device must be addressed by a higher-level structure, the drive letter. For example, your primary hard drive would be called the C drive, as shown in Exhibit 7-5. When you insert a DVD disc, its file system is identified by your system as drive D. The file systems on drives C and D are distinct and separate.

In Linux and Mac OS X, there is a single directory tree for all devices. Those operating systems do not use a letter to identify drives. Let's say you insert a DVD disc into your drive. To make its file system available, you must mount it to the tree. The contents of the DVD are then made available as if they were within a directory on your hard drive. Exhibit 7-6 shows the root directory on a Linux system.

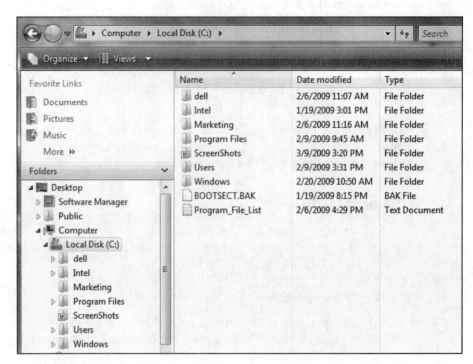

Exhibit 7-5: Windows Explorer identifies the root directory of C: as "Local Disk (C:)"

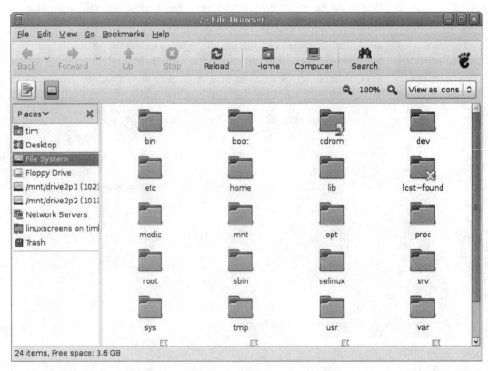

Exhibit 7-6: Browsing the root directory of a Linux computer

The format and mkfs commands

For DOS and Windows 95 systems, you use the MS-DOS `format` command to format a hard drive partitioned with the FAT16 file system. You can use the Windows 98/Me `format` command to format FAT16 and FAT32 partitioned hard drives. Windows NT Workstation, Windows 2000 Professional, Windows XP, and Windows Vista include a command-line utility, also named `format`, which you can use to format FAT32 and NTFS partitioned hard drives. More commonly, you use the graphical Windows Disk Management tool to format drives.

For Linux, you use the `mkfs`, make file system, command to create file systems. In other words, you use `mkfs` to format your partition. In general, you use the command like this:

```
mkfs -t filesystem_type /dev/hdX#
```

You specify the file system type as ext2, ext3, and so forth. (See the man pages for a full list of supported file system types.) Then, you specify the device file, usually a hard drive partition such as /dev/hdb1. You must run `mkfs` as root or via `sudo`.

Do it!

A-2: Partitioning and formatting a hard drive

Questions and answers

1 Give at least one reason you might choose to use the FAT32 file system rather than NTFS on a Windows Vista system.

2 List at least two advantages of NTFS over FAT32.

3 When do you assign the file system that's used on the disks in your PC?

4 Boot your PC	If necessary.
5 Log on	If necessary.
6 Open Server Manager	Click the Quick Launch icon; or click Start, right-click Computer, and choose Manage.
7 In the left pane, expand **Storage**	
Select **Disk Management**	To display disk and partition information. You should have space that is listed as Unallocated.
8 Select the Unallocated space	
9 Right-click the Unallocated space and choose **New Simple Volume...**	
10 In the "Simple volume size in MB" box, enter a number that is approximately half the current value	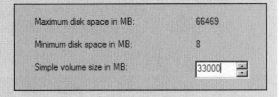
11 Click **Next**	

Installing data storage devices

12 Click **Next**

> ○ Assign the following drive letter: `F` ▾
> ○ Mount in the following empty NTFS folder:
>   `Browse...`
> ○ Do not assign a drive letter or drive path

To accept the default drive-letter assignment.

13 In the Volume label box, type
    My Drive

> ● Format this volume with the following settings:
>   File system: `NTFS` ▾
>   Allocation unit size: `Default` ▾
>   Volume label: `My Drive`
>   ☐ Perform a quick format
>   ☐ Enable file and folder compression

14 Observe the options

A quick format doesn't scan the disk for bad sectors like a normal format does. You can choose this option if your hard disk has been formatted before and you're sure that the hard disk isn't damaged.

The file and folder compression feature decreases the size of files and folders, reducing the amount of space they use on your storage devices.

15 Click **Next**

16 Record the drive letter of your new drive

Drive letter: _____

17 Click **Finish**

> 32.23 GB
> Formatting : (3%)

To proceed with partitioning and formatting. When formatting is complete, the new volume opens in Windows Explorer.

18 Close all open windows

Installation of external drives

Explanation

Installing an external hard drive involves most of the same steps as installing an internal drive. You won't need to open your PC's case to install an external drive, but the rest of the procedure is similar:

1 If appropriate, set jumpers or switches on the drive to enable drive identification (such as setting an appropriate SCSI ID).

2 If you're installing a non-hot-plug drive, such as an external ATA/IDE or older SCSI drive, shut down your system.

3 If you're installing a SCSI drive, you might need to configure bus termination. The bus must be terminated on both ends. It cannot have extra termination installed in the middle of the chain. You might need to set switches or jumpers, or install or remove terminator blocks to set termination.

4 Connect the data cable to the computer and the external drive.

5 Connect the drive's power cable.

6 Turn on the drive.

After you have physically installed the drive, you might need to partition and format it, as appropriate to your operating system. Obviously, such steps would be unnecessary with an optical drive. Additionally, most USB flash drives are formatted at the factory.

Hot-plug and hot-swap considerations

Some interface technologies, such as USB, FireWire, SATA, and serial SCSI, support the hot-swapping of components, as do some expansion-bus backplane designs. Also called hot plugging, hot swapping enables you to plug in or unplug devices without shutting down the computer. Hot plugging requires the following considerations to be handled by designers and users:

• Physical connections

• Dynamic bus configuration

• Software enabling and disabling

Physical connections

A hot-plug device must be able to be connected and removed without being damaged by electrical surges. Of course, such devices must not damage the computer's electronics. Designers must ensure that both ground and "hot" connections can be made safely and easily.

Typically, ground wires are connected first to ensure that the device's electronics have a suitable electrical ground before voltage is applied. Such a scheme prevents component damage and lessens the risk of electrical shock as you connect the device. Longer pins, a staggered arrangement of pins, and edge connector traces are common ways that device designers make sure ground wires connect first.

Special current-limiting circuitry is added inline with power pins to prevent inrushing voltage from damaging the electronics. Additionally, circuits are designed to operate over a range of voltages because voltages will vary for a few hundred milliseconds—a long time for electronics—as you plug in the device.

With some bus technologies, such as USB and FireWire, the size and shape of the connectors enable you to quickly and safely connect external devices. For SCSI bus or internal (backplane) connectors, designers might fashion a slide or lever mechanism to make it easier for you to quickly connect a new device to the bus.

Dynamic bus configuration

Once you have physically connected the device, and it has received power (from the bus or external source), it will need to be configured to participate in communications. This function is handled by bus and operating system designers. The USB specification, for example, describes how devices identify themselves and their needs. The operating system uses this information to configure the new device to coexist with other devices.

Software enabling and disabling

Modern operating systems use caching, logging, and journaling to improve the perceived performance of the system and to add fault tolerance. With such operating systems, you must disable a device in the operating system before removing it. Doing so forces the operating system to write cached and journaled files to the disk and to close log files. Windows, for example, provides the Safely Remove Hardware Wizard, which you use to safely disable a hot-plug device before physically disconnecting it.

Optical drives

Optical drives can be internal or external devices. Internal devices can be connected via IDE, Serial ATA, or SCSI. External drives are most often FireWire (IEEE 1394) or USB devices. Some external drives might also be connected via SCSI, or even by a parallel connection for older drives. External versions aren't as popular as they were in the past because computers now come with internal optical drives as standard components. Optical drive connections are shown in Exhibit 7-7.

Exhibit 7-7: Optical drive connections: here, for a CD drive

Drivers

IDE, SCSI, and USB optical drives might require drivers for your operating system. If so, Windows should detect the drive after you install it and either load the drivers automatically or prompt you for an installation source. FireWire storage devices don't require drivers for most operating systems.

Flash drives

For quick data transfers, a removable media device such as a flash drive, shown in Exhibit 7-8, is hard to beat. Few systems still use floppy drives for removable storage. In fact, many modern motherboards don't even contain a floppy controller. If you need to use a floppy, you will probably have to use a USB-based external floppy drive.

Capacities of modern flash drives rival those of DVD media. Multi-gigabyte flash drives are inexpensive and widely available. Incidentally, while you might call these "jump drives" or "thumb drives," those terms are actually trademarked product names. Generically, you should call such devices "flash drives" or "USB drives."

Exhibit 7-8: USB flash drives

Do it!

A-3: Installing and removing an external drive

Here's how	Here's why
1 Following the steps appropriate to your external storage device, physically install the drive	
2 Partition and format the drive	If appropriate.
3 Explore the drive's contents	
4 Safely remove the drive	For example, use the Safely Remove Hardware Wizard, if appropriate.

External storage technologies

Explanation

You will encounter various storage technologies used in conjunction with servers. You should be able to differentiate between them, describe their purposes, and select the appropriate technology for your needs. These technologies include:

- Network attached storage
- Storage area networks
- Tape libraries
- WORM drives
- Optical jukeboxes

Network attached storage (NAS)

Network attached storage (NAS) is in essence a self-contained file server that you connect to your network rather than to an expansion bus. NAS devices provide file-level access via their integrated operating system, such as an embedded Linux version. That software enables you to either manage access and allocation directly, or integrate such management with your existing network operating system and infrastructure.

A NAS unit can use a single hard drive or implement a drive array (RAID). You connect the NAS device to your network, using your existing media (10BaseT, fiber optic cabling, and so forth). The NAS makes files available via standard file sharing protocols, such as SMB/CIFS (Windows) or NFS (Linux/UNIX).

Storage area network (SAN)

A storage area network (SAN) is a device or system that provides block-level access to external storage. In essence, a SAN is a self-contained external hard drive. A SAN is typically made up of multiple drives (typically in a RAID configuration), a master control computer, and other devices.

Unlike NAS, a SAN can act as your server's primary hard drive—to your server, the SAN appears to be a local hard drive. Typically, your server communicates with the SAN by using SCSI techniques, though not typically using the Physical or Transport layer SCSI (e.g. cabling) components. Most often, you connect SANs via one of these low-level storage network technologies:

- **AoE** — ATA over Ethernet, a protocol that enables access to SATA (not IDE/PATA) devices over an Ethernet physical layer.
- **iSCSI** — SCSI over TCP/IP.
- **SAS** — Serial attached SCSI, which permits SCSI connectivity over cables up to 8 meters long.
- **HyperSCSI** — SCSI over Ethernet.
- **FCP** — Fiber Channel Protocol (a mapping of SCSI over Fiber Channel) over various transports, including FCoE (Fiber Channel over Ethernet), iFCP (Fiber Channel over IP), and SANoIP (also Fiber Channel over IP).

Software on the SAN enables you to divide the total storage space into multiple virtual drives (or use just one virtual drive). You can also expand or shrink drives dynamically via the SAN's management software. Typically, you can perform backups, drive replacement, RAID rebuilds, and other operations via the SAN's console without interrupting your server's operations.

Tape libraries

A tape library is a device that provides more storage capacity than a single tape cartridge could hold. A tape library might do so by using a robotic mechanism to switch cartridges in and out as needed. Alternatively, a tape library might use multiple drives, each with its own cartridge, presenting the combined storage space to the operating system as if it were a single large tape cartridge. Tape libraries automate the task of manually inserting and removing cartridges, as you must do with a single drive.

You use tape libraries to back up and archive large data sets. For example, the typical SAN provides more live storage space than can fit on a single backup tape. Such SANs require a tape library for any backups and restores you perform.

Optical jukeboxes

Optical jukeboxes are like tape libraries, but they use optical discs instead of tapes. An optical jukebox might include many CD or DVD drives. You can insert a disc into each of the drives and make the contents individually available.

Optical jukeboxes can also be used in mass-duplication systems. To record multiple copies of a disc, you could insert a master copy in one of the jukebox's drives and insert blank discs in the other drives. A click of a button would duplicate the master onto each of the blanks simultaneously.

In some situations, you can span storage across multiple, writable discs. You would use that sort of system for backing up or archiving onto optical, rather than tape, media.

WORM drives

Write once, read many (WORM) devices permit you to store information permanently, or at least in a form that does not permit the reuse of the media. Most people think of the specialized optical drive, often called a WORM drive, when considering this type of device. But other devices enable WORM functionality. Tape drives and punched paper cards are two other types of devices that can provide WORM functionality.

Companies use WORM devices to archive data to comply with government or industry regulations. For example, medical companies might record patient records on WORM devices to comply with HIPAA requirements. Once stored, the data could not be altered, so its legal status and legitimacy would be preserved according to the regulations.

WORM media can be destroyed and sometimes overwritten. But such alterations are typically obvious. You could rip up a punch card or melt an optical disc, for example. WORM optical drives typically record data by melting spots on the disc to form binary zeros or ones. Although you could melt all the zeros to transform them to ones, you could not write new usable data to the disc.

Do it!

A-4: Comparing external storage technologies

Questions	Answers
1 True or false? A SAN is essentially a self-contained file server that you attach to your network.	
2 A NAS is a _____-level storage device, while a SAN is a _____-level storage device.	
3 Which can replace your server's primary hard drive, a SAN or a NAS device?	
4 Describe the purpose of a tape library.	
5 What is one way you would use WORM storage in your environment?	

Topic B: Selecting RAID technologies

This topic covers the following CompTIA Server+ (2009 Edition) exam objectives.

#	Objective
1.3	**Differentiate between memory features/ types, and given a scenario, select an appropriate processor** • RAID and hot spares
3.1	**Describe RAID technologies and its features and benefits** • Hot spare • Software vs. hardware • Cache read/write levels (data loss potential) • Performance benefits and tradeoffs
3.2	**Given a scenario, select the appropriate RAID level** • 0, 1, 3, 5, 6, 10, 50 • Performance benefits and tradeoffs

Disk arrays

Explanation

Modern disk drives are very reliable. Yet, for the most critical server environments, even a rare failure can be a catastrophe. To reduce the potential for downtime, you can implement a drive array. A *drive array* is a collection of two or more drives that work in unison to provide a single point of data storage. A drive array appears to the operating system to be a single drive, no matter how many hard drives are actually in the array.

Various drive array schemes have been developed. In general, arrays are called Redundant Arrays of Independent Disks (RAID), formerly called Redundant Arrays of Inexpensive Disks. RAID exists in various implementations, using differing numbers of disks and various techniques to ensure reliability. These variations are called the *RAID levels*. Many RAID levels have been developed or proposed, but just a few are used widely.

Primary RAID levels

There are seven primary RAID levels. They are numbered RAID levels 0 through RAID level 6.

RAID level 0

RAID level 0 is also called *striping*. In this scheme, data is divided into blocks, and the blocks are distributed across the drives in the array. Most commonly, two disks are used. So, half of the data is written to one disk, with the other half written to the second disk. Striping is illustrated in Exhibit 7-9.

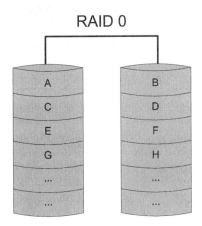

Exhibit 7-9: RAID level 0: striping

Striping improves read and write performance because only half of the data must be read or written to each drive for each operation. Striping does not provide data redundancy, however. The failure of either drive results in the total loss of data stored on the whole set.

RAID level 1

There are two implementations of RAID level 1: mirroring and duplexing. With both techniques, data is duplicated onto a second disk, as illustrated in Exhibit 7-10. With *mirroring*, a single drive controller is used; *duplexing* uses two controllers.

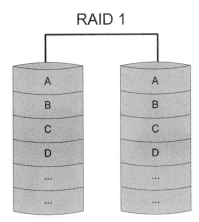

Exhibit 7-10: RAID level 1: mirroring or duplexing

RAID level 1 provides data redundancy. If either drive fails, data can be read or written to the other drive. With duplexing, even the failure of a drive controller won't interfere with the continued operating of the disk subsystem.

RAID level 1 does not provide any performance improvement. In fact, there can be a slight decrease in write performance if one drive performs more slowly than the other.

RAID level 2

RAID level 2 is an array of disks in which the data is striped at the bit level across all disks in the array. Error correction information, in the form of a Hamming code, is stored on multiple parity disks. The spindles of each disk in the array are synchronized to spin at the exact same rate.

RAID level 2 offers high performance and the ability to recover from single-bit error conditions. This level is rarely used because modern hard drives automatically include Hamming code error correction bits. Using RAID 2 would add unnecessary complexity and duplication.

RAID level 3

RAID level 3 is also called *striping with parity*. In this scheme, data is striped byte by byte onto separate drives. Parity—or more accurately, error detection and correction code—is stored on an additional, dedicated parity disk. As illustrated in Exhibit 7-11, parity for bytes A0 through A3 is calculated and stored on the parity disk.

If any one drive in the set fails, data can be recovered by examining the remaining blocks plus the parity information. Read and write operations can continue in this state until you have the time to replace the failed drive. RAID level 3 is illustrated in Exhibit 7-11.

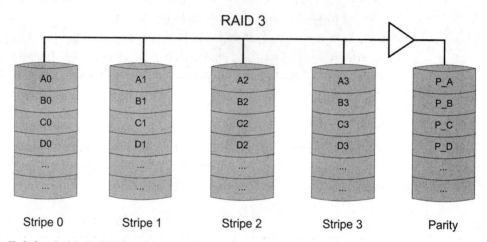

Exhibit 7-11: RAID level 3: striping with parity

RAID level 3 provides improved read times when large chunks of data are retrieved, such as with video or other large files. This improvement occurs because data blocks can be read simultaneously from the multiple drives in the set. However, because there is only one parity drive, write operations must be performed one at a time.

RAID level 4

RAID level 4 is similar in concept to RAID level 3, except that data is striped by the block rather than by the byte. This method permits simultaneous reads of small files if those files fit within a single block. Thus, RAID 4 can offer higher read performance than RAID 3 in some circumstances. As with RAID 3, however, RAID 4 write performance can suffer because of the bottleneck caused by the single parity drive.

RAID level 5

RAID level 5 is known as *striping with distributed parity*. In this scheme, data is divided into an even number of blocks. These blocks, along with an additional parity block, are striped across an odd number of disks. RAID level 5 is illustrated in Exhibit 7-12.

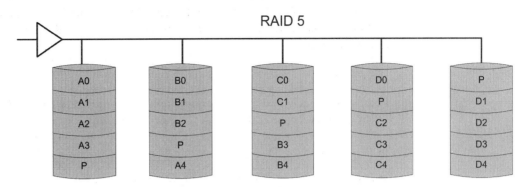

Exhibit 7-12: RAID level 5: striping with distributed parity

If any one drive in the set fails, data can be recovered by examining the remaining blocks plus the parity information. Read and write operations can continue in this state until you have the time to replace the failed drive.

RAID level 5 provides improved read and write times because data blocks can be read or written simultaneously to the multiple drives in the set. Because parity is not kept on a single drive, writing that information is not the bottleneck that it is with RAID level 3 or 4.

RAID level 6

RAID 6 is nearly identical to RAID 5, except that two parity drives are used instead of one. This setup permits you to recover from the failure of two drives in a set rather than just one.

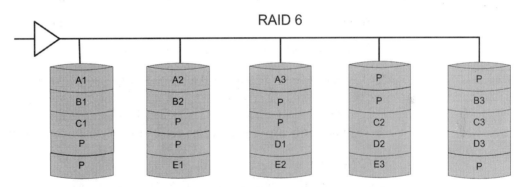

Exhibit 7-13: RAID 6 adds another parity drive to RAID 5

RAID 6 offers similar performance benefits as RAID level 5. It offers faster recovery after the failure of a single drive because you can begin operating again by using the data drives and the remaining parity drive. The rebuilding of the duplicate parity information can proceed while your system is live and in use.

Hybrid RAID levels

Many of the preceding RAID levels can be combined to create hybrid levels. The most common of these hybrids combine block-level striping (RAID level 0) with another RAID level. For example, RAID 0+1, RAID 1+0 (also called RAID 10), and RAID 5+0 (also called RAID 50) are common hybrid levels.

RAID level 0+1

RAID level 0+1 is an array in which drives are striped and then mirrored. Put another way, you create two striped arrays, one of which becomes the mirror of the other. This type of array requires a minimum of four drives as well as an even number of drives.

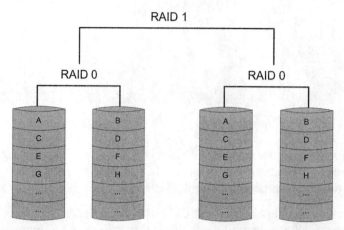

Exhibit 7-14: RAID 0+1 combines striping and mirroring

RAID level 1+0 (RAID level 10)

RAID level 1+0 is an array in which data is both mirrored and striped simultaneously. A RAID level 1 mirrored set of drives is then striped (RAID level 0) to provide fault tolerance and high performance. RAID level 1+0 is commonly implemented with four drives.

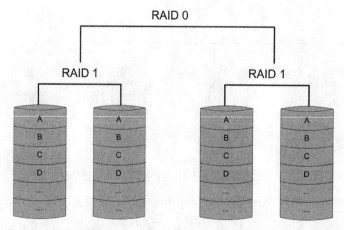

Exhibit 7-15: RAID 1+0 combines mirroring and striping

RAID level 50 (RAID 5+0)

In RAID level 50, also called RAID level 5+0, data is striped at the block level (RAID level 0 striping) across multiple RAID 5 arrays. This RAID level requires at least six drives (three in each RAID 5 array). One drive from each of the RAID 5 arrays could fail, and operations could continue.

RAID 50 offers better performance than RAID 5, particularly during write operations. It also provides better fault tolerance than either RAID 0 or RAID 5. This is an expensive RAID level to operate, given the number of drives required. But it is suitable when performance and fault tolerance are critical.

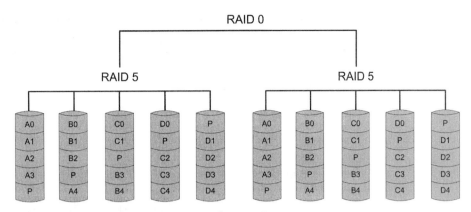

Exhibit 7-16: RAID 50 stripes sets of RAID 5 arrays

Software vs. hardware RAID

You can implement RAID by using software or dedicated hardware solutions. Software-based RAID is typically slower than hardware solutions because the operating system must perform parity calculations, divide data into blocks for striping, handle recovery operations, and so forth. Dedicated hardware performs those functions in a hardware-based RAID solution.

Software-based RAID

Software-based RAID is sometimes called "operating system–based RAID," as it is typically a function of the operating system. The RAID levels you can implement vary by operating system, as described in the following table.

Operating system	RAID levels	Notes
Windows XP, Windows Vista, and Windows Server	0, 1, 5	You might need to apply Service Packs or patches to support all three levels on the client operating systems. Additionally, you will need to use dynamic disks to implement software-based RAID in Windows.
Linux	0, 1, 4, 5, 6, 0+1, 1+0, 5+0	Check with your distribution's publisher to determine the exact RAID levels it supports.
Mac OS X	0, 1, 1+0	Some sources claim that OS X also supports RAID 5, though that level is not listed on Apple's Web site.

Hardware-based RAID

Hardware-based RAID can be implemented with a specialized disk controller that supports the desired RAID level. For larger disk sets, or for more complete and complex solutions, you can purchase a dedicated RAID unit that features special disk controllers, power supplies, cooling units, and the necessary bays for installing each of the component drives.

Hardware RAID is more expensive than software RAID, but offers many advantages over software RAID:

- Read and write responses are faster.

- You can place boot and system files on different RAID levels, such as RAID levels 1 and 5.

- You can hot-swap a failed disk with one that works or is new, thus replacing the disk without shutting down the server. (This option can vary by manufacturer.)

- Some hardware-based solutions enable you to implement a *hot spare drive*. Such drives are installed in the RAID chassis, powered, and connected to the data bus, but not actively used. If either a data drive or parity drive fails, you can use management software to enable the hot spare and assign it a role as data or parity drive. Then, when time permits, you can replace the failed drive, with the replacement becoming the new hot spare.

- There are more setup options to retrieve damaged data and to combine different RAID levels within one array of disks. For example, you can mirror two disks using RAID 1 and set up five disks for RAID 5 in a seven-disk array. (The RAID options depend on what the manufacturer offers.)

- Many hardware-based RAID systems provide a high-performance cache to improve read and write performance. Typically, this cache is battery-protected so that data in it won't be lost if a power failure occurs.

Do it!   ## B-1: Exploring storage fault tolerance

Questions and answers

1 Describe the advantages of RAID 10 over either RAID 0 or 1.

2 What term is used to describe disk mirroring when each drive is connected to its own hard disk controller?

   A Disk mirroring

   B Disk duplexing

   C Shadowing

   D Controller mirror

3 Which of the following RAID levels provides no fault tolerance?

   A RAID 0

   B RAID 1

   C RAID 4

   D RAID 5

4 Why might you choose software-based RAID over hardware-based RAID? What might you have to give up for the benefits of software-based RAID?

5 Describe a benefit of RAID 5 over RAID 3.

6 Why is caching of data in a hardware-based RAID system more fault tolerant than caching in a software-based RAID system?

Topic C: Troubleshooting data storage

This topic covers the following CompTIA Server+ (2009 Edition) exam objectives.

#	Objective
6.2	**Given a scenario, effectively troubleshoot hardware problems, selecting the appropriate tools and methods**
	• Common problems
	– Incorrect boot sequence
	– Operating system not found
	– Drive failure
	– I/O failure
6.3	**Given a scenario, effectively troubleshoot software problems, selecting the appropriate tools and methods**
	• Common problems
	– User can't access resources
	– OS boot failure
	– Cannot mount drive
	– Cannot write to system log
	• Cause of common problems
	– Corrupted files
	– Lack of hard drive space
	– Virtual memory (misconfigured, corrupt)
	– Fragmentation
	– Encryption
	• Software tools
	– System logs
	– Monitoring tools (resource monitor, performance monitor)
	– Defragmentation tools
6.5	**Given a scenario, effectively troubleshoot storage problems, selecting the appropriate tools and methods**
	• Common problems
	– Slow file access – Cannot access logical drive
	– OS not found – Data corruption
	– Data not available – Slow I/O performance
	– Unsuccessful backup – Restore failure
	– Error lights – Cache failure
	– Unable to mount the device – Multiple drive failure
	– Drive not available

#	Objective
6.5	**Given a scenario, effectively troubleshoot storage problems, selecting the appropriate tools and methods (continued)**

- Causes of common problems
  - Media failure
  - Drive failure
  - Controller failure
  - HBA failure
  - Loose connectors
  - Cable problems
  - Misconfiguration
  - Improper termination
  - Corrupt boot sector
  - Corrupt file system table
  - Array rebuild
  - Improper disk partition
  - Bad sectors
  - Cache battery failure
  - Cache turned off
  - Insufficient space
  - Improper RAID configuration
  - Mismatched drives
  - Backplane failure
- Storage tools
  - Portioning tools
  - Disk management
  - RAID array management
  - Array management
  - System logs
  - Net use / mount command
  - Monitoring tools

Hard drive maintenance

Explanation

Computer hard disks, like automobiles, benefit from regularly scheduled maintenance. Windows operating systems include utilities you can use to keep a hard disk's performance at an optimal level. These disk maintenance utilities can:

- Remove unnecessary files from a hard disk.
- Scan a disk for errors.
- Defragment a disk.

Disk Cleanup

Client versions of Windows include the Disk Cleanup tool, which you can use to remove unnecessary files from a hard disk. Such files use space on the hard drive that could better be used by applications or for the user's data files. Removing them is at least a temporary fix for problems with insufficient disk space (ultimately, adding disk space is the best solution to that problem).

Unnecessary files are grouped into the following categories:

- Downloaded program files
- Temporary Internet files
- Files in the Recycle Bin
- Windows temporary files
- Optional Windows components that you aren't using
- Installed programs that you no longer use
- Offline Web pages in client operating systems before Windows Vista
- The hibernation file in Windows Vista
- Setup log files in Windows Vista
- Archive files in Windows Vista
- Thumbnails of picture, video, and other documents in Windows Vista

Checking a disk for errors

Viruses, poorly written programs, and disk-write errors can break the chain of clusters that make up a file. For example, a rogue application might change or remove the marker in one cluster that points to the file's next cluster.

You can use a tool, such as Windows chkdsk (Check Disk), to scan a hard disk for physical errors and damaged files. If the tool finds a physical disk error, it:

- Moves any data stored on that area of the disk.
- Marks the disk so the operating system doesn't store additional data in the damaged area.

The chkdsk command checks files and folders for invalid file names, dates, or times. It can also check for data fragments that don't belong to any file. You'll hear these data fragments called "lost file fragments," "lost file allocation units," or "lost clusters." When it finds a data fragment, chkdsk can do any of the following:

- Automatically delete the fragment.
- Attempt to fix the fragment.
- Convert the data to a file so you can view its contents.

To check your disk for errors in Windows XP, Windows Vista, and Windows Server:

1 Click Start and choose Computer (or My Computer in OSs before Windows Vista).
2 Right-click the drive you want to check for errors, and choose Properties.
3 Activate the Tools tab and click Check Now.
4 If prompted by UAC (User Account Control), click Continue.
5 Check "Automatically fix file system errors" and/or "Scan for and attempt recovery of bad sectors."
6 Click Start.
7 Click "Schedule disk check." The scan will be scheduled for the next time you boot Windows. This enables Windows to check system files that are open and in use when Windows is running.
8 Restart your computer.

Do it!   ## C-1:   Scanning a disk for errors

Here's how	Here's why
1 Click **Start** and choose **Computer**	
Right-click **Local Disk (C:)** and choose **Properties**	
2 Activate the Tools tab	In the Local Disk (C:) Properties dialog box. In this activity, you'll check your C: drive for errors by using the Check Disk utility.
Under Error-checking, click **Check Now**	
3 Check **Automatically fix file system errors**	If necessary. This option is typically selected automatically.
Check **Scan for and attempt recovery of bad sectors**	
Click **Cancel**	Rather than running this check now, you'll explore the chkdsk command and use it to schedule a boot-time check in the next activity.
4 Close the Local Disk (C:) Properties dialog box and the Computer window	

The chkdsk command

You use the chkdsk command to search FAT and NTFS disks for file system errors. All Microsoft client operating systems—from MS-DOS through Windows Vista—ship with command-line versions of chkdsk. The version included with the operating systems that support NTFS is different from the DOS-based version used in operating systems that support only FAT.

The syntax of the chkdsk command is

```
chkdsk drive:
```

where *drive* is the drive letter of the volume you want to check for errors.

Optional parameters and switches include those shown below and described in the following table:

```
chkdsk drive:path\filename /f /v /r /x /i /c /l:size
```

Parameter or switch	Description
Path\filename	Specifies a particular file to check for errors. You can use the * and ? wildcards to check multiple files.
/f	Fixes any errors it finds with the file system on the specified disk. The file system must be locked to allow chkdsk to fix errors. You're prompted to schedule chkdsk to run the next time you restart the computer.
/v	Invokes verbose mode, which displays the path and name of each file as it's checked.
/r	Locates bad sectors on the disk and recovers any data that it can.
/x	Used with NTFS disks to dismount the volume before the check; includes the functionality of the /f switch. The file system must be locked for this process. You're prompted to schedule chkdsk to run the next time you restart the computer.
/i	Performs a scaled-down index check, which reduces the amount of time needed to check NTFS disks. This switch is available only in Windows NT Workstation with SP4, Windows 2000 Professional, Windows XP, and Windows Vista.
/c	Excludes the checking of cycles within the folder structure, thereby reducing the amount of time needed to check NTFS disks. This switch is available only in Windows NT Workstation with SP4, Windows 2000 Professional, Windows XP, and Windows Vista.
/l:size	Specifies the size of the log file on NTFS disks.

Windows NT Workstation, Windows 2000 Professional, Windows XP, and Windows Vista include a chkntfs command, which is similar to the chkdsk command. The chkntfs command is used at bootup on NTFS volumes. You can find out more about chkntfs at *http://support.microsoft.com/kb/160963*.

Third-party utilities, such as Norton Disk Doctor, are sometimes better at determining which disconnected clusters belong to which files. You can use these utilities to scan a disk for errors and correct them.

Do it!

C-2: Running chkdsk.exe

Here's how	Here's why
1 Click **Start**, and in the search box, enter **cmd**	To open a Command Prompt window.
Enter **chkdsk c: /i**	To check your C: drive for errors, without fixing any problems that might be found.

```
The type of the file system is NTFS.

WARNING! F parameter not specified.
Running CHKDSK in read-only mode.

WARNING! I parameter specified.
Your drive may still be corrupt even after running CHKDSK.

CHKDSK is verifying files (stage 1 of 3)...
  132352 file records processed.
File verification completed.
  63 large file records processed.
  0 bad file records processed.
  2 EA records processed.
  60 reparse records processed.
CHKDSK is verifying indexes (stage 2 of 3)...
  122015 index entries processed.
Index verification completed.
  5 unindexed files processed.
CHKDSK is verifying security descriptors (stage 3 of 3)
```

2 Run the same command in verbose mode	Repeat the command with the /v switch.
What is the difference in the reports?	
3 Enter **chkdsk c: /f**	

```
C:\Windows\system32>chkdsk c:  /f
The type of the file system is NTFS.
Cannot lock current drive.

Chkdsk cannot run because the volume is in use by another
process.  Would you like to schedule this volume to be
checked the next time the system restarts? (Y/N) _
```

Enter **Y**	To schedule the check for the next system restart.
4 Enter **exit**	To close the Command Prompt window.
5 Restart the computer	After the POST, chkdsk checks the file system on C: and then restarts the computer.
6 Log on	

Disk Defragmenter

Explanation

The Disk Defragmenter utility is included with all versions of Windows from Windows 95 on. This utility helps to improve hard disk performance by reorganizing the files on the disk.

Files can be divided across multiple clusters on the disk. From a speed perspective, the optimal arrangement is to have all of a file's clusters located contiguously on the disk. However, as you add, remove, and change the contents of files, they grow or shrink. Files can become fragmented into many clusters spread across discontinuous portions of the disk.

Fragmentation isn't as much of a problem in Windows Server and newer client operating systems, such as Windows Vista, as it was in earlier operating systems. However, you can still use a file defragmentation utility to move file clusters and return the disk to a less fragmented state. Using such a utility is sometimes called *defragging* the disk.

To defrag a disk, open its Properties dialog box, activate the Tools tab, and click Defragment Now. Windows will analyze the disk and present its assessment of whether you can improve performance by defragging. Windows Server also enables you to configure automatic defragging on a schedule you define. Make sure to schedule automatic defragging because of the intensive disk activity involved in defragmenting.

Unlike some previous versions of Windows, the current versions of Disk Defragmenter do not display a graphical progress window.

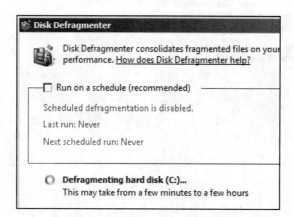

Exhibit 7-17: Defragmentation in process in Windows Server 2008

Do it!

C-3: Defragmenting a disk

Here's how	Here's why
1 Click **Start** and choose **Computer**	
Right-click **Local Disk (C:)** and choose **Properties**	
Activate the Tools tab	
2 Click **Defragment now**	Windows analyzes your disks. Most likely, in the classroom environment, your disks will not need defragmentation.
3 In the Disk Defragmenter window, click **Defragment now**	
Click OK	⟳ **Defragmenting hard disks...** This may take from a few minutes to a few hours
4 Close all open windows	

Storage monitoring and logging

Explanation

The tools you use to monitor resource usage vary by operating system and version. Windows offers various tools, though not all tools are available in all versions of Windows. Linux distributions vary significantly, and each one includes its own selection of tools. The following sections describe common tools that you can use to monitor storage. Check your operating system version to confirm their availability or to locate other tools that provide similar functionality.

Windows monitoring tools

Windows offers various tools for monitoring system resources and disk usage. Helpful tools include Reliability and Performance Monitor and Performance Monitor.

Resource monitoring

Reliability and Performance Monitor contains an important tool called Resource Overview, which you can use to assess and maintain the health of your system. As shown in Exhibit 7-18, Resource Overview is the first tool you see when you open Reliability and Performance Monitor. It provides real-time graphs and detailed information about four key components:

- **CPU** — Displays CPU utilization.
- **Hard disk** — Displays the disk input/output statistics.
- **Network** — Details network traffic.
- **Memory** — Displays memory statistics, including the percent of memory used and the number of hard page faults.

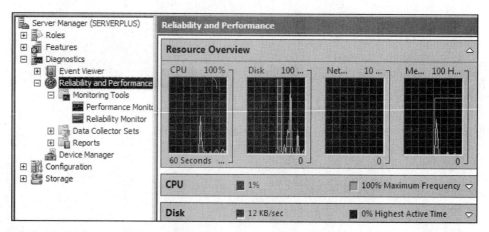

Exhibit 7-18: Resource Overview

Performance Monitor

You use Performance Monitor, shown in Exhibit 7-19, to monitor computer performance in real time (in one-second intervals), or in the form of saved reports of real-time data. Hundreds of computer performance variables called *counters* are available for measuring and assessing a computer's performance. For example, you can:

- Create a baseline to compare system performance over time.
- Monitor system resource use.
- Locate performance problems.
- Identify performance bottlenecks.

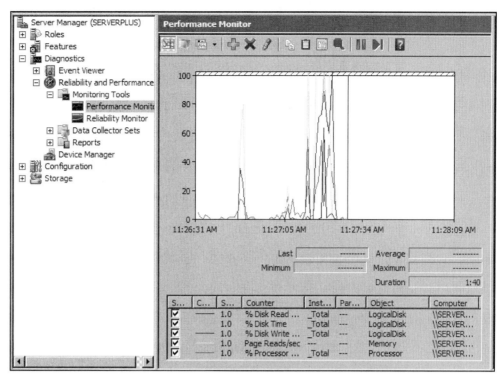

Exhibit 7-19: A real-time graph in Performance Monitor

Linux monitoring tools

The various Linux distributions each offer their own set of tools for system monitoring. In general, any of the GUI environments (Gnome, KDE) will include a resource monitoring tool. In Debian Linux, the tool is called System Monitor. You can use it to view CPU, memory, swap (virtual memory), and network information, and more. System Monitor, shown in Exhibit 7-20, presents information similar to that provided by Windows Task Manager.

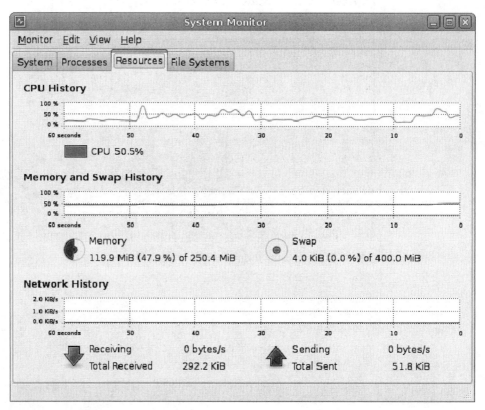

Exhibit 7-20: Debian's System Monitor shows CPU, memory, network, and disk statistics

Linux also offers many command-line tools, such as the input/output statistics program, `iostat`. Without command switches, the program outputs CPU utilization, disk utilization, and network utilization statistics, as shown in Exhibit 7-21. Using command switches, you can view any one of those three categories individually. For example, the `iostat -d` command outputs only disk performance information. In addition, you can add the `-x` option to display "extended" information.

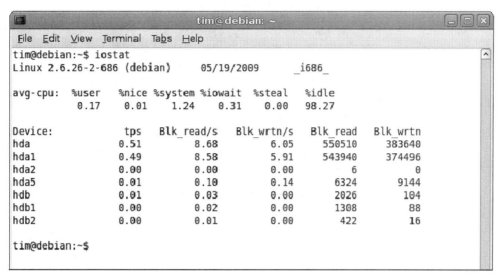

Exhibit 7-21: Output of the iostat command

For each device, `iostat` lists the following information:

- **tps** — The number of transfers per second.
- **Blk_read/s** — The number of blocks read per second.
- **Blk_wrtn/s** — The number of blocks written per second.
- **Blk_read** — The total number of blocks read.
- **Blk_wrtn** — The total number of blocks written.

What to watch for:

- A high number of read or write operations per second indicates a busy disk. Continually high levels indicate a slow disk that should be replaced by a faster one. Steadily increasing values indicate a disk that is trending toward being a bottleneck. Consider moving data to another device or upgrading the disk or controller.
- A high iowait value indicates that a drive is a bottleneck because the CPU is spending a lot of time waiting for I/O.

Windows logging

Event Viewer is a Windows GUI utility that enables you to monitor events that occur on your system. The events that are recorded can help you determine the cause of problems you're having with a particular application, a component of the operating system, or a suspected security breach.

Event Viewer is available in Windows 2000 Professional, Windows XP, Windows Vista, and Windows Server (all versions). You can access it through the Administrative Tools in the Control Panel. Event Viewer is also a System Tools component of the Computer Management console.

There are five types of events; they are described in the following table.

Event type	Description
Error	A significant problem; for example, a service fails to start.
Warning	An event that isn't a significant or immediate problem but could become a significant problem in the future. For example, disk space is running low.
Information	The successful operation of a task; for example, a network driver loads successfully.
Success Audit (Security Log only)	A successful security event; for example, a user logs on successfully.
Failure Audit (Security Log only)	An unsuccessful security event; for example, a user attempts to log on but fails to submit proper credentials.

Linux logging

Many Linux processes create log files detailing the actions they have taken, events that have occurred, and processes that have failed. You should monitor these log files to keep tabs on your system and catch little problems before they become big ones.

Most logs are stored as text files in the /var/log directory and its subdirectories. The following table lists a few of the log files you might find there.

Log file	Contains information about...
boot.log	System boot and daemon startup.
cron	The operation or failure of scheduled jobs.
dmesg	Hardware detection successes and failures.
lastlog	Users and their last logon times.
messages	Daemon startup and system-level messages produced since booting.

Network file access

When monitoring storage on your server, you might need to remotely access the file system of another computer. Perhaps you need to copy a file to that computer or remove unnecessary files from it. You can use GUI tools to browse and connect to remote file systems. But you can also use command-line tools.

In Windows, you can use the `net use` command, as shown here:

```
net use X: \\computer\share
```

Of course, various security considerations come into play, depending on whether your systems are part of a Windows domain or a workgroup. The command offers various ways to provide a domain name, user name, and password. For further help on syntax, enter the following command:

```
net use ?
```

In Linux, you can use the mount command to access NFS (Network File System) shared volumes. You must be logged in as root or use sudo to mount an NFS file system. The file system will remain mounted until you shut down the computer or use the umount command to unmount the file system.

```
mount -t nfs computer:/file_system mount_point
```

In the preceding syntax statement, *computer* is the name of the NFS server, *file_system* is the remote file system you're mounting, and *mount_point* is the directory to which you're mounting that file system. As with other uses of mount, when you mount an NFS file system to a directory, any existing contents of that directory are hidden until you unmount the file system.

Do it!

C-4:   Monitoring and logging storage use

Here's how

1 Use Resource Overview to view the current CPU and disk activity. Identify any signals that might identify a current or pending storage problem, such as high swap activity, high disk utilization, insufficient disk space, and so forth.

2 Using Performance Monitor, create a real-time graph that provides a snapshot of disk activity. Add the counters shown in Exhibit 7-19. Monitor performance for a few minutes and then identify any signals that might indicate a current or pending storage problem.

3 If you have a Linux server available, use System Monitor (or your distribution's similar tool) and iostat to monitor disk usage. Identify any signals that might indicate a current or pending storage problem.

4 Examine your computer's logs to find warning or error-level events related to disk storage. Are there any indications of a pending problem?

5 Close all open applications.

Storage hardware troubleshooting

Explanation   The following table describes hard drive storage–related problems you might encounter.

Symptom	Probable cause	Suggested solution
Can't access drive at all; cannot mount a drive	Cables disconnected; master/slave or SCSI ID conflict; dead drive; drive controller disabled in BIOS.	Confirm that all cables are connected fully and properly. Check the master/slave or SCSI settings. Try replacing the drive with a known good drive to see if that drive works in the system. Try the suspect drive in another system to see if it works there. These steps help you determine if the drive is good or bad. Confirm that the controller is enabled in the BIOS.
Can't boot from the hard drive	BIOS drive order prevents booting from hard drive; non-bootable disk used; another drive set to be bootable; corrupt boot sector.	Confirm the boot drive order in the BIOS. Make sure the drive is set to be bootable and is formatted as a bootable disk. Make sure you haven't set another drive to be the boot drive, or installed another boot drive into a higher-priority position on the drive chain.
Space on drive doesn't match advertised space	Disk unit misunderstanding; file system limitations; space being used by system recovery programs.	Sometimes the M in MB or the G in GB refers to a decimal measurement (multiples of 1000), and sometimes it's a binary measurement (multiples of 1024 based on powers of 2). Perhaps you have just misunderstood which units are being used. The FAT32 file system is less efficient with very large drives compared to NTFS. You can also "lose" space with some sector and cluster size combinations.
Files becoming corrupted	Drive failing; bad data cable; terminator missing.	Try replacing the data cable with a new, high-quality cable. Make sure all connectors are seated fully. Confirm that the SCSI chain is terminated properly. Use a disk testing utility, such as Windows Check Disk, to determine if the drive is failing.
System boots from hard drive when you do a warm restart, but doesn't do a cold boot	System booting too quickly.	Sometimes the motherboard portions of the boot process can move too quickly for a slower hard drive, which isn't ready when the CPU tries to access it. Use the BIOS setup utility to disable the Quick Boot option and, if available, enable the boot delay time option.
Drive letter incorrect	Cables connected incorrectly or master/slave set incorrectly; drive letters reassigned with Windows.	Confirm that you have installed the drive in the correct location on the cable and configured the master/slave settings correctly. Use Windows Disk Manager (part of the Computer Management console) to change drive letter assignments.
Can't use the full space of a very large hard drive	BIOS or operating system can't support very large drives.	Install a BIOS update from your motherboard or drive controller's manufacturer. Install the BIOS patch included with many extremely large drives.
Drive not auto-detected during boot process	BIOS settings incorrect; bad data cable connection; failing drive.	Confirm that the BIOS settings controlling the disk drive detection are set correctly. Make sure the cables are connected properly and fully seated. Try using a different data cable. Test the drive with a diagnostic utility to confirm that the drive is functioning correctly.
User cannot access files or resources	File permissions don't permit access; files are encrypted by another user or with an old key.	Test user permissions and update user or file permissions as necessary and appropriate. Check for encryption problems; restore the old key or use a master override key if one is available.

Symptom	Probable cause	Suggested solution
Disk performance decreases	Files are fragmented; drive is beginning to fail; cabling or controller failure is causing data transfer errors; array member rebuild is in process.	Examine system logs for drive failure–related messages. If none are found, defragment the hard drive. Check for loose or damaged cables. Replace controller and cables. Schedule an array member rebuild for low-use hours.
Backup fails	Insufficient capacity on backup medium; bad backup medium; insufficient time allotted for backup.	Confirm that the backup will fit onto the medium; divide backup set into smaller parts to fit, or replace the drive with a larger-capacity unit. Test the medium by writing to and reading from it. Replace the backup medium. Confirm that the backup has sufficient time to finish; if not, divide the set or upgrade the backup device with a faster unit over a faster bus.

Troubleshooting CD and DVD drives

The following table describes CD and DVD drive–related problems you might encounter.

Problem	Probable cause	Suggested solutions
No audio plays from CD.	Volume turned down; speakers disconnected; CD drive not connected to sound card.	Make sure you check the volume on both the volume control (in the Windows system tray) and the speakers. Make sure the speakers are plugged in and turned on. Make sure the CD-to-sound-card cable is connected. Check Device Manager to see if a resource conflict is preventing Windows from accessing the drive properly.
CD drive not found.	Drive disabled in BIOS; driver problem; wrong drive letter.	Check your system BIOS settings to confirm that the drive is enabled. Make sure you're using the newest drivers. CD drives often get assigned the last drive letter, but can be assigned other letters. Make sure the drive is truly not being found, rather than just being assigned an unexpected drive letter.
Disc can't be read.	Disc scratched or damaged; DVD disc inserted in a CD drive.	Treat all optical discs gently and store them in suitable cases or sleeves. If you must set one down without a case, lay it label side down. Make sure the disc type matches the drive type.
Buffer underrun occurring.	Buffer empties before you've finished recording.	Check the Buffer Underrun Protection checkbox in your software, if it's available.
		Record from an image on disc rather than directly from some other source.
		Don't run anything else on the computer while recording. Disable antivirus, screensaver, or other software that might wake and disrupt the CD burning process. Adjust virtual memory settings to prevent swapping.
Write process fails several minutes after starting.	The data source can't keep up with the CD-R.	Try recording at 1X and write from a disc image by using disc-at-once writing mode.
	It might be a bad batch of CDs.	Try another package of CDs or another brand of CDs.

Problem	Probable cause	Suggested solutions
Zip files are corrupted when recorded on a SCSI CD-RW drive.	Most files have redundant information in them. Compressed files use every bit, so any lost information causes a problem.	Check the SCSI cable, connection, and termination for the drive. Also, check L2 cache and memory settings for potential problems.
Burned CD-RW disc can't be read on another computer.	The CD-ROM drives on the other computers aren't MultiRead-compliant or can't read CDs created with packet-writing utilities.	Check media compatibility. Some players and CD drives read only pressed CDs or CD-Rs, and not CD-RW discs. With Windows 95/98/Me, you can change the recording mode. Instead of packet-based writes, try recording with No Read Ahead enabled. (In Control Panel, Performance, File System, CD-ROM, set Access Pattern to No Read Ahead.)
DVD can't be played when two displays are being used.	On a laptop or other system with two displays, the overlay can't be created to play on both devices.	Use only one display when playing video in Windows Media Player. Refer to *support.microsoft.com/kb/306713* for more information.
UDF-formatted discs can't be read. You might be able to read some files or none, or the disc might not show up in Explorer.	The latest Windows XP service pack needs to be installed.	Apply the latest Windows XP service pack; make sure recording software is up-to-date. Refer to *support.microsoft.com/kb/321640* for more symptoms, causes, workarounds, and other information.
DVD movie won't play.	No DVD playback software installed; decoders missing.	You must have special software for playing DVD movies on a PC. Make sure you have such a program installed. Movies are encoded in various formats, and it's possible that you don't have the correct type installed. You might find a suitable decoder at *www.free-codecs.com*.

Do it!   **C-5:   Interpreting hardware symptoms and their causes**

Questions and answers

1 You just installed a new SCSI hard disk as a second drive in a computer, but Windows doesn't recognize it. What are probable causes?

2 You have installed a second hard disk in a computer. When you boot the computer, the operating system doesn't recognize the second hard disk. What are probable causes and solutions?

3 Users are calling to complain that access to files on the file server is slower than normal. You had recently started rebuilding a failed drive array member. What should you do?

4 What would the consequences be from the failure of the battery that backs up the cache in your drive array?

Unit summary: Installing data storage devices

Topic A   In this topic, you examined **data storage device types**. You installed a hard drive and prepared it for use by the operating system. You also examined external storage technologies, such as NAS, SANs, and tape libraries.

Topic B   In this topic, you learned about **RAID** storage technologies. You explored the various RAID levels so that you're prepared to select the correct level for a given scenario.

Topic C   In this topic, you identified common symptoms of **hardware-related problems**. You examined probable causes of those symptoms and identified possible resolutions to the problems.

Review questions

1   You can configure an IDE drive to be _master, slave_, or _backup_ by using jumpers or switches on the drive.

2   Partitioning divides a drive into one or more logical drives, also called _volumes_

3   Partitions that are directly accessed as volumes by the operating system are which type?

   A Extended

   B Logical

   C Primary

   D Secondary

4   Which file system has a maximum file size of 4 GB?

   A FAT16

   B FAT32

   C NTFS

5   Which file system supports file-level security?

   A FAT16

   B FAT32

   C NTFS

6 The following graphic is an example of which RAID level?

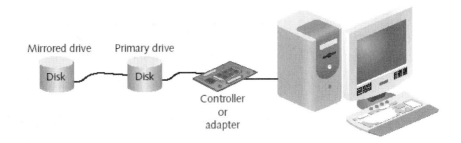

A Level 0

B Level 1

C Level 3

D Level 5

7 The following graphic is an example of which RAID level?

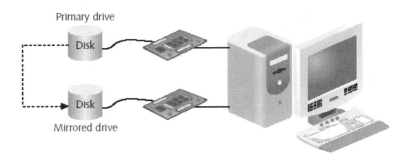

A Level 0

B Level 1

C Level 3

D Level 5

8 The following graphic is an example of which RAID level?

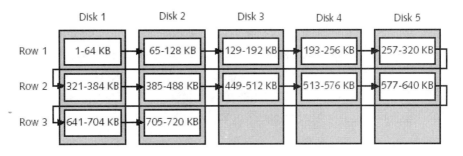

A Level 0

B Level 1

C Level 3

D Level 5

9 In Windows Vista, which disk maintenance utility runs on a reboot?

A The `chkdsk` command

B Disk Cleanup

C Disk Defragmenter

D ScanDisk

10 Which disk maintenance utility identifies files that can be deleted to recover space on a hard disk?

A The `chkdsk` command

B Disk Cleanup

C Disk Defragmenter

D ScanDisk

11 Which disk maintenance utility writes data in clusters sequentially on the disk?

A The `chkdsk` command

B Disk Cleanup

C Disk Defragmenter

D ScanDisk

12 You have a computer that boots from the hard drive when you do a warm restart, but doesn't boot from a cold boot. Which of the following causes might you suspect?

A BIOS settings are incorrect.

B Cables are connected incorrectly.

C The drive is failing.

D The system is booting too quickly.

Independent practice activity

In this activity, you'll practice cleaning up, checking, and defragging a hard drive.

1 Using Disk Management, partition and format the remaining unallocated space on your hard drive.

2 Schedule and run a check of your NTFS volume at system boot.

3 Use the Disk Defragmenter to analyze your hard disk. If you completed the defragmentation activity in this unit, it should report that defragmenting your drive is not recommended at this time.

Unit 8

Installing a network operating system

Unit time: 180 minutes

Complete this unit, and you'll know how to:

A Explain different server roles.

B Summarize virtualization concepts.

C Install a Linux distribution.

D Install Windows Server 2008.

Topic A: Server roles

This topic covers the following CompTIA Server+ (2009 Edition) exam objectives.

#	Objective
2.4	**Explain different server roles, their purposes, and how they interact**
	• File and print server
	• Database server
	• Web server
	• Messaging server
	• DHCP server
	• Directory services server
	• DNS server
	• Application server
	– Update server and proxy server
	– Filtering server
	– Monitoring server
	– Dedicated
	– Distributed
	– Peer to peer
	• Remote access server
	• Virtualized services
	• NTP server
	• Explain the difference between a workstation, a desktop, and a server
	• Server shutdown and startup sequence (one server vs. multiple servers vs. attached components)

Nowadays, networks make the world go 'round. From the small home network to the larger networks at your doctor's office or your bank to the world-wide Internet, networks are involved in some way in almost all of the business activities and a good part of the leisure activities in the world today. A CompTIA Server+ technician must be able to support the interrelationships of all types and sizes of networks and servers.

Local area networks

A *local area network* (LAN) is a specifically designed configuration of computers and other devices located within a confined area, such as a home or office building, and connected by wires or radio waves that permit the devices to communicate with one another to share data and services. Computers and other devices connected on a LAN can send and receive information from one another without confusion.

Each device with an address that can be accessed for sending or receiving information is a *node*. A node can be a computer, router, printer, video camera, controller, or other kind of electronic device.

A *host* is always a computer. The network directs the communication passing through it and acts as a sort of electronic traffic cop to prevent collisions or mixing of data.

A LAN can be connected to the Internet, either through a direct cable connection or by a telephone link through a modem, so that workstations on the LAN have access to all of the networks and sites linked to the global Web. Exhibit 8-1 shows the components of a simple LAN. On the middle right is the server. The computers are workstations on the LAN and are connected with a cable of some type. The second laptop is also a workstation on the LAN, but it's connected through a wireless access point. The printer is a shared network printer available to clients on the LAN.

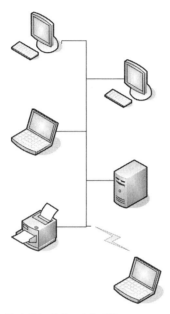

Exhibit 8-1: A LAN

A host requires an operating system to manage its applications, hardware, and connection to the network. The operating system is also responsible for enabling the computers on the LAN to share their resources. The term *resource* refers to any file, database, or printer installed on or attached to a host.

Basic network types

There are two basic types of networks that you'll encounter:

- **Peer-to-peer network** — Usually consists of several client computers that are connected for simple file and printer sharing in a small office or home office, as shown in Exhibit 8-2. Each computer has a network card, which is connected to the network by a network cable or wireless network medium. All communication occurs between the client computers, although there might be one or two server computers that also participate in peer-to-peer computing.

  There are often fewer than a dozen hosts on this type of network. You might also hear a peer-to-peer network described as a decentralized networking model because you must administer each user and computer on the network individually.

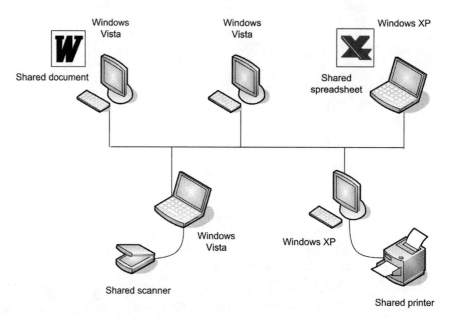

Exhibit 8-2: A peer-to-peer LAN

- **Client/server network** — Consists of client computers and servers. *Servers* are computers that hold data and provide services that users can share. Most of the communication occurs between the client computers and the servers, as shown in Exhibit 8-3.

  Client/server networks can be much larger than peer-to-peer networks. You might also hear a client/server network described as a centralized networking model because it enables you to administer computers and users as a group, instead of individually.

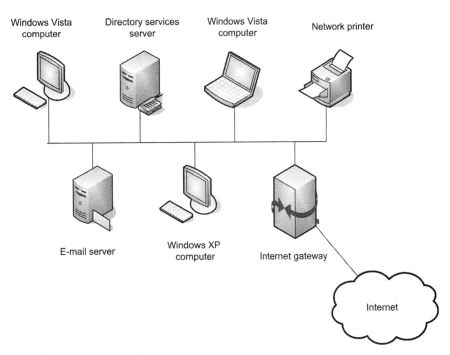

Exhibit 8-3: A client/server LAN

Peer-to-peer authentication

In a peer-to-peer LAN consisting of Windows computers, each user has his or her own computer and must enter his or her valid user ID and password in order to use the computer. If the user doesn't enter a valid user ID and password, he or she can't use the computer. The process of entering a correct user ID and password to gain access to a computer is called *authentication*, *validation*, or *logging on*. In the peer-to-peer model, the local client operating system authenticates the user ID and password.

User IDs and passwords allow users to access only their own computers. Their user accounts exist only on their own computers, so they can't authenticate and gain access to someone else's computer.

Client/server authentication

In the client/server model, the local client operating system does not authenticate user IDs and passwords. Instead, the client OS sends the logon information to the NOS on the server, which verifies it based on the information stored in its database. The NOS does this by using a *network client* that's installed on the client computer. The network client is responsible for communicating with the NOS on the server.

In the client/server model, an administrator assigns user IDs and passwords to users. Users can then authenticate against the NOS and log on to access network resources. (This process is called "logging onto the network.")

The logon process goes something like this:

1. The network client on the client computer displays a logon screen.
2. The user enters his or her user ID and password and clicks OK.
3. The network client sends this information to the NOS for authentication.
4. After the user ID and password have been authenticated, the user can gain access to the computer and the network resources.

Do it!

A-1: Describing networking models

Questions and answers

1 How are client/server networks different from peer-to-peer networks?

2 Why would a company want to implement a client/server network?

3 What kind of company would implement a peer-to-peer network?

Do it!

A-2: Identifying the basic components of a network

Here's how	Here's why
1 Identify the server computer in your classroom	You'll identify components of your classroom network.
2 Identify any client workstations on your classroom network	
3 Identify nodes on your classroom network	
4 Determine whether you're using a physical or wireless communication channel in your classroom	

Server roles

Servers play a variety of roles in an organization's network. The following table describes common server roles and their functions.

Server role	Provides...
File and print server	Access to shared files, such as documents, pictures, spreadsheets, and graphics; and access to laser and inkjet printers.
Database server	Access to databases, including those for customer information, provided by database software such as Oracle or SQL Server.
Web server	Access to personal, corporate, or education Web sites. This service is provided primarily to external users, such as customers or students, who access the Web services from the Internet. Web servers typically provide Web services to external users, although intranet servers can provide Web services to internal users.
Messaging server	Instant messaging, primarily for internal users. Some organizations have dedicated messaging servers, giving users a secure way to send and receive messages without using less-secure Internet instant-messaging services.
DHCP server	IP addressing information for network computers. This information includes IP addresses, subnet masks, default gateways, and DNS server addresses.
Directory services server	Authentication services across an organization, providing access via a single logon to servers and computers within the organization. Directory services servers also authenticate incoming connections, providing remote access to users outside the network. These include users who are traveling or who work remotely from home or other organizational sites.
DNS server	Name resolution services for users accessing Internet resources. Name resolution allows users to use familiar Web names, such as *www.microsoft.com*, instead of using IP addresses, to access Web sites. DNS servers also point users to internal resources, such as directory services, file and print servers, and database servers.
Application server	Access to shared applications, including data warehousing, data processing, and other applications shared among multiple users. Some application servers are dedicated servers, meaning that they provide only one type of application service to network users. Applications that are large or very sensitive might be distributed across multiple servers to provide fast access to resources and to prevent a critical system failure if one server goes offline.
Update server	Updates, including service packs and hotfixes, for operating systems and applications in the organization. Although these updates are available from the software vendors, for larger organizations it's more efficient to provide update services locally, rather than require users to access multiple Web sites.

Server role	Provides...
Proxy server	Web requests on behalf of clients. With a proxy server, a client's request is not sent directly to the remote host. Instead, the request goes to the proxy server, which then sends the request to the remote host on behalf of the client.
	Before sending the packet, the proxy server replaces the original sender's address and other identifying information with its own. When the response arrives, the proxy server looks up the original sending node's information, updates the incoming packet, and forwards it to the client. By these actions, a proxy server masks internal IP addresses, like a NAT device. It also blocks unwanted inbound traffic—there will be no corresponding outbound connection data in its tables, so the packets will be dropped. Many proxy servers also provide caching functions, which speed up Web page access for internal users.
Filtering server	Services that block user access to specific Web sites or content that the organization deems inappropriate for the work or educational environment.
Monitoring server	Network monitoring statistics to help server and network administrators optimize network usage.
Remote access server	Access to internal network services and computers to employees working outside the network, such as those who are traveling or working from home.
Network Time Protocol (NTP) server	Time synchronization services for computer clocks. This server provides the mechanisms to synchronize time and coordinate time distribution in a large network. Correct times are important for authentication services.

The server shutdown and startup sequence

When you're shutting down a single server, such as a print server, for maintenance or updates, there's no requirement for how you shut it down. However, when you're restarting certain servers—such as a directory server, a DNS server, or application servers with a distributed application—the shutdown and restart sequence plays an important role.

Keep these general rules in mind.

- Make sure the directory servers and the DNS servers are the last ones shut down and the first ones restarted. As you restart other servers, they'll need access to the DNS server and the directory server to register their services and accounts in the directory and the DNS database.

- Ensure that DHCP servers are started before the client computers or any other computers or servers that depend on the DHCP servers for networking information.

- Restart distributed-application servers according to the software manufacturer's instructions.

- You'll need to restart proxy servers before any clients can access the Web.

Do it!   ## A-3: Discussing server roles

Here's how

1 True or false? All networks require a directory services server.

2 What's the difference between a file server and a database server?

3 What functions do DHCP servers and DNS servers provide?

4 Why would a network have its own messaging and update servers?

5 What is the difference between a proxy server and a Web server?

6 What services do remote access servers provide?

7 True or false? NTP servers provide a location for file downloads.

8 True or false? When restarting servers, you must restart the DNS server as early as possible.

Topic B: Virtualization

This topic covers the following CompTIA Server+ (2009 Edition) exam objectives.

#	Objective
2.1	**Install, deploy, configure, and update the NOS (Windows / *nix)** • Imaging – system cloning and deployment (Ghost, RIS/WDS, Altiris, virtualization templates)
2.5	**Summarize server virtualization concepts, features, and considerations** • Resource utilization • Configuration • Interconnectivity • Management server • Reasons for virtualization – Cost benefits – Redundancy – Green initiative – Disaster recovery – Testing environment • Ease of deployment

Overview of virtualization

Explanation

Virtualization is a technology through which one or more simulated computers run within a physical computer. The physical computer is called the *host*. The simulated computers are typically called *virtual machines (VMs)*, although other terms are sometimes used.

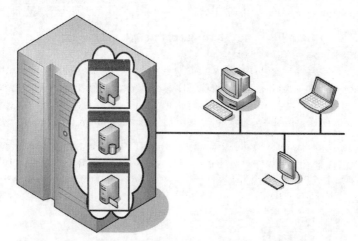

Exhibit 8-4: Multiple VMs on a single physical host

Virtualization is generally categorized into three levels:

- Virtual servers
- Virtual applications
- Virtual desktops

Virtual servers

Virtual servers apply virtualization to the data center. One or more servers are implemented as virtual machines within a single host. Server virtualization offers many benefits, such as better hardware utilization, but can come at the cost of additional administration complexity.

Virtual applications

With virtual applications, users share a pool of software licenses. The company saves money by purchasing enough licenses to service average demand (or peak demand), rather than one license per employee. Beyond cost savings, virtual applications provide centralized control over applications. Users cannot make changes or install their own software, and the threat of viruses can be reduced.

Virtual desktops

Virtual desktops go beyond virtual applications to provide an entire computing environment, including multiple applications, a logon environment, and local user preferences. Essentially, a virtual desktop is a virtualized PC running within a VM on a host computer. End-users connect to their own virtual desktops by using a "thin" terminal or specialized Windows software.

As with virtual applications, virtual desktops provide centralized administration and additional security. Furthermore, virtual desktops empower a mobile workforce whose members can access their personal workspaces from anywhere on the network.

Server virtualization

Currently, one of the biggest applications of virtualization is in the computer room. Companies use server virtualization to consolidate servers onto fewer physical hosts to save money.

Virtualizing servers and running them within a VM host is a bit different than simply configuring a single server to handle multiple roles. Consider that you could combine the functions of a file, print, and application server onto a single network server. By doing so, you would consolidate services that might have been performed by multiple physical servers. However, you wouldn't gain all of the benefits of server virtualization.

Virtualization enables you to prioritize server functions and dynamically reassign those priorities. You have fewer options for prioritization when you simply combine services onto a single server. Additionally, with virtualization, you can assign resources such as CPU and RAM as needed, and *provision* (that is, set up) new virtual servers on the fly.

Server virtualization benefits are described in the following table.

Benefit	Considerations
Reduced power and cooling requirements	Fewer physical computers use less electricity and require less cooling. Virtual servers are therefore a greener choice to meet both organizational and governmental green initiatives, as well as to reduce utility expenses.
Reduced infrastructure costs	Having fewer physical computers to purchase, set up, and configure means a reduction in both capital and operating expenses. You can use a smaller computer room to house your servers. You will need fewer networking components, and you can save on seemingly trivial tasks such as installing and labeling cables and wiring racks. You might also reduce your software licensing costs.
Centralized administration	You can administer many virtual servers from a single console. Often, you can do so from across the network. This capability can reduce travel time or enable an administrator to manage more computers than he or she could handle if the servers were physically distributed throughout your company's premises.
Faster deployment	Virtual servers can be deployed via software with the click of a few buttons. Deploying a server no longer requires someone to physically assemble a computer, install it into a rack, connect it to the physical network, and so forth. Virtualization templates make it even easier to deploy pre-configured servers with the exact configuration settings and software that you need.
Improved hardware utilization	You can reduce capital expenses by using the full capabilities of the hardware you already own, rather than buying more. According to *Enterprise Systems Journal*, the typical x86-based server uses 5–10% of its computing capacity on average. Given the journal's assertion that 80% of servers are x86-based servers, you can see that there is an incredible opportunity for hardware consolidation.
Reduced disposal	Using fewer physical components—computers, wiring components, racks, and so forth—means you will have less to dispose of when that equipment reaches the end of its usable life. Using less equipment further reduces production- and distribution-related pollution. Source reduction is a great way to reduce your environmental footprint.
Testing environment	You can install multiple operating systems on a single computer to test new software or updates.

Server virtualization is not without downsides, however. Some of the reasons that server virtualization might not be suitable are described in the following table.

Downside	Considerations
Increased administration complexity	Increased administration complexity can slow response time and increases the skills needed by administrators. For example, to manage a particular virtual server, the administrator will need to know how to use both the server virtualization product's management server console and the server operating system's tools. He or she will have to log onto the virtualization consoles, and then onto the operating system.
Single point of failure	Consolidation of multiple servers onto a single host increases your risk of loss. When a physical host fails, it brings down all of the virtual servers running on it. A single hardware failure in a VM host can affect many more services than would a similar failure in a physical server.
Increased data throughput demands	Increased traffic on backbone network segments slows response times. Network traffic for all of the virtual servers must flow over a single network segment. Multiple network adapters can be installed in the host, with each adapter connected to its own network segment. That setup just moves the bottleneck to the host's I/O bus. You will need to provision servers accordingly to avoid or minimize resource contention problems.
Reduced performance	Running multiple servers on a single host can reduce the performance of each server, though you can enforce prioritization rules to mitigate some of the consequences. If your database server is already using all or most of the computing resources of a physical server, implementing its functions in a virtualized environment will only reduce performance, making users wait longer or limiting the number of new user accounts that can be attached to that server.
High initial investment	You will need to invest in more powerful servers to act as your VM hosts. Virtualization software can be expensive. You will also need a high-quality and high-capacity network infrastructure. All of these are expensive items, at least initially. You might also need to over-buy to provide capacity for future growth.

Server virtualization products

Currently, the most popular virtualization products fall into two general categories:

- Bare metal hypervisors
- Host-based hypervisors

A *hypervisor*, or virtual machine manager, is the core virtualization software that enables multiple virtual computers to run on a single physical host. A *bare metal hypervisor* is one you install directly on the server's hardware—you don't install an operating system first. A *host-based hypervisor* is one that runs within an operating system—you install the OS first and then install the hypervisor.

The primary vendors of bare metal hypervisors are VMWare and Citrix. VMWare's offerings are built around the ESXi Server. This is the main virtualization engine for which VMWare offers a suite of tools. For example, the Virtual Center management console is the tool you use to create virtual machines, move them between hosts, monitor resource usage, and so forth. The VMotion add-on component enables you to move VMs between hosts while those VMs are actively being used. The LabManager add-on component enables you to set up self-serve lab computer provisioning that will let end-users set up virtual computers without administrator involvement. The VMWare File System (VMFS) is available for use in ESXi Server, but it's not required.

Citrix's XenServer is also a bare metal hypervisor. Citrix purchased the open-source Xen project. For a while, you could still download a free, limited-feature version of Xen from Citrix or purchase the full-featured XenServer product. In early 2009, Citrix surprised industry watchers by releasing the full XenServer product for free. Citrix's virtualization management suite is called "Essentials for XenServer," and you can purchase editions with various levels of capabilities. For example, both the Enterprise and Platinum editions offer the XenMotion migration tool (equivalent to VMotion from VMWare). However, you have to purchase the Platinum version to get the automated lab management functionality like that offered by VMWare's LabManager.

Microsoft's Hyper-V is a bare metal hypervisor that requires one guest virtual machine running Windows Server 2008. That "parent partition" has full access to all of the hardware and serves as the management entry point for all of the other VMs. Hyper-V is a new product that currently has more limitations than the products from Citrix and VMWare. For example, at the time of this writing, you could not move running virtual machines from one host to another without using third-party software.

Of the hosted hypervisors, Sun Microsystems' VirtualBox is a popular choice. This product is not an enterprise-level virtualization solution, at least not at the level of VMWare and XenServer. However, it does provide a powerful and free solution for test environments, client operating system virtualization, classroom and development lab environments, and more. It is available in commercial and open-source editions at *www.virtualbox.org*.

Microsoft's Virtual PC is an emulator rather than a hypervisor. This application is aimed primarily at end-users who need to simulate desktop environments. The current version, called "Windows Virtual PC," runs only on Windows 7 hosts and requires a CPU with either AMD-V or Intel VT hardware-based virtualization support. This package is mostly meant to simulate a Windows XP guest to provide backward compatibility. Although you can run a server operating system within Virtual PC, this emulator is not suitable for a serious server virtualization project.

Do it!

B-1: **Exploring the purposes and application of virtualization**

Questions	Answers
1 Describe the differences between virtual servers and virtual desktops.	
2 Why is server virtualization a "green" activity?	
3 What are "non-green" benefits of server virtualization?	
4 List two downsides of server virtualization and describe how you could mitigate those concerns.	
5 What is a benefit of using a bare metal hypervisor instead of a host-based hypervisor?	

Storage virtualization

Local storage for virtual machines resides on the host's drives. The hypervisor simulates disk storage within a binary file on the host's disk drives. Opening bytes serve the same function as file system tables on a physical hard drive. The remainder of that host file holds the sectors and clusters of data stored by the VM.

Some virtualization systems enable you to change the size of a VM's drives on the fly. They do so by increasing the size of the file on the host's disk while updating the guest operating system with the new size. This feature is possible because most modern operating systems support dynamic drives and support modifications of disk space without restarting or reconfiguring the OS.

The integrity of the host file containing a VM's drive is critical. If the host file is corrupted, all VM disk information could be lost. For example, if even a few bytes of the opening-file-system table data become corrupt, the rest of the file will be unusable. The VM will lose all access to the disk. Worse yet, typical file-system forensics tools cannot read or recover the remaining data. This vulnerability makes disk backups, as well as redundancy, a critical feature in any production virtual environment. You should use RAID to protect your system from data loss.

In addition to this local virtual storage, you can use standard network storage systems with your VMs. You can use both *network attached storage* (NAS) devices and *storage area networks* (SANs). Some such systems offer virtualization-specific features.

NAS

Network attached storage (NAS) is in essence a self-contained file server that you connect to your network, rather than to an expansion bus. A NAS device provides file-level access via its integrated operating system, such as an embedded Linux version. That software enables you to either manage access and allocation directly, or integrate such management with your existing network operating system and infrastructure.

A NAS unit can use a single hard drive or implement a drive array (RAID). You connect the NAS device to your network, using your current media (10BaseT, fiber optic cabling, and so forth). The NAS makes files available via standard file-sharing protocols, such as SMB/CIFS (Windows) or NFS (Linux/UNIX).

A NAS device cannot replace or act as the system disk for a server. A server must have a local disk to boot from. This restriction exists whether you're considering a virtualized server or a physical server. User and application data could be stored on a NAS device.

SAN

A storage area network (SAN) is a device or system that provides block-level access to external storage. In essence, a SAN is a self-contained external hard drive. A SAN is typically made up of multiple drives, usually in a RAID configuration, along with a master control computer and other devices.

Software on the SAN enables you to divide the total storage space into a single or multiple virtual drives. You can also expand or shrink drives dynamically via the SAN's management software. Typically, you can perform backups, drive replacement, RAID rebuilds, and other operations via the SAN's console without interrupting your server's operations.

A SAN can act as a server's primary drive. It is accessed as if it were a local disk. This is true for both virtual servers and physical servers.

Benefits of storage virtualization

Some of the benefits of storage virtualization are listed in the following table.

Benefit	Considerations
Dynamic provisioning	With virtualized storage, you can typically increase a server's storage capacity dynamically from the administration console. This capability saves downtime (you don't have to shut down the server to physically install a new drive) and permits you to adjust storage to meet needs.
Centralized administration	You manage virtualized storage devices through a central administration console. This saves time for an administrator who doesn't need to physically visit a server to manage the storage.
Reduced infrastructure costs	Multiple servers sharing storage capacity will often require less total disk space and fewer actual hard drives, controllers, and cables. By reducing hardware, you'll have to buy fewer components, and you might need less physical space for housing your computers.
Reduced power and cooling consumption	More efficient use of available storage can reduce power use and require less cooling. Typically, you'll reduce the total number of physical disks needed to provide the storage space required for your servers.
Backup consolidation	Consolidating storage will likely lead to a larger data set to be backed up. However, all that data will be located on a single system, making the task of backing up easier to administer.

Storage virtualization is not without downsides, however. Some of the reasons that storage virtualization might not be suitable are described in the following table.

Downside	Considerations
Increased administration complexity	Increased administration complexity can slow response time and increase the skills needed by administrators. Administrators might need to learn VM console software functions or NAS or SAN administration tools and techniques.
Single point of failure	As noted previously, the corruption of a host's virtualized local storage devices can be devastating to VMs. Even worse would be the failure of a host's drive. Such a failure with destroy the virtual drives used by all of the VMs running on that host.
Increased data throughput demands	Data for all of the VMs must pass over the host's I/O bus. You must ensure that the bus is capable of transmitting that data, or it will be a bottleneck in the performance of all VMs on that host.
Reduced performance	With virtualized local disks (implemented as files on the host), actual reads and writes for all of the VMs are all performed by the same physical disk. Its rotation speed, seek time, and data transfer rate limit the overall performance and thus the performance of each VM.
High initial investment	SANs in particular can be very expensive. But outfitting high-performance local storage with redundancy and proper backups can also require expensive equipment.

Do it!

B-2: Investigating storage virtualization

Questions	Answers
1 Why does the hypervisor virtualize local drives for the VMs it hosts?	
2 When you back up a hypervisor host's hard drive, what considerations must you account for to be sure you correctly back up all of the virtual drives it hosts?	
3 True or false? A SAN is essentially a self-contained file server that you attach to your network.	
4 A NAS is a(n) _____ -level storage device. A SAN is a(n) _____ -level storage device.	
5 Which can replace your server's primary hard drive: a SAN or a NAS device?	

Security considerations

Explanation

You must carefully consider security as part of your overall virtualization strategy. An attack on a VM host can affect far more users than an attack on a physical server would. For example, a denial-of-service attack on your host could block access to all of the virtual servers it runs.

Normally, a virtual machine doesn't "know" that it is running on virtual hardware within another computer. The hypervisor should fully contain each virtualized computer, segregating it from all the other VMs and from the hypervisor itself. However, virtualization limitations or simple programming errors can provide a means for a process running within a VM to access other VMs or, worse yet, the hypervisor itself. This type of failure is called *VM escaping*. If a process can escape and access the hypervisor, it will have access to the data and resources accessible to all the other VMs.

The current crop of viruses and malware can determine whether they are running within a virtualized environment. Most of these programs use this information to hide themselves or alter their behavior because IT staff often test new software in virtual environments, looking for viruses and malware. By being virtual-aware, viruses can hide themselves during such tests and then wreak their havoc when implemented on physical hardware. The next breed of malware will likely begin exploiting vulnerabilities in hypervisors to escape the VM and infect the host.

A virus that overwrites the boot sector or file tables on a physical hard drive is certainly a headache. However, many file-system forensics tools enable you to detect, block, and sometimes recover from such problems. In a virtualized environment, local disks are just files on the host. When the boot sector and file table data within those dynamic files are altered, the remainder of the host file, and thus the VM drive it virtualizes, is rendered utterly useless. Normal tools likely provide little or no value in blocking or recovering from such attacks.

Most existing intrusion detection and prevention systems don't run at the hypervisor level. This means you cannot run a single tool to monitor all of the VMs. Instead, you must monitor each VM individually.

Data on physical servers is segregated, and transfers between servers can be monitored with network management tools. Data flow between virtual servers running on the same host is more difficult to manage. Furthermore, VMs can be moved between hosts and even merged. This means that data, users, and processes that originally were physically segregated can be brought together, sometimes inadvertently. A programming error or security breach can enable a malicious process to access data that it wouldn't have access to in a physically separated environment.

Human factors

The preceding concerns ignore the human aspects of a virtualized environment. System administrators with access to the hypervisor management consoles will have far-reaching powers to affect the VMs that run on a host. Organizations should carefully limit access to key, trusted personnel, and should routinely audit and monitor operations to make sure that the administrators don't overstep their duties.

The organization should implement strong policies related to upgrading and patching the hypervisor software and any components that run at the hypervisor level. For example, the entire virtualized environment would be put at risk if an administrator could be tricked into installing a Trojan horse. More likely, installing an untested and unstable upgrade to the hypervisor could cause it and all of its VMs to fail.

Do it!

B-3: Considering the security implications of virtualization

Questions	Answers
1 What is "VM escaping" and why is it a concern?	
2 Speculate on the attack vectors that a virus could use to infect the hypervisor.	
3 Speculate on ways that security concerns would affect the "greenness" of a virtualization initiative.	

Best practices

Explanation   Virtualization is complex. You should plan carefully before implementing a virtualized environment. Once you have an environment up and running, you should continually evaluate the system to make sure that it meets your needs and goals. When planning and evaluating virtualization for your organization, consider the following factors.

High-level considerations

- Determine your virtualization goals. For example, determine whether you want to consolidate servers, save space in your data center, or speed the provisioning of new servers.

- Prioritize your needs. You will likely select different products and implement them differently if you value power and cooling savings over high performance.

- Determine your current challenges and pains. Virtualization might not be the solution. For example, you might save thousands on hardware costs by implementing virtual servers. However, you could also lose far more than that in lost time and productivity if your virtualization effort results in slower performance for your users.

- Plan what will be virtualized and what will remain deployed as physical hardware. Planning will help you avoid "VM sprawl," in which you end up with too many virtual servers and a management headache.

- Implement virtualization in non-critical and test areas first. You can then apply what you learned when you deploy virtualization on a wider scale.

- Build a detailed baseline for each server that is a candidate for virtualization. Not every server should be virtualized. For example, you wouldn't want to virtualize servers that are using a high proportion of system resources, such as CPU time or disk I/O. Doing so would only reduce performance.

- Set performance goals for each server to be virtualized. Once you have virtualized a server, monitor its ongoing performance and compare that to its baseline specifications. Tune the VM (memory, CPU, and so forth) until you achieve your goals.

- Before implementing virtualization, determine how you will handle disaster preparedness and recovery. Investigate backup and restore options. Determine whether your current physical plant (fire suppression, power conditioning, cooling) systems are sufficient. Make sure you determine whether current failover systems (hot sites, cold sites) are sufficient, and if they are not, include such considerations when selecting a virtualization solution.

  On the positive side, recovering from a disaster with a virtual infrastructure can be faster and simpler. Using provisioning or migration tools, you can often quickly move a VM from a failed host to a working host, minimizing downtime. Should you need to restore a failed host entirely, then once it's up and running, all the VMs it hosted will probably be running, too. You could get more servers up and running in less time with a virtualized infrastructure than with a physical implementation.

Implementation-level considerations

- Carefully plan for and manage access to your VM management consoles. This will limit the opportunities for inadvertent or malicious changes in your virtualized environment.

- Use separate network interfaces and network segments for management and business-use data. This way, your access to the management consoles won't be limited by regular network traffic.

- Make sure that all of the hardware used in your virtualization hosts is fully compatible with both your virtualization platform and your guest operating systems.

Only after you have fully planned a virtualization project should you begin the product selection process. Most of the vendors have free or limited-time trial versions that you can use to confirm that a selected product meets your needs. Most of the vendors are willing to work with you if you need longer or more detailed trials of their products.

Do it!

B-4: Evaluating virtualization best practices

Questions	Answers
1 Of the best practices listed in this section, which are most important to you and your company?	
2 How can you determine if a server is a good candidate for virtualization?	
3 After you implement a virtualized environment, what is the purpose or benefit of evaluating your implementation and its performance?	

Topic C: Installing Linux

This topic covers the following CompTIA Server+ (2009 Edition) exam objective.

#	Objective
2.1	**Install, deploy, configure, and update the NOS (Windows / *nix).**
	• Installation methods (optical media, USB, network share, PXE)
	• Bootloader
	• File systems
	– FAT – VMFS
	– FAT32 – ZFS
	– NTFS – EXT3
	• Configure the NOS
	– User – Device

Linux overview

Explanation

Linux is a UNIX-like operating system originally developed by Linus Torvalds, starting in 1991 while he was a student at the University of Helsinki. Like all operating systems, Linux enables the most basic common system operations, such as file management, user account management, and so forth. It provides a means for users to interact with their computer's hardware and software.

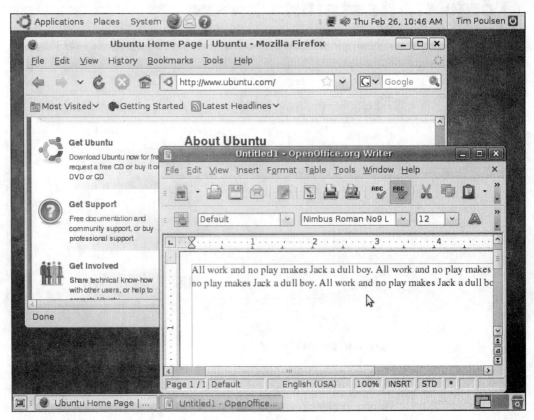

Exhibit 8-5: Ubuntu Linux with OpenOffice Writer and Mozilla Firefox open

Linux is perhaps most notable because it is free and open source. Programmers have made versions of Linux available for nearly every computer hardware platform in current use. Linux is available for:

- Network servers and enterprise-class computing environments

- Desktop and end-user computers

- "Non-computer" devices, such as cell phones, automobile control systems, network routers, and alarm system controllers

Linus Torvalds wrote the original Linux kernel. The *kernel* is the software component that provides the core set of operating system functions. These include features for managing system hardware and for communicating between software and hardware.

The Linux kernel is the base on which various versions, or *distributions*, are built. Each Linux distribution (often abbreviated as *distro*) bundles a specific set of features, software components, and a design philosophy that targets a particular use or market segment. The following table describes some of the distributions in common use as of this writing.

Distribution	Description
Ubuntu	Ubuntu is a community-developed distribution coordinated by Canonical, Ltd. It is currently one of the most popular end-user versions of Linux. Ease-of-use and multi-language support are two key goals of Ubuntu's developers. Linux Mint (*http://linuxmint.com/*) is a popular variant of Ubuntu.
Red Hat Enterprise	Red Hat, Inc., creates the Red Hat Enterprise Linux distribution in versions for servers and desktops. Red Hat also provides middleware software components and consulting, support, and education services. Red Hat is one of the largest Linux distributions in the business marketplace.
Fedora	Fedora is Red Hat's end-user Linux distribution. Red Hat engineers participate, but Fedora development is community driven.
SUSE and openSUSE	Developed by Novell Corporation, SUSE is released in two major versions: SUSE Linux Enterprise Desktop (SLED) and SUSE Linux Enterprise Server (SLES). They are built atop the open-source openSUSE core. Novell adds interoperability, virtualization, and enterprise service features for its commercial distributions.
Debian GNU/Linux	Debian is a community-developed distribution managed by The Debian Project. Debian is regarded as highly customizable and powerful. Generally, Debian would be described as an intermediate user's version of Linux: slightly harder to use and more customizable than some versions, but less feature rich than others.
Slackware	Slackware Linux is one of the oldest distributions that is still undergoing active development. It is a popular, highly technical distribution aimed at experienced Linux "power users."

You can get detailed information about most of the top Linux distributions at *http://distrowatch.com/*. The *http://en.wikipedia.org/wiki/List_of_Linux_distributions* entry at Wikipedia lists even more distributions.

Do it!

C-1: Exploring Linux distributions

Here's how	Here's why
1 Open your Web browser	
2 Visit **www.distrowatch.com**	
3 Scroll as necessary to find the table titled "Page Hit Ranking"	
4 What is currently the most popular distribution according to this table?	
5 At the top of the page, click **Major Distributions**	To view the "top ten" distribution list, as compiled by this Web site.
6 Compare the descriptions of at least two distributions. Would this information help you select the best Linux version to use?	

Pre-installation tasks

With older versions of Linux, and with a few of the technically complex distributions such as Slackware, you used to have to gather all sorts of technical details about the hardware in your computer. You needed to know the interrupts and IO addresses of the various adapters in your system, the graphics chipset your video adapter used, and so forth. Arguably, one of the largest advancements in "modern" Linux distributions has been improved installers that detect all these values for you. In this way, modern Linux distributions are now like Windows and Mac OS X in their ability to auto-detect and auto-configure hardware.

Another way installers have improved is in their ability to work cooperatively with operating systems already installed on your computer. Before, you had to install on an empty hard drive, or partition your drive before installing Linux in an empty partition. Modern desktop distributions in particular now handle such details for you.

During an installation, you can often specify to resize an existing Windows partition in order to make room for running Linux side by side with Windows on the same PC. Or you can use the installer to erase a Windows partition for a "clean install" of Linux. Most Linux distributions include *boot loaders*, which enable you to select which operating system to load when you boot your PC.

Before you can install Linux, you will generally perform the following tasks:

- Select the installation type.
- Download the appropriate installation files.
- If necessary, burn an ISO image to disc.

Installation types

To install Linux, you will need the installation files. Depending on the installation type, this set of files might comprise a set of DVD discs containing every possible application and package supported by the distribution. Or it might include just the minimal files needed to boot your PC, connect to the Internet, and download the files required to run your distribution.

The following table describes the primary installation types you must choose between.

Install type	With this option...
CD/DVD media	You purchase or receive CDs or DVDs and install Linux in much the same way you would install any retail software application.
ISO file	You download an "image" of a CD or DVD. Using disc burning software, you create your own CD or DVD installation media and then install from those discs. ISO files are large, typically 700 MB per CD and multiple gigabytes for DVD images.
Installable live CD	You download an ISO file, burn a disc, and then boot. Unlike the "plain" ISO file install option, a live CD provides a fully working Linux environment. You don't actually have to install anything to run Linux if you have an available hard drive on which to store your files (the live CD is unwritable). Installable live CDs include programs you can use to install Linux on your computer.
Netinst	You download a small bootable file, which you store on a USB drive, an optical disc, or even a floppy disk. You boot from that medium, at which point the installation begins. All of the remaining files needed to install Linux on your computer are downloaded from the Internet, typically over an HTTP or FTP connection.
NFS	You connect to a network drive that contains your Linux installation files and load the installer from there. The Network File System (NFS) is a means of file sharing across the network, akin to Windows shares.

Installation files

Most Linux distributions are available for multiple hardware platforms. Additionally, many are available in both 32-bit and 64-bit versions. You must choose the installation file set that matches your hardware.

For most distributions, all Intel-compatible platforms are supported through a single release. This means that you use the same file whether you are running an Intel Pentium or an AMD clone system. You will see such download files identified with abbreviations such as x86, i386, i686, and so forth. The 32-bit and 64-bit versions will typically be identified with a suffix: for example, x86_32 or x86_64.

Sometimes a distribution will take advantage of specific CPU optimizations; thus you will see processor-specific downloads. For example, you might see an AMD-specific version identified by the abbreviation amd64.

Usually, you can run a 32-bit version on a 64-bit CPU. The reverse is not true, however. You will get the best performance and optimized feature set by using the exact version for your platform (use the 64-bit version on a 64-bit platform whenever possible).

Partitioning

Partitions define the type of file system that will be used on your hard drive. They also specify the tables that describe where files are stored on the volume and the size of the various volumes on your computer.

Hard drive file systems

Popular hard drive file systems for Windows computers include NTFS (the Windows NT File System) and FAT32. The older 16-bit FAT (file allocation table) file system is not used on hard drives anymore. The *virtual FAT* (VFAT) system introduced with Windows 95 is still used on some removable media, such as USB drives and camera memory cards. Sun Microsystems also has a file system for its Solaris systems; it's called ZFS, and it's also supported on Mac OS X Server.

Linux cannot use NTFS, FAT32, or FAT/VFAT file systems for its hard disks, and support for ZFS is virtually impossible to find. (Linux can use FAT/VFAT and FAT32 on removable media, though.) Natively, Linux distributions use one or more of the following file systems:

- **ext2** —The "second extended file system" is an older type of Linux file system. It is still supported in the kernel, but it's rarely used on hard drives. It offers benefits for removable media, particularly flash memory–based devices. Such devices have a limited number of rewrite/erase cycles before they fail. Ext2 requires fewer writes than ext3 and some other file systems.

- **ext3** — The "third extended file system" is a journaling file system. It is the primary file system used by many Linux distributions at the time of this writing. In general, journaling file systems log changes before actually writing them to the file system, making them less likely to become corrupted during a system crash.

  The successor, ext4, was released as part of the Linux kernel (version 2.6.28) on December 25, 2008. Ext3 and ext4 support 32-bit and 64-bit namespaces, respectively. This means that ext4 can support volumes of up to 1 exabyte and files of up to 1 terabyte. (An *exabyte* is 1,152,921,504,606,846,976 bytes, or $1024 \times 1024 \times 1024$ gigabytes.)

- **JFS** — This is the IBM Journaling File System. IBM has released its JFS under the GPL and makes versions available for Linux, OS/2, and AIX. Most Linux distributions include support for JFS, though it could be omitted to save space.

  HP-UX, Hewlett-Packard's UNIX, uses a file system also called JFS, but it is not the same JFS as IBM's. According to Wikipedia, it is a licensed version of the Veritas VxFS file system.

- **ReiserFS** — This journaling file system was created by programmer Hans Reiser at Namesys. Once the native file system of SUSE Linux, it is not commonly used in current distributions.

- **XFS** — This journaling file system was created by Silicon Graphics (SGI) for its IRIX operating system. XFS is a high-performance file system with features to support large files. SGI ported the file system to the Linux kernel, which has included XFS support since kernel version 2.4.

Partitioning utilities

Partitioning utilities are the software you use to create and manage partitions and their file systems. Typically, these utilities are built into the installer or are run automatically during installation. You can also download and use some separately. For example, you can use *GParted*, the GNOME Partition Editor, to manage Windows and Linux partitions without actually running Linux.

With GParted, you download an ISO file image, create a CD, and boot with that disc. Your system loads a minimal Linux environment from that disc and opens the GParted utility automatically. You can use GParted to resize Windows partitions before installing Linux or perform other file system management tasks with Windows and Linux volumes.

Once your Linux computer is up and running, you can use GParted or its command-line equivalent, parted (for "partition editor"), to modify your existing partitions. When creating new partitions with parted, you might also need to use the `mkfs` ("make file system") command to create your file system. You can execute this command as part of your `parted` command. For more information on parted, see your system's man pages or visit *www.gnu.org/software/parted/manual/html_mono/parted.html*.

Linux partitions

At a minimum, most Linux distributions require two distinct partitions:

- **The root partition** — Stores the operating system, application, and data files.
- **The swap partition** — Stores virtual memory data, similar to the pagefile.sys file on Windows computers.

You can create additional partitions. For example, you could create a volume for just your data files. Doing so would making backing up your data files a bit easier—you would simply back up that entire volume.

Unless volumes are on distinct hard drives, there is generally no performance advantage to maintaining separate partitions. The primary reason to put root and swap volumes on separate partitions is so that you can use different file systems for each one. Swap data, specifically, does not need or benefit from journaling. There is no value in logging changes for recovery. That's because swap data is dynamic data that will be re-created the next time you boot.

Exhibit 8-6: The initial Debian installation screen

Do it!   ## C-2:   Installing Linux

Here's how	Here's why
1 Insert your Linux installation CD into your CD drive	Use the CD provided by your instructor.
2 Restart your computer	
Press a key to boot from the CD	(If necessary.) For Intel architectures, Debian offers a text or graphical installer, each of which offers the same options and capabilities.
3 Press ⬇ and then ↵ ENTER	To start the graphical installer.
4 Select your language and click **Continue**	
Select your country and click **Continue**	
Select your keyboard layout and click **Continue**	Debian detects your hardware and loads the appropriate components.
Select your primary network interface and click **Continue**	If necessary.
5 In the Hostname box, enter **linserver##**	Where ## is the lab station number assigned by your instructor; for example, linserver01.
Click **Continue**	
Click **Continue**	You're leaving the domain name box empty.
6 Select your time zone and click **Continue**	Debian detects the disk drives in your system.
7 Follow your instructor's directions to select the partitioning method appropriate for the computers in your classroom	For example, select "Guided – use entire disk" and press Enter.
Install all files onto a single partition	Debian partitions your drive and begins installing the base components of the operating system.

8	Enter **p@ssword** into the Root password and Re-enter password boxes, and press (↵ ENTER)	*Root password:* [ ] *Please enter the same root passı Re-enter password to verify:* [ ]
		This is not a strong password but will suffice for classroom use.
9	In the Full name box, enter your full name, and click **Continue**	To begin creating a user-level account for your general use.
	In the username box, enter your first name, and click **Continue**	
	Set **p@ssword** as the password	Debian creates the account. Then it prompts you for the location of the package manager mirror.
10	Select your location and click **Continue**	
	In the archive list, select a mirror near you, and click **Continue**	The mirror is the location from which application files will be loaded. You might be able to tell from the domain name which ones are located nearby.
	Enter the HTTP proxy information as directed by your instructor, and click **Continue**	Debian configures apt, the package manager, to download necessary files from the mirror you specified.
11	Select **No** and click **Continue**	To opt out of participating in the package usage survey.
12	On the Software Selection screen, click **Continue**	☑ Desktop environment ☐ Web server ☐ Print server ☐ DNS server ☐ File server ☐ Mail server ☐ SQL database ☐ Laptop ☑ Standard system
		To install the desktop environment and standard system components. You will install other packages later.
13	Install the GRUB boot loader	When prompted.
14	When the installation is complete, click **Continue**	To restart your computer and load Debian. If you had multiple distributions, you'd be asked to choose one from the boot loader menu.

Exhibit 8-7: The Debian log on screen

Do it!

C-3: Logging on to Debian

Here's how	Here's why
1 Enter your user name	It should be your first name.
Press (← ENTER)	
2 Enter your password	It should be p@ssword.
Press (← ENTER)	You are logged on and the Debian desktop is displayed.
3 Examine the desktop	Like Windows or Macintosh OS X, this Linux graphical user interface uses icons, a menu bar, and a notification area to enable you to interact with your computer.
4 Click **Applications** and then point to each of the submenus in turn	To display the applications menu. The entries on this menu represent the standard set that come with Debian. Other distributions include other default applications. You can install more with Debian as well.
5 Click a blank area of the desktop	To close the menu.
6 Choose **System**, **Log Out**	To log out. You should log out when you're done using your computer. Alternatively, you can lock the screen if you plan to be away for just a short time.

Topic D: Installing Windows Server

This topic covers the following CompTIA Server+ (2009 Edition) exam objectives.

#	Objective
2.1	**Install, deploy, configure, and update the NOS (Windows / *nix)**
	• Installation methods (optical media, USB, network share, PXE)
	• Imaging – system cloning and deployment (Ghost, RIS/WDS, Altiris, virtualization templates)
	• File systems
	– FAT
	– FAT32
	– NTFS
	• Driver installation
	– Driver acquisition
	– Installation methods
	– Required media
	• Configure the NOS
	– Initial network – Roles
	– User – OS environmental settings
	– Device – Applications and tools
	• Patch management
4.4	**Implement and configure different methods of server access**
	• KVM (local and IP based)
	• Direct connect
	• Remote management
	– Remote control
	– Administration
	– Software deployment
	– Dedicated management port

Pre-installation tasks

Explanation

Before you start the actual operating system installation, there are several steps you must take to gather necessary information and make decisions. Pre-installation tasks you should complete include:

- Backing up files, if necessary
- Verifying that hardware requirements are met and checking for hardware compatibility
- Identifying the appropriate partition size and file system
- Choosing an installation method

File backup

Before you perform a clean installation on a server, if there are any data files you want to save, you should back them up to a secure location. When the clean installation is complete, you can restore the data files on the server.

Hardware requirements

Not all servers can run Windows Server 2008 operating systems. You need to match the computer's hardware capabilities with the hardware requirements of the Windows Server 2008 OS you've chosen to install. The following table outlines the minimum hardware configurations for Windows Server 2008.

Component	Minimum
Processor	1 GHz 32-bit and 1.4 GHz 64-bit
Memory	512 MB
Hard disk	20 GB or greater
Graphics	Super VGA
Optical drive	CD-ROM

Not only must your computer's hardware meet the minimum requirements, but it must also be compatible with the version of Windows you're going to install. Most systems today designate which version of Windows they're designed for. If you're adding additional hardware, be sure it has a logo that tells you it's approved for the Windows version you're installing. You can also check the HCL (Hardware Compatibility List) on Microsoft's Web site at *http://www.microsoft.com/whdc/hcl* and select the correct compatibility center.

Partitions and formatting

Before beginning the installation, you must decide which file system you're going to use. Windows Server supports FAT and FAT32 for removable storage, but you'll use NTFS for server installations because of its increased performance and security.

If the hard disk doesn't already have an appropriately formatted partition, you must prepare the hard disk before you can install the operating system. You can use Windows Setup on your installation disc to create, delete, and format partitions on the hard disk. To use Windows Setup, insert the bootable Windows setup disc and start the installation. When prompted, partition the hard disk and format the drive where you plan to install Windows.

Installation methods

Several methods are available for installing Windows, depending on which operating system, if any, is already on the computer. The easiest way to install Windows Server is from the installation disc. When you insert the disc into a computer, Setup runs automatically and a wizard guides you through the steps.

You can also access the Windows installation files from a network share. To start Setup from across the network, locate the network share that contains the installation files and double-click the executable file.

It's important to note that a network installation is not the same as a remote installation using Microsoft's Remote Installation Services or Windows Deployment Services from a Windows server or a third-party deployment application, such as Altiris. These programs use an image of the original cloned computer and copy it over to the installation server, where you can make changes as needed based on the configuration of the installation server.

You can also use disk-imaging software, such as Norton Ghost, to create and deploy operating system images. There are many requirements you have to meet to use disk images, so be sure to investigate and fulfill all requirements before you begin to clone computers and distribute images. The image distribution process includes making a clone or image of a computer that has a version of Windows installed. You can configure this computer with hardware similar to that of the computers on which you install Windows, and you can install common applications that you want to distribute with Windows. After the image is created, it's stored on a network server and used to install Windows on computers across the network.

Servers equipped with compatible *Preboot eXecution Environment (PXE)* hardware can boot to the network directly and obtain DHCP addressing information and information about the network location of an image distribution server. The server will then contact the distribution server and begin to load the image that you've specified for it.

Devices and drivers

Windows Setup loads the default drivers from the Windows installation CD. After the installation is complete, you might discover that certain devices aren't functioning properly. You're probably going to have to install drivers for at least one device, especially for devices that are newer than the operating system you're installing. You should also obtain the latest drivers for any installed hardware or any hardware you plan to install; you can usually get drivers from the hardware manufacturer's Web site. It's a good idea to find updated drivers and have them available to save time.

Although most devices are packaged with drivers, some of the drivers might not be the most up-to-date ones. Most manufacturers offer free downloads of drivers and utilities for their devices. Determine the name of the manufacturer, and visit the appropriate Web site. Look for a link that offers drivers, support, or downloads. Then download the driver, which is often zipped, to a local hard disk, from which you can install it on the appropriate computer.

After you've found an updated device driver, you can install it. If one is provided, use the installation file provided with the device. If you have the device driver file without an installation program, use Device Manager. In Device Manager, choose to update the driver for a device, and then point the wizard to the location of the new driver.

Do it!   **D-1:   Installing Windows Server 2008**

Here's how	Here's why
1 Insert the Windows Server CD into your computer, and press any key to boot from CD when prompted	
2 Select the appropriate language, time and currency format, and keyboard layout	
Click **Next**	
3 Click **Install now**	
4 If prompted, select **Windows Server 2008 Standard (Full Installation)** and click **Next**	
5 Accept the license terms and click **Next**	
6 Select **Custom (advanced)**	
Click **Drive options (advanced)**	
7 Select any existing partitions, click **Delete**, and click **OK**	You're going to create a partition on which to install the operating system.
8 Click **New**	
Create a partition sized according to your instructor's directions, and click **Apply**	
Click **Next**	To continue with the installation wizard.
9 Click **OK**	To change the Administrator user's password.
Enter and confirm a new password of **!pass1234**	
Click **OK**	To acknowledge the password change.
10 If prompted, install the driver	To ensure that all devices are working. Any devices on the HCL should be fully functional or require just the installation of a driver.
11 At the network selection screen, choose Work and click OK	
12 Observe the Initial Configuration Tasks window	You can follow these steps to complete your server installation.

Do it!

D-2: Configuring computer information

Here's how

1 In the Initial Configuration Tasks window, under section 1, click **Set time zone**. Set the appropriate time zone, and correct the time if necessary.

2 Next to Configure networking, verify that you have an IPv4 address assigned by DHCP. If you don't, notify your instructor.

3 Click **Provide computer name and domain**. Click **Change**, and enter a computer name of **WINSRV##**, where ## is your unique number. Restart when prompted, and log back on as Administrator.

4 Open Server Manager, expand Diagnostics, and select **Device Manager**. Install any new or updated drivers necessary to ensure that your devices are working. If necessary, search for drivers on the Internet.

Updating the server

Explanation

Windows Server computers are the most vulnerable immediately after you complete their installation. This is because the computers typically have the original Windows Server files without any of the updates that Microsoft has released since the release of the version you just installed. You might need to install hotfixes, patches, or full updates.

- *Hotfixes* fix errors in the operating system code. These errors are discovered after the operating system has been released. The hotfixes often replace specific files with revised versions.

- *Patches* are temporary or quick fixes. They are designed to fix security vulnerabilities. Patches can also be used to fix compatibility or operating problems.

- *Updates* enhance the operating system and some of its features. In addition, updates are issued to improve computer security, improve ease of use, add functionality, and/or improve the performance of the operating system.

You can install the latest service pack and hotfixes from *download.microsoft.com* or from *update.microsoft.com*. Updates might also be stored locally on an update server on your network—check with your network administrator.

You can use the Windows Update feature to automatically manage patches, hotfixes, and other updates. When configuring Windows Update, you have the following options:

- **Install updates automatically (recommended)** — Configures Windows to automatically download and install updates each day. After you select this option, you can configure a custom schedule for applying updates.

- **Download updates but let me choose whether to install them** — Configures Windows to download the necessary updates. However, Windows does not automatically install them. Instead, you must install them manually. You might select this option if you run a custom application that might conflict with specific Windows updates.

- **Check for updates but let me choose whether to download and install them** — Configures Windows to obtain a list of the latest updates (without downloading them). You must open the list and select the updates you want to install. Windows will then download and install the selected updates. You might choose this strategy if you need to minimize the impact of updates on your network traffic.

- **Never check for updates (not recommended)** — Prevents Windows from checking for updates. You might select this option if you have your own update scheme and update server.

If Windows Update reports that it failed to install an update, you can manually download and install the update directly from Microsoft's Downloads site. The update should refer to a Microsoft Knowledge Base article, such as KB947562. Use this number to find the update on Microsoft's site. If, after installing an update, you start to experience problems with specific devices or software, you might need to back out the update installation by using Programs and Features in the Control Panel.

Do it!

D-3: Configuring Windows Update

Here's how	Here's why
1 In the Initial Configuration Tasks window, under Update This Server, observe the current settings	You can see that updates have not yet been enabled.
2 Click **Enable automatic updating and feedback**	
3 Click **Manually configure settings**	To open the Manually Configure Settings dialog box.
Click **Change Setting**	To open the Windows Update settings in the Control Panel.
4 Select **Check for updates but let me choose whether to download and install them**	
Click **OK**	
Click **Close**	To close the Manually Configure Settings dialog box.
5 Observe the settings	Windows Update will only check for updates; it will not download or install them.
6 How can you remove updates that are causing problems on your server?	

Do it!

D-4: Searching for updates

Here's how	Here's why
1 Click **Download and install updates**	Under Update This Server, in the Initial Configuration Tasks window.
Click **Check for Updates**	
2 Click **Install now**	(If necessary.) To install a new version of Windows Update software. After the Windows Update window closes and re-opens, it will check for updates.
3 Observe the results	Windows Update likely found a significant number of updates for you to install.
4 Click the link for the important updates	To view the updates Microsoft suggests you install. You'll see a list of security updates and other updates.
5 Click **Cancel** and then close the Windows Update window	There are too many updates to install at this time.

Customizing Windows Server

After you've installed the operating system, configured its name and networking settings, and installed any updates, you can customize the server by installing roles and features and configuring Remote Desktop and Windows Firewall.

Server roles

You learned about server roles earlier in this unit, and those same roles are available for installation here. They include directory services (Active Directory domain controller), application servers, DHCP and DNS servers, and Web servers. You can even install Windows Deployment Services to help manage Windows operating system deployment throughout the network. If you want to add a server role later, you can do so in Server Manager.

Features

Features are add-ons that can enhance server functionality. You could run your server without ever adding any of the features, but there might be times you need to support a specific function, such as Telnet or a basic SMTP e-mail server. You can add features at any time in Server Manager.

Remote Desktop

You can use Remote Desktop and the Remote Desktop Protocol (RDP) to connect to remote Windows computers—"remote" meaning a computer that is on another desk, in another building, across a campus, on a different floor in the same building, or almost anywhere in the world. Using Remote Desktop, you can access any program or folder, the Control Panel, network configuration tools, and just about any other feature on the remote computer.

To enable Remote Desktop connections to the Windows Server, click Enable Remote Desktop (under Customize This Server in the Initial Configuration Tasks window). Then select one of the options to allow connection. Not every user can connect remotely with Remote Desktop. By default, computer administrators already have permission, but you can click the Select Users button, select other users, and allow them to make remote connections.

Windows Firewall

Microsoft includes its software firewall, called Windows Firewall, in Windows Server 2008. Windows Firewall is turned on by default. Windows Firewall offers many features, such as allowing incoming network connections based on software or services running on a server, and the ability to block network connections based on the source—the Internet, your local area network, or a specific range of IP addresses. Also, unlike most firewalls, Windows Firewall can be configured to block only incoming network traffic on your computer. All outgoing network traffic is allowed to travel, unrestricted, from your computer to its destination.

When a software firewall like Windows Firewall filters ports, it prevents software on the outside from using certain ports on the network, even though those ports have services listening to them. For example, if you have an intranet Web site, used only by your employees inside the network, you can set your firewall to filter port 80. Those on the intranet can access your Web server using port 80 as normal, but those outside can't reach your Web server.

If a server is having trouble sending or receiving data, it's possible that the current firewall settings are preventing the communication from passing through. You might need to allow a specific type of communication—that's prohibited by default—to pass through the firewall.

When you need to configure Windows Firewall, open the Control Panel. Double-click Windows Firewall and then click Change settings to open the Windows Firewall dialog box. You can turn the firewall on and off, and you can create what are known as *exceptions* to allow or deny specific types of network communication. You can also configure firewall protection for multiple network connections, manage the log file, and configure Internet Control Message Protocol (ICMP) settings.

Do it!

D-5:   Customizing a Windows Server installation

Here's how	Here's why
1 Under Customize This Server, view the roles currently installed	Because this is a new installation, no roles have been added yet.
2 Click **Add Roles** and click **Next**	
Select (but don't check) **Active Directory Domain Servers** and read the description to the right	This is Microsoft's directory services server role.
3 Check **File Services** and click **Next**	You're going to install the file server role.
Read the Introduction to File Services, and click **Next**	
4 On the Select Role Services page, click **Next**	To accept the defaults.
Click **Install**	To complete the installation of the file server role.
Click **Close** and view the roles installed	File Services is now installed. You can manage this service in Server Manager.
5 Click **Add features**	
Select various features and read their descriptions	There's a wide variety of features you can add to enhance the server's function.
6 Install the Remote Assistance feature	Check the feature's box and complete the Add Features Wizard.
In the Initial Configuration Tasks window, view the installed feature	Remember, you can add and remove features and roles in Server Manager.

7	Click **Enable Remote Desktop** and view the dialog box	In the Remote Desktop box, you can allow remote connections to this server. You can click Select Users to allow non-Administrator users to access the server remotely.
	Click **Cancel**	
8	Click **Configure Windows Firewall** and view the firewall status	The firewall is enabled.
	Click **Change settings**	To view the status of the firewall and access options to disable and configure it.
9	Click the **Exceptions** tab	You can create exceptions to allow specific types of communication through the firewall. You can allow exceptions for the listed programs and services, or you can create your own by using the buttons at the bottom of the page.
	Click **Cancel** and close the Windows Firewall window	
10	At the bottom of the Initial Configuration Tasks window, select **Do not show this window at logon**	To prevent the window from opening when you log on.
	Click **Close**	
11	In Server Manager, under Security Information, click **Configure IE ESC**	"Internet Explorer Enhanced Security Configuration is enabled by default. It increases the security of your server's Web browser, but for this course you will leave it disabled.
	Select **No** under both Administrators and Users, and click **OK**	
12	Close any open windows	

Malware

Explanation

Viruses are one of the biggest threats to network security. Network administrators need to keep a constant lookout for them and prevent their spread. They are designed to replicate themselves and infect computers when triggered by a specific event. The effect of some viruses is minimal and only an inconvenience, but others are more destructive and cause major problems, such as deleting files or slowing down entire systems.

Worms

Worms are programs that replicate themselves over the network, without user intervention. A worm attaches itself to a file or a packet on the network and travels of its own accord. It can copy itself to multiple computers, bringing the entire network down. One method worms use to spread themselves is to send themselves to everyone in a user's e-mail address book. The intent of a worm infiltration is to cause a malicious attack. Such an attack often uses up computer resources to the point that the system, or even the entire network, can no longer function or is shut down.

Trojan horses

Trojan horses are delivery vehicles for destructive code. They appear to be harmless programs but are enemies in disguise. They can delete data, mail copies of themselves to e-mail address lists, and open up other computers for attack. Trojan horses are often distributed via spam—a great reason to block spam—or through a compromised Web site.

A *logic bomb* is code that is hidden within a program and designed to run when some condition is met. For example, the code might run on a particular date, or the bomb's author might set some sort of condition that would be met after he or she is fired, at which time the code would run. Because a logic bomb is contained within another, presumably useful, program, you can consider it a type of Trojan horse.

Zombies and botnets

The goal of malware is often to turn compromised systems into *"zombies*, sometimes called *bots*. At a signal from the malware author, these zombies are made to attack some computer or group of computers. For example, in a distributed denial-of-service (DDoS) attack, a collection of zombies overwhelms a system with bogus requests. A collection of zombies is sometimes called a *botnet*, although that term is also used to describe collections of uninfected computers working together to perform a distributed computing task.

Rootkits

A *rootkit* is software that grants full system control to the user. The term comes from the UNIX/Linux environment, where the highest level of system administrator is the user called "root." Viruses, worms, and other types of malware sometimes act as rootkits, granting the malware author full access to the compromised system.

Rootkits are a specific example of a type of program that seeks privilege escalation. Many forms of malware seek to gain higher privileges in order to modify user or system files. Users themselves attempt a privilege escalation attack when they try to log on with someone else's account.

Antivirus software

To stop viruses and worms, you should install antivirus software on individual servers. Most antivirus software runs a *real-time antivirus scanner*, which is software that's designed to scan every file accessed on a computer so it can catch viruses and worms before they can infect a computer. This software runs each time a computer is turned on.

Definition files

Antivirus software must be updated to keep up with new viruses and worms. The software can find only threats that it knows to look for; therefore, the antivirus software manufacturer constantly provides software updates, called *virus definitions*, as new viruses and worms are discovered. It's important to use antivirus software that automatically checks and updates its virus definitions from the manufacturer's Web site. Having outdated virus definitions is the number-one cause of virus or worm infection.

Antivirus products

The following table lists several antivirus software products and their manufacturers' Web sites. Most of these sites offer detailed information about common viruses and worms. They even offer removal tools you can download for free and use to remove worms and viruses from infected computers.

Software	Web site
Norton AntiVirus by Symantec, Inc.	www.symantec.com
ESET Smart Security	www.eset.com
McAfee VirusScan by McAfee Associates, Inc.	www.mcafee.com
ESafe by Aladdin Knowledge Systems, Ltd	www.esafe.com
F-Prot by FRISK Software International	www.f-prot.com
PC-cillin by Trend Micro (for home use); NeaTSuite by Trend Micro (for networks)	www.trendmicro.com
avast! by ALWIL Software	www.avast.com

One of the best ways to protect your computers against viruses and worms is to stay informed. Web sites like *www.datafellows.com* and *www.symantec.com* provide descriptions of the latest threats.

E-mail servers should also have antivirus software installed to protect computers on your local area network. Microsoft Forefront is an example of network antivirus software that scans all inbound and outbound e-mail, filters e-mail based on attachment type, and blocks spam.

Spyware

Spyware is software that gets installed on your system without your knowledge. It can cause a lot of problems for the user, including gathering personal or other sensitive information. Spyware can also change the computer's configuration. For example, it might change the home page in your browser. In addition, it often displays advertisements, earning this type of spyware the name *adware*.

All of this can slow down your computer's performance, and the pop-ups can occur so frequently that you can't really do any work. Spyware is often installed when you are installing another application, especially free applications that you download from the Internet. For this reason, you need to be sure that you know exactly what you are installing. Sometimes the license agreement and privacy statement state that the spyware will be installed, but most people tend not to read those documents very closely. Spyware is often found on peer-to-peer and file-sharing networks. Spyware can also integrate itself into Internet Explorer, causing frequent browser crashes.

Windows Server includes anti-spyware software called Windows Defender. This real-time protection software alerts you when it detects spyware. You can also schedule it to perform scans. When Windows Defender detects spyware on your computer, it displays information about the threat, including the location on your computer, a rating of the risk it poses to you and your information, and its recommendation as to what action you should take.

Do it!   ### D-6:   Discussing anti-malware software

Questions	Answers
1 Explain the purpose of antivirus software	
2 Compare and contrast Trojan horses and logic bombs	
3 Is every program that attempts privilege escalation a rootkit?	
4 What does it mean to say your system is part of a botnet?	
5 Explain the purpose of antispyware software	
6 Are all examples of spyware also adware?	

Server connections

Explanation

There are multiple ways to connect to a server after you've installed it and put it into service on the network.

- You can access the server directly by sitting down at the server console, logging on, and using a keyboard, mouse, and monitor. This is the easiest method, but it might not always be available, especially if you have multiple servers or the servers aren't easily accessible from your current location.

- A keyboard, video, and mouse (KVM) switch can be used to access multiple servers. The switch is a box or small unit to which the servers are connected through USB or other cabling. You can use buttons on the box or keyboard commands to switch from one server to another, each time gaining keyboard, mouse, and video capability from the server you've switched to, while losing the same from the server you were just working on.

  KVM is also available over an IP network. You can make the connection via just about any computer through a browser window or proprietary software.

- You can connect to servers from a remote location by using remote control software and a network connection. Software includes the built-in Microsoft Remote Desktop, Symantec pcAnywhere, Timbuktu, and TightVNC. To make a remote connection, you need to deploy software on the server to accept the connection and allow remote management, and you need to deploy software on the computer from which you're making the connection, typically a desktop client. In addition, the server often has a dedicated port that accepts incoming connections for remote management. From the remote location, you can do anything you could if you were sitting at the server console.

Do it!

D-7: Implementing server access methods

Here's how
1 Shut down your computer. Follow your instructor's directions to disconnect the mouse, keyboard, and monitor connections.
2 Obtain a KVM switch from your instructor and follow the instructions to connect the appropriate cables on your server. Then connect the cables to the KVM switch.
3 Power up the servers and use the KVM switch to display Server Manager on both servers.
4 Shut down and remove the KVM switch cables. Return the KVM switch to your instructor.
5 Open Server Manager. Select the Server Manager console root. In the details pane, click **Configure Remote Desktop**. Configure the service to allow connections from computers running any version of Remote Desktop.
6 Observe your instructor use the Remote Desktop Connection client to connect to servers in the classroom. When the connections are complete, close all open windows.

Unit summary: Installing a network operating system

Topic D   In this topic, you learned about basic **networking models**, including peer-to-peer and client/server networking. You also learned about **server roles**, such as the directory service, DNS, file/print, and NTP roles. You also learned how the servers interact on the network and which services they provide.

Topic E   In this topic, you learned that **server virtualization** enables you to implement the functionality of multiple servers via software running on one **physical host**. You also learned that server virtualization can be **environmentally friendly** because of power, cooling, and disposal reductions, and it can be **budget-friendly** thanks to reduced procurement and licensing costs. You also learned that virtualization has **downsides**, such as heightened security concerns, up-time concerns, and increased complexity.

Topic F   In this topic, you learned how to install **Linux**. You learned about the pre-installation tasks, installation methods, and file systems. Then you installed Linux and signed on to the server.

Topic G   In this topic, you learned how to install **Windows Server 2008**. You learned about the pre-installation tasks, installation methods, and file systems. Then you installed Windows Server 2008 and logged onto the server to perform post-installation tasks, such as updating device drivers and installing **operating system updates**. You also learned about **antivirus** and **antispyware** software, and you learned about different methods of **server access**.

Review questions

1 Which of the following server roles manages network access through user names and passwords?

A DNS

B DHCP

C Directory service

D NTP

2 Which server role is used to ensure that clocks are synchronized across the network?

A DNS

B DHCP

C Directory service

D NTP

3 The physical computer running one or more virtual computers is called a(n)

host

4 Define "hypervisor."

virtual connection

5 What is a bare metal hypervisor?

on the server

6 What is a host-based hypervisor?

hyper-v on the server *user pc*

7 What is the VMWare product that enables on-demand labs?

8 Microsoft's Hyper-V requires you to install Windows Server 2008 into the _____ partition.

system

9 To provide local storage, the hypervisor simulates disk storage within what?

virtual environment

10 True or false? You can use a NAS device in place of local storage for a server.

true

11 True or false? You can use a SAN in place of local storage for a server.

true false

12 What is the Linux kernel?

bare bones linux

13 Name at least three Linux distributions in common use.

ISO, disk, internet

14 True or false? Installing Linux always begins with burning an ISO image to disc.

false

15 What is the practical result of this statement? Ext3 volumes use 32-bit namespaces, and ext4 volumes use 64-bit namespaces.

64bit is more secure

16 What is the benefit of creating separate root and swap partitions on the same physical drive?

redundancy

17 How does antivirus software recognize new viruses and worms?

updated definitions

18 What is the Windows Server built-in spyware protection function called?

window defender

19 What is a program that poses as something else, causing the user to "willingly" inflict the attack on himself or herself?

trojan

20 Which of the following are typically designed to fix security vulnerabilities?

    A Hotfixes

    B Patches

    C Updates

    D BIOS updates

Independent practice activity

In this activity, you will update Windows Server 2008 and perform remote management.

1 Use Windows Update to download and install all important updates. Restart your server when prompted.

2 Connect to another student's server by using the Remote Desktop Connection client. Open Windows Update to verify that all important updates have been installed.

Unit 9

Networking

Unit time: 120 minutes

Complete this unit, and you'll know how to:

A Compare wired network connections. Describe how various types of addresses are used to identify devices on a network.

B Select and use the appropriate TCP/IP utility to test network connectivity issues.

C Troubleshoot network and resource problems.

Topic A: Networking essentials

This topic covers the following CompTIA Server+ (2009 Edition) exam objective.

#	Objective
2.6	**Describe common elements of networking essentials** • TCP/IP – Subnetting – Gateways – DNS – Static vs. dynamic – DHCP – IP stack – Classes – Ports • Ethernet – Types – Speeds – Cables • VPN • VLAN • DMZ

Network wiring

Explanation

The computers in the network need a pathway to connect to each other. This pathway can be a physical connection, using cabling. The connection can also be made through radio waves, infrared light, or other wireless methods.

Twisted-pair cable

Many networks use *unshielded twisted-pair (UTP)* or *shielded twisted-pair (STP)* cabling to connect the nodes in the network. Both types of cable are composed of four pairs of wires. The wires in each pair are twisted around each other, and the pairs are twisted together and bundled within a covering, as shown in Exhibit 9-1. The two wires (two halves of a single circuit) are wound together to cancel out electromagnetic interference (EMI) from external sources. The shielding for STP can be either foil or braided wire.

Exhibit 9-1: UTP cable

UTP cable comes in categories. Each category has a specific use, number of twists per foot, and speed. The more twists there are, the less crosstalk and EMI will affect the data on the cable. All twisted-pair cabling has a maximum run length of approximately 100 meters.

- **Cat3** — For networking, Cat3 cable used to be acceptable. However, Cat3 operates at up to only 10 Mbps with about two or three twists per foot.

- **Cat5/5e** — Most networks now use at least Cat5 cable, which operates at up to 100 Mbps, or Cat5e, which operates at up to 1 Gbps (gigabits per second). Cat5 and Cat5e cables have 20 twists per foot.

- **Cat6/6a** — Cat6 cables use higher-quality materials and can operate at up to 2.5 Gbps. The number of twists in Cat6 cable can vary. There is also a Cat6a cable that provides performance of up to 10 Gbps.

- **Cat7** — Cat7 is an emerging standard that will support 10 Gbps transmissions and higher. Research suggests that Cat7a, an amendment to the Cat7 specification, will support 100 Gbps transmissions.

Twisted-pair connectors

UTP cabling uses four types of connectors: RJ-11, RJ-14, RJ-25, and RJ-45. The "RJ" in the jack's designation simply means "registered jack," and the number refers to the specific wiring pattern used for jacks and connectors. You'll find RJ-11, RJ-14, and RJ-25 connectors used for telephone and dial-up modem connections. Twisted-pair network cables use RJ-45 connectors, which look a lot like the other RJ snap-in connectors except that they're larger. Exhibit 9-2 shows RJ-45 and RJ-11 connectors.

Exhibit 9-2: RJ-45 connector, left, and RJ-11 connector, right

The RJ-45 connector attaches to eight wires, as opposed to the four or six in the RJ-11. The jacks, with which the two types of connectors mate, have corresponding conductor counts and are different sizes. An RJ-45 connector won't fit into an RJ-11 jack.

The EIA/TIA-568-A standard defines two wiring patterns for Ethernet cabling: T568A and T568B. These standards specify the pattern in which the color-coded wires in a twisted-pair cable are connected to the pins of the RJ-45 connector or the jack. The T568A standard is preferred for residential applications, and T568B, for commercial applications. Both, however, are electrically identical as long as you use the same color pattern to connect both ends of a given cable. If you're consistent in this, pin 1 at one end of the cable is always connected to pin 1 at the other end, and pin 2 on one end is connected to pin 2 on the other end, and so on, regardless of which of the two color patterns you use.

If you hold an RJ-45 connector in your hand with the tab side down and the cable opening toward you, the pins are numbered, from left to right, 1 through 8, as shown in Exhibit 9-3. The pin numbers connect to the following colored wires in the cable for T568A or T568B.

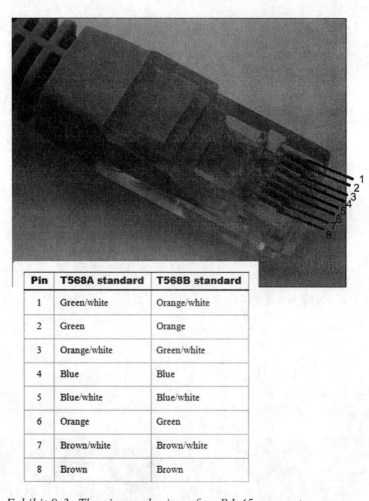

Pin	T568A standard	T568B standard
1	Green/white	Orange/white
2	Green	Orange
3	Orange/white	Green/white
4	Blue	Blue
5	Blue/white	Blue/white
6	Orange	Green
7	Brown/white	Brown/white
8	Brown	Brown

Exhibit 9-3: The pin numbering of an RJ-45 connector

Do it!

A-1: Examining twisted-pair cables and connectors

Here's how	Here's why
1 Locate a segment of twisted-pair cabling	
2 Verify that it has an RJ-45 connector	RJ-45 has eight wires, whereas RJ-11 has only six.
3 If the connector is clear, examine the color of each wire to the pins	
What T568 standard is being used?	

Fiber optic cable

Explanation

Fiber optic cabling, which carries light-based data through strands of glass or plastic no thicker than a human hair, is currently the fastest and most expensive network transmission medium. Fiber optic cables are composed of a glass or plastic strand through which light is transmitted. This core is clad in a glass tube designed to reflect the light back into the core, as the light bounces while moving through the fiber core. An outer insulating, rubberized jacket covers the entire cable to protect it. A single-strand fiber optic cable is shown in Exhibit 9-4.

Exhibit 9-4: A single-strand fiber optic cable

There are two types of fiber optic cable: single-mode fiber (SMF) and multi-mode fiber (MMF).

- *Single-mode* optic fibers support only a single transmission path. They are used for most communication links longer than 300 meters.

- *Multi-mode* optic fibers support many transmission (propagation) paths. Multi-mode optic fibers generally have a large-diameter core and are used for short-distances, typically less than 300 meters.

Fiber optic cable is used by the telephone and cable companies to deliver information across long distances. Fiber optic cabling is also used as the backbone for networks. For end-users to use fiber optic cabling, they must purchase conversion equipment that changes electrical impulses into photons. At present, this equipment is expensive, but as the technology matures, the price is certain to decline, making widespread use of fiber optics more likely in the future.

Coaxial cable

Coax cables contain a layer of braided wire or foil between the core and the outside insulating layer. The shielding provided by this layer helps protect the data from EMI problems. Another layer of plastic or rubberized material separates the central core from the shielding layer, because if these two layers touch, the data signal will be damaged or lost. The type of coax cable used for Ethernet networking is marked *RG-58*, as shown in Exhibit 9-5. It's important that you don't mistake RG-59 cable for RG-58.

RG-59 coaxial cable is used for low-power video and RF signal connections. You'll find these cables shipped with consumer electronic equipment, such as VCRs or digital cable and satellite receivers. In recent years, RG-6 cables have become the standard for cable TV, replacing the smaller RG-59. RG-6 cables are most commonly used to deliver cable television signals to homes, and they aren't suitable for networking.

Exhibit 9-5: Thin Ethernet, or Thinnet, cable

Thicknet cables are *RG-8* or *RG-11* cables. RG-8 cables, shown in Exhibit 9-6, are 50-ohm stranded core cables, and RG-11 cables are 75-ohm solid-core cables with dual shielding (foil and braided wires). Neither RG-8 nor RG-11 bends easily, because both are 10 mm in diameter (four-tenths of an inch). These cables can carry signals up to about 500 meters, so they're typically used for Ethernet network backbones rather than for drops to network nodes.

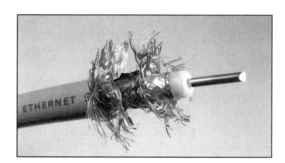

Exhibit 9-6: Thick Ethernet, or Thicknet, cable

Thin Ethernet designs, wired with RG58/U coaxial cable, are limited by the attenuation of signals in the cable and can support network segments up to only 185 meters long. (*Attenuation* is a weakening of signal strength due to distance traveled.) Thick Ethernet designs, wired with 50-ohm RG8/U coaxial, are more resistant to attenuation and can span up to 500 meters. Neither of these is being widely used now, because more advanced cable types can span distances up to 1000 meters with less attenuation of network signals.

Duplex data transmission

Data transmission can be simplex, half-duplex, or full-duplex. In simplex, data is transmitted in only a single direction. In half-duplex, data is transmitted across the medium in both directions, but in only one direction at a time. In full-duplex, data can be transmitted across the medium in both directions at the same time. Network transmissions can be half-duplex or full-duplex, but the majority are half-duplex.

Do it!

A-2: Identifying cable types

Here's how	Here's why
1 Examine the cable used to connect your computer to the network	
Identify its type	Cable type: _____
2 Record the backbone cabling used	Your instructor will describe the backbone cable used to connect network segments. _____

Ethernet

Explanation

Ethernet is the most popular form of LAN in use today. It's popular because it strikes a good balance between ease of setup and use, speed, and cost. Four types of Ethernet architecture are available now. Each type is distinguished primarily by the speed at which it operates.

- **10 Gigabit Ethernet** (also called **10GbE**) — Is the fastest of the Ethernet standards. With a data rate of 10 Gbps (gigabits per second), it is 10 times faster than Gigabit Ethernet.

- **1000-Mbps Ethernet** (or **Gigabit Ethernet**) — Operates at a speed of 1000 Mbps (1000 megabits per second = 1 gigabit per second). It's used for large, high-speed LANs and heavy-traffic server connections. Few, if any, home networks require Gigabit Ethernet.

- **100-Mbps Ethernet** (or **Fast Ethernet**) — Operates at a speed of 100 Mbps. It can also handle data at 10 Mbps, and this feature allows devices running at the slower speed to operate on the same network as devices operating at 100 Mbps.

- **10-Mbps Ethernet** (or **Twisted-Pair Ethernet**) — Operates at a speed of 10 Mbps. The first Ethernet version was developed by the Xerox Corporation in the 1970s and later became known as Ethernet IEEE 802.3.

Each Ethernet version can be set up with various types of wire or cable. However, the different speeds of the versions and the conditions in which they operate usually dictate what type of connecting wires you need to use. Designations for the different Ethernet standards are based on the medium each standard uses:

- **BASE-X** and **BASE-R** standards — Run over fiber optic cable.

- **BASE-W** standards — Run over fiber optic cables; referred to as *Wide Area Network Physical Layer (WAN PHY)*. BASE-W standards use the same types of fiber and support the same distances as 10GBASE-R standards; however, with BASE-W, Ethernet frames are encapsulated in SONET frames.

- **BASE-T** standards — Run over twisted-pair cable, either shielded or unshielded.

- **BASE-CX** standards — Run over shielded copper twisted-pair cable.

Most current Ethernet installations use shielded twisted-pair (STP), unshielded twisted-pair (UTP), or fiber optic cable. Older Ethernet installations used either 50-ohm RG58/U coaxial cable (also known as thin Ethernet or 10Base2) or 50-ohm RG8/U coaxial (known as thick Ethernet or 10Base5). However, these are both obsolete now.

10 Gigabit Ethernet standards

The following table lists the 10 Gigabit Ethernet standards and their specifications.

Standard	Medium	Distance: up to	Notes
10GBASE-T	Copper twisted-pair, shielded or unshielded	100 meters with CAT6a; up to 55 meters with CAT6	
10GBASE-SR, 10GBASE-SW	Multi-mode fiber	26 or 82 meters, depending on cable type 300 meters over 50 microns at 2000 MHz per km with OM3 multi-mode fiber	Preferred choice for optical cabling within buildings.
10GBASE-LR, 10GBASE-LW	Single-mode fiber	10 km	Used to connect transceivers.
10GBASE-ER, 10GBASE-EW	Single-mode fiber	40 km	
10GBASE-ZR, 10GBASE-ZW	Single-mode fiber	80 km	Not specified in standards; built to Cisco optical specifications.

Gigabit Ethernet standards

The following table lists the Gigabit Ethernet standards and their specifications.

Standard	Medium	Distance	Notes
1000BASE-T	Unshielded twisted-pair: CAT5, CAT5e, or CAT6	100 meters per network segment	Requires all four wire pairs.
1000BASE-CX	Balanced copper shielded twisted-pair	25 meters	An initial standard for Gigabit Ethernet connections.
1000BASE-LX	Single-mode optic fiber	5 km*	See paragraphs following this table.
1000BASE-LX10	Single-mode optic fiber	10 km	Wavelength of 1270 to 1355 nm.
1000BASE-BX10	Single-mode fiber, over single-strand fiber	10 km	Different wavelength going in each direction: 1490 nm downstream, 1310 nm upstream.
1000BASE-LH	Single-mode optic fiber	10km	Wavelength of 1300 or 1310nm. Non-standard implementation. Similar to 1000BASE-LX, but achieves longer distances due to better optics. 1000BASE-LH is backward-compatible with 1000BASE-LX.
1000BASE-ZX	Single-mode optic fiber	70 km	1550 nm wavelength. Non-standard implementation.

Standard	Medium	Distance	Notes
1000BASE-SX	Multi-mode optic fiber	500 meters	

* The 1000BASE-LX standard specifies transmission over a single-mode optic fiber, at distances of up to 5 km over 9 μm (micron or micrometer). In practice, it often operates correctly over a much greater distance. Many manufacturers guarantee operation at 10 to 20 km, provided that their equipment is used at both ends of the link.

1000BASE-LX can also run over multi-mode fiber with a maximum segment length of 550 meters. Link distances greater than 300 meters might require a special launch conditioning patch cord, which launches the laser at a precise offset from the center of the fiber. This spreads the laser across the diameter of the fiber core, reducing differential mode delay. *Differential mode delay* occurs when the laser couples onto a limited number of available modes in the multi-mode fiber.

Fast Ethernet standards

Standard	Medium	Distance	Notes
100BASE-TX	Twisted-pair copper: CAT5 or above	100 meters per network segment	Runs over two pairs: one pair of twisted wires in each direction. The most common Fast Ethernet.
100BASE-T4	Twisted-pair copper: CAT3		Requires four pairs: one pair for transmitting; one for receiving; and remaining pairs switch direction as negotiated. An early implementation of Fast Ethernet.
100BASE-T2	Twisted-pair copper		Runs over two pairs.
100BASE-FX	Singe- or multi-mode fiber	400 meters for half-duplex 2 km for full-duplex over MMF	Uses two strands: one for receiving and one for transmitting. Not compatible with 10BASE-FL.
100BASE-SX	Multi-mode fiber	300 meters	Uses two strands of MMF: one for receiving and one for transmitting. Backward-compatible with 10BASE-FL.
100BASE-BX	Single-mode fiber	20 km	Uses a single strand of SMF.

Do it!

A-3: Describing Ethernet standards

Questions	Answers
1 Which is the fastest Ethernet standard?	
2 Which Ethernet standards run over fiber optic cables?	
3 What type of cabling do most current Ethernet networks use?	
4 Which 10 Gigabit Ethernet standard can be run the longest distance?	
5 What type of cabling would you use for a 1000BASE-T Ethernet network?	
6 What's the difference between 100BASE-TX and 1000BASE-T cabling?	

The Internet Protocol suite

Explanation

Most networks use the Internet Protocol suite for network communications. It is commonly referred to as "TCP/IP" because these are the two best known protocols in the suite (TCP and IP).

TCP

The Transmission Control Protocol (TCP) provides connection-oriented, acknowledged communication. It provides guaranteed delivery, performs data integrity checks, and ensures the proper sequence of packets. If an error occurs during transmission, TCP ensures that the sender resends the data. This is a Transport-layer protocol in the OSI reference model.

IP

Internet Protocol (IP) is a routable, unreliable, connectionless protocol. Its sole function is the addressing and routing of packets. IP doesn't verify that data reaches its destination. It relies on other protocols to ensure proper data sequence and data integrity. This is a Network-layer protocol in the OSI reference model.

UDP

The User Datagram Protocol (UDP) is used for connectionless, unacknowledged communication. It uses IP as the protocol carrier, and then UDP adds source and destination socket information to the transmission. UDP is also a Transport-layer protocol and is used by applications as an alternative to TCP. TCP has a lot of overhead due to the acknowledgement packets. Applications use UDP when they don't need guaranteed delivery. For example, DNS uses UDP instead of TCP.

DNS

Domain Name System (DNS) is a protocol that provides common naming conventions across the Internet. This distributed database supports a hierarchical naming system.

NFS

Network File System (NFS) is the standard distributed file system for UNIX- and Linux-based environments. NFS allows users to share files on both similar and dissimilar hardware platforms.

ICMP

The Internet Control Message Protocol (ICMP) controls and manages information sent using TCP/IP. ICMP enables nodes to share error and status information. The ICMP information is passed on to upper-level protocols to let the transmitting node know of hosts that can be reached and to provide information that can be used to figure out and resolve the cause of the transmission problem. ICMP also handles the rerouting of messages to get around failed or busy routes. The ping command uses ICMP.

ARP and RARP

The maintenance protocols Address Resolution Protocol (ARP) and Reverse Address Resolution Protocol (RARP) translate between IP addresses and MAC addresses. ARP is used to request a MAC address when the IP address of a node is known. The information is stored in cache for use later on.

Additional protocols

Some of the other protocols in the IP suite are covered in the following table.

Protocol	Description
Telnet	The Telnet utility enables a host to connect to and run a session on another host through remote terminal emulation. It uses TCP for acknowledgement.
HTTP, HTTPS, SHTTP	Hypertext Transfer Protocol is the standard for transferring data been Web servers and Web browsers. HTTPS uses SSL (Secure Sockets Layer) to encrypt TCP/IP communications. Files exchanged via Secure HTTP are either encrypted or contain a digital certificate, or both.
FTP, SFTP, TFTP	File Transfer Protocol is used to support unencrypted file transfer between similar or dissimilar systems. Secure FTP is used for secure, encrypted file transfers. (Secure FTP is officially FTP over SSH.) Trivial FTP uses UDP for less overhead and thus is faster than FTP. However, TFTP is less reliable than FTP, is less secure than FTP, and doesn't enable you to list the contents of a directory.
SNMP	Simple Network Management Protocol uses UDP to collect management statistics and trap error-event information between TCP/IP hosts. SNMP enables remote device control and management of parameters.
SMTP	Simple Mail Transfer Protocol enables the transfer of mail between Internet users. SMTP manages outgoing mail.
POP3	Post Office Protocol version 3 receives and holds e-mail at the Internet mail server. POP3 manages incoming mail.
IMAP4	Internet Mail Access Protocol version 4 enables users to store, read, and organize messages on the e-mail server from any computer. It supports authentication.
SSH and SCP	Secure Shell (SSH) enables users to securely access a remote computer. All passwords and data are encrypted. A digital certificate is used for authentication. Secure Copy (SCP) uses SSH for data encryption and authentication when copying data between computers.
NTP	Network Time Protocol synchronizes networked computers' clocks.

Do it!

A-4:   Examining protocols in the TCP/IP suite

Questions and answers

1 Which protocol provides connection-oriented, acknowledged communications? Which protocols provide connectionless, unacknowledged communications?

2 Which protocols are used for e-mail, and what are their purposes?

3 Compare ARP and RARP.

4 Why would you use SSH?

Identifying addresses

Every device on a network must have a unique address. Many times, you'll find that a device has more than one of the following types of unique addresses:

- **Media Access Control (MAC) address** — A unique address permanently embedded in a NIC by the manufacturer. It identifies devices on a LAN. A MAC address is a unique value expressed as six pairs of hexadecimal numbers, often separated by hyphens or colons. (Hexadecimal numbers use a base of 16 rather than 10, and consist of a combination of numerals and letters.) Part of the MAC address contains the manufacturer identifier, and the rest is a unique number.

  No two NICs have the same identifying code. The MAC address is used only by devices inside the LAN and isn't used outside the LAN. MAC addresses are also referred to as "physical" or "adapter addresses" or "Ethernet addresses."

- **IPv4 address** — A 32-bit address consisting of a series of four 8-bit numbers separated by periods. An IP address identifies a computer, printer, or other device on a TCP/IP network, such as the Internet or an intranet. The largest possible 8-bit number is 255, so each of the four numbers can be no larger than 255. An example of an IP address is 109.168.0.104. Think of a MAC address as a local address, and an IP address as a long-distance address.

- **IPv6 address** — A 128-bit address, which can support a much bigger pool of available addresses than IPv4 can. IPv6 addresses are written in the hexadecimal-equivalent values for each of the 16 bytes.

- **Character-based names** — Domain names, host names, and NetBIOS names used to identify a computer on a network, using easy-to-remember letters rather than numbers.

- **Port address** — A number between 0 and 65,535 that identifies a program running on a computer.

MAC addresses

MAC addresses function at the lowest networking level. If a host doesn't know the MAC address of another host on a LAN, it uses the operating system to discover the MAC address. Computers on different networks, however, can't use their MAC addresses to enable communication because the hardware protocol (for example, Ethernet) controls traffic on only its own network. For the host to communicate with a host on another LAN across the corporate intranet or Internet, it must know the IPv4 or IPv6 address of the host.

There are three important things to remember about MAC addresses:

- Unlike other addresses, MAC addresses are absolute. A MAC address on a host normally doesn't change as long as the NIC doesn't change.

- All hosts on a local area network must communicate by their MAC addresses, which are managed by the Data Link–layer protocol that controls the network.

- MAC addresses alone can't be used to communicate between two computers on different LANs.

IPv4 addresses

Version 4 of the Internet Protocol (IPv4) has been the standard since September of 1981. This is the protocol that all Internet traffic was based on until recently.

Every piece of information stored in a computer can be broken down into a series of on/off conditions called *bits*. This type of information is called "binary" data because each element has only two possible values: 1 (on) and 0 (off). In the binary system, a byte (or octet) is a string of eight bits. An IPv4 address is made up of 32 bits of information. These 32 bits are divided into four octets.

There are two main methods of depicting an IP address:

- **Binary IP addresses** — What the computer reads. A binary IP address has the following format: 11001010 00101101 11100001 00001111.
- **Dotted-decimal IP addresses** — Widely used to show IPv4 addresses. A dotted-decimal IP address has the following format: 208.206.88.56.

You write IP addresses in dotted-decimal notation. With IPv4 32-bit IP addresses, you can uniquely identify up to 2^{32} addresses, for a total of 4.3 billion potential IP addresses ($256 \times 256 \times 256 \times 256$). However, some of those addresses are unavailable for general use. The largest possible 8-bit number is, in binary form, 11111111, which is equal to 255 in decimal notation. Therefore, the largest possible decimal IP address is 255.255.255.255. In binary notation, it's 11111111.11111111.11111111.11111111.

All IP addresses are composed of two parts: the network ID and the host ID. The *network ID* represents the network on which the computer is located; the *host ID* represents a single computer on that network. No two computers on the same network can have the same host ID; however, two computers on different networks can have the same host ID.

The first part of an IP address identifies the network, and the last part identifies the host. When data is routed over interconnected networks, the network portion of the IP address is used to locate the right network. After the data arrives at the LAN, the host portion of the IP address identifies the one computer on the network that's to receive the data. Finally, the IP address of the host must be used to identify its MAC address so the data can travel on the host's LAN to that host.

IPv4 classes

The Internet Assigned Numbers Authority (IANA) implemented classful IPv4 addresses in order to differentiate between the portion of the IP address that identifies a particular network and the portion that identifies a specific host on that network. These classes of IP addresses are shown in the following table.

Class	Addresses	Description
A	1.0.0.0 – 126.0.0.0	First octet: network ID. Last three octets: host ID. Default subnet mask: 255.0.0.0.
B	128.0.0.0 – 191.255.0.0	First two octets: network ID. Last two octets: host ID. Default subnet mask: 255.255.0.0.
C	192.0.0.0 – 223.255.255.0	First three octets: network ID. Last octet: host ID. Default subnet mask: 255.255.255.0.
D	224.0.0.0 – 239.0.0.0	Multicasting addresses.
E	240.0.0.0 – 255.0.0.0	Experimental use.

When a business, college, or other organization applies for an IP address, a range of addresses appropriate to the number of hosts on the organization's networks is assigned. IP addresses that can be used by companies and individuals are divided into three classes: Class A, Class B, and Class C. Each class is based on the number of possible IP addresses in each network within the class, as shown in Exhibit 9-7. The group of IP addresses assigned to an organization is unique among all other IP addresses on the Internet and is available for use on the Internet. The IP addresses available to the Internet are called *public IP addresses*.

The following table describes the three classes of IP addresses.

Class	Network octets	Possible number of networks	Host octets	Possible number of addresses in network
A	1.___.___.___ to 126.___.___.___	127	___.0.0.1 to ___.255.255.254	16 million
B	128.0.___.___ to 191.255.___.___	16,000	___.___.0.1 to ___.___.255.254	65,000
C	192.0.0.___ to 223.255.255.___	2,000,000	___.___.___.1 to ___.___.___.254	254

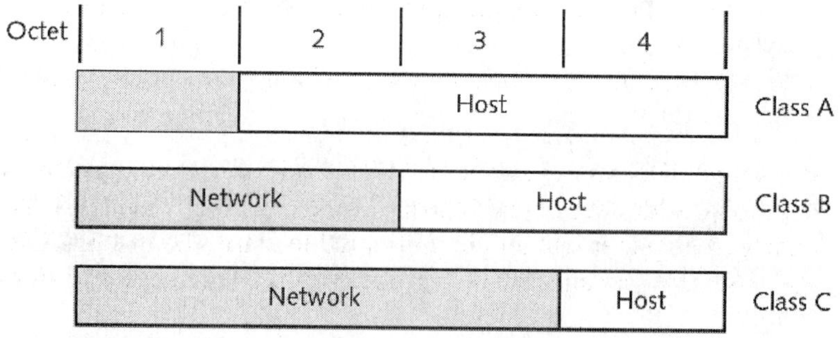

Exhibit 9-7: Network and host portions of an IP address

Subnet masks are used to identify the network-ID portion of an IP address. You can use it to infer the host-ID portion of the IP address. Subnet masks allow additional addresses to be implemented within a given address space. The default mask for each class is listed in the previous table.

The following table shows two examples of how the network ID and host ID of an IP address can be calculated by using the subnet mask.

IP address	Subnet mask	Network ID	Host ID
192.168.100.33	255.255.255.0	192.168.100.0	0.0.0.33
172.16.43.207	255.255.0.0	172.16.0.0	0.0.43.207

No matter how many octets are included in the network ID, they are always contiguous and start on the left. If the first and third octets are part of the network ID, the second must be as well. The following table shows examples of valid and invalid subnet masks.

Valid subnet masks	Invalid subnet masks
255.0.0.0	0.255.255.255
255.255.0.0	255.0.255.0
255.255.255.0	255.255.0.255

Reserved addresses also take up some of the available addresses. About 18 million addresses are reserved for private networks. About 16 million addresses are reserved for multicast addresses. The number for "this network" is also reserved. It is 0.0.0.0. The local loopback address is another reserved address: 127.0.0.1.

An IPv4 broadcast address sends information to all machines on a given subnet. The broadcast address is the last address in the range belonging to the subnet. On a Class A, B, or C subnet, the broadcast address always ends in 255. For example, on the subnet 192.168.157.0, the broadcast address would be 192.168.157.255.

CIDR

In the early 1990s, it became apparent that the number of available unique IP addresses would be used up soon. Several methods were developed to cope with the need for more addresses while a new IP version was being developed and implemented.

Classless Inter-Domain Routing (CIDR) was implemented in 1993 to help alleviate the problem. CIDR allows you to use variable-length subnet masking (VLSM) to create additional addresses beyond those allowed by the IPv4 classes. You can group blocks of addresses together into single routing-table entries known as CIDR blocks. These addresses are managed by IANA and Regional Internet Registries (RIRs).

CIDR addresses are written in the standard four-part dotted-decimal notation, followed by /N, where N is a number from 0 to 32. The number after the slash is the prefix length. The prefix is the number of bits (starting at the left of the address) that make up the shared initial bits (the network portion of the address). The default for a Class B address would be /16, and for a Class C address, it would be /24.

IPv6

Internet Protocol version 6 *(IPv6)* development began in the mid-1990s. IPv6 uses 128-bit addresses, providing many more possible addresses than IPv4 provided. Ipv6 provides 2^{128} addresses.

IPv6 addresses include eight 16-bit fields. They are written as eight groups of four numbers in hexadecimal notation, separated by colons. You can replace a group of all zeros by two colons. Only one set of colons (::) can be used per address. Leading zeros in a field can be dropped. However, except for the :: notation, all fields require at least one number. For example, fe80:0000:0884:0e09:d546:aa5b can be written as fe80::884:e09:d546:aa5b.

You indicate the network portion of the address by a slash and the number of bits in the address that are assigned to the network portion. If the address ends with /48, the first 48 bits of the address are the network portion. An example of a link-local IPv6 address is fe80::884:e09:d546:aa5b.

Just as with IPv4, the loopback address is a local host address. The IPv6 loopback address can be written as ::/128. The address fe80::/10 is equivalent to the IPv4 address 169.254.0.0.

In IPv4, the first octet of the address denotes the network's class. However, classes are no longer formally part of the IP addressing architecture, and they have been replaced by CIDR. With IPv6, there are five types of addresses:

- **Link-local** — The IPv6 version of IPv4's APIPA. Link-local addresses are self-assigned using the Neighbor Discovery process. You can identify them by using the `ipconfig` command. If the IPv6 address displayed for your computer starts with `fe80::`, then it's a self-assigned link-local address.

- **Site-local** — The IPv6 version of an IPv4 private address. Site-local addresses begin with FE and use C to F for the third hex digit—FEC, FED, FEE, or FEF.

- **Global unicast** — The IPv6 version of an IPv4 public address. A global unicast address is identified for a single interface. Global unicast addresses are routable and reachable on the IPv6 Internet.

  All IPv6 addresses that start with the binary values 001 (2000::/3) through 111 (E000::/3) are global addresses, with the exception of FF00::/8, which are addresses reserved for multicasts. Those bits are followed by 48 bits that designate the *global routing prefix*—the network ID used for routing. The next 16 bits designate the subnet ID. The last 64 bits identify the individual network node.

- **Multicast** — An address that identifies a multicast group. Just as with IPv4, an IPv6 multicast sends information or services to all interfaces that are defined as members of the multicast group. If the first 16 bits of an IPv6 address are `ff00n`, the address is a multicast address.

- **Anycast** — A new, unique type of address in IPv6. An anycast address—a cross between unicast and multicast addressing—identifies a group of interfaces, typically on separate nodes. Packets sent to an anycast address are delivered to the nearest interface, as identified by the routing protocol's distance measurement.

  Multicast addresses also identify a group of interfaces on separate nodes. However, the packet is delivered to all interfaces identified by the multicast address (instead of to a single interface, as with anycast addresses).

IPv6 doesn't use broadcast addresses; that functionality is included in multicast and anycast addresses. The all-hosts group is a multicast address used in place of a broadcast address.

IPv6 address scopes

Address *scopes* define regions, also known as *spans*. Addresses are defined as unique identifiers of an interface. The scopes are link-local, site network, and global network. A device usually has a link-local address and either a site-local or global address.

A network address can be assigned to a scope zone. A link-local zone is made up of all network interfaces connected to a link. Addresses are unique within a zone. A zone index suffix on the address identifies the zone. The suffix follows a % character. An example is fe80::884:e09:d546:aa5b%10.

Ports

If you imagine a packet of data traveling from one computer to another, the addresses described so far help route that packet to the correct computer. The MAC address identifies nodes on the local segment. The IP address handles transmissions between segments. But once the packet arrives at its destination computer, how does that computer determine which application should handle it?

Port numbers, or simply *ports*, are numeric addresses between 0 and 65,535 that identify applications. Both the originating (sending) application and the target application are identified by ports. They might not be the same.

Commonly used port numbers are listed in the following table.

Port	Protocol and purpose
20	FTP for file transfer services. Port 20 is used for transmitting the data.
21	FTP for file transfer services. Port 21 is used for transmitting commands between clients and servers.
22	Secure Shell (SSH) for secure login and file transfers.
23	Telnet for remote terminal access.
25	SMTP (Simple Mail Transport Protocol) for sending e-mail.
53	DNS for name resolution messaging.
80	HTTP for Web server traffic.
110	POP3 for incoming mail services.
123	NTP (Network Time Protocol) for time synchronization services.
143	IMAP4 for incoming mail services.
443	SSL (Secure Sockets Layer) for secure connections over HTTP.
631	IPP (Internet Printing Protocol) for network printing services.
3306	MySQL database system messaging.

Default gateways

In TCP/IP jargon, "default gateway" is another term for "router." If a computer doesn't know how to deliver a packet, it gives the packet to the default gateway to deliver. This happens every time a computer needs to deliver a packet to a network other than its own.

The one consistent feature of routers is that they can distinguish between different networks and move (or route) packets between them. Routers can also figure out the best path to use to move a packet between different networks.

A router has an IP address on every network to which it is attached. Remember that routers keep track of networks, not computers.

When a computer sends a packet to the default gateway for further delivery, the router's address must be on the same network as the computer, because computers can talk directly to only the devices on their own network. Exhibit 9-8 illustrates a computer using a default gateway to communicate with another computer on a different network; the example uses IPv4 addresses.

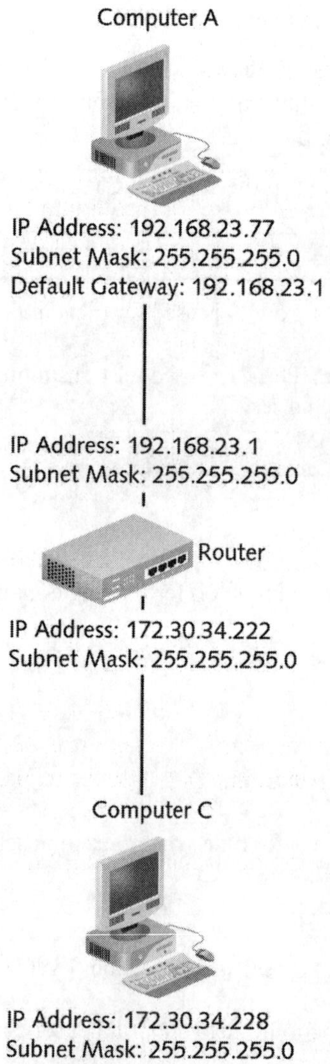

Computer A

IP Address: 192.168.23.77
Subnet Mask: 255.255.255.0
Default Gateway: 192.168.23.1

IP Address: 192.168.23.1
Subnet Mask: 255.255.255.0

 Router

IP Address: 172.30.34.222
Subnet Mask: 255.255.255.0

Computer C

IP Address: 172.30.34.228
Subnet Mask: 255.255.255.0

Exhibit 9-8: A routed network

In Exhibit 9-8, Computer A is sending a packet to Computer C. Computer A uses its subnet mask to determine whether the default gateway is required. In this example, IPv4 addresses are used, but the process is the same for IPv6.

1   Computer A compares its subnet mask and IP address to find its own network ID. The following table shows the calculation of the network ID for Computer A.

IP address	Subnet mask	Network ID
192.168.23.77	255.255.255.0	192.168.23.0

2   Computer A compares its subnet mask and the IP address of Computer C to see if it is on the same network. This step does not calculate the network ID for Computer C. It only tests whether it is the same as for Computer A. Computer A is not configured with the subnet mask of Computer C, so it is impossible for Computer A to find the network ID for Computer C.

The following table uses the subnet mask of Computer A to test the network ID for the IP address of Computer C.

IP address	Subnet mask	Network ID
172.30.34.228	255.255.255.0	172.30.34.0

3   The two network IDs are different, so Computer A sends the packet to the router (default gateway) for delivery.

4   The router looks in its routing table to see if it knows where the network 172.30.34.0 is located.

5   Because the router is attached to network 172.30.34.0, it delivers the packet to Computer C. If the router were not attached to network 172.30.34.0, it would forward the packet to another router, and this process would continue until the network was reached.

In an IPv6 network, network segments are identified by the IPv6 network prefix and the prefix length.

Address assignment

MAC addresses are assigned by the manufacturer and "burned" into network adapter firmware during the manufacturing process. You cannot typically change the MAC address. In the rare instances that you can, you must use special software designed to modify the non-volatile memory of the network adapter to assign a new MAC address.

Computers and devices on your networks can get their IPv4 or IPv6 addresses by either static or dynamic assignment. In other words, you can manually assign each node a computer, or you can set up a service to assign those addresses automatically.

The Dynamic Host Control Protocol (DHCP) is an Internet standard for dynamically assigning IP addresses to network nodes. When a device starts, it searches the local network for a DHCP server and requests an IP address. The DHCP server assigns one or more IP addresses (IPv4, IPv6, or both), along with other required addresses, such as the default gateway and DNS server's addresses.

Private IP addresses

Computers connected to a home or office network are typically assigned private IP addresses. Such addresses are unique and valid within that network, but not outside of that network. *Network Address Translation (NAT)* services provide the means for such internal computers to communicate with the outside world.

NAT services run on your router. When an internal computer tries to reach an outside address, the NAT services modify the packets to replace the private internal address with a valid public IP address. The NAT services monitor return traffic to send such packets to the internal node for which they are bound. NAT services, along with your firewall, typically don't permit outside computers to initiate a communication session with an internal node.

APIPA

The network 169.254.0.0 (addresses 169.254.0.1 through 169.254.255.254 inclusive) is reserved for *Automatic Private IP Addressing (APIPA)*. Windows operating systems (Windows 2000 and later) automatically generate an address in this range if they are configured to obtain an IPv4 address from a DHCP server and are unable to contact one.

APIPA is a Microsoft proprietary technology. Due to Microsoft's market dominance, many other operating systems have adopted similar technologies. The Internet Engineering Task Force eventually formalized APIPA in RFC 3927 Dynamic Configuration of IPv4 Link-Local Addresses. Linux and other operating systems support RFC 3927.

Automatic private IP addresses are not routable on the Internet. They are for local network use only.

Character-based names

Computers use numeric network addresses to communicate with each other. People prefer to use names, such as host or NetBIOS names, to refer to computers on a network. Most likely, when you direct your computer to connect to a remote computer, you provide a name for that remote computer. Your computer must determine the name of the target computer.

- TCP/IP supports a naming service called the Domain Name System (DNS). DNS servers resolve (translate or convert) host names to IP addresses.
- Windows computers support NetBIOS names. A NetBIOS name has 16 characters, with the first 15 characters available for the name and the 16th character reserved to designate a particular service or functionality.

The Domain Name System

DNS servers match host names to IP addresses. These specialized servers maintain databases of IP addresses and their corresponding domain names. For example, you could use DNS to determine that the name `www.microsoft.com` corresponds to the IP address 207.46.19.60.

The DNS naming hierarchy

DNS names are typically composed of three parts: a computer name, a domain name, and a top-level domain name. For example, in the name `www.microsoft.com`, `www` is the computer's name (or an alias for the actual name), `microsoft` is the domain, and `com` is the top-level domain.

With this scheme, many computers can be called "www" without causing naming conflicts. Additionally, there can be many computers within the Microsoft domain, each with a different name. There can also be more than one Microsoft domain, as long as each one is contained in a different top-level domain.

You can also use subdomains. For example, in `www.corporate.microsoft.com`, "corporate" is a domain within the Microsoft domain. Four-part names such as this aren't rare, but you probably won't see divisions beyond that.

Top-level domains

Top-level domains (TLDs) constitute the suffix at the end of a DNS name. The original specifications called for the following TLDs, each meant to contain domains with the following purposes:

- .com for general business
- .org for nonprofit organizations
- .edu for educational organizations
- .gov for government organizations
- .mil for military organizations
- .net for Internet organizations (hosting companies and ISPs)
- .int for international

As more countries joined the Internet, new TLDs were added for each country. A few examples of these two-letter (digraph) TLDs are in the following list, and a complete list can be found at *www.iana.org/cctld/cctld-whois.htm*:

- .ar for Argentina
- .be for Belgium
- .ca for Canada
- .de for Germany
- .cn for China
- .ve for Venezuela

The Internet Corporation for Assigned Names and Numbers (ICANN) regulates TLDs. It has recently created several new TLDs to keep pace with the demands of the growing Internet. These include:

- .biz for businesses
- .name for individuals
- .museum for museums
- .pro for professionals
- .aero for aviation
- .coop for cooperatives
- .info for general information

NetBIOS

NetBIOS name is 16 characters, with the first 15 characters used for the name and the 16th character used to designate a particular service or functionality. A NetBIOS name can consist of letters, numbers, and the following special characters:

> ! @ # $ % ^ & ( ) - _ ' { } . ~

NetBIOS names must be unique. They cannot contain spaces or any of the following special characters:

> \ * + = | : ; " ? < > ,

NetBIOS names aren't case-sensitive, so "A" is equivalent to "a." Some examples of valid NetBIOS names are SUPERCORP, SERVER01, and INSTRUCTOR.

In a NetBIOS name, the reserved 16th character is typically expressed as a hexadecimal number surrounded by angle brackets at the end of the name. For example, the NetBIOS name SUPERCORP<1C> would represent a request for the SUPERCORP domain controllers. When you try to access a given service, you don't have to append a NetBIOS suffix manually; Windows does this automatically. When you're setting the NetBIOS name on a domain or computer, you enter it without the 16th character because a single NetBIOS name can be used to represent many different services on the same system.

NetBIOS names exist at the same level—a concept referred to as a *flat namespace*—even if the computers to which they're assigned are arranged in a network hierarchy. All NetBIOS names are in one big pool, without anything that identifies what part of the network the names belong to. For example, SERVER01 and SERVER02 are both valid NetBIOS names. By looking at them, however, you can't tell that SERVER01 is a member of the domain CHILD01, and SERVER02 is a member of CHILD02. With the flat-namespace structure, managing a large network environment becomes much more difficult.

Resolving NetBIOS names

The simplest way for a computer to resolve a NetBIOS name to a numeric address is to send a network broadcast, as shown in Exhibit 9-9. A *broadcast* is a message destined for all computers on a given network. The name-request broadcast message includes the NetBIOS name the computer is looking for, the type of service (represented by the 16th character), and the address of the computer sending the broadcast. The computer with the requested NetBIOS name can respond to the request. If a computer with a matching NetBIOS name and service type receives the broadcast message, it responds directly to the computer that sent the broadcast message.

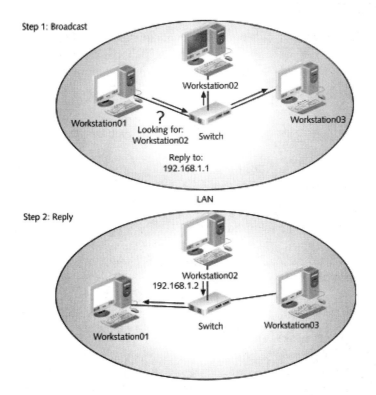

Exhibit 9-9: NetBIOS name resolution, using a broadcast

Once the two computers know each other's IP addresses, they can communicate directly with one another. In order to improve performance and reduce network traffic, IP addresses associated with resolved NetBIOS names are cached for 10 minutes.

Although using broadcasts to resolve NetBIOS names is simple, it isn't efficient. Network devices such as routers, which are used to control traffic among various parts of a network, usually don't forward broadcasts. Two computers on different physical networks separated by a router can't resolve each other's NetBIOS names. To overcome some of these problems, Microsoft introduced the *Windows Internet Name Service* (WINS).

WINS is a database with which all computers on a network register their NetBIOS names. In order for computers to register with WINS, they must be configured with the IP address of one or more WINS servers on the network. When a computer needs to resolve a NetBIOS name to an IP address, it sends a request directly to a WINS server, instead of sending a broadcast to the entire network. If the WINS server finds a matching name in its database, it responds with the IP address of the computer being sought.

Due to such problems as excessive broadcasts and the inability of broadcasts to cross routers, and in acknowledgement of the dominant role the Internet plays in today's networks, Microsoft switched to DNS as the primary name-resolution system on Windows networks, starting with Windows 2000.

A-5:   Examining addresses

Here's how	Here's why
1 On your Windows Server 2008 computer, click **Start** and right-click **Computer**	
Choose **Properties**	To open the System window.
2 Examine the "Computer name" and "Full computer name" lines	You might need to scroll down to see this information. These are the character-based names your computer is using.
3 Close the System window	
4 Click **Start** and choose **Network**	If this option isn't on your Start menu, right-click the network connection icon in the notification area of the status bar and choose Open Network and Sharing Center.
Click **Network and Sharing Center**	To open the Network and Sharing Center. This utility gives you a summary of your computer's network connectivity.
5 Under "View your active networks," observe your network connection information	You should be connected to a Work or Home network.
6 Next to Connections, click **View status**	
Click **Details**	
7 Examine the Physical Address line	This is your network card's MAC address.
8 Examine the DHCP Enabled line	This value is Yes, so your computer gets its IP address from a central server. If this value were No, a computer administrator would manually assign your computer an IP address.
9 Examine the IPv4 Address line	This is the IP address your computer is using. The IP address can be manually assigned to your computer, or it can be assigned dynamically.
10 Examine the IPv4 Subnet Mask line	This number works with the IP address to separate the network portion of the address from the host portion.
11 Examine the IPv4 Default Gateway	This is the router your computer uses to send data to computers that aren't on the same network.
12 Examine the IPv4 DNS Server line	This is the IP address of the server your computer is using to resolve DNS character-based names to IP addresses.

13 Examine the IPv4 WINS Server line	In the classroom, your computer is using broadcasts on the local subnet to resolve NetBIOS names. Your computer isn't configured to use a WINS server.
14 Examine the "NetBIOS over Tcpip Enabled" line	It is set to Yes. NetBIOS is an older application programming interface. Examples of Windows applications and services that use NetBIOS are file and printer sharing and the Computer Browser service.
15 Examine the IPv6 address	The address begins with fe80:, indicating that it is a self-assigned address.
16 Click **Close** twice	
Close the Network and Sharing Center window	
Close the Network window	If necessary.
17 Open Internet Explorer and verify that you have Internet connectivity	(Enter a URL of your choice.) Your computer can connect to other computers on the Internet because it is using a routable protocol and has the appropriate physical connections to internetworking devices.
18 Close all open windows	

Network security options

Explanation
Network security is typically the domain of dedicated network engineers. However, as a server administrator, you should be familiar with a few of the most common network security techniques. These include:

- Demilitarized zone (DMZ) configurations
- Virtual local area networks (VLANs)
- Virtual private networks (VPNs)

DMZ configurations

A DMZ is an area between the private network (intranet) and a public network (extranet) such as the Internet. A DMZ isn't a direct part of either network, but is instead an additional network between the two networks.

Computers in the DMZ are accessible to nodes on both the Internet and the intranet. Typically, computers within the DMZ have limited access to nodes on the intranet, but direct connections between the Internet and nodes on the internal network are blocked. For example, you might put your company's mail server in a DMZ. Users on both the internal network and the Internet will need access to the mail server. The mail server might need to communicate with internal storage servers to save files and other data. But Internet users shouldn't have access to your internal network.

Typically, a router is used to filter all traffic to the private intranet while allowing full access to the computer in the DMZ. The router is solely responsible for protecting the private network (see Exhibit 9-10). The IP address of the DMZ host is entered in the router configuration. This IP address is allowed full Internet access, but other computers on the network are protected behind the firewall provided by the router. The disadvantage of this setup is that sometimes a router firewall can fail and allow traffic through to the intranet.

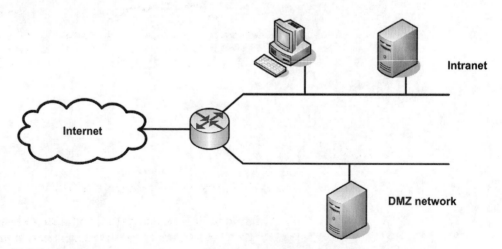

Exhibit 9-10: A router separates the DMZ and the intranet from the Internet

Virtual LANs

A *virtual LAN (VLAN)* is a virtual network segment enabled by a Layer 2–compatible switch. Nodes on the same physical segment can be made to interoperate as if they were on separate segments, or various physical network segments can be made to appear as if they were on the same segment. By formal definition, a VLAN is a distinct broadcast domain within a larger network.

Bridging between virtual segments can be restricted or permitted as needed. In this way, nodes can co-exist on the same wire, yet be logically separated and protected from each other.

Furthermore, broadcasts are limited to a VLAN. A broadcast on one virtual segment is not transmitted to other segments. This setup reduces overall traffic and enables subsets of nodes to communicate more efficiently.

VLANs increase security by clustering users in smaller groups, thereby making the job of the hacker harder. Rather than just gaining access to the network, a hacker must now gain access to a specific virtual LAN as well.

VLAN configurations are often used with VoIP (Voice over IP) telephony systems. Distinct VLANs are created for voice and data traffic. In this way, traffic on each VLAN is isolated and protected from the other. For example, if someone launched a denial-of-service attack against one of your servers, your VoIP phones will continue to operate.

Virtual private networks

A *virtual private network (VPN)* is a private communications network transmitted across a public, typically insecure, network connection. With a VPN, a company can extend a virtual LAN segment to employees working from home by transmitting data securely across the Internet. A VPN, illustrated in Exhibit 9-11, is a means of providing secure communications across the extranet zone.

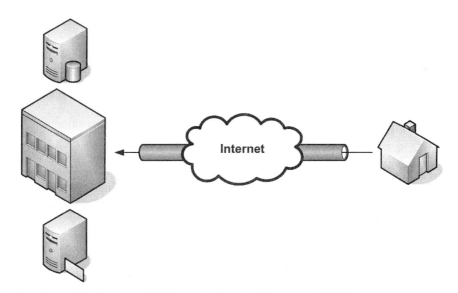

Exhibit 9-11: A typical VPN using Point of Presence (POP)

With a VPN, TCP/IP communications are encrypted and then packaged within another TCP/IP packet stream. The VPN hardware or software can encrypt just the underlying data in a packet or the entire packet itself before wrapping it in another IP packet for delivery. If a packet on the public network is intercepted along the way, the encrypted contents cannot be read by a hacker. Such encryption of data or packets is typically implemented by using a protocol suite called *Internet Protocol Security (IPSec)*.

IPSec was initially developed for IPv6, but many current IPv4 devices support it as well. IPSec enables two types of encryption. With transport encryption, the underlying data in a packet is encrypted and placed within a new packet on the public network. With *tunnel encryption*, the entire packet, including its header, is encrypted and then placed in the public network's packet.

With IPSec in place, a VPN can virtually eliminate packet sniffing and identity spoofing. Only the sending and receiving computers hold the keys to encrypt and decrypt the packets being sent across the public network. Anyone sniffing the packets would have no idea of their content and might not even be able to determine the source and destination of the request.

Do it!

A-6: Identifying network security options

Questions and answers

1 Some of the features of a DMZ are:

  A   It is a network segment between two routers.

  B   Its servers are publicly accessible.

  C   Its servers have lower security requirements than other internal servers.

  D   All of the above.

2 A feature available in some switches that permit separating the switch into multiple broadcast domains is called a(n) _____.

3 What could you use a VPN for?

4 Which encryption method encrypts the entire packet, including its header, before packaging it into the public network's packet stream?

  A   CHAP

  B   IPSec

  C   Tunneling

  D   Transport

5 Do you have to use IPSec to enable a VPN?

Topic B: Networking utilities

This topic covers the following CompTIA Server+ (2009 Edition) exam objective.

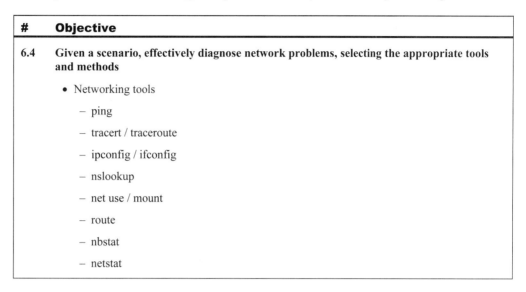

#	Objective
6.4	**Given a scenario, effectively diagnose network problems, selecting the appropriate tools and methods**
	• Networking tools
	– ping
	– tracert / traceroute
	– ipconfig / ifconfig
	– nslookup
	– net use / mount
	– route
	– nbstat
	– netstat

Network tools

Explanation

One of the most common complaints you'll hear from users is that they can't get to something on the network, or "the Internet is down." When you hear a complaint about network connectivity, your first step should be to check the user's network connection and TCP/IP settings.

If you find a problem on the client computer, it's your job to fix it, usually by correcting TCP/IP properties. If you suspect a problem with the network as a whole or with a particular server on the network, you'll need to contact the appropriate individual, typically the network administrator, to escalate the problem.

TCP/IP utilities

Most operating systems include various utilities that you can use to configure or troubleshoot TCP/IP connectivity. The following table describes the most important of these utilities. Consult your system documentation to determine which ones are available on your platform.

Utility	Platform	Used to...
IPConfig	Windows	Display the host's IP address and other information.
Ifconfig	Linux, UNIX, Mac OS X	Display or configure the host's IP address and other information associated with a wired network interface.
Iwconfig	Linux, UNIX, Mac OS X	Similar to ifconfig, but for wireless connections.
Ping	All	Test connectivity by sending and monitoring ICMP echo requests.
Route	All	View or manually configure network routing tables.
NSLookup	All	Look up the IP address for a named host, or the host name associated with an IP address.
Tracert	All	Trace the route over which packets flow from one host to another on a network.
Arp	All	Display the contents of your ARP cache, which saves MAC (hardware) address information for the nodes your station has communicated with in the past few minutes.
Hostname	All	Display the computer's host name, which is either defined locally or set by a network service such as DNS.
Nbtstat	Windows	Display NetBIOS over TCP/IP statistics, NetBIOS name tables, and the NetBIOS name cache. You can use this utility with switches to remove or correct NetBIOS name cache entries.
Netstat	Windows	Display a list of a computer's active incoming and outgoing connections.
Telnet	All	Open a terminal session with a remote host.
FTP	All	Transfer files to and from an FTP file server.

To open a Command Prompt window in any version of Windows, run the `cmd` command. From the Command Prompt, you can enter a Windows or DOS command, including any of those in the previous table.

At Linux, UNIX, and OS X stations, you will need super-user (root) privileges to run some of the previous commands. You can use the `su` or `sudo` commands to temporarily elevate your permissions on such systems.

Do it!

B-1:   Identifying TCP/IP utilities used for troubleshooting

Questions and answers

1 A user opens a browser window and tries to contact your intranet server. The user receives a message that it can't be found. What's the first TCP/IP utility you should try?

2 Which other utility could you use to ensure that the computer is properly connected to the network?

The IPConfig command

When a user complains of network problems, you should first check the TCP/IP settings on the user's computer. In any version of Windows, use `ipconfig`, as shown in Exhibit 9-12, to display and modify the current TCP/IP configuration, including the IP address, subnet mask, default gateway, and DNS server address.

Several switches can be added to the `ipconfig` command to display the current IP information (`ipconfig /all`), release the IP address (`ipconfig /release`), and renew the IP address (`ipconfig /renew`) for all connections. The following table describes some common switches.

Switch	Use to...
`/release [adapter name]` `/release6 [adapter name]`	Release a leased IPv4 or IPv6 address (respectively) so that it returns to the pool of available addresses on the DHCP server. You can specify the name of the network connection for which you want to release the leased address. If you don't specify a connection name, Windows Server 2008 releases the leased IP addresses for all network connections. You might use this option when a computer cannot obtain an address from a DHCP server (typically when the server is unavailable) or if you want to force the computer to obtain a new lease (because the DHCP server's IP addressing parameters have changed).
`/renew [adapter name]` `/renew6 [adapter name]`	Renew a leased IPv4 or IPv6 address. You can specify the name of the network connection for which you want to renew the IP address lease. If you don't specify a network connection name, Windows Server 2008 attempts to renew all leased IP addresses for all network connections configured to use DHCP. Use this option to try to renew a computer's IP address lease. If the computer can't communicate with the DHCP server from which it obtained its IP address, or you have disabled the scope (pool) of IP addresses from which the computer obtained its IP address, the DHCP server will deny the computer's lease renewal request. The computer will then start over with the IP address leasing process by broadcasting a DHCP request packet.
`/flushdns`	Delete all name resolution information (host names and their IP addresses) from the client's DNS Resolver cache. For example, you might use this parameter to troubleshoot name resolution problems that occur after you change a server's IP address. If computers still have the server's name and old IP address in the DNS Resolver cache, they won't be able to communicate with the server until this cache is deleted.
`/displaydns`	Display the contents of the DNS Resolver cache.
`/registerdns`	Renew all IP address leases from DHCP servers, and re-register the computer's host name and IP address on your network's DNS servers.

The ifconfig command

On Linux and UNIX systems, you can use the `ifconfig` command to view or change your NIC's configuration. You use it in this form:

```
ifconfig [interface] [new_settings]
```

In Linux, network interfaces are assigned names such as `eth0`, `eth1`, and so forth. Thus, to check the state of your primary network connection, you would enter:

```
ifconfig eth0
```

The `ifconfig` command will not display your default gateway's address. Instead, you can use the `route` command with no options to see your current gateway address. You might need to use `sudo` or `su` to use the `ifconfig` and `route` commands.

Troubleshooting with IPConfig or ifconfig

Check to see if the IP address and subnet mask are correct, and verify the default gateway and DNS server addresses. When you do this, you might find that the computer has no IP address configured or has configured itself with an automatic private address. If so, this gives you a couple of options:

- If IP addressing information is assigned by a DHCP server, suspect a problem with a DHCP server itself or with the network between the user's computer and the DHCP server. First, verify that the network card is working correctly and is attached to the network cable, which is in turn plugged into the appropriate network port on the wall or floor. Try to release and then renew the IP address from the DHCP server. If you can verify these things, and you can't get an IP address from the DHCP server, then escalate the call to the appropriate network administrator.

- If IP addressing is assigned manually, then assign the correct information, such as IP address, default gateway, subnet mask, or DNS server address, and test to see if connectivity is restored.

```
Command Prompt

Microsoft Windows [Version 6.0.6001]
Copyright (c) 2006 Microsoft Corporation.  All rights reserved.

C:\Users\Host Administrator>ipconfig /all

Windows IP Configuration

    Host Name . . . . . . . . . . . . : nethost01
    Primary Dns Suffix  . . . . . . . : networkplus.class
    Node Type . . . . . . . . . . . . : Hybrid
    IP Routing Enabled. . . . . . . . : No
    WINS Proxy Enabled. . . . . . . . : No
    DNS Suffix Search List. . . . . . : networkplus.class

Ethernet adapter Local Area Connection:

    Connection-specific DNS Suffix  . :
    Description . . . . . . . . . . . : Intel(R) 82566DC-2 Gigabit Network Connec
tion
    Physical Address. . . . . . . . . : 00-1D-09-24-F5-97
    DHCP Enabled. . . . . . . . . . . : No
    Autoconfiguration Enabled . . . . : Yes
    Link-local IPv6 Address . . . . . : fe80::690e:5c3a:7771:89b6%8(Preferred)
    IPv4 Address. . . . . . . . . . . : 192.168.100.214(Preferred)
    Subnet Mask . . . . . . . . . . . : 255.255.255.0
```

Exhibit 9-12: Output from the ipconfig command

Do it!

B-2: Using IPConfig to display TCP/IP settings

Here's how	Here's why
1 Click **Start** and enter **cmd**	To open a Command Prompt window. You're going to use `ipconfig` to view your IP address settings.
2 At the command prompt, enter **ipconfig**	To display your current IP address, subnet mask, and default gateway, as shown here.

```
C:\Users\hostadmin01>ipconfig

Windows IP Configuration

Ethernet adapter Local Area Connection:

   Connection-specific DNS Suffix  . : networkplus.class
   Link-local IPv6 Address . . . . . : fe80::3585:ffb7:fa18:8e72%11
   IPv4 Address. . . . . . . . . . . : 192.168.157.17
   Subnet Mask . . . . . . . . . . . : 255.255.255.0
   Default Gateway . . . . . . . . . : 192.168.157.1
```

This is a quick way to find a computer's basic IP address information.

| 3 At the command prompt, enter **ipconfig /all** | To display extended IP addressing information, as shown here. |

```
C:\Users\hostadmin01>ipconfig /all

Windows IP Configuration

   Host Name . . . . . . . . . . . . : nethost01
   Primary Dns Suffix  . . . . . . . : networkplus.class
   Node Type . . . . . . . . . . . . : Hybrid
   IP Routing Enabled. . . . . . . . : No
   WINS Proxy Enabled. . . . . . . . : No
   DNS Suffix Search List. . . . . . : networkplus.class

Ethernet adapter Local Area Connection:

   Connection-specific DNS Suffix  . : networkplus.class
   Description . . . . . . . . . . . : Broadcom NetXtreme Gigabit Ethernet
   Physical Address. . . . . . . . . : 00-1E-C9-47-59-31
   DHCP Enabled. . . . . . . . . . . : Yes
   Autoconfiguration Enabled . . . . : Yes
   Link-local IPv6 Address . . . . . : fe80::3585:ffb7:fa18:8e72%11(Preferred)
   IPv4 Address. . . . . . . . . . . : 192.168.157.17(Preferred)
   Subnet Mask . . . . . . . . . . . : 255.255.255.0
   Lease Obtained. . . . . . . . . . : Monday, December 08, 2008 1:43:26 PM
   Lease Expires . . . . . . . . . . : Sunday, December 14, 2008 1:43:25 PM
   Default Gateway . . . . . . . . . : 192.168.157.1
   DHCP Server . . . . . . . . . . . : 192.168.157.5
   DNS Servers . . . . . . . . . . . : 192.168.157.5
   NetBIOS over Tcpip. . . . . . . . : Enabled
```

It can be easier to view this information at the command prompt than to click through a few dialog boxes to find the same information in the Windows GUI.

| 4 What Linux command should you use to display your default gateway's address? | |

Ping and basic TCP/IP connectivity

Explanation

Ping (Packet Internet Groper) is a simple program that allows one computer to send a test packet to another computer and then receive a reply. You use `ping` to determine whether another computer is available for communication on a TCP/IP network. After you have verified that the computer has a valid IP address, you can use the `ping` command to see if you can communicate with another computer on the network. You'll need to know the NetBIOS name, DNS name, or IP address of the other computer—perhaps a router or server that you know is operational.

At the MS-DOS or command prompt, enter

```
ping computer
```

where `computer` is the other computer's name or IP address. A successful result looks similar to Exhibit 9-13.

```
C:\Users\Host Administrator>ping 192.168.100.214

Pinging 192.168.100.214 with 32 bytes of data:
Reply from 192.168.100.214: bytes=32 time<1ms TTL=128
Reply from 192.168.100.214: bytes=32 time<1ms TTL=128
Reply from 192.168.100.214: bytes=32 time<1ms TTL=128
Reply from 192.168.100.214: bytes=32 time<1ms TTL=128

Ping statistics for 192.168.100.214:
    Packets: Sent = 4, Received = 4, Lost = 0 (0% loss),
Approximate round trip times in milli-seconds:
    Minimum = 0ms, Maximum = 0ms, Average = 0ms

C:\Users\Host Administrator>_
```

Exhibit 9-13: Successful ping results

When you issue the `ping` command from the command prompt, followed by an IP address or a domain name, `ping` communicates over a TCP/IP network to another node on the network. It sends an Internet Control Message Packet (ICMP) Echo Request and expects to receive an ICMP Echo Reply in return. Packets are exchanged and then reported on screen to verify connectivity on the network.

If you can't use `ping` successfully, try the following:

- If you used `ping` with a domain name, use the IP address of the remote host instead. If that works, the problem is with name resolution.
- Try to ping a different computer. Can you communicate with any other computer on the network? Ping the loopback address, 127.0.0.1, to see if you have any connectivity on the network.
- If you can't communicate with any other computer on the network, use `ipconfig` or `ifconfig` to verify that the computer has been assigned an IP address.
- Verify all network configuration settings, including IP address, subnet mask, and default gateway.
- Reboot the computer to verify that TCP/IP has been loaded.
- Try removing TCP/IP and reinstalling it. Perhaps the initial installation was corrupted.
- Check the physical connections. Is the network cable plugged in or is there a telephone connection? Do you get a dial tone?

If all of these methods fail to produce results, you might need to escalate the issue.

Do it!

B-3: Testing TCP/IP connectivity

Here's how	Here's why
1 In the Command Prompt window, type **ping 127.0.0.1** and press (↵ *ENTER*)	(The window should still be open from the previous activity.) This is the *loopback address*, which verifies that TCP/IP is working on this computer. Pinging the loopback address tests a computer's basic network setup.
	You should receive four successful responses.
2 Type **ipconfig /all** and press (↵ *ENTER*)	Record your IP address and your default gateway address.
	IP address: _____
	Default gateway address: _____
3 Ping your IP address	To verify that TCP/IP communication can be sent out on the network cable from your NIC and come back in again.
	You should receive four successful responses.
4 Ping the instructor's computer	To verify that you have connectivity to other computers on your local subnet.
	You should receive four successful responses.
5 Ping the IP address of your classroom's gateway	To verify that you can reach the gateway that connects you to other subnets.
	You should receive four successful responses.
6 How does being able to successfully ping the IP address of your default gateway help you when troubleshooting?	

7 Users tell you that they cannot access one of your organization's file and print servers (even though they had just been using this server). You discover that another person in Desktop Support moved the server to a new subnet. What might be the cause of the current problem? How can you resolve the problem?

NSLookup

Explanation

When two computers communicate with each other by using TCP/IP across the network, the DNS server is responsible for resolving the names you specify to their associated IP addresses. Active Directory domains also use DNS to provide users and computers with access to the network's resources.

To verify that your computer can communicate with its DNS server(s), enter nslookup [*host or FQDN*]. Your computer has succeeded in communicating with the DNS server if the server responds with the IP address of one or more computers. You'll sometimes see multiple IP addresses for a given *fully qualified domain name* (FQDN), such as *www.cnn.com*. In this example, the Web site administrators have configured multiple Web servers to host its content. DNS servers then use a technique referred to as "round-robin" to balance the workload across those servers.

Tracert

If a user tells you that he or she can't access resources on the network, you should verify that the user's client software is configured properly. You should also verify that File and Printer Sharing is installed and enabled on the computer the user is trying to access.

You can also perform a test on the network by using the tracert command to check the network path between two computers. At an MS-DOS or command prompt, enter tracert *computer* where *computer* is the name or IP address of a destination.

Do it!

B-4:   Using NSLookup and Tracert

Here's how	
1 At the command prompt, enter **nslookup**	To test your DNS configuration. In class, the classroom DNS server's IP address will be returned. In other environments, depending on the configuration, you might see a DNS server name and IP address returned, or you might see just an IP address and an error message telling you that NSLookup can't find the server name. This is a DNS server configuration issue.
2 Enter **nslookup** followed by a Web address	Try www.yahoo.com. You should see DNS addressing information for that domain.
3 Enter **exit**	To exit NSLookup.
4 Enter **tracert [IP_address of a classroom server]**	To trace the path to a server in your network. This is a short path, so the results are returned promptly.
5 Enter **tracert www.yahoo.com**	To trace the route to Yahoo's Web server. This takes a while longer.
6 Close the Command Prompt window	

The net command

Explanation
Windows versions since Windows NT have included the net command-line utility, which you can use to manage and monitor the operating system. The net command provides a quick way to get specific information and perform several functions at the command line. The following table describes some of the parameters that are available for this command.

Parameter	Description
continue	Restarts a paused service.
pause	Pauses a service.
print	Displays print jobs and queues.
session	Lists or disconnects sessions between the computer and other computers.
share	Lists shares on the local computer, and shares local resources.
start	Lists running services, and starts a service.
stop	Stops services.
use	Connects the computer to and disconnects it from a network share.
view	Displays a list of computers on the network. When used with a computer name, lists the shared resources on a specific computer.

The administrative command prompt

Some net command operations, such as starting and stopping services, require you to use an administrative command prompt. To open an administrative command prompt, click Start, right-click Command Prompt, and choose "Run as administrator."

Do it!

B-5:   Using the net command

Here's how	Here's why
1 Click **Start** and choose **All Programs, Accessories**	
Right-click **Command Prompt**	
Choose **Run as administrator**	To open the Command Prompt window with administrative privileges.
2 Enter **net view**	To see a list of computers on the network.
3 Enter **net share**	To see a list of shared folders on your computer.
Do you have any shared folders?	

4	Create a directory named **Marketing** in the root directory of your C drive	Type *md c:\Marketing* and press Enter.
5	Enter **net share Marketing=C:\Marketing**	
		To share the Marketing folder.
6	Enter **net share**	To confirm that you've shared the folder and the share name is Marketing.
7	Enter **net use *computername*\Marketing**	
		To connect to the shared Users folder on another computer in the classroom.
	Enter a user name when prompted	
	Enter a password when prompted	
8	Enter **net use**	To confirm that you've connected to the shared folder.
9	Enter **net use *computername*\Marketing /delete**	
		To remove the connection.
10	Enter **net use**	To confirm that you've removed the connection to the shared Marketing folder on the other computer.
11	Enter **net share marketing /delete**	
		To stop sharing the Marketing folder.
12	Enter **net share**	To verify that the folder is no longer shared.
13	Enter **net start**	To display the list of services running on your computer.
14	Enter **net stop spooler**	To stop the Print Spooler service.
	Enter **net start spooler**	To start the service again.

Network statistics

Explanation

You can use the `nbtstat` and `netstat` commands to display information about network connections. Both commands offer various command-line switches. You can get a list by typing the command's name followed by /? and pressing Enter.

The nbtstat command

This Windows command displays NetBIOS over TCP/IP statistics. This information can include NetBIOS name tables and the NetBIOS name cache. You can use this command with switches to remove or correct NetBIOS name cache entries.

The netstat command

This command displays a list of a computer's active incoming and outgoing TCP/IP connections. Versions of the command are available in Windows and Linux. The output from this command typically includes the local and remote computers' IP addresses, the port number associated with each computer, and the state of the connection (established, waiting to close, and so forth).

Do it!

B-6:   Checking network connections

Here's how	Here's why
1 Enter **nbtstat -c**	To display a list of names your computer has cached. This list should include the names of any computers you have connected to on the local network within the cache period (5 minutes). The remaining time within this period is shown in the Life [sec] column.
2 Enter **nbtstat -R**	To purge (empty) the name cache and reload it from the WINS server, if one is available.
3 Enter **nbtstat -c**	Most likely, the name cache will be empty now.
4 Enter **netstat -a**	To display your active TCP/IP connections. You will probably see a long list of connections. For each one, the command outputs the protocol (TCP or UDP), the local address with port number, the remote or "foreign" address and port, and a state.
5 Enter **netstat -b**	This time, the command lists the name of the executable ("binary") file associated with each connection.
6 Enter **exit**	To close the Command Prompt window.

Topic C: Troubleshooting

This topic covers the following CompTIA Server+ (2009 Edition) exam objective.

#	Objective
6.4	**Given a scenario, effectively diagnose network problems, selecting the appropriate tools and methods** • Common problems – Internet connectivity failure – E-mail failure – Resource unavailable – DHCP server misconfigured – Non-functional or unreachable – Destination host unreachable – Unknown host – Default gateway misconfigured – Failure of service provider – Can reach by IP, not by host name • Causes of common problems – Improper IP configuration – VLAN configuration – Port security – Improper subnetting – Component failure – Incorrect OS route tables – Bad cables – Firewall (misconfiguration, hardware failure, software failure) – Misconfigured NIC, routing / switch issues – DNS and/or DHCP failure – Misconfigured hosts file

Troubleshooting TCP/IP

Explanation

In this section, you'll examine some common networking failures. There can be no single "laundry list" of potential problems. You'll need to be prepared to follow a standard, methodical troubleshooting process to discover the causes and solutions to the problems you'll encounter. But these scenarios will lay the groundwork for at least some of the more common issues you'll face.

Destination host unreachable

When a user reports that he or she cannot reach a particular host, you must determine the scope of the problem. Is this person the only user experiencing the problem? Can the affected users access other hosts? Is the host local or remote (on the Internet)? A few of the more common symptoms and causes are listed in the following table.

Symptom	Scope	Causes
Users can't reach a host on the LAN or Internet	Single user	TCP/IP misconfigured (invalid IP address, improper subnet mask, failure to obtain DHCP lease).
		Local routing tables or host tables misconfigured.
		Default gateway misconfigured in that user's static IP assignment.
		Network adapter failure (misconfigured NIC, bad driver, failed board).
		Bad network cable.
	Multiple users	Host failure.
		DHCP server misconfigured to hand out invalid default gateway address.
		Improper subnet assignments.
		Gateway failure.
		DNS failure preventing name-based access (IP-based access would work in this case).
		Router failure.

Resource unavailable

Users might tell you that a particular resource is unavailable. For example, they can't access a shared folder or a particular service on a server, or can't use e-mail for some reason. A few of the more common symptoms and causes are listed in the following table.

Symptom	Scope	Causes
Resource unavailable	Single user	Permission problem.
		Network configuration problem.
		Port configuration problem (using the wrong port number to access the outgoing mail server, for example).
		Local firewall software failure.
	Multiple users	Service failure or misconfiguration.
		Port security on host or intervening firewall blocking access.
		VLAN configuration problem.

Internet connectivity failure

When users tell you that they cannot access the Internet, you must first determine the scope of the problem. Can some users access the Internet but not others? Can users access local resources? Can users access some Internet destinations but not others? When did the problem start—and then what happened or changed at about that time?

Your answers to these questions will help you determine the scope and cause of the problem. That information will help you narrow the range of possible causes. A few of the more common symptoms and causes are listed in the following table.

Symptom	Scope	Causes
Users can access hosts on the local segment but not other segments or the Internet	Single user	Default gateway misconfigured in that user's static IP assignment.
	Multiple users	DHCP server misconfigured to hand out invalid default gateway address.
		DCHP server failure.
		Switch failure.
Users can access hosts on the LAN (intranet) but not on the Internet	Single user	Default gateway misconfigured in that user's static IP assignment.
	Multiple users	Internet service provider failure (line outage, service failure, and so forth).
		Switch or router (gateway) failure, or routing misconfigured.
		Firewall issues (misconfiguration, hardware or software failure, improper rules).

Do it!

C-1: Determining problems and their causes

Questions and answers

1 Why must you determine the scope of the problem before attempting a solution?

2 Users report an Internet outage. You troubleshoot and determine that the problem is with your Internet service provider. Is your job done?

3 Once you have solved a problem, what should you do?

4 Troubleshooting reveals that the cause of a problem was a router misconfiguration. By examining the logs, you identify who made the changes. How is this information helpful?

Do it!

C-2:   (Optional) Troubleshooting network problems

Here's how

1 As your instructor describes the troubleshooting scenario she or he has implemented, record the pertinent facts here that will help you troubleshoot the problem.

2 Determine the scope of the problem. How many users are affected? What resources are unavailable?

3 Speculate on the cause of the problem and a probable solution.

4 Using the networking tools described in the preceding topic, test your assumptions and fix the problem. If your changes didn't solve the problem, undo them and try again.

5 Confirm that everything is working as it should, according to the scenario.

Unit summary: Networking

Topic A   In this topic, you learned about **network cabling** types, features, and specifications. You examined the **TCP/IP protocol stack**. Then you learned how various types of **addresses**—MAC addresses, IP addresses, character-based names, and port addresses— are used to identify computers on a network. You also learned how the **DNS** service resolves character-based host names to IP addresses.

Topic B   In this topic, you learned about the tools available to **test** the functionality of the components of a TCP/IP network connection. You used ping, NSLookup, Tracert, and various other tools to examine the classroom network.

Topic C   In this topic, you learned about common **networking problems**. You learned that you must first assess the scope of the problem, and then systematically **troubleshoot** the problem to determine the root cause and the solution.

Review questions

1 At a minimum, which IPv4 address components must you configure in order to communicate on your local subnet? [Choose all that apply.]

    A IP address

    B Subnet mask

    C Default gateway

    D DNS server address

2 Which unique address is permanently embedded in a NIC by the manufacturer?

    A Character-based address

    B IPv4 address

    C IPv6 address

    D MAC address

    E Port address

3 Which unique address is a 128-bit address written in hexadecimal?

    A Character-based address

    B IPv4 address

    C IPv6 address

    D MAC address

    E Port address

4 Which address is a number between 0 and 65,535 that identifies a program running on a computer?

    A Character-based address

    B IPv4 address

    C IPv6 address

    D MAC address

    E Port address

5 How many addresses can IPv6 provide?

   A 2^{32}

   B 2^{64}

   C 2^{128}

   D 2^{256}

6 Which IPv6 address type is similar to an IPv4 APIPA address?

   A Anycast

   B Global unicast

   C Link-local

   D Multicast

   E Site-local

7 Which IPv6 address type is similar to an IPv4 private address?

   A Anycast

   B Global unicast

   C Link-local

   D Multicast

   E Site-local

8 What scheme enables many computers to be called "www" without causing naming conflicts?

   A DHCP

   B DNS

   C TCP/IP

   D WINS

9 True or false? NetBIOS names can't contain spaces.

false

10 Which command displays the IP address of the host and other configuration information?

   A `getmac`

   B `ipconfig`

   C `nslookup`

   D `ping`

11   What information does the `ipconfig` command report?

IP and mac address default gateway

12   What command should you enter to view the Host Name and DNS Server address?

who , nslookup

13   Which command would you use to verify name resolution (DNS) settings?

    A   `ipconfig`

    B   `ping`

    C   `nslookup`

    D   `tracert`

14   What is the difference between SMTP and POP3?

Outgoing Incoming

15   _____ is the decrease in signal strength along the length of a network wire.

Attenuation

16   Which `ipconfig` switch is used to delete all name resolution information from the client's DNS Resolver cache?

/dump

Independent practice activity

In this activity, you'll practice identifying the unique addresses used by a computer.

    1   Switch computers with another student. Identify the following information for the computer:

      MAC address:

      IP version(s):

      IP address(es):

      Character-based names (type and name):

      Gateway address:

      DNS server address:

2 Go back to your computer and answer the following questions about its configuration.

a   What operating system are you running on your computer?

b   How does your computer connect to the Internet (for example, telephone line to ISP, company LAN to ISP, cable modem)?

c   If you use a telephone line to connect to the Internet, what's the telephone number you dial to your ISP?

d   Does your computer use a NIC to connect to the Internet? If so, what's the MAC address of the NIC?

e   What are your current IP address and subnet mask?

f   What class of IP address does the computer use?

g   Does your computer use static or dynamic IP addressing to connect to the Internet? List the steps you used to determine this answer.

Unit 10

Managing a network server

Unit time: 120 minutes

Complete this unit, and you'll know how to:

A Implement and manage user accounts on a network operating system.

B Implement and manage disk resources on a network operating system.

C Monitor your server and network's components.

Topic A: User management

This topic covers the following CompTIA Server+ (2009 Edition) exam objectives.

#	Objective
2.3	**Given a scenario, implement and administer NOS management features based on procedures and guidelines** • User management – Add and remove users – Setting permissions – Group memberships – Policies – Logon scripts • Resource management – ACLs
6.3	**Given a scenario, effectively troubleshoot software problems, selecting the appropriate tools and methods** • Common problems – User unable to logon – User can't access resources • Cause of common problems – User account control (UAC/SUDO)

System security

Explanation

Ensuring the security of system resources generally follows a three-step process of authentication, authorization, and accounting (AAA).

Step	Description
Authentication	Positive identification of the entity, either a person or a system, that wants to access information or services that have been secured. This could be done through a user name and password, a smart card, or a fingerprint scan. At the end of this stage, you know that the user either is who he or she claims to be or is an imposter.
Authorization	The stage in which a predetermined level of access is granted to the entity so that it can access the resource.
Accounting	The stage that involves tracking the user's actions. It could include determining how long he or she was connected, what systems were accessed, how much data was transferred, and so forth. While such information is great if you plan to bill users based on usage, it's also helpful in determining if you have sufficient bandwidth, optimal connectivity, and so forth.

Authentication factors

There are several factors that can be used to authenticate you to the system when you log on. These are:

- Something you know
- Something you have
- Something you are

One-factor authentication

One-factor authentication typically consists of only something you know—your user name and password. When you log into your Windows computer, using the logon box, you are using one-factor authentication. Even if you had to log in a second time to gain access, you are still using one-factor authentication. The user name and password combination is not a very secure type of authentication, compared to two- or three-factor authentication.

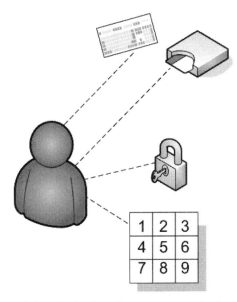

Exhibit 10-1: One-factor systems include user name and password combinations, keycards, locks and keys, and PIN pads

If you use only something you have or only something you are, that is also one-factor authentication. Any time you use just one type of authentication, you are using one-factor, also known as single-factor, authentication.

If you use only a fingerprint sensor or a card reader, that is also one-factor authentication. If you combine the fingerprint sensor with a password, that is two-factor authentication. If you combine a card reader with something else, such as a fingerprint scan or password, that is also considered two-factor authentication.

Opening a door with a PIN pad is also considered one-factor authentication. However, if you first need to swipe a card through a reader before entering your PIN, that is considered two-factor authentication.

A token that generates new passwords every few seconds is another form of one-factor authentication. In this case, it is not being combined with anything that you know.

Two-factor authentication

Two-factor authentication consists of something you know, *plus* either "something you have" or "something you are."

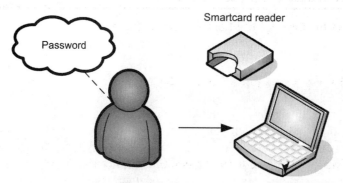

Exhibit 10-2: A smart-card plus password is a form of two-factor authentication

For something you know plus something you have, something you have is a token of some sort, such as a card that you swipe through a reader. One example of this is an ATM card. When you go to the bank's ATM, you use the ATM card along with something you know—your personal identification number (PIN).

For something you know plus something you are, the something you are includes things like your fingerprint, voice print, retinal scan, or something else unique on your body that can be measured. When combined with a password or PIN, this is another example of two-factor authentication. Another example of two-factor authentication consists of a token that creates new passwords every few seconds, combined with a PIN to access the passwords.

Three-factor authentication

Three-factor authentication uses something you know, something you have, and something you are. In addition to having a token, such as a card and a PIN, you also use a biometric scan of your fingerprint, voice, retina, or other uniquely distinguishing body feature to provide a third authentication factor in order to gain access to the system.

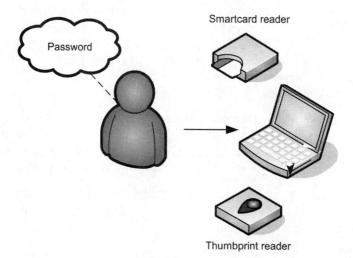

Exhibit 10-3: Add a biometric reader to create a three-factor authentication system

Do it!   **A-1:   Comparing one-, two-, and three-factor authentication**

Questions and answers

1 List the three types of authentication factors.

2 List two types of one-factor authentication.

3 What is combined to create two-factor authentication?

4 Three-factor authentication makes use of what types of authentication methods?

User accounts

Explanation

A *user account* is a collection of all the information that pertains to a user, such as his user name, password, access rights, and permissions. User accounts reside either in a local database on an individual computer or in the *network directory service (NDS)* database on the *network operating system (NOS)* installed on your server. Any person who requires access to network resources needs a user account. By creating user accounts in the NDS, you can centrally administer and maintain the security of the network. Through user accounts, you can:

- Require authentication for users connecting to the network.
- Control access to network resources such as shared folders or printers.
- Monitor access to resources by auditing the actions performed by a user.

User names and passwords

Throughout the ages, secret codes have been used for access to things and locations that only those with the secret code can get into. The secret code can be simple and easily guessed or extremely complicated. In the computing environment, these secret codes are what we use to gain access to files and systems.

A *user name* uniquely identifies the user to a computer or network system when the person logs in. The user name assigned is often simple and might even be based on the user's name; other times, it's a complex string of characters that users need to memorize.

The *password* is the secret code. In some cases, it can be very simple, although this isn't a good practice because someone else could easily guess the password. Usually, network administrators will require users to create a complex password that consists of letters, numbers, and possibly special characters. Often, network administrators will also recommend a minimum password length. When the password is combined with the user name, it authenticates the user.

Password protection

Weak passwords are a major problem. Hackers have tools that help them quickly retrieve passwords from a compromised system. Users need to create stronger passwords and protect them diligently, and administrators need to use every tool available to them to protect password files.

Some steps users should take to protect their passwords include:

- Memorizing passwords rather than writing them down.
- Using a different password for every account that requires a password.
- Creating a password at least eight characters long. Longer passwords are harder to crack.
- Using a mixture of upper- and lowercase letters, numbers, and special characters in a password.
- Changing passwords frequently.
- Avoiding using the same password again within a year.

Strong passwords

When users create a password, they need to balance the ability to remember it with the complexity of it. If the password is so complex that the only way to remember it is to write it down, then you are sacrificing the security of the password.

The way some people create passwords is to take the first letter of a song title, book title, or phrase and use it as the basis of a password. The result is often referred to as a *passphrase*. They make some of the letters uppercase and some lowercase, and add numbers and special characters to make it more secure. This scheme gives you something that is easily remembered, along with the more secure password created with numbers and special characters.

Make sure to teach users not to include any personal information, such as their name or pet's name, in their passwords. Also, they shouldn't use any word that can be found in the dictionary, because hackers routinely perform dictionary-based attacks.

Multiple passwords

If users have multiple passwords to remember for different systems and Web sites, it can be difficult to remember all of the user name and password combinations. One way to record them is to use a password management tool, which is a program in which you store your passwords in an encrypted format. Users just need to remember a single password to access the file. Some of the password management tools will create complex passwords for you, using rules that you define.

User account guidelines

It's important that your organization set standards for the various elements of a user account. Some of these standards might include:

- **Establishing a naming convention** — Each user account name should follow a consistent format. Common examples include:

Naming convention	Example for Kirk Jeffries
First name and last initial	KirkJ
First initial and last name	KJeffries
Last name and first initial	JeffriesK

A small company might be fine using only the user's first initial and last name, but a larger company might end up with multiple users with the same combination of first initial and last name. For you to give every user a unique user name, your naming convention should describe what to do if multiple users have similar—or even the same—names. For example, if the user name *bsmith* is already taken and Barbara Smith joins the organization, the naming convention could specify that the first two letters (or more if necessary) of the person's first name be used. Alternatively, the user's middle initial or nickname, or even a number, could be used.

- **Controlling password ownership** — You need to decide whether you control the password for each user or allow users to maintain their own passwords. Many organizations establish policies for the format of the passwords, such as requiring a password to have at least eight alphanumeric characters. Having passwords expire on a regular schedule helps maintain security.

- **Including additional required attributes** — You can include additional information about users when creating the user accounts. This information might include phone numbers and e-mail addresses. The type of information you can attach to the user account will vary based on the NOS. Keep in mind that every additional attribute requires additional replication bandwidth and storage space within your network directory service.

- **Determining the location for user accounts** — When your network size goes beyond a small peer-to-peer network, having user accounts in the NOS's directory services makes user management and access control much easier. For small networks, you might be able to create local user accounts on your file and print servers to grant users access.

The exact steps to create and manage user accounts will vary based on the network operating system you have installed on your server. You should refer to the Help system for your network operating system.

Client/server authentication

In the client/server networking model, user accounts are created centrally and stored on a server. A trained system administrator is usually responsible for maintaining the server and NOS while managing resources to meet user needs. Each user can authenticate and gain access to any resource on the LAN by entering his or her network user ID and password. The local client operating system isn't responsible for authenticating user IDs and passwords. Instead, the client OS uses its *network client* software to send this information to the NOS on the server. The directory service verifies the user ID and password based on the information stored in its database.

The logon process goes something like this:

1 The network client on the client computer displays a logon screen.

2 The user enters his or her user ID and password on the logon screen and clicks OK.

3 The network client sends this information to the NOS for authentication.

4 After the user ID and password have been authenticated, the user can gain access to the computer and to the network resources.

The server uses a database to store user account information, user permissions, security policies, printer information, and other configuration settings. This information is used to control which resources on the LAN are shared and who can use them. The system administrator assigns user permissions that specify which resources users can access on the LAN. Software, files, printers, and other resources can be accessed by a user on the LAN only when the system administrator has granted specific permission to that person's user account. You might also hear a client/server network described as a *centralized networking* model because it enables you to administer computers and users as a group instead of individually.

Active Directory domain controllers

In Windows Server 2008, a domain controller is configured to store a copy of the Active Directory database (the NDS for Windows Server) and to service user authentication requests or queries about domain objects. You promote servers to the role of domain controller by using the Active Directory Installation Wizard (dcpromo.exe).

Active Directory is made up of several components that provide a way to design and administer the hierarchical, logical structure of the network. To install a domain controller, you need to know the topmost component (the forest name) and the next level (the domain name). Active Directory uses the DNS naming standard.

Many network directory services support a number of open standards and interfaces which enable you to programmatically create user accounts. Many Web resources are available to help you develop a script for creating user accounts in your environment. Using a search engine, you should be able to find scripts that can perform all but the most unusual tasks.

Creating and managing an Active Directory structure is beyond the scope of this course. For additional information, you can take courses in the MCSE line.

Account logon problems

If a user is unable to log on, there are several things you need to investigate:

- Has the user entered the correct user name and password? Be sure the Caps Lock key is not on. And remember, user names are not case-sensitive, but passwords are.

- Does the user have a valid user account? Is the account disabled?

- Is the user's computer connected to the network, and are the networking settings correct? Can the computer "see" the directory server? Is the directory server online?

By working your way through these questions, you should be able to solve just about any logon problem.

Do it!

A-2: Adding the Directory Services role

Here's how	Here's why
1 If necessary, log on to your Windows Server 2008 computer	
2 In Server Manager, in the navigation pane, select **Roles**	You will make your Windows Server 2008 computer an Active Directory domain controller, allowing you to create network user accounts instead of local user accounts.
3 In the details pane, under Roles Summary, click **Add Roles**	
Click **Next**	
4 Check **Active Directory Domain Services**	
Click **Next** twice	
5 Click **Install**	
6 Click **Close this wizard and launch the Active Directory Domain Services Installation Wizard (dcpromo.exe)**	
7 Click **Next** twice	
8 Select **Create a new domain in a new forest**	Currently there isn't an Active Directory structure set up in the classroom.
Click **Next**	
9 In the FQDN of the forest root domain, type **DOMAIN##.CLASS**	Where ## is a unique number. .CLASS is not a currently recognized top-level DNS name, so we don't have to worry about the names you assign conflicting with a computer on the Internet.
Click **Next**	
10 Open the Forest functional level list	If you have domain controllers running Windows Server 2000 or Windows Server 2003, you can allow them to continue to provide services in your forest. The functional level you choose doesn't affect member servers.
Select **Windows Server 2008**	
Click **Next**	

11 Click **Next**	To install the DNS server role on this computer. DNS is important for most network services, including processing user logons. If a user cannot log on, verify that the network settings, including the DNS server address, are correct.
12 Click **Yes**	If necessary, to say that you wish to use a dynamic IP address.
13 Click **Yes**	To acknowledge that no action is needed because you aren't integrating with an existing DNS zone.
14 Click **Next**	To accept the default locations for the database, log files, and the SYSVOL folder.
15 Enter and confirm a password of **!pass1234** Click **Next**	For the Directory Services Restore Mode Administrator password.
16 Review the Summary information Click **Next**	If the information isn't correct, you can click the Back button to make corrections.
17 Click **Finish** Click **Restart Now**	
18 Log back on Close Server Manager	

A-3: Creating user accounts

Here's how	Here's why
1 Click **Start** and choose **Administrative Tools, Active Directory Users and Computers**	
2 In the navigation pane, expand **DOMAIN##.CLASS**	
Select **Users**	There are two users in Active Directory for your domain: administrator and guest.
3 Right-click **Users** and choose **New**, **User**	
4 Enter the following information and then click **Next**	
First name: *Your first name* Last name: *Your last name* User logon name: *Your first initial, middle initial, and last name*	Notice that your full name is filled in automatically as you type your first name and last name. For the User logon name, don't include spaces. For example, Sara Ann Carson would be *sacarson*. An incorrectly entered user logon name could prevent the user from logging on.
5 Click **Next**	
6 In the Password and Confirm password boxes, enter **pa$$321**	
7 Observe the options	In Active Directory, there are four: • User must change password at next logon • User cannot change password • Password never expires • Account is disabled Other NDSs might have similar options.
8 Click **Next**	
Click **Finish**	Your new user account is listed in the details pane.
9 Create two more user accounts	You can use any two names of your choosing. Use *pa$$321* as the password.

User properties

Explanation

There are potentially hundreds of other attributes you can set for each user account. Many of the attributes configured as part of creating a user object are fairly limited. You can quickly create the basic components needed for a user account to give the person network access, and then add information as your company requires when time allows. You can add information by modifying the properties of the user account.

In many NDSs, you can include additional user information, such as:

- Telephone numbers
- E-mail addresses
- Web page addresses
- Physical address
- Job information, such as title and department
- Group memberships
- Remote access conditions
- Operating system environment settings

Other options will be available based on the NDS you are running. Many times, you can modify multiple user accounts simultaneously with the same information either programmatically or by using the NDS interface. This method can save you time when you need to enter common information, such as your company's mailing address for all employees at a particular location or a department name for a specific group of employees.

In a Windows domain environment, you modify user accounts by using the Active Directory Users and Computers administrative tool.

Do it!

A-4: Modifying user properties

Here's how	Here's why
1 In the details pane, right-click your user name and choose **Properties**	
2 Observe the series of tabs on the page	The information on these tabs is unique to Active Directory, but similar user properties are found in other NDSs.
3 Activate each tab and observe the information it contains	
4 On the General tab, in the E-mail box, type *your user name*@**DOMAIN##.CLASS**	
Click **OK**	

Disabling and removing user accounts

Explanation

As a network administrator, you need to closely monitor the user accounts in your organization. If a user is going on leave and won't be accessing the network remotely, it's a good security precaution to disable the account until the user returns to work. This prevents someone from using the account to gain unauthorized access during the user's absence. Because the user is out, there's a high likelihood that any security breach won't be noticed until he or she returns.

The exact steps to disable a user account depend on the NDS. In Active Directory, it's a property of the user account. When you disable an account, the settings, group memberships, and permissions assigned to the account remain intact. You don't have to reconfigure the account once you re-enable it.

When a user has left the company, you don't want to disable the account; you want to delete it. Deleting an account removes all configuration information attached to the account—group memberships, permissions, and so on. If you need to reinstate the user for some reason, you'll have to start from scratch with a brand new user account.

Do it!

A-5: Disabling and removing a user account

Here's how	Here's why
1 In the details pane, right-click one of the three user accounts you created and choose **Properties**	
2 Activate the Account tab	
3 Scroll through the Account options list	
4 Check **Account is disabled**	
Click **OK**	The account is still in the NDS's database. All settings, group memberships, and permissions are maintained, but the account can't be used to log on.
5 Right-click the disabled user account and choose **Delete**	
Click **Yes**	

Group memberships

Explanation

Administrators might be responsible for thousands of user accounts and hundreds of resources. Trying to manage each individual account is not very efficient. If you had 5 printers, 10 file shares, 2 SQL database servers, and 150 users in your company, you would have at least 2500 sets of permissions to manage. However, if those 150 users all required the same level of access, then assigning permissions to a group, which could encompass all of those users with the same access needs, would take only a few minutes.

Some NDSs offer different types of groups you can create. For example, Active Directory has *distribution groups*, which have no security functions and are used with e-mail applications, and *security groups*, which can be used to grant permissions to network resources. Security groups can also be used with e-mail applications to send an e-mail message to all members of the group.

NDSs will provide groups that are created automatically with assigned permissions and rights based on their functions. For example, in Active Directory, the Domain Admins group is assigned complete unrestricted access to the local computer and the domain. When you hire a network administrator who will be responsible for your Active Directory domain, instead of granting individual permissions and rights to her user account, you add her account to the Domain Admins group. If she later takes a different position in the company, you don't need to change all of her individual permissions and rights; instead, you simply remove them from the Domain Admins group and put them in another group with permissions and rights appropriate for her new position.

Again, creating and managing an Active Directory structure is beyond the scope of this course. For additional information, you can take courses in the MCSE line.

Do it!

A-6: Creating a group

Here's how	Here's why
1 With the Users container selected, observe the Security Groups listed in the details pane	These groups were created automatically when you installed Active Directory.
	• Domain Local groups can be used to assign permissions to resources within the local domain. Remember that Active Directory is hierarchical. There can be other domains in the forest. Members of these groups would not have rights in other domains.
	• Global groups can be used to assign permissions to resources in any domain within the forest. Members come from only the domain in which the group was created.
	• Universal groups can be used to assign permissions to resources in any domain within the forest. However, members can come from any domain within the forest.
2 In the navigation pane, select **Builtin**	The Builtin container contains a number of domain local group accounts that allocate user rights based on common administrative or network-related tasks. For example, members of the Backup Operators group can override security restrictions for the purpose of backing up or restoring files.
	These groups were created for this domain only when you installed Active Directory.
3 In the navigation pane, select **Users**	
4 Right-click **Users** and choose **New**, **Group**	
5 In the Group name box, type **Marketing Dept ##**	Where ## is your unique number. The group name (pre-Windows 2000) is filled in automatically.
6 Observe the Group scope and Group type boxes	By default, the new group is a Global Security group. You can assign permissions to this group for resources within any domain in the AD forest, but you can add members from only this domain.
Click **OK**	
7 Double-click **Marketing Dept**	
Activate the Members tab	There are no members in this group.

8 Click **Add**	If you know the name of the user or group account you want to add, you can type it in the "Enter the object names to select" box.
9 Click **Advanced**	
10 Click **Find Now**	To display all user and group accounts that you can add to this group.
11 Select the two user accounts you created	Press and hold the Ctrl key to select multiple accounts.
Click **OK** three times	To add the two user accounts you created to the Marketing Dept group. You can now use this group to assign rights or permissions to shared resources within domains in your AD forest.
12 Right-click either user account and choose **Properties**	
Activate the Member Of tab	It shows that this user is a member of Domain Users (added by default when you created the account) and Marketing Dept.
13 Click **Cancel**	
14 Close Active Directory Users and Computers	

User privilege escalation

Experts have recommended for years that administrative users log on and work with a standard user-level account unless they actually need special administrative privileges for certain tasks. This security scheme protects a computer in a number of ways, including the following:

- Administrators can't inadvertently change system settings, delete important files, or do other system harm, as they could if they logged on regularly as an administrative user.

- Unauthorized users can't walk up to an unattended administrator computer and make system changes on it or on other computers on the network.

Escalation in Windows

The *User Account Control (UAC)* feature, introduced in Windows Vista and Windows Server 2008, is designed to make it convenient to follow Microsoft's security recommendation. You are permitted to make more system changes than you could before when logged on as a standard user. More important, whenever you attempt an action that requires administrative privileges, you are prompted for credentials; this step helps protect against malware being installed or making changes without your permission. If you supply appropriate administrative credentials, you are permitted to perform the action. You don't need to log out and log back in as an administrator.

Windows displays different elevation prompts based on the privileges of the user account that is logged on when an application needs administrative privileges. When you are logged on to Windows as a local administrator, it displays a consent prompt whenever a program needs elevated privileges to accomplish a task.

If you're logged on as a standard user and try to perform a task that requires administrative privileges, you'll see a credential prompt. This prompt requires you to enter the user name and password for a local or domain administrator account before Windows will grant the necessary privileges for the application to run.

When elevated permissions are required, UAC will present one of the alerts in the following table. You'll need to provide the appropriate administrative credentials or speak to an administrator to continue.

Alert	You'll see this alert when...
Windows needs your permission to continue	The operating system wants to perform a function that will modify the computer or operating system settings.
A program needs your permission to continue	A program with a valid digital signature wants to start.
An unidentified program wants access to your computer	A program without a valid digital signature wants to start. A program without a valid digital signature is not necessarily a malicious program.
This program has been blocked	The computer administrator has blocked you from starting the program you're trying to start.

Escalation in Linux

Generally, regular users do not have the permissions needed to perform administrative tasks, such as mounting file systems. That is a privilege reserved for the root user. If you have root access, such as when you're operating your own computer, you can log on as root to mount the file system or perform other administrative tasks. However, the better option is to use the su or sudo command to temporarily raise your privileges; you then perform the administrative command and return to your normal operating level.

The su command, an abbreviation for "switch user," is the traditional command used for privilege escalation. In its default form, to run this command, you must enter the root user's password. Then you can work at a terminal or shell as the root user until you exit that shell.

You can also use the su command to impersonate another user. You would enter su *username* and then that user account's password. Then you would be able to operate as that user until you exited that shell.

The sudo command, a concatenation of "su do," is like su. However, you use it to run a single command as another user. In addition, the system administrator has fine-grained control over which commands you can run via the sudo command. Usually, it's better to run the sudo command, rather than the su command, because there is a smaller chance of inadvertently damaging your system by forgetting to return to a normal user level.

You run the privileged command through sudo in this way:

```
sudo [-u username] command
```

You are then prompted to enter *your* password, not the root user's (or other user's) password. Typically, your system will cache your authentication criteria for 15 minutes. Within that timeframe, you can execute further sudo commands without re-entering your password. Because it requires you to enter your own password, sudo does not require you to know, or the administrator to share, the root password. This makes sudo a more secure option than the su command.

The commands you are allowed to execute are stored in the /etc/sudoers file. To get a list of the commands you are permitted to execute, enter sudo -l (that's an "L" for list, not a one).

In Debian, standard user-level accounts are not listed in the sudoers file; even the initial account you create during installation is not listed. In Ubuntu, the user-level account you create during installation is added to the sudoers file with permissions to execute all commands. To edit the sudoers file, you must use the visudo command while logged in as root.

Do it!

A-7: Discussing privilege escalation

Questions and answers

1 You are logged on to a Windows server with a standard user account. All default User Account Control settings are enabled. What happens when you attempt to run a task that requires administrative privileges?

2 Which activities require you to respond to elevation prompts in Windows?

    A   Changing your password

    B   Using Windows Defender to scan for malware

    C   Configuring a Windows Firewall exception

    D   Modifying the screen resolution for your monitor

3 Why did Microsoft incorporate User Account Control into Windows?

4 Why would you run `sudo` instead of `su` on a Linux server?

Permissions

Explanation

Resources are secured on a server through the use of permissions. By configuring various permissions on a particular resource, you can grant a certain group of users the ability to access the resource and complete tasks with it. You can also use permissions to deny access or the ability to complete particular tasks. Common network resources you want to secure with permissions include files and printers. Examples of other network resources include e-mail and database servers.

The steps to assign permissions will vary based on the resource. All resources that can be secured have an *access control list (ACL)* associated with them. The ACL is a list of *access control entries (ACEs)*, each of which specifies a "who" and a permission. Most resources will be able to access your NDS database and use the user and group accounts as the "who."

One important thing to remember is that there are two types of permissions: local access and remote access. Local access permissions are applied on only the computer where the resource is located. Remote access permissions are applied on top of the local access permissions when you connect to the resource over the network. The most restrictive of the two sets are the permissions a user will have when connecting remotely.

Most operating systems have the following types of permissions you can assign (the names might vary slightly):

- **Read** — Grants the user the ability to view the contents of a folder or file. However, the user can't add files to or remove files from the folder, or change the files.

- **Write** — Grants the user the Read permissions, plus the ability to add files to or remove files from a folder, and change files.

- **Full control** — Grants the user full control over a folder or file, including the ability to delete the folder and its contents.

Implicitly and explicitly denying access

Shared resources will also implement what is called an *implicit deny*, which occurs when a user who hasn't explicitly been assigned an entry allowing access is automatically denied access. Because the user isn't in the ACL, the resource denies the user access. You can think of this as being like security at a private event—if someone isn't on the list, he isn't allowed in.

You can also create ACEs that specifically deny access. You might wonder why you should explicitly deny access if the system will automatically implicitly deny it. The biggest reason for assigning a deny ACE is to change the effect of permissions that a user would otherwise have as a member of a group or by permissions inheritance, where access is granted to a subfolder based on the permissions assigned to its parent folder. It's important to remember that an explicit deny ACE overrides all other ACEs.

Troubleshooting permissions

A particular user can have permissions assigned to him individually or through group membership. One of the more complex tasks that an administrator is responsible for is determining a user's effective permissions for a network resource. Because the permissions that actually apply to a user can result from membership in various groups, this task can be complex. In environments with thousands of users and shared resources, the amount of time and effort required to do this could quickly become unmanageable. Some resources, such as shared folders in Windows operating systems, will have a tool you can use to see the effective permissions of a particular user or group.

A-8: Creating a shared resource and assigning permissions

Here's how	Here's why
1 Click **Start** and choose **Computer**	You'll create a shared folder where users can access files.
2 In the details pane, double-click **Local Disk (C:)**	
3 Click **Organize** and choose **New Folder**	
Type **Marketing Documents**	
4 Right-click **Marketing Documents** and choose **Share...**	Currently only the Administrator user has share permissions on the folder.
5 Click the down-arrow and choose **Find...**	
6 In the "Enter the object names to select" box, type **Marketing**, and then click **Check Names**	The Marketing Dept group is displayed.
Click **OK**	
7 Click **Share**	The folder is now shared over the network. If you had an e-mail server set up, you could use e-mail to notify group members that the folder is available.
Click **Done**	
8 Right-click **Marketing Documents** and choose **Properties**	
9 Activate the Sharing tab	
Click **Advanced Sharing**	
Click **Permissions**	
10 If necessary, select **Marketing Dept ## (DOMAIN##\Marketing Dept ##)**	This shows you that members of the Marketing group can read the contents of the shared folder via the network share.
Check **Change**	To increase the permissions for members of this group so they can change files in the folder.
11 Click **OK** twice	

12	Activate the Security tab	This shows the local permissions for the folder. If they are more restrictive than the ones you set on the share, users won't be able to complete the restricted tasks via the network share.
13	Select **Marketing Dept ##** **(DOMAIN##\Marketing Dept ##)**	Members of this group have local Read permissions. They won't be able to change the files in the folder.
14	Click **Advanced**	
15	Select **Marketing Dept ##** **(DOMAIN##\Marketing Dept ##)**	
	Click **Edit**	
16	Select **Marketing Dept ##** **(DOMAIN##\Marketing Dept ##)** again	
	Click Edit	
17	In the Allow column, check: **Create files / write data** **Create folders / append data** **Delete subfolders and files Delete**	
18	Click **OK** three times	
19	Click **Close**	The local permissions and the share permissions are now similar. The users in the Marketing Department group should be able to change the files in the folder via the network share without problems.
20	Close Local Disk (C:)	

Policies

Explanation

Many NOSs include policy features that allow you to easily manage and control various computer configurations. You can choose to apply the policies you create to all users, to all computers, to a subgroup of users, or to a subgroup of computers. Administrative tasks you can automate with policies include:

- Controlling users' computer settings, such as the desktop configuration in Windows.
- Controlling security settings for users and computers.
- Running scripts when events—such as user logon or logoff, or computer startup or shutdown—occur.
- Redirecting folders from a local drive to a network location.
- Distributing software installations and updates to computers throughout the network.

In Windows Server 2008, you use the Group Policy Management utility to create and manage your policies. To implement a group policy, you must create a *group policy object* (GPO) or modify one of the default GPOs to meet your requirements. When you install Active Directory, two default GPOs are created. The first GPO is linked to the domain and is called the Default Domain Policy. This policy will be applied to all computers and users in the domain. The second GPO is linked to the AD domain controllers and is called the Default Domain Controllers Policy. This policy will be applied to all domain controllers in your AD domain. You can also create custom GPOs that are applied to subgroups of users or computers.

If you have the capacity, you should set up a test environment where you can test your policies before you deploy them in your enterprise. You can then troubleshoot any problems or unintended results of the policies before they reach your users.

Again, creating and managing an Active Directory structure is beyond the scope of this course. For detailed information on AD group policies, you can take courses in the MCSE line.

Do it!

A-9: Exploring policy settings

Here's how	Here's why
1 Click **Start** and choose **Administrative Tools**, **Group Policy Management**	In Windows Server 2008, you use the Group Policy Management utility to create and manage your group policies.
2 In the navigation pane, expand Forest: DOMAIN##.CLASS, Domains, DOMAIN##.CLASS	A shortcut to the Default Domain Policy is located at the root of the DOMAIN##.CLASS container.
3 Expand Domain Controllers	A shortcut to the Default Domain Controllers Policy is located in the Domain Controllers container.
4 Expand Group Policy Objects	The Default Domain Policy and Default Domain Controllers Policy objects are located in this container.
5 Under Group Policy Objects, select **Default Domain Policy**	
Observe the Scope	This policy is applied to all authenticated users in the DOMAIN##.CLASS domain.
6 Activate the Details tab	This policy is enabled.
7 Activate the Settings tab	Only computer security settings are defined for this policy. No user configuration settings have been defined.
8 Click **show**	
Review the policy settings that are being applied	
9 In the navigation pane, right-click **Default Domain Policy** and choose **Edit...**	You'll review the other settings you can configure.
10 Observe the navigation pane	The policy is divided into two sections: settings that apply to computers, and settings that apply to users.
11 Under Computer Configuration, expand Policies	This item is divided into three sections: Software Settings, Windows Settings, and Administrative Templates.
12 Select and observe Software Settings	You use this policy section to centralize the management of software installation and maintenance. You can control the installation, upgrades, and removal of applications from one central spot.

13 Expand and select Windows Settings	You use this policy section to manage the deployment and management of scripts and security settings.
Expand and select Security Settings	The details pane lists the types of security settings you can apply to computers in your domain.
14 Explore the various security categories	
15 Expand and select Administrative Templates	You use this section to set Registry-based values that configure application, network, and user desktop settings.
16 Explore the various Administrative Templates categories	
17 Select **Preferences**	Preferences provide more than 20 group policy extensions that allow you to manage drive mappings, Registry settings, local users and groups, services, files, and folders without scripting.
Explore the settings in Preferences	
18 Explore the User Configuration settings	You'll find that some are similar to those that can be applied to computers.
	Keep Group Policy Management open for the next activity.

Scripts

Explanation

You can automate routine administrative tasks by using various types of scripts or files that issue commands. With many NOSs, you can assign scripts to run when a trigger event occurs. Common trigger events include the following:

- A user logs on
- A user logs off
- A computer starts up
- A computer shuts down

For example, a very popular option is to use logon scripts to automate such tasks as drive mappings or application updates. You can typically create scripts in any language supported by the client computer. In the Windows Server 2008 environment, the most common are Windows Script Host (WSH)–supported languages and command files, such as VBScript and Jscript. You can assign multiple scripts to be applied to the same user or computer. Once you've assigned scripts, you can configure options such as the order in which they run, script time-outs, whether the scripts run synchronously or asynchronously, and whether they are hidden to the user when they are executed. (Scripting languages are beyond the scope of this course.)

The exact steps to assign scripts will vary based on the NOS you have installed. However, you should always test each script individually in a non-production environment to make sure it functions correctly before you deploy it in your organization. If possible, deploy to a small group as a second test before deploying to the entire company. You don't want to arrive at work and find that when users logged on, an untested script caused a problem that prevents them from working.

In Windows Server 2008, you use Group Policy Management to assign scripts. You first need to copy your scripts and any dependent files to the Netlogon shared folder on the AD domain controller. This is where clients will run the script files from. You must be a member of the Domain Administrators security group to configure scripts on a domain controller.

After you have your scripts in the Netlogon shared folder, you need to assign them by using Group Policy Management Console. You can assign scripts to any GPO you have established, or you can create a new GPO specifically for scripts. You'll find computer startup and shutdown script configuration under Computer Configuration, Policies, Windows Settings, Scripts (Startup/Shutdown). You'll find user logon and logoff script configuration under User Configuration, Policies, Windows Settings, Scripts (Logon/Logoff).

Do it!

A-10: Setting up a logon script

Here's how	Here's why
1 Click **Start** and choose **Administrative Tools, Share and Storage Management**	
Observe the Shares on your computer	The NETLOGON share is assigned to the local folder C:\Windows\SYSVOL\sysvol\▶ DOMAIN##.CLASS\SCRIPTS.

2	Close Share and Storage Management	
3	Click **Start** and choose **Computer**	
	Navigate to **C:\Windows\SYSVOL\sysvol\DOMAIN##.CLASS\SCRIPTS**	This is the location to which you would copy your script and supporting files.
4	Close the scripts window	
5	In the Group Policy Management Editor, under Default Domain Policy, Computer Configuration, Policies, Windows Settings, select **Scripts (Startup/Shutdown)**	
6	In the details pane, double-click **Startup**	
7	Click **Add**	You won't do this now, but to assign a script, you would do the following:
		In the Script Name box, browse to select the script file in the Netlogon shared folder on the domain controller.
		In the Script Parameters box, type any parameters you need applied to the script. Type them just as you would at a command line.
	Click **Cancel** twice	You would assign Shutdown scripts in the same manner.
8	Navigate to User Configuration, Policies, Windows Settings, and select **Scripts Logon/Logoff)**	
	In the details pane, double-click **Logon**	User scripts are specified in the same way as computer scripts.
	Click **Cancel**	These scripts would be applied to all computers or users in the domain, but you can assign scripts to smaller groups of computers or users by creating a GPO that is assigned to specific users, groups, and computers.
9	Close Group Policy Management	

Topic B: Resource management

This topic covers the following CompTIA Server+ (2009 Edition) exam objectives.

#	Objective
2.3	**Given a scenario, implement and administer NOS management features based on procedures and guidelines**
	• Resource management
	– Quotas
	– Shadow volumes
	– Disk management
6.3	**Given a scenario, effectively troubleshoot software problems, selecting the appropriate tools and methods**
	• Common problems
	– Users cannot print
	• Cause of common problems
	– Print server drivers/services
	– Print spooler

Disk and volume information

Explanation
Many NOSs provide a utility you can use to view disk-related information and to perform such tasks as creating and deleting partitions and volumes. The disk-related information provided typically includes status messages on the health of disks and volumes to help you monitor the overall health of the disk subsystem. Some of the more common volume-status messages you might encounter include the following (exact wording can vary by NOS):

- **Failed** — Indicates that a volume could not be started automatically or that the disk is damaged. If this status message appears, verify that the disk is properly connected to the system.

- **Failed Redundancy** — Indicates that the fault tolerance provided by a RAID or mirrored volume is unavailable. This problem can be caused by one of the disks in the volume being offline. Different sub-status messages might appear next to the message, indicating that the volume at risk is the system or boot volume, holds the paging file, and so forth.

- **Formatting** — Indicates that a volume is being formatted.

- **Healthy** — Indicates that a volume is functioning as it should, and no additional administrative actions are required. If this message is followed by a sub-status message indicating that the volume is at risk, I/O errors may have been detected. Run a disk check/verification program.

- **Regenerating** — Indicates that a missing disk in a RAID volume has been reactivated and is regenerating its data. Once this process is complete, you should see the status of this volume return to Healthy.

- **Resyncing** — Indicates that a mirrored volume is synchronizing information as part of maintaining identical data on both disks. This message may also appear when mirrored disks are imported, or when an offline disk in a mirrored volume is brought back online. Once the process is complete, the status of the volume should return to Healthy.

- **Unknown** — Indicates that the boot sector for the volume is corrupted, and data on that volume is not accessible.

Common status messages that you may encounter for a disk include:

- **Audio CD** — Indicates that an audio CD is located in a CD or DVD drive.

- **Foreign** — Designates the disk as a disk imported from another computer.

- **Initializing** — Is displayed when you're converting a basic disk to a dynamic disk.

- **Missing** — Indicates that the disk has been removed, is not properly connected, or has been corrupted.

- **No Media** — Indicates that the CD, DVD, or other removable media drive is empty.

- **Not Initialized** — Indicates that a new disk has been added to the system without a valid disk signature.

- **Online** — Indicates that the disk is functioning normally, and no additional actions are required.

- **Online (Errors)** — Indicates that I/O errors have been detected on a disk. Use a disk check/verification program to scan the disk for errors.

- **Offline** — Indicates that a disk is no longer accessible. The problem might be related to the connection or a problem with the drive controller.

- **Unreadable** — Typically indicates I/O errors or corruption on certain portions of the disk. Try to repair the problem with a disk check/verification program.

For a complete list of the various disk and volume status and sub-status messages available in your NOS, refer to the Help system. In Windows Server, you use the Disk Management utility to view the status of your disks and volumes. The Disk Management node of the Computer Management tool is shown in Exhibit 10-4.

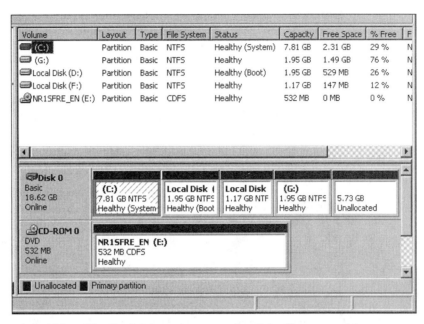

Exhibit 10-4: The Disk Management node of the Computer Management tool

Do it!

B-1:   Viewing the status of a server's disks and volumes

Here's how	Here's why
1 Click **Start** and choose **All Programs**, **Administrative Tools**, **Computer Management**	Disk Management is located in the Computer Management Microsoft Management Console (MMC).
2 In the navigation pane, under Storage, select **Disk Management**	Hard drives and removable drives are listed in the bottom center pane.
3 Observe the information provided for each disk	For the hard disks in your system, you'll see whether they are basic or dynamic, what their sizes are, and whether they are on- or off-line. To the right, you will see the volumes (partitions) that have been created on the drive, along with their sizes, their file formats, whether they are healthy, and what types of volume they are (for example, system, boot, page file, or active).
	Removable drives are also listed, along with their drive letters, whether there are media in them, and if so, the size of the media loaded.

Shadow volumes

A *shadow volume* is a read-only copy of files—including open files—on a selected volume at a particular point in time. You can use shadow volumes to back up open files and applications.

Shadow volumes allow users to restore previous versions of files without the administrator involvement that a backup restore would require. In Windows Server 2008, Shadow Copies for Shared Folders uses the Volume Shadow Copy service to provide point-in-time copies of files located in a network share.

Using Shadow Copies for Shared Folders, users can:

- Recover files that have been accidentally deleted
- Recover a previous version of a file
- Compare versions of a file while working

A shadow volume copy is unlike a traditional file copy. You cannot select specific folders and files on a volume to be copied (or not copied), as you could with a backup. A shadow volume copy applies to an entire volume.

A volume shadow copy sets aside a specified amount of disk space to store file changes that have occurred since the shadow volume was created. Only files that have changed take up additional disk space. In Windows, a certain amount of disk space is allocated for storing the file changes made after a shadow volume is created. If the amount of space allocated is not enough to hold all of the changes, older changes are overwritten. You can change the storage location, space allocation, and schedule of your shadow copies. There is a limit of 64 shadow copies per volume. When this limit is reached, the oldest shadow copy is deleted and you can't retrieve it.

Best practices

Microsoft recommends the following guidelines when you're implementing shadow volumes on Windows Server 2008:

- To ensure that your file server's performance doesn't suffer, select a volume on another disk as the storage area for shadow copies.
- Adjust the default shadow copy schedule so that it doesn't interfere with high access times on the volume you want to shadow.
- Don't implement the shadow volume feature on volumes that have mount points. (A *mounted drive* is one that appears as a folder and is accessed through a path like any other folder. Mounting a drive is an alternative to giving it a drive letter.) Mount drives aren't included in shadow copies.
- Back up your file server regularly. Shadow volumes aren't a replacement for backups.
- Don't schedule shadow copies to occur more than once per hour. More storage space is used and performance of the file server degrades as the number of shadow copies increases.

Steps to enable a shadow volume will vary based on NOS, if the feature is included. In Windows Server 2008, you use the Disk Management utility to enable and configure shadow volumes. If you want users to be able to access previous versions of files via the Shadow Copies of Shared Folders feature, you can have them use either Previous Versions or the Shadow Copy client.

Here's the recommended method:

1 Right-click the share for which you want to access previous file versions and choose Properties.

2 Select the desired folder version based on its date and time stamp.

3 Click the desired button: click Open to open the shadow copy in Windows Explorer; click Copy to copy the selected folder's snapshot image; or click Restore to roll back the shared folder to its state at the time of the snapshot image you selected.

Do it!

B-2: Exploring shadow volumes

Here's how	Here's why
1 In the navigation pane, right-click **Disk Management** and choose **All Tasks**, **Configure Shadow Copies...**	
2 If necessary, select **C:**	
Click **Settings**	
3 Observe the Storage area settings	Microsoft recommends selecting a volume on a disk other than the one where the original volume resides.
	You can change the maximum size of the shadow volume or set it to No limit.
4 Click **Schedule**	
Open the drop-down list	By default, shadow copies are made at 7:00 a.m. and noon every weekday. You can alter this schedule if you need to.
5 Click **Cancel** twice	To enable shadow copies using the settings you just reviewed, you would click Enable and then click Yes to confirm. That would create the shadow volume and enable the copy schedule.
6 Click **OK**	To close the dialog box without enabling a shadow volume.

Disk quotas

Explanation

In all server environments, available disk space eventually becomes an issue. This is often a result of users storing large data files or archiving e-mail messages (which may include attachments) in their home directories. Depending on the number of users on the network and the amount of data they are storing, disk space can easily become scarce, and you will have to impose rules to control its use.

You can use *disk quotas* as a means of monitoring and controlling the amount of disk space available to users. Administrators can use disk quotas as a capacity-planning tool or as a way of managing data storage. Using disk quotas has the following advantages:

- It prevents users from consuming all available disk space.
- It encourages users to delete old files as they reach their disk quotas.
- It allows an administrator to track disk usage for future planning.
- It allows administrators to track when users are reaching their limits.

Most NOSs have the ability to implement disk quotas. In Windows Server 2008, you can enable disk quotas on any NTFS volume, but they are disabled by default. By enabling disk quotas, you can see the amount of disk space being consumed by users.

To use disk quotas as a management tool, you can specify the maximum amount of space allocated to network users. This is particularly useful for volumes hosting home folders, which tend to consume a lot of disk space. Many organizations establish a quota on users' home folder volumes.

The following table summarizes the options available on the Quotas tab of an NTFS volume in Windows Server 2008. Other NOSs with the disk quota feature will have similar options that you can configure.

Parameter	Description
Enable quota management	Tracks disk space on the volume and allows for the configuration of disk quotas.
Deny disk space to users exceeding quota limit	Causes users to be denied access to additional disk space after they reach their quota limits.
Do not limit disk usage	Tracks disk usage, but does not limit disk space available to users.
Limit disk space to	Sets the default amount of disk space that is available to users.
Set warning level to	Sets the default amount of disk space that a user can consume before a warning message is sent to the user, stating the quota is being reached.
Log event when user exceeds their quota limit	Causes an event to be entered in the system log to notify the administrator that the user has reached his or her quota.
Log event when a user exceeds their warning level	Causes an event to be entered in the system log to notify the administrator that the user is approaching his or her quota.

Exceptions can be created for users who require more disk space than others. In Windows Server 2008, you can set disk quotas for specific user accounts. On the Quota tab of the Properties dialog box, click the Quota Entries button to open the Quota Entries window; then choose New Quota Entry from the Quota menu. You can then choose the user account for which you want to establish a quota and configure appropriate quota limits for that user.

It's important to keep in mind that the amount of disk space that someone uses changes when ownership of files is transferred from one user account to another. For example, suppose that Moira creates a database called Clients.mdb that occupies 1022 KB on a volume with disk quotas enabled. After Moira creates and saves the database, her available disk space is decreased by 1022 KB. If Moira later changes job roles within the company and John takes ownership of the database, Moira's available disk space would increase by 1022 KB, while John's would decrease by the same amount.

B-3: Implementing disk quotas

Here's how	Here's why
1 In Disk Management, right-click **(C:)**	In either the volume list or disk list.
Choose **Properties**	
2 Activate the Quota tab	The status notice and icon both indicate that disk quotas are disabled for the partition.
3 Check **Enable quota management**	
4 Select **Limit disk space to**	
From the drop-down list, select **GB**	You'll allow each user 1 GB of space.
5 In the "Set warning level to" boxes, enter **800** and select **MB**	
6 Check **Log event when a user exceeds their quota limit**	
7 Check **Log event when a user exceeds their warning level**	Although quota information is tracked for this volume, the option to "Deny disk space to users exceeding quota limit" was not selected. Therefore, these quotas settings would be considered "soft" because they do not actually deny disk space to users and would instead be used for monitoring purposes.
8 Click **OK**	The Disk Quota message box appears.
9 Click **OK**	Allow a few minutes for the disk to be rescanned and quota information gathered if necessary.
10 Open Properties for drive C:	
Activate the Quota tab	The disk quota system is now active and the quota icon has changed.
11 Click **Quota Entries**	To open the Quota Entries window.
12 Double-click the entry that appears for the DOMAIN##\Administrator user account	To display information about the amount of quota used and amount remaining.

13 Change the quota entry for
Administrator such that the
warning levels are both set to
1 KB

Click **OK**

The icon next to the quota entry changes to a
warning because this user is now over the quota
limit.

14 Close the Quota Entries for (C:)
window

15 Clear **Enable quota
management**

Click **OK** twice

Printing

Explanation

Printing is a critical business task throughout an organization. You will need to be able to set up printers, manage print queues, and manage print jobs on the print servers in your network.

Windows printing

The Windows print process can be divided into three major processes. Each of these processes is composed of several sub-processes involved in getting the print request from the user to the printer. The three main processes are:

- Client
- Spooler
- Printer

The client processes include the following:

1 A user sends a print job from within an application.
2 The application calls a *graphics device interface* (GDI).
3 The spooler receives the print job from the GDI.

The spooler processes include the following:

1 Winspool.drv issues a *remote procedure call* (RPC) to Spoolsv.exe. Winspool.drv is on the client side. Spoolsv.exe is on the server side.
2 Spoolsv.exe calls Spoolss.dll, the print router.
3 Localspl.dll routes the print job.
4 The local print provider finds a print processor capable of handling the job's data type and then sends the job to the print processor.
5 The print processor makes any necessary modification for printing the job.
6 The page-separator processor receives the print job from the print processor and, if necessary, adds a separator page.
7 The job is sent either directly to the appropriate port monitor or to a language monitor and then on to the port monitor. The port monitor is responsible for communications between the PC and the printer. A language monitor is responsible for translating the print job into code that the printer understands.

The printer processes include the following:

1 The print spooler sends the job to the printer.
2 The print language is translated into information that the printer can print.

When you're troubleshooting the Windows print process, first ensure that the client is sending valid print jobs. Troubleshoot the Windows client operating system, the application from which the user is trying to print, and the network connection between the client and the print server. Then check the print server to see if any print services or the print spooler has stalled, and check that the print server has the correct printer driver installed. If necessary, restart the print services and the print spooler, or install or reinstall the print driver.

Linux printing

Linux supports printing operations via a few system components, the most popular of which are:

- Line Printer Daemon (LPD)
- Application-specific printing systems
- Common UNIX Printing System (CUPS)

All of these printing subsystems share some common concepts. Each subsystem uses the components described in the following table.

Item	Description
Printer	The physical printing device, such as an HP LaserJet printer.
Queue	A holding place for jobs waiting to be printed. Technically, a queue is a temporary file on the server hosting the printer. Depending on your printing system, it is likely to be something like /var/spool or var/spool/cups.
Job	The document being printed. Sending a job to the queue is called *spooling*. Sending a job from the queue to the printer is formally called printing, though that's also the term you understandably use for the whole process.
Print device	The device file you print to; for example, /dev/lp0.

The traditional Linux (and UNIX) printing system is the lpd daemon. This system is interchangeably called the LPD or LPR (taking its initials from "line printer") system. It is now largely replaced by CUPS because of many limitations.

LPD has significant security holes, has limited support for modern printers, and for the most part, doesn't handle graphics well. Various enhancements over the years, including LPRng and PDQ, attempted to rectify these issues. In most cases, however, the overall deficiencies remained.

To address the limitations of LPD, some applications provided their own printing systems. Examples include StarOffice and WordPerfect. Although these systems provided higher-quality printouts that included fonts, colors, and graphics, they were limited to those applications. For example, you could not print a log file via StarOffice's printing system without using StarOffice to open and view the file first.

Currently, the most popular and capable printing system is the Common UNIX Printing System (CUPS). It is installed by default on most modern distributions and is available as a package or source download for many other distributions.

CUPS addresses the security vulnerabilities of LPD and offers greatly increased controls for limiting who can print to your printers. It supports the Internet Printing Protocol (IPP) and is compatible with the Samba component, which provides interoperability with Windows-based networks. Many printer manufacturers have adopted support for CUPS, giving you a much wider range of printers to choose from (though that selection is still far smaller than for Windows and Macintosh computers).

Do it!

B-4: Examining the printing process

Questions and answers

1 List the three main processes of the Windows print process.

2 Which process does this step fall into? A graphics device interface (GDI) is called by the application.

3 Which process does this step fall into? The print language is translated into information the printer can print.

4 Which process does this step fall into? The print processor makes any necessary modifications for printing the job.

Topic C: Monitoring and management

This topic covers the following CompTIA Server+ (2009 Edition) exam objective.

#	Objective
2.3	**Given a scenario, implement and administer NOS management features based on procedures and guidelines** • Resource management – Performance monitoring – Baselining • Monitoring (tools and agents) – SNMP (MIBs) – WBEM (WMI)

Monitoring tools

Explanation

In this topic, you will examine three features for system and network monitoring and management. They are:

- Performance monitoring and baselining
- SNMP
- WBEM

Performance Monitor

You use Performance Monitor, shown in Exhibit 10-5, to monitor computer performance in real time (in one-second intervals) or in the form of saved reports of real-time data. Hundreds of computer performance variables called *counters* are available for measuring and assessing a computer's performance. For example, you can:

- Create a baseline to compare system performance over time.
- Monitor system resource use.
- Locate performance problems.
- Identify performance bottlenecks.

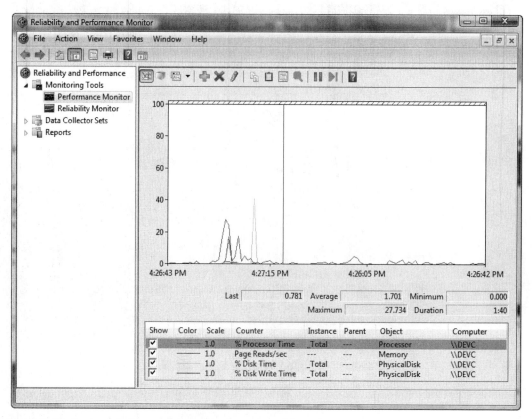

Exhibit 10-5: A real-time graph in Performance Monitor

The counters are categorized by *performance object*, which is any resource that you can measure. Here are some of the commonly used performance objects:

- Cache
- Memory
- Objects
- Paging File
- PhysicalDisk
- Process
- Processor
- System
- Thread

Bottlenecks

A bottleneck occurs when a shortage of a particular system resource causes a performance problem. You can identify some common system-resource shortages by using the counters described in the following table.

Counter	Description
Processor: % Processor Time	Monitors how hard your processor is working. A number consistently exceeding 75% indicates that the processor is being overworked. If purchasing a new system with a more powerful processor is not an option, you can try to take some of the burden off the processor by: • Adding more RAM to the system • Reducing the number of programs that run simultaneously • Verifying that an individual program is not taking control of the processor and then not releasing it
Process: Thread Count	Displays the numbers of threads active in a process. *Threads* are pieces of software code that are loaded into memory. When an application opens, it can take control of multiple memory threads to accomplish its tasks. When the application closes, it should release the threads, thereby freeing them up for other applications. When an application opens threads in memory but fails to close them, this situation is called a *memory leak*. (It's typically caused by poor application programming.) Monitoring the Thread Count can help you identify memory leaks in applications.
Memory: Pages/sec	Monitors the rate at which pages are read from or written to disk. This counter can point to page faults that cause system delays. You might need to add RAM.
PhysicalDisk: Disk Transfers/sec	Records the rate of read and write operations on the disk. If the value recorded exceeds 25 disk I/Os per second, you have poor disk-response time. This can cause a bottleneck that affects response time for applications running on that system. It might be time to upgrade the hardware to use faster disks or scale out the application to better handle the load. (*Scaling out* an application means adding one or more servers to your distributed software application.)

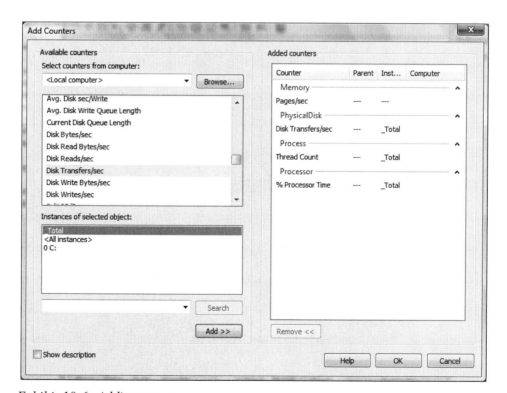

Exhibit 10-6: Adding counters

Real-time monitoring

To monitor resources in real time, you add counters to the Performance Monitor graph. Right-click the graph and choose Add Counters to open the dialog box shown in Exhibit 10-6. You can also click the Add button on the toolbar—it's a green plus sign. Then, in the Add Counters dialog box:

1 Specify whether you want to monitor resources on the local computer or a remote computer.

2 In the list of performance objects, expand the performance object that contains the counter you want to add.

3 Select the desired counter.

4 Select an instance of the counter. *Instances* are unique copies of a performance object (for example, a network card or hard disk).

5 Click Add.

6 When you've added all the counters you want, click OK.

Do it!

C-1:   Monitoring performance with Performance Monitor

Here's how	Here's why
1 Under Monitoring Tools, select **Performance Monitor**	In Reliability and Performance Monitor.
2 Observe the graph	After you add counters, this is where the real-time data will be displayed. Under the graph is a list of the counters it shows.
3 Right-click the empty graph and choose **Add Counters...**	
4 Scroll the Available counters list until you see Process	
5 Click the down-arrow next to Process	To expand that performance object and display its associated counters.
6 Scroll through the Process list	
Select **Thread Count** and observe the list of instances	You can see a list of all of the process threads. If you need to monitor a specific thread, you can select it from the list.
Verify that **_Total** is selected, and click **Add**	
7 Add **Memory: Pages/sec**, **Processor: %Processor Time**, and **PhysicalDisk: Disk Transfers/sec** to the Added counters list	Repeat the procedure of expanding the performance object, selecting the counter, and clicking Add.

Counter	Parent	Inst...	Computer	
Memory				⊟
Pages/sec	---	---		
PhysicalDisk				⊟
Disk Transfers/sec	---	_Total		
Process				⊟
Thread Count	---	_Total		
Processor				⊟
% Processor Time	---	_Total		

8 After you've added all four counters, click **OK**

9 Observe the graph	The real-time monitoring has begun. In a moment, you'll generate some activity to see how the graph spikes when you use the computer.
Observe the list of counters	You can see the four counters you added, Each counter has been assigned a different color. You can uncheck one of the checkboxes to remove the counter's display from the graph. The counter will be temporarily hidden, but not deleted.
10 Open Internet Explorer, and then open the Control Panel and the Documents folder	To generate activity on the computer.
Switch to Computer Management and observe the graph	The activity has generated some data, so you might see counters you didn't see just a few minutes ago.
11 Switch to Internet Explorer and browse to a couple of Web pages	To generate more activity and some network traffic.
Switch to Computer Management and observe the graph	

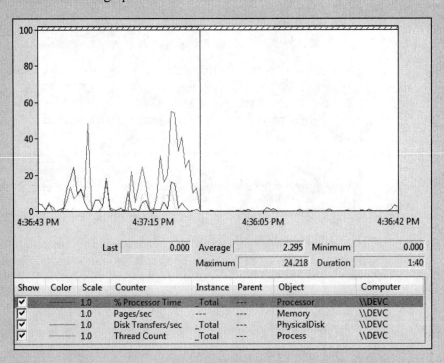

You can use this data to help determine where there might be some performance bottlenecks on your computer. Depending on the information you're trying to find, you can add or remove dozens of counters to measure a computer's performance.

12 Close all open windows

SNMP

Explanation

SNMP, the Simple Network Management Protocol, is a standard technology for managing devices connected to a network. SNMP defines two basic roles: manager and agent. The *manager* is the central system that collects information from agents and presents that information in reports, console screens, and so forth. The manager can also send configuration changes to agents. *Agents* are the managed devices.

Technically, an agent is SNMP-compatible software running on the device. Your router, for example, might run an SNMP agent. That agent collects data, such as routing tables, free memory, workload, and so forth, from the hardware. Then the agent packages that information into a standard format for sending to the manager.

Agents are available for internetworking devices, such as switches, routers, and hubs. Many server operating systems, such as Windows Server 2008, include SNMP agents. There are even SNMP agents for computer racks and HVAC equipment so that you can monitor the temperature, humidity, and power use of your computer room's equipment.

SNMP is part of the TCP/IP family of protocols. The first version of SNMP was released in 1998. Before the current version (SNMP version 3), it was possible for an agent to be "fooled" into sending data to an unauthorized network manager. Data could be read by a network analyzer because it was sent in plain text. To prevent such problems, SNMPv3 adds three important security features:

- **Message integrity** — To detect messages that are tampered with en route, SNMPv3-compatible systems monitor message integrity.

- **Authentication** — Managers and agents can authenticate each other to make sure that sensitive data is not transmitted to unauthorized systems.

- **Encryption** — SNMPv3 supports packet encryption to thwart hackers who use protocol analyzers to read "raw" data off the network.

MIBs

Each agent defines what data it collects from a device and what configuration settings can be changed via SNMP commands. Due to this freeform nature of information collection and distribution, the SNMP specification describes a common form in which an agent lists such configuration information. A *management information base (MIB)* is a hierarchical database of information managed by an agent.

Traps

Usually, contact within the SNMP environment is initiated by the network management system. It sends a message to the agents it monitors that essentially says "send me your data." You can, however, define *traps*, which are messages sent by network devices to the management system to alert you of specific events based on criteria that you define. For example, you might define a trap on your router that specifies that it should send a message if one of its network interfaces fails. Rather than waiting for the manager to poll, the router will alert your network management system if a NIC fails.

If you define a trap, you must specify a community name. A *community name* is a string used as if it were a password. Only managers and agents configured with a matching community name can share trap notifications. SNMPv3-compatible systems also let you define a list of hosts to which an agent can send traps.

SNMP management applications

The SNMP manager is typically provided as a component in a larger network management system. Open-source software, such as OpenNMS (www.opennms.org), and Splunk (www.splunk.com), enable you to gather SNMP information as part of the software's routine monitoring of your network. Some networking equipment vendors provide free or low-cost software for monitoring and managing their devices via SNMP. Systems software vendors, such as IBM and Cisco, include SNMP support in their enterprise-class network management systems.

Do it!

C-2: Enabling the Windows Server 2008 SNMP agent

Here's how	Here's why
1 Log on to your server as an administrator	
2 Open Server Manager	If necessary.
3 In the left pane, select **Features**	
4 In the Details pane, click **Add Features**	In Windows Server parlance, the SNMP agent service is a Feature.
Check **SNMP Services**	
Click **Next**	
Click **Install**	
Click **Close**	When the wizard is done.
5 In the left pane, expand **Configuration**	
Select **Services**	
6 In the list of services, double-click **SNMP Service**	To open the service's Properties dialog box.
7 Activate the Agent tab	You configure the agent from this tab.
8 In the Contact field, enter your name	If requested by the network management system, the SNMP agent will return the name of the person who manages this system.
Observe the services list	By checking or clearing these boxes, you can control what information is recorded by the SNMP agent.

9 Activate the Traps tab

   Observe the Community name list | To send traps, you must enter the community name configured on your network management system into this box.

   Observe the Trap destinations box | You could define a list of hosts to which this agent will send traps by entering them in this box.

10 Activate the Security tab

   Observe the Accepted community names list | By adding community names to this list, you can define the communities that this agent participates in.

   Observe the Accept SNMP packets options | You can specify which hosts can send this agent SNMP get and set requests by adding those hosts to this list.

11 Click **OK** | To save your changes.

12 Close Server Manager

WBEM and WMI

Explanation

Web-based Enterprise Management (WBEM) is a standards-based architecture for application and systems management. For example, using a WBEM-compatible network management system, you could remotely reconfigure servers and workstations, start and stop services, share and stop sharing folders, and so forth.

Microsoft's implementation of WBEM is called *Windows Management Instrumentation (WMI)*. WMI enables you to use scripts, .NET-based applications, and graphical tools to remotely query and manage Windows computers. Additionally, most Windows versions include the WBEMTest.exe application for testing individual WMI operations. Windows XP Professional, Windows Vista, Windows 7, Windows Server 2003, and Windows Server 2008 include the Windows Management Instrumentation command-line tool (http://technet.microsoft.com/en-us/library/bb742610.aspx). It eases the task of developing and testing WMI scripts.

Apple includes WBEM support in OS X as part of its Apple Remote Desktop tools. WBEM is also widely implemented in the UNIX and Linux operating systems, including Ubuntu, SuSE, Red Hat Enterprise, and HP-UX. Enterprise software vendors, including IBM, HP, and Computer Associates, offer WBEM-based solutions for centralized systems management. Purgos, from SoftTulz (http://softulz.net/products.shtml), is a free, open-source WBEM-based systems management application.

CIM

The *Common Information Model (CIM)* describes how IT resources—including applications, servers, and hardware devices—are represented as programming objects. It also describes the relationships between those objects. Although CIM is a common standard, it is extensible so that manufacturers can include devices and software-specific information into the schema.

The overall CIM repository is divided into namespaces. Each namespace corresponds to a management area, such as Active Directory, Internet Information Services, and so forth. Within each namespace, a provider—implemented as a DLL or similar software component—serves as the access point for collecting information or updating configuration settings for the components within that namespace.

Scripting

The *WMI Query Language (WQL)* is a SQL-like query language you can use to search for manageable objects within a namespace. You can also use WQL in the management scripts you write. If you do write such scripts, it will be critical that you understand the difference between classes and instances. In programming terminology, a *class* is a type or category, and an *instance* is a specific item in a class. Think of a class as being like the generic term "cell phone," and an instance as being the specific iPhone attached to your belt.

Do it!

C-3: Exploring WBEM and WMI with Wbemtest.exe

Here's how	Here's why
1 Open a command prompt	
2 Enter **wbemtest**	Wbemtest is a complex application. In fact, a TechNet article states, "Wbemtest was not designed for mere mortals or even savvy system admin scripters ... the interface is difficult to use, even for experts."
3 Click **Connect**	The first step is to connect to a provider.
Where indicated, enter **root\cimv2**	
Click **Connect**	
4 Click **Enum Classes**	To see what classes are available.
Leave the superclass box empty	
Select **Recursive**	
Click **OK**	To retrieve a list of classes you could manage.
5 Click anywhere in the list of classes	
Type **win**	To jump to the beginning of the list of Win32-related objects.
6 Explore the list of Win32-related classes	These classes represent Windows components that you could view or manage with a WMI script.
7 Scroll to and double-click **Win32_OperatingSystem (CIM_OperatingSystem)**	
	This class represents your operating system itself. Keep in mind that classes are abstract generalizations. Most of the properties listed in this dialog will have null or meaningless values.

8 Click **Instances**

To display the list of specific instances of operating systems running on your computer (as if there could be more than one).

Double-click the instance

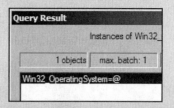

9 In the list of properties, scroll to and double-click **CSName**

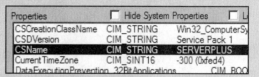

This property corresponds to your operating system's name. In a script, you could use a statement such as the following to output the name of the computer on which the script was running:

```
WScript.echo "Name: " &
objOperatingSystem.csname
```

10 Close all dialog boxes

Close Wbemtest

Close the command prompt window

Do it!

C-4: (Optional) Writing a script that uses WMI

Here's how	Here's why
1 Open Notepad	

2 Enter the following text:
 	
``
set objWMISvc = GetObject("Winmgmts:\\.")
set colOSes = objWMISvc.InstancesOf("win32_OperatingSystem")
For each objOS In colOSes
    WScript.echo "Name: " & objOS.csname & vbcrlf & _
    "OS: " & objOS.caption & vbcrlf & _
    "Version: " & objOS.version
Next
``
	Case doesn't matter, but spelling and punctuation do.

3 Save the file as **wmitest.vbs**	This script reads values from instances of the Win32_OperatingSystem class, which represents the operating system running on your computer.
4 Open your **Documents** folder	The wmitest file should be listed as a VBScript Script File and not a text document. If it is not, then the .txt extension was incorrectly added to the file's name. Rename the file.
5 Double-click **wmitest.vbs**	**Windows Script Host** Name: WINSRV01 OS: Microsoft® Windows Server® 2008 Standard Version: 6.0.6002 OK You should get a message box as shown here. If you don't, check your script for errors and try again.
6 Close all windows	

Unit summary: Managing a network server

Topic A   In this topic, you learned how to implement and manage **user accounts** on a network operating system. You created user accounts in Active Directory, the network directory service (NDS) for Windows Server. You changed the properties of, disabled, and removed a user account. You also created a group account in AD and added users to it. You then used those accounts to secure a network resource. You also learned how to control the user accounts by using a group policy and scripts.

Topic B   In this topic, you learned how to implement and manage **disk resources** on a network operating system. You used Disk Management to determine the status and other properties of your server's disks and volumes. You learned how to create shadow volumes and set up Shadow Copies of Shared Folders. You also implemented disk quotas.

Topic C   In this topic, you learned that **Performance Monitor** enables you to examine system performance and compare it to a baseline. You also learned that **SNMP** is a standard protocol for monitoring and managing network devices, servers, and equipment. Finally, you learned that you can write system management scripts and automate management through **WBEM** and **WMI**.

Review questions

1   What's the difference between one-factor and two-factor authentication?

two is more methods sor more secure

2   Where do user accounts reside?

directory service

3   What are some benefits of using user accounts?

can hold people accountable

4   What are some recommended steps users should take to protect their passwords?

make complex dont write down

5 What's a passphrase?

memory technique to help users remember passwords

6 What's the benefit of using passphrases?

helps bad memories

7 What are some things you need to decide before creating user accounts for your organization?

naming structure
password life

8 When would you want to disable a user account versus removing it?

when something useful may still be on the account

9 What is the main benefit of groups?

organizes directory
can assign policy to multi people

10 What is an access control list?

list of ~~user~~ things authorized to access the network

11 Why would you want to explicitly deny access for a user or group?

when they dont need access

12 What are some of the administrative tasks you can automate with policies?

updates
backups
maintenance

13 What are some of the common script trigger events?

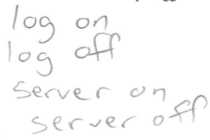

log on
log off
server on
server off

14 If a disk status reads Failed in Disk Management, what does it indicate?

did not boot properly

15 Using the following graphic, answer the following questions.

Volume	Layout	Type	File System	Status	Capacity	Free Space	% Free	F
(C:)	Partition	Basic	NTFS	Healthy (System)	7.81 GB	2.31 GB	29 %	N
(G:)	Partition	Basic	NTFS	Healthy	1.95 GB	1.49 GB	76 %	N
Local Disk (D:)	Partition	Basic	NTFS	Healthy (Boot)	1.95 GB	529 MB	26 %	N
Local Disk (F:)	Partition	Basic	NTFS	Healthy	1.17 GB	147 MB	12 %	N
NR1SFRE_EN (E:)	Partition	Basic	CDFS	Healthy	532 MB	0 MB	0 %	N

Disk 0
Basic
18.62 GB
Online

(C:) 7.81 GB NTFS Healthy (System	Local Disk (1.95 GB NTFS Healthy (Boot	Local Disk 1.17 GB NTF Healthy	(G:) 1.95 GB NTFS Healthy	5.73 GB Unallocated

CD-ROM 0
DVD
532 MB
Online

NR1SFRE_EN (E:) 532 MB CDFS Healthy

■ Unallocated ■ Primary partition

A) How many disks are there?

4

B) How many volumes are on the hard disk?

2

C) Which volume has the least percentage of free space remaining?

F

16 What's the benefit of shadow volumes for users?

Can restore lost files

17 Why should you store your shadow copies on a volume separate from the one being copied?

So if you lose a volume you can still restore

18 What are some of the benefits of using disk quotas?

maintains drive space

19 In Performance Monitor, hundreds of computer performance variables, called
tickers , are available for measuring and assessing a computer's
performance.

20 If you wanted to identify a memory leak, which performance variable would you
monitor?

A Memory: Pages/sec

B PhysicalDisk: Disk Transfers/sec

C Process: Thread Count

D Processor: % Processor Time

21 The software that runs on an SNMP-enabled network device is called the ~~IDS~~ _agent_

22 List two or more devices or network components typically manageable with SNMP.

Switches, routers, hubs

23 Define MIB.

Management information base

24 True or false? WBEM is a standardized architecture for applications and systems
management.

true

25 Microsoft's implementation of WBEM is called:

A WBEM

B WBEMTest

C Purgos

D WMI

Independent practice activity

In this activity, you'll practice managing a Windows 2008 network server.

1 Create the following user accounts:

Name: Carl Dietz
User logon name: CDietz
Password: !pass1234
Job Title: HR Specialist

Name: Sierra Drake
User logon name: SDrake
Password: !pass1234
Job Title: HR Specialist

Name: Merriam Pultz
User logon name: MPultz
Password: !pass1234
Job Title: HR Director

2 Create a group called **Human Resources**. Add CDietz, SDrake, and MPultz to the group.

3 On the server, create a shared folder called **HR Docs**. While creating the share, grant the Human Resources group Contributor rights. Grant Merriam Pultz Co-owner rights.

4 View the Share permissions for HR Docs. What permissions are given to the Human Resources group as Contributors? What permissions are given to Merriam Pultz as Co-owner?

5 If you wanted to restrict users' ability to add or remove Windows components from their computers, how would you do that?

6 Use Disk Management to determine the configuration of the hard disk(s) on your system. How many disks are there? Are they basic or dynamic? How much used and free space is there on each disk?

7 Enable quotas for users. Limit disk usage to **2 GB**. Set a warning level at **1.5 GB**. Set the system to log events when both the warning and usage limits are reached.

Unit 11

Documenting and planning

Unit time: 60 minutes

Complete this unit, and you'll know how to:

A Document your computing infrastructure.

B Manage change within your IT infrastructure through proper planning and procedures.

C Manage physical security and access to your computing infrastructure.

Topic A: Documenting the IT environment

This topic covers the following CompTIA Server+ (2009 Edition) exam objectives.

#	Objective
4.1	**Write, utilize, and maintain documentation, diagrams, and procedures** • Follow pre-installation plan when building or upgrading servers • Labeling • Diagram server racks and environment topologies • Hardware and software upgrade, installation, configuration, server role, and repair logs • Document server baseline (before and after service) • Original hardware configuration, service tags, asset management, and warranty • Vendor-specific documentation – Reference proper manuals – Web sites – Support channels (list of vendors)
4.2	**Given a scenario, explain the purpose of the following industry best practices** • Follow vendor-specific server best practices – Documentation – Tools – Web sites • Comply with all local laws/regulations, and industry and corporate regulations • Purpose of Service-Level Agreements (SLAs)
4.5	**Given a scenario, classify physical security measures for a server location** • Secure documentation related to servers – Passwords – System configurations – Logs

System documentation

Explanation

System documentation serves many purposes. However, when creating your system documentation, you should identify a primary purpose. Your target audience and intended use will dictate what you document, how you write that documentation, and what level of detail you record.

IT system documentation could serve as:

- An introduction or overview of your systems, their configuration, and their purposes, which you share with a new hire or consultant.
- A disaster recovery guidebook that describes the state to which you must rebuild systems.
- A troubleshooting aid that helps you determine if the current operating state matches a baseline recorded during normal operations.
- A planning tool for upgrades, moves, or changes.
- A component of an application for certification in a program, such as ISO 9000/9001, or record of compliance with a law or regulation.

Characteristics of good documentation

Regardless of how you plan to use it, high-quality documentation typically includes the following characteristics. It is:

- Written with sufficient detail to satisfy its intended audience.
- Up-to-date and accurate.
- Accessible in a convenient location and format (even if systems have crashed or are inaccessible).
- Secure from unauthorized users. For example, passwords and system configuration information in your documentation represent key points of vulnerability and must be protected carefully.

Typical contents of documentation

The exact contents of your system documentation will vary according to your specific needs. Typically, though, documentation will include the following:

- Lists of servers and the primary purpose of each of those servers. Additionally, for each one, you should record the operating system version, patch levels, and any specific needs, such as proprietary hardware drivers.

- Lists of key client workstations that must be accessible or quickly restored. These might include executive staff workstations, IT system consoles, and so forth. As with key servers, this documentation should note operating system details, key applications, drivers, and other necessary details.

- Network diagrams, cabling diagrams, server rack diagrams, and building maps.

- Automatically generated documentation, including logs, system inventories, and system update reports. If you use a problem tracking and resolution system, be it paper based or electronic, your documentation should include either a copy of such records or a notation that such records are available.

- Contact information for key personnel, along with your policies about whom to call in various situations and your escalation policy.

- Vendor-specific documentation, including product manuals, warranty information, and support contract details (procedures and contact details). In general, you should also maintain a list of all key vendors and their support channels.

- Descriptions and details of local laws and regulations, industry-specific regulations, and corporate policies you must comply with. Details of how you currently meet those regulations will help if you need to change or move systems while continuing to meet regulations. Note contact information for compliance officers, inspectors, and other key personnel.

- Purchase records, such as packing lists and the documentation of initial hardware configuration.

- Vendor repair logs, if your vendors supply you with such reports.

Service-level agreements

Service-level agreements with internal and external customers and vendors are another record of system configuration that should be part of your documentation. A *service-level agreement* (SLA) is a contract between a service provider and the end-user. This document specifies the service levels for support, documents any penalties for the service level not being met by the provider, and describes disaster recovery plans.

SLAs often contain details that will be helpful when your organization is recovering from a disaster, upgrading systems, or confirming proper operations. Although SLAs are typically created outside of a documentation process, copies should be made available within your documentation set. Alternatively, your documentation can note the existence of and official location of SLAs.

Non-documentation records

You can document your environment in various other ways that are not part of a written set of documentation. For example, you might label each rack and the server or network appliance it contains. Cabling installers should label each connection block and cable in wiring closets and racks. You might post network diagrams or even facilities maps in a location central for your IT staff. Such labels and diagrams would help a new technician, contractor, or consultant find the specific system he or she needs to work on.

Do it! **A-1: Considering IT documentation**

Questions	Answers
1 With your classmates, or by yourself, debate the pros and cons of the following documentation recording options:	
Writing your documentation in Microsoft Word versus another word processing program	
Printing your documentation versus maintaining it as electronic files	
2 Consider a server inventory section of your documentation with a target audience of experienced technicians who might use the details to restore servers after a system failure. What sorts of details would such documentation include?	
3 Consider this scenario: Your documentation is in printed form. It contains user names and passwords for master administrator accounts in case your primary system administrator is unavailable during a disaster.	
How would you secure the password information contained in the documentation?	
What additional security measures should you take with the documentation?	
4 Is it necessary to secure system configuration or logs that are part of your inventory? Why or why not?	
5 What value would network diagrams, equipment labels, and facilities maps offer after a physical disaster (earthquake, flood, fire)?	

Documentation tools

Documenting every system on your network is a time-consuming and cumbersome process. Many companies start with good intentions but become overwhelmed trying to describe every server and workstation, myriad applications, user environment settings, and so forth. Fortunately, you can turn to automated documentation tools to build a record of your environment. Such tools include:

- Logging software
- Provisioning systems (such as Altiris or Xen Enterprise)
- Inventory software

Logging software

Logging software and operating system components typically gather a significant collection of hardware and software details. Yet such programs are rarely set up to output such information in a format easily used for creating documentation. If you're skilled with scripting tools, such as PERL scripts, you might be able to automate the process of scanning log files and extracting the necessary details.

Another form of log file might be a bit more useful. That would be the automated setup log files, such as the setup.log file created by some Windows operating systems. Such files contain many configuration details. However, they sometimes lack the hardware details that would be required to fully replace a failed system.

Provisioning systems

Provisioning systems are software tools that enable you to quickly clone or set up new computers. Some systems, like Xen Enterprise, are designed to operate within a virtualized environment. Others, such as Altiris, are designed to set up physical computers.

In either case, these tools can often create reports of system template configurations or details of systems that the tool has been used to set up. The usefulness of these tools depends entirely on the features they offer. And of course you must have the tools in place and use them consistently when setting up computers in order to get value from the information they record.

Inventory software

Many applications have been written to automate the inventorying process. Typically, you install a small component on each PC to be inventoried. Then, from a central computer, you initiate an inventory sweep. Software on the central station queries the agents on each of the networked PCs to gather system specifications.

A few examples of inventory software include:

- Lansweeper (www.lansweeper.com) — Free and paid versions
- Zenoss (www.zenoss.com) — Commercial open source
- Spiceworks (www.spiceworks.com) — Free and paid versions

The information gathered by these tools varies. The reports they generate also vary in detail. Most provide a list of systems on your network and the hardware those systems contain. Some pull vendor-specific information, such as service tag numbers, which can then be associated with vendor-support Web sites and documentation.

Do it!

A-2:   **Exploring an inventory application**

Here's how	Here's why
1 With your browser, visit **www.lansweeper.com/demo/**	
	This Web site demonstrates the information gathered by the free Lansweeper inventory application.
2 Under Domains, click the first domain listed	Clicking the name will display a list of computers in that domain. In the resulting list, you will see an inventory of computers, their operating systems, installed memory, IP addresses, and more.
3 Click the name of the first computer listed	To load the detailed information page, which lists the type of computer, an asset tag, Active Directory information, network information, and security and application configuration status.
Observe the vendor-specific support link, as shown	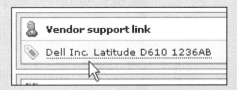
	Based on the computer's asset tag number, the tool has built a link to the vendor's support Web site specific for this computer.
4 Near the top of the page, click **Computer Report**	
	The resulting page lists extensive computer, hardware, and operating system details.
5 Based on your quick exploration of this reporting application, what critical feature do you think is missing?	
6 Close your browser	

Topic B: Planning and implementing change

This topic covers the following CompTIA Server+ (2009 Edition) exam objectives.

#	Objective
4.1	**Write, utilize, and maintain documentation, diagrams, and procedures** • Hardware and software upgrade, installation, configuration, server role, and repair logs • Document server baseline (before and after service)
4.2	**Given a scenario, explain the purpose of the following industry best practices** • Explore ramifications before implementing change; determine organizational impact • Communicate with stakeholders before taking action and upon completion of action • Comply with all local laws/regulations, and industry and corporate regulations • Follow change control procedures • Equipment disposal
4.3	**Determine an appropriate physical environment for the server location** • Check for adequate and dedicated power, proper amperage and voltage – UPS systems (check load, document service, periodic testing) – UPS specifications (runtime, max load, bypass procedures, server communication and shutdown, proper monitoring) • Server cooling considerations: HVAC – Adequate cooling in room – Adequate cooling in server rack – Temperature and humidity monitors

Change management

Explanation

Whenever an IT change is made, a set of procedures called *change management* should be followed. You should develop such procedures with your network staff, systems engineers, IT planning team, management, and end-user departmental representatives. Document and publish your change management procedures, and then insist that such procedures always be followed.

Typically, the change management process is initiated with a "request for change" (RFC) document. This document records the change, the category that the change falls into, and any other items the change might affect.

Next, the RFC is sent through a review and approval process. A priority is set, and it is assigned to whoever will make the change. Decisions on whether to proceed should be made with representatives from various departments affected by the change. All of the discussions related to the RFC should be documented.

The RFC is scheduled and a proposed completion time is set. The change is then planned, developed, tested, and implemented by the person or team to which the RFC was assigned. All of this is documented in the RFC log.

The change is complete when both the change owner and the requester verify that the change has been successfully implemented. Finally, the RFC is reviewed by all parties involved, and the change is closed.

Your change management process should ensure that you:

- Communicate with all stakeholders involved with or affected by the change.
- Determine if infrastructure modifications are required as part of the change. These would include updates to power, backup power, and cooling systems to accommodate new or changed equipment.
- Document the system state before (for a baseline) and after any changes. This includes recording the details of the change itself and recording the details of the new system configuration state after the change is implemented.
- Remain in compliance with any applicable laws and regulations after the change is implemented.
- Dispose of obsolete equipment in accordance with your equipment disposal process.

Benefits of a formal change management process

A formal change management process has many benefits. It ensures that all of the effects of a change are examined before the change is actually implemented. A formal process makes sure that a consistent set of procedures is followed so that steps aren't forgotten. It ensures that security and downtime risks are considered and managed. And finally, a natural offshoot of a formal procedure is that your system documentation will be updated to include not only a record of the change, but also the details associated with the resulting new conditions.

Change documentation

In addition to architecture documentation, each individual system should have a separate document that describes its initial state and all subsequent changes. This document includes configuration information, a list of patches applied, backup records, and even details about suspected breaches. Printouts of hash results, last modification dates of critical system files, and contents of log files may be pasted into this book.

System maintenance can be made much smoother with a comprehensive change document. For instance, when a patch is available for an operating system, it typically applies in only certain situations. Manually investigating the applicability of a patch on every possible target system can be very time consuming; however, if logs are available for reference, the process is much faster and more accurate.

Do it!

B-1: Exploring change management

Here's how	Here's why
1 With your browser, visit **www.sunviewsoftware.com/products/plus.aspx**	
	You will examine an example of change management software.
2 Activate each of the tabs	To examine the features and benefits of this company's product.
3 How would you use this product to manage changes?	

Disposal of electronics

Explanation

You might need to dispose of obsolete equipment after implementing a change. When possible, you should repurpose such equipment internally. For example, a decommissioned application server might be usable as a print server or departmental-level file server.

When reuse isn't feasible, you must dispose of the equipment in accordance with local laws and regulations. Corporate "green" policies might also dictate specific disposal procedures.

Electronic components and equipment can't be sent to the landfill along with the rest of the trash because of the many hazardous materials they contain. Hazardous materials in electronic equipment include lead, mercury, cadmium, phosphorus, fire-retardant chemicals, and other substances. Some electronics contain trace amounts of gold, platinum, and other valuable metals, which can be recovered and reused.

Be sure to check the MSDSs (material safety data sheets) for safety and disposal information. Also check for OSHA and EPA regulations, as well as local laws and corporate or industry regulations.

Methods of disposal

Some municipalities offer local electronic-equipment recycling services. These might be available year round or offered periodically. There's often a small fee for disposing of the equipment. Considering the amount of manual labor involved in recycling these materials, the fees aren't exorbitant.

If no local service is offered, you can check the Web for recyclers. If you have pallet upon pallet of equipment, a recycler might be able to pick it up from you or arrange to have it picked up.

Do it!

B-2: Selecting proper equipment disposal methods

Here's how	Here's why
1 In your browser, use your favorite search engine to search for computer recyclers in your area	
2 Determine whether the recycler you find offers equipment for reuse	
3 Determine whether the organization recycles other electronic components or batteries	
4 Determine how to get the equipment to the recycler	
When you're done, close the browser	

Topic C: Managing physical access and security

This topic covers the following CompTIA Server+ (2009 Edition) exam objective.

#	Objective

4.5	**Given a scenario, classify physical security measures for a server location**
	• Physical server security
	  – Locked doors
	  – Rack doors
	  – CCTV
	  – Mantraps
	  – Security personnel
	• Access control devices (RFID, keypads, pinpads)
	  – Biometric devices (fingerprint scanner, retina scanner)
	• Security procedures
	  – Limited access
	  – Access logs
	  – Limited hours
	• Defense in-depth – multiple layers of defense
	• Reasons for physical security
	  – Theft
	  – Data loss
	  – Hacking
	• Secure documentation related to servers
	  – Passwords
	  – System configurations
	  – Logs

Physical access control

Explanation

The data on the network needs to be secured through network access controls. The facility housing the network also needs access control. Physical access security protects the data, the employees, power sources, utility lines, the equipment, and the building. This control can come in the form of security guards, ID badges, security cameras (CCTV), lighting, locks, fences, and other physical barriers. Failure of any of these barriers can result in a breach that compromises the organization's information.

The level and number of physical access controls should be in direct proportion to the importance of the information and assets you are trying to protect. For example, a government organization with top-secret information is going to need much stricter security controls than will the local baseball team league headquarters.

Physical tokens

A physical token, also known as a hardware token or cryptographic token, can be required in order to access a computer. This token might take the form of a smart card and a reader or a USB token. Both of these tokens contain a microcontroller and operating system, a security application, and a secured storage area. The device stores a cryptographic key, which might be a digital signature or biometric data.

Physical tokens sometimes contain a method for the user to enter additional information, such as an account number. They can be used in single-sign-on environments. Single sign-on lets the user log on once to gain access to multiple systems, instead of being required to log on each time another system is accessed. Because single sign-on gives the user access to so many resources, it is imperative that strong authentication be used. Using a physical token along with a user name and password helps provide strong authentication.

Locks

Locks are the most common physical access control method. The lock is a good first line of defense against break-ins. An attacker needs the key or a set of lock picks to gain access through a locked door or locked device.

Most homes, many office doors, and small business offices usually use preset locks. These are opened or closed with metal keys or by turning or pressing a button in the center of the lock. These locks are not very secure because keys can be duplicated, lost, or stolen, and such locks are easily picked with a set of picks. A door-knob lock has a bolt, or locking bar, that is held in place by a spring in the knob. It is pulled in by turning the handle on the door. The bolt secures the door by fitting into a strike plate on the door jamb. The lock prevents the bolt from being withdrawn into the door, allowing it to open. A preset lock is shown in Exhibit 11-1.

Exhibit 11-1: A preset lock

A deadbolt can be added. Instead of using spring pressure, it uses the weight of the bolt. Deadbolts are more secure than standard preset locks. Some deadbolts are installed in a vertical position at the top of the door, rather than in the typical placement at the side of the door. Vertical placement makes the lock more difficult to pry open.

A more secure type of lock is a cipher lock. This is an electronic, programmable locks, using either a keypad or a card reader. Cipher locks, which are more expensive, provide better security than standard preset or deadbolt locks. There is no need for everyone requiring access to the building or room to have a key; they just need to know the combination to enter to open the lock. A cipher lock is shown in Exhibit 11-2.

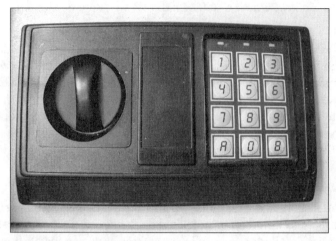

Exhibit 11-2: A cipher lock

The risk of one of these locks is that the person might write down the combination and it might be found by an intruder. The main risk in using a cipher-lock card reader is that the user might lose his or her card to an intruder. The card often doubles as the user's ID badge for the organization.

Some of the features that make cipher locks better options than preset locks are described in the following table.

Feature	Description
Door delay	An alarm is triggered if the door is held open or propped open after a specified time.
Key override	A special code can be set for use in emergencies or for management needs.
Master key ring	This function enables management to change access codes or other features.
Hostage alarm	If the user is being forced to enter a PIN into the cipher lock, he or she can enter a special code that notifies security or law enforcement of the attempted break-in.
Logging	Many cipher locks record the date and time of entry, along with the person's ID. Security administrators can review these logs to determine who entered (and maybe left) the secure area.

Locks can also be used to secure devices. These device locks are often vinyl-coated steel cables that attach the devices to stationary objects. There are also switch controls to cover the power switches on devices, slot locks to cover open expansion slots in devices, and port locks to block access to drives or ports. Cable traps prevent cables from being removed. Rack locks prevent unauthorized access to the components mounted in equipment racks.

The various locking methods can be combined to increase security. For example, you might need a key or card along with a PIN or a biometric access device to gain entry. You can expect to pay more for multi-criteria locks, but you need to weigh the cost and inconvenience for employees with the level of security needed by your organization.

Man-traps

A *man-trap* is a set of doors that are interlocked. When one door is opened, the other door can't be opened. Using this security method provides secure access control. It is usually configured as two doors at one entrance with a space between them. You can also configure it so that when one entrance is being used, another entrance can't be used.

Fences

A fence around the facility is a good deterrent to casual entry. Local zoning laws might forbid the installation of fencing or might specify the maximum height of installed fences and the type of fencing allowed. Security fences range from simple chain-link fencing to razor-wire-topped eight-foot fences. You will need to do a cost analysis to determine whether the expense of installing the fence is worth the security it would provide for the perimeter of your facility.

Lights

A well-lit area around your facility will make employees feel more secure and will deter intruders. It is recommended that key areas have illumination at least eight feet up and two feet out. You might want full illumination. You can install flood lights, street lights, or spot lights, depending on the location of the lights and the needs of the organization.

Do it!

C-1: Identifying the risks associated with physical access to systems

Here's how	Here's why
1 Determine the cost of various types of door locks	Use your favorite search engine to locate and price locks.
2 Compare the cost of a lock to the cost of the potential loss of data	Usually, the cost of locks can easily be justified.
3 Determine whether fencing is allowed by the zoning laws where your organization does business	
Determine what types of fencing are allowed and whether there are any ordinances regarding lighting in your area	
4 If you are required to carry or wear a security ID badge at your workplace, examine the badge and the policies that describe its use. How could you improve the security provided by the ID badge?	

Surveillance

Explanation

Surveillance is another important part of physical security. A security guard is a good deterrent to intruders. Guards might be stationed at fixed locations, or they might patrol around the facility. A fully trained guard will know the procedures to follow and the actions to take if an emergency occurs.

Surveillance with cameras, such as in a *closed-circuit television* (CCTV) system, can be used along with or in place of security personnel. These cameras are connected to one or more monitors that a central security guard watches. Video from such cameras is usually recorded for later review. Cameras should be placed both inside and outside the facility, aimed at key entry points and critical equipment.

Guard dogs are very effective deterrents to intrusion. Trained guard dogs know how to take down intruders and hold them until human help arrives. Just their very presence is a deterrent to casual intrusion, and their barking alerts others of the potential threat that they sense. Guard dogs are usually used along with security guards.

Logging

When users log onto the network, you can create a log file of their activity. When the server is shut down, you can create a log file with the reason for the shutdown. When intrusion detection software detects an intruder, it writes the incident to a log file. There are many network log files for various events.

You can also keep logs regarding the physical security of a facility. When a card-reader cipher lock is used, it can create a log file of who enters the building, because the card identifies the user. When visitors come to your building, they can be required to sign into a log book at the front desk. Security guards are often required to create a log that states that everything was okay on their last shift.

These various logs can be used to identify potential suspects when an incident occurs. They can also help identify potential threats if anomalies are noted in any of the logs.

Do it!

C-2: Examining logging and surveillance best practices

Here's how	Here's why
1 Determine the cost of hiring a security guard with a guard dog	Use the Web to search for firms offering such services or for articles describing these options.
2 Determine the cost of a surveillance system composed of:	
Four cameras at each outside entrance	The system should use a DVR to record information to a hard drive, and a monitor that can be split to see four cameras at a time.
A camera at the front lobby	
A camera at the door to the server room	
A camera at the accounting office	
3 To maintain physical security, what kinds of logging does your organization need to do?	

Biometrics

Explanation
Sometimes it is not enough to secure an account by using just a user name and password. Even good authentication and encryption might not be enough to protect the information that is being secured. In such cases, a biometric device can be employed to further secure the information. A biometric device uses a person's physical trait—such as a fingerprint, retinal scan, or voice print—to authorize access to the information.

Fingerprint scanners

One of the most common biometric devices is a fingerprint scanner. The user places his finger over a sensor window, and the fingerprint is compared to data in a database. If it matches, the user is granted access to the resource. Fingerprint scanners can be used to secure resources such as computers, Web pages, or applications. A fingerprint scanner is shown in Exhibit 11-3.

Exhibit 11-3: A fingerprint scanner

You usually connect these devices via USB. They come with software to gather, verify, and store fingerprints. They are usually used in combination with user names and passwords that users enter with their keyboards. Sometimes these scanners are used in place of user names and passwords.

Hand geometry scanners

Another biometric device is the hand geometry scanner, which scans the entire hand of the user. This device measures the length and width of the fingers and hand. The information scanned is compared to the data stored in a database. If it matches, the user is granted access to the secured resource.

Eye scanners

A retina scanner scans the surface of the retina to obtain the blood vessel patterns found there. This information is stored in a database, and when the user needs to gain access to the secured resource, her retina is scanned and compared to the database. If a match is found, access is granted.

An iris scanner uses the same idea, but captures and compares the color, shape, and texture of the user's iris. These attributes include the rings and furrows found in the iris, along with variations in the coloring.

Voice verification

A user's speech patterns can also be used for authentication. A phrase is stated by the user and recorded, and it is archived in a database. The user's intonation, pitch, and inflection are used to identify him to the system. If the user has a cold that affects his voice, he might not be granted access. If you foresee such potential problems, you might want to provide an alternate access method.

Signature verification

Signature cards have long been used by banks when people open accounts. You sign a card, which the bank stores in a file cabinet. When you come in to make a transaction, they can pull out your signature card to compare the signature to the one you signed for the transaction. This process can be moved to the digital arena by storing user signatures in a database and having users sign in with a stylus, writing their signatures on a pad connected to the computer. The software needs to account for the variations that occur in a person's signature because people often do not use the exact same strokes when signing their names. Instead, the software looks for general characteristics in the way a name is signed.

DNA scans

DNA scanning is a promising biometric authentication method. A DNA sample's analysis is stored in a database. The user requesting access provides another DNA sample for comparison. Every person has a unique DNA structure.

Pros and cons of biometrics

Biometrics can provide strong authentication because they are unique to an individual. However, they have been prone to produce both false negatives and false positives. They have gotten better over time, but as soon as they are strengthened, attackers come up with ways of thwarting the systems.

Biometric access is being included on portable devices. Even if someone steals the device, such as a laptop or removable drive, the data cannot be accessed without the biometric access being successfully negotiated. However, if an alternative access is allowed through a user name and password, the attacker could potentially still access the secured information.

Most biometric systems store the data as clear text because encryption would result in the stored data not being identical to the original scan. Storing data as clear text leaves the database vulnerable. One method created by Mitsubishi Electric Research Laboratories overcomes this problem by transforming the data into a binary vector, which is then multiplied by the parity check matrix of a publicly known parity check code. The output, which is compressed and scrambled, is referred to as the biometric's *syndrome*. The syndrome doesn't contain all of the information from the original scan, so if only the syndrome is stolen without the original scan, the original biometric scan can't be recovered.

One way that fingerprint and hand scanners are deceived is through the use of gel-filled devices that can mimic fingerprints. Just as a paper check can be forged, so can a digital signature. If someone obtains a DNA sample of a valid user, he can present the sample as his own to fool the system into giving the attacker access to the secured resource.

Do it! **C-3: Identifying biometric authentication systems**

Questions and answers

1 What is different about using biometric authentication as compared to using other authentication methods?

2 What is a benefit of a fingerprint scanner over a hand geometry scanner?

3 What types of scans can be used on eyes? What features do the scans measure and record?

4 What voice features are analyzed in voice verification?

5 What vulnerabilities can be found in signature authentication?

6 Each person's DNA is unique, so why is DNA authentication vulnerable?

Unit summary: Documenting and planning

Topic A　　In this topic, you learned that no matter why you **document your IT environment**, you must make sure such information is sufficiently detailed, up-to-date, accessible, and secure. You learned that such documentation typically describes systems and their components, network diagrams and maps, contact information, and vendor-specific information. Finally, you learned about the various tools, including logs and dedicated inventory software, for creating such documentation.

Topic B　　In this topic, you learned why electronic components and equipment cannot be sent to landfills. You examined options such as reusing and recycling **decommissioned hardware**.

Topic C　　In this topic, you examined how to establish **physical access security**. You started by identifying risks associated with physical access to systems. These systems include various types of locks, fencing, and lighting. Then you examined how logs can be used to increase physical security and surveillance methods. Finally, you identified biometric authentication systems, such as fingerprint scanners, hand geometry scanners, retina scanners, iris scanners, voice analyzers, and signature verification.

Review questions

1　To be useful, documentation must be _____ even if systems have crashed or power is unavailable.

　　accessable

2　Why must you keep your IT documentation secure from unauthorized users?

　　can provide vulnerabilities

3　True or false? To be useful, your IT systems documentation must contain recent log file contents.

　　true

4　List the three categories of software that you can use to generate portions of your IT systems documentation.

　　logging, provisioning, inventory

5　What kind of policies describe the set of procedures followed whenever an IT change is made?

　　change management

6　List at least two practices that a formal change management policy helps ensure that you follow.

　　remain in compliance
　　determine obsolete equipment

7　Ideally, rather than disposing of equipment, you should first try to do what?

　　repurpose

8　Why can't you simply throw electronics in the trash?

　　hazmat + security threat

9 True or false? Fingerprint scanners can be used in combination with having users enter a username and password.

true

10 What does a hand geometry scanner measure?

hand outline

11 List two types of eye scanners and what they scan for.

retina, iris, scan for patterns

12 What is a security drawback to using DNA scans?

~~*time consuming*~~

can get a sample easily

13 Why are preset locks considered less secure than cipher locks?

spare key could have been made, company security might be poor

14 List three types of surveillance that you might implement.

~~*audio*~~   *dog*

~~*visual*~~   *guards*

~~*discreet*~~   *cameras*

Independent practice activity

In this activity, you will research access security measures that can be implemented at the organization described in the following scenario.

XYZ Corporation has recently downsized its workforce from 100 employees to 75 and moved into a smaller building. Some of their new neighbors have experienced break-ins and minor vandalism on their properties. One of the former employees has made threats against the organization, but nobody is sure which employee it was. You have been hired as a security manager by XYZ to secure the network and the facility. Your first task is to figure out how much it would cost to implement appropriate security measures. You also must prioritize the measures so that if the budget doesn't cover all of your recommendations, you will still be able to provide a safe, secure workplace.

1 What facility entry method would you recommend? Determine the cost of procuring and installing your choice.

2 Would you recommend hiring a security guard? Why or why not?

3 What biometric authentication device would you recommend if it fit within the allotted budget? Determine the cost of procuring and installing your choice.

4 You checked with the local zoning office and found that a six-foot security fence can be installed. The entry areas and parking lot currently have little lighting. What types of fencing and lighting would you recommend? Determine the cost of procuring and installing your choice.

5 Prioritize your solutions.

6 At the meeting where you present your findings, management determines that you are about 20% over budget. Determine which of the solutions you would eliminate or change.

Unit 12

Preparing for disaster

Unit time: 120 minutes

Complete this unit, and you'll know how to:

A Compare and contrast backup and restoration methodologies and media types.

B Identify server redundancy and other disaster precautions.

C Develop a disaster recovery plan.

Topic A: Backing up data

This topic covers the following CompTIA Server+ (2009 Edition) exam objectives.

#	Objective
5.1	**Compare and contrast backup and restoration methodologies, media types, and concepts**
	• Methodologies
	– Snapshot
	– Copy
	– Bare metal
	– Open file
	– Databases
	– Data vs. OS restore
	– Rotation and retention (grandfather, father, and son; leaning tower)
	• Media types
	– Tape – Optical
	– Disk – Flash
	– Worm
	• Backup security and off-site storage
	• Importance of testing the backup and restore process
5.2	**Given a scenario, compare and contrast the different types of replication methods**
	• Disk to disk
5.3	**Explain data retention and destruction concepts**
	• Differentiate between archiving and backup

Importance of backups

Explanation

An important role of any server administrator is to ensure that system and user data remain available, even under adverse circumstances. Although fault-tolerant hardware and devices can reduce system downtime, the greatest potential loss in the event of a system failure is data loss. Even during normal day-to-day operations, data can become corrupt or lost. For example, users sometimes accidentally overwrite their own files with blank data, or an application crashes while a file is open, resulting in a corrupt file. Server operating system files are just as vulnerable to loss or corruption as application and user data are. One of your main tasks as a server administrator is to make sure that all necessary data is kept safe from loss and that server systems can be quickly restored.

The best way to secure data is to back it up by copying files to other media, which you then store securely. The basic theory behind backing up data is simple: never put yourself in a position where data that's critical to the survival of your network or business is permanently unavailable. That sounds easy, but the more you look at what's involved in backing up user data and system data, and strategies for restoring data and systems, the more complex the job becomes.

Backups must be performed regularly, or the possibility exists that newer or updated files will not be saved. There are many backup devices to choose from, and several backup methods you can employ, with the ultimate goal of never being without your mission-critical data. Commercial backup software packages provide a great deal of flexibility, allowing different types of backups to be performed according to the needs and requirements of your organization. Most network server operating systems include a number of tools, utilities, and features that can be used as part of your backup and disaster recovery strategy.

For example, Windows Server 2008 includes a backup utility that allows you to restore an operating system or data in the event of a total hardware or storage media failure. Using the Windows Backup utility, you can perform a variety of tasks, including:

- Backing up and restoring files and folders
- Scheduling backups
- Backing up Windows Server 2008 system state data
- Restoring the Active Directory database
- Creating an Automated System Recovery (ASR) backup

Backup hardware

Factors to consider when you purchase a backup unit include:

- The amount of data you need to back up
- Whether your backup software supports the backup device and media type you're considering
- The amount of money you want to spend
- The amount of time it takes to back up and restore data

The amount of data that needs to be backed up varies according to the size and nature of an organization. For example, a small company might be able to back up user files to a single tape or a couple of CDs. In larger organizations that have many servers, hundreds of gigabytes of storage space might be required. In these situations, companies typically invest in sophisticated, automated tape devices in large, centralized storage systems. Deciding which files are backed up, how often, and with what storage methods is all part of implementing your strategy.

There are many types of backup media and devices, ranging from removable media cartridges to CD-ROMs and magnetic tape. When deciding on the best backup media and device for your organization, you need to find the best balance between various factors: the speed of backing up the data, the speed of restoring data, the quality and function of supported backup programs, and the storage media requirements. Then choose a unit that provides the technology you need to back up and restore data efficiently and effectively within the parameters of your situation.

For example, some products use optical disks, which are a great solution for *Hierarchical Storage Management (HSM)*, in which infrequently used data is moved from fast, expensive hardware (hard disks) to slower, less expensive media, such as optical disks or magnetic tape. However, optical disks are a poor solution if you want to back up large amounts of data quickly. If speed is an issue, you will usually turn to the ubiquitous and cost-effective tape drive. Tape drives offer the lowest cost per megabyte of storage and the greatest degree of flexibility compared to comparable-capacity devices, and they are very portable.

The choices available in backup devices have greatly expanded over the last few years due to advances in technology. The following table compares the most common backup solutions in the server realm: tape and optical devices.

Device (Category)	Pros	Cons
Tape drives (magnetic)	Inexpensive media, faster transfer rate	Expensive drives
Optical: CD and DVD (laser)	Inexpensive media	Limited software support for drive interface; not as flexible as other solutions for recording data; slower than tape

Tape drives

Tape drives are generally the most popular server backup devices. You use tape drives to create backups of data from hard drives. Then you typically move the tapes to an off-site location for storage. This way, if a disaster occurs in the building the computer is in, the tapes are safe in another location. There are companies you can contract with for secure, fireproof storage of your tapes. You can also use a safety deposit box at a bank or a fireproof safe if you don't have more stringent storage requirements for the tapes.

Tape is a low-cost, high-capacity storage solution for data backups. Magnetic tapes are used to record information in *burst mode*, in which data is written in blocks. Burst mode results in faster data transfer. An *interblock gap* is a physical space between blocks on the tape. These gaps help prevent blocks of data from being overwritten.

Various types of compression are used to fit more data onto the tape at a faster rate. Most data backup algorithms use lossless compression so that reconstructed data is the same as the original. Most of these algorithms compress data at a 2:1 ratio or better.

Some devices support multiple tape formats, and others support only one. Some are very expensive, and some are not. The faster units are more expensive, as are units that have larger media capacities and/or automated handling of multiple media. One factor that often forces you to choose the large, more expensive drives is the backup window. The *backup window* is the optimal period of time in which you can perform a backup, and it's usually when most files are closed. If your organization has a very small backup window, you need a very fast (and expensive) tape backup solution.

Tape drives are sequential-access devices. Instead of being able to go directly to a specific file when you need to restore it, you must read all of the files before that file on the tape.

Tape drives are known for their long-lasting performance between hardware failures, due to the reliability of tape drive mechanics and robotics that some systems include. Despite this reliability, you should research a vendor's service contract to ensure that it includes same-day on-site or overnight cross-shipping service if the unit fails.

Competition in the tape backup arena has created an abundance of dubious performance claims. You need to determine the type of files the vendor used to test the drive and the type of test the vendor ran, because many claims are a result of using totally compressible files. These tests don't take into account that many file types can't be compressed, so the tests don't simulate real-world scenarios.

Tape formats

Backup tapes come in various cartridge formats. The original tapes were reel-to-reel tapes on mainframes; then came cassette tapes, and then DAT tapes. The tapes have gone from relatively slow devices with low capacity to the high speeds and capacities of the current tapes.

QIC

Quarter-inch cartridge, or QIC (pronounced "quick"), tapes are belt-driven, rather than having the tape attached to the reels. Because of this setup, the tapes need to be retensioned periodically. *Retensioning* means winding the tape end to end and then rewinding it in a single operation. This process resets the belt to the proper equalized tension.

The tape contains holes at the ends to prevent it from being unwound completely. Going to the end would cause the tape to come off the reel, making it unusable.

The Travan version of QIC uses a miniature cartridge and was developed for the home market. This cartridge's capacity ranges from 400 MB to 10 GB. The SLR (scalable linear recording) drive is the only type of drive still being manufactured that uses QIC tapes, so this format is also known as SLR.

DDS

The digital audio tape (DAT) format was designed for audio recording. It has been adapted for data storage with the digital data storage (DDS) format. This format uses tape that's 4 mm wide. DDS recorders contain two read heads and two write heads. The tape is read, and if errors are detected, the data is rewritten.

The cartridges are expected to last for approximately 2000 passes and should be replaced after that. That should be good for about 100 backups. The cartridges are rated for a 10-year shelf life. However, the technology is rather old and the tape drives require frequent cleaning. A DDS2 tape is shown in Exhibit 12-1.

Exhibit 12-1: A DDS2 tape

The capacities of DDS tapes range from 2 GB without compression for DDS-1, to 20 GB without compression for DDS-4. Compression can double the capacity of your tape.

DLT and SDLT

The DLT (digital linear tape) standard was created by DEC and was later sold to Quantum. It uses linear serpentine recording with multiple tracks on 12.6mm wide tape. With *linear serpentine recording*, data tracks are written in alternating bands from the beginning of the tape to the end and back again. A DLT cartridge contains a single reel, and it pulls the tape out of the cartridge, using a leader tape attached to a take-up reel inside the drive. You attach the drive leader tape to the cartridge leader during the load process. The reel motors control tape speed and tension. The tape is guided by four to six rollers that touch only the back side of it. After data is written across a single band from beginning to end, the write head drops down and writes another band of data in the opposite direction. This process continues until the tape has no more room for data bands.

Super DLT (SDLT) is a higher-capacity version of DLT. Capacities range from 15 GB to 1200 GB.

LTO

The LTO (linear tape open) format was developed by HP, IBM, and Certance, and it's an open format. Tapes created on one brand of drive can be used on drives from another manufacturer if they're LTO-compatible. That isn't the case with other tape formats.

LTO comes in two formats: Accelis and Ultrium. Accelis uses an 8mm tape and a dual-reel cartridge. However, licenses for Accelis are no longer available, so you won't find Accelis drives and media available commercially. Ultrium uses a 0.5" tape and a single-reel cartridge. Ultrium is the high-capacity version of LTO. The third generation of Ultrium, Ultrium format generation 3, has a data storage capacity of up to 800 GB and a maximum transfer rate of 80 to 160 MBps.

AIT and SAIT

The AIT (Advanced Intelligent Tape) format and its successor, SAIT (Super AIT), were developed by Sony. AIT and SAIT use helical-scan recording, in which the head is tilted and data is recorded in diagonal stripes across the head.

AIT uses 8mm tape in a 3.5" drive. Its capacities range from 20 GB to 400 GB, depending on the specific tape. SAIT uses single-reel, 0.5" tape. Its capacities range from 500 GB, uncompressed, to 1 TB, compressed. Data transfer rates are 30 MBps, uncompressed, and 78 MBps, compressed. SAIT technology includes Memory-in-Cassette (MIC)—a 64 KB memory chip used to store the cartridge's system log and file search information.

Whichever type of tape drive you install, consider the importance of the tape drive's driver. Plug and Play operating systems might automatically detect hardware and install drivers of their own for the tape device. However, there might be features of the device that do not become available until you install the driver supplied directly from the manufacturer. For example, many tape drives include hardware compression, in which tape drive electronics compress data as it writes to tape, relieving the compression burden from the processor. However, unless you use the vendor drivers, the feature might not be available and you would then have to fall back to software compression utilizing the processor.

Be sure to upgrade tape drivers when upgrading from one drive to another. For example, upgrading from a standalone tape device to an autoloader without also upgrading the driver will likely result in a unit that will not back up at all or might back up to only a single tape.

No matter what type of drive you choose, versions of most backup products are available with a choice of SCSI, EIDE, or parallel port interfaces, except for the very high-end products, which all have SCSI interfaces. Additionally, some older, low-end products, particularly tape drives, also come in versions that connect to the floppy disk controller. Parallel port and floppy disk interfaces will not be considered further in this discussion of server backup solutions.

Departmental servers that might not require extremely high-capacity backup solutions might only require a single standalone EIDE tape device. These devices provide reasonably good performance at up to about 20 GB of compressed data. For the best backup performance, especially for use on higher-end workstations and certainly for all servers, the interface option of choice is SCSI.

When assessing the cost of your backup solution, you'll need to add the price of a good-quality SCSI interface card for your server if you don't have one already, though most high-end workstation PCs and servers are already based on SCSI disk subsystems and therefore won't require an additional interface. In either case, check the type of physical SCSI connector fitted to a drive before buying to make sure you won't need additional cables or adapters.

An additional benefit of SCSI is system responsiveness. With EIDE tape drives, some tape operations, such as cataloging the contents of the tape or re-tensioning, will temporarily dominate the system and affect responsiveness. Because of the nature of SCSI, you can perform nearly any tape function with minimal impact on overall system responsiveness.

If it is not cost prohibitive, take performance a step further and choose a tape solution that is Fiber Channel–compatible.

Optical media

CDs are 120mm plastic discs that contain a layer of reflective metal-alloy foil encased in transparent plastic. The CD contains a single spiral track. A 74-minute CD can hold 650 MB of data; an 80-minute CD can hold 700 MB of data. Exhibit 12-2 illustrates the components of a CD.

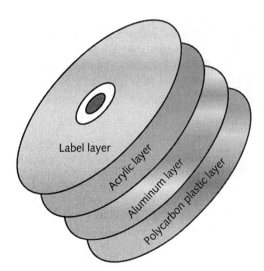

Exhibit 12-2: Components of a CD

Recordable CDs

Writable CDs are written using a process called burning. This is what you do when you write to CDs with your PC. CD-R discs can be read many times but written to just once. These CDs are also referred to as single-session discs for this reason. They're composed of a gold metal alloy and an organic dye. The dye can be cyan (cyan blue), phthalocyanine (aqua), metalized azo (dark blue), or formazan (green). The dye is heated with the laser, and this process causes pits and bumps. CD-R discs are an example of a write once, read many (WORM) medium.

CD-RW discs have a silver alloy layer. The alloy has a polycrystalline structure. The laser melts the crystals in the alloy, creating the land areas. CD-RW discs can be written to multiple times and are thus referred to as multisession discs.

CD drives

CD drives are standard on computer systems today. In fact, many computers no longer contain a floppy drive unless the buyer selects it as an option. CD drives come in two types:

- **CD-ROM drive** — Can only read CDs.
- **CD-RW drive** — Can read from and write to CDs.

When a CD contains computer data, the data stays in digital format. If the CD is an audio CD, a digital-to-analog converter converts the digital information into analog sound.

CD drives contain three major parts.

- **The drive motor** — Spins the disc.
- **The laser lens and laser pickup** — Focuses in on and reads the disc.
- **The tracking drive and tracking motor** — Moves the laser to follow the track on the CD.

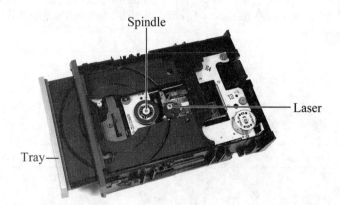

Exhibit 12-3: CD drive components

CD drive speeds

The speed of a CD drive is expressed in #X, where # is the number of times faster than the rate at which an audio CD spins. A 1X CD spins from approximately 210 to 539 RPM. The rate varies depending on where on the disc the information is being read.

A 2X CD is twice as fast as a 1X CD. This power of X is accurate up to 12X. After that, to increase the access speed, various methods are used that don't actually produce speeds directly X-times faster than a 1X CD. Access time is affected by how many times the read head has to move to various locations on the CD.

DVDs

DVDs are 12cm-diameter discs like CDs but are often thinner than CDs. DVDs use a different encoding method than the one CDs use, and DVDs are higher-density discs. The higher density requires a narrower laser beam than CDs require. A DVD track is 0.74 microns wide, whereas a CD track is 1.6 microns wide.

DVD drives are becoming standard devices on computers, often replacing CD drives. They're often DVD-Rewritable drives. If they're players only, then there's often a CD-RW drive in addition to the DVD drive on the computer.

A DVD drive running at 1X transfers data at 1.38 MB per second. DVD drives are available in higher speeds, up to 16X. They come in read-only, write-once, and rewritable versions.

DVD drives use red and infrared lasers with a 650 nm laser beam. Compare this to the longer-wavelength 780 nm laser used for CDs.

DVD media

A standard DVD disc has a 4.7 GB capacity. This DVD is also known as a DVD-5; the "5" refers to the DVD holding almost 5 GB of data. Discs can be single-sided and single-layered, as the DVD-5 disc is. A 3" mini-disc is also available; it holds 1.5 GB of data. DVDs use the UDF (universal disc format) file system.

DVDs can also be double-sided, double-layered, double-sided single-layered, or any combination of single and double sides and layers. Double layering is achieved by having two layers of pits, one deeper than the other. The laser is refocused on the deeper layer to read the second layer.

The following table summarizes the number of sides and layers and the capacities of various types of DVDs.

DVD type	Sides	Layers	Capacity
DVD-5	Single	Single	4.7 GB
DVD-9	Single	Double	8.5 GB
DVD-10	Double	Single on both sides	9.4 GB
DVD-14	Double	Double on one side, single on the other side	13.3 GB
DVD-18	Double	Double on both sides	17.1 GB

DVD standards, which were created by the DVD Forum, include DVD-R, DVD-RW, and DVD-RAM. Media created according to these standards can display the DVD logo. Full details can be found on the DVD Forum Web site, at *dvdform.org/forum.shtml*. Another source for further information about DVDs is *dvddemystified.com/dvdfaq.html*.

The DVD+R Alliance created standards for DVD+RW, DVD+R, and DVD+ R DL media. These aren't official DVD standards and can't display the DVD logo. Instead, they display the RW logo. Details can be found at the dvdrw.com Web site.

DVD-Rs and DVD+Rs are write-once, read-many media. DVD-RW and DVD+RW are rewritable discs, with the latter being faster to format. A DVD-RAM holds up to 9.4 GB of data. This standard isn't well established at this time, and few systems can use it.

Blu-ray discs

Blu-ray discs are optical discs created with a "blue" (actually, violet) laser. Because of the violet laser's shorter wavelength, dual-layer Blu-ray discs can hold up to 50 GB of data, and single-layer Blu-ray discs can hold up to 25 GB of data. This capacity is significantly higher than a DVD's capacity.

Currently, Blu-ray discs are primarily used to store high-definition video or large amounts of data. The Blu-ray disc was developed by the Blu-ray Disc Association, a group of representatives from consumer electronics manufacturers, computer hardware manufacturers, and the motion picture industry. The Blu-ray standards were finalized in 2004.

USB flash drives

For small-scale backups, USB flash drives are a popular storage solution. They are about the size of an adult person's thumb or a pack of gum, and they weigh about as much as a car key. They come with capacities from a few megabytes to many gigabytes. Their capacity is much greater than that of a floppy disk, and many flash drives can hold more than a CD can. Flash drives are a popular option for users to back up important data files on their own.

Flash drives are designed to be *hot-swappable*, meaning that you can attach the device to or detach it from your computer without shutting the PC down and restarting it. This functionality is part of the USB specification.

When hot-swapping, be sure that the drive has finished writing before you remove it. If the drive is in the middle of a write operation when you disconnect it, the file that was being written, or even the entire directory structure, can become unreadable. An LED light on the drive typically indicates when a write operation is in progress. Generally, you should use the Safely Remove Hardware icon to stop the device before removing it from the computer. Some computer makers recommend ejecting the drive instead. To do so, right-click the USB flash drive in Windows Explorer and choose Eject.

Exhibit 12-4 shows three USB flash drives. Notice that the top one is made to look like a pen, and the drive is contained in half of the pen. Most drives have a size and shape similar to these examples, but some have slightly different shapes. Some drives have bulges and ridges to make them easier to grip when you're inserting them in and removing them from the USB port.

Exhibit 12-4: USB flash drives

The technical specifications of USB flash drives can be found at the *usb.org* Web site. The USB Flash Drive Alliance is a good resource for information on USB flash drives; its Web site is *usbflashdrive.org*. In general, USB flash drives are typically composed of:

- A controller with a USB interface
- A non-volatile memory interface connected to memory
- An LED to indicate drive activity

Many flash drives come with one or more security features. These include:

- Encryption
- Password protection
- A fingerprint sensor

Optionally, USB flash drives might include:

- A crystal for external clock generation on high-speed drives
- A write-protect switch
- An integrated MP3 player

The drivers that support USB flash drives have been included in Windows client and server operating systems since Windows 2000. Drivers are also included in Macintosh OS 9 and OS X or later, as well as Linux kernels 2.4 and later.

Floppy disk storage

A floppy disk is a removable data storage medium composed of a thin, typically brown, plastic disk contained within a stiff or rigid plastic case. Floppy disks are also called floppies or diskettes. A floppy disk drive (FDD) is the PC component that reads data from and writes data to floppies. This drive can be internally connected, typically through a 34-pin data connector on the motherboard. External FDDs are available with USB, IEEE 1394, and eSATA connections.

Data is stored on the disk using magnetism—the disk is coated with a magnetic material that retains its magnetic polarization even when power isn't present. Read/write heads, which are small electromagnets, either sense the current polarization to read the data or set new polarization to write data to the disk. A small opening or door on the case permits the associated drive components to access the inner disk. The read/write heads actually touch the surface of the disk as it's spun by the drive's motor. The disk spins at 300 revolutions per minute (RPM).

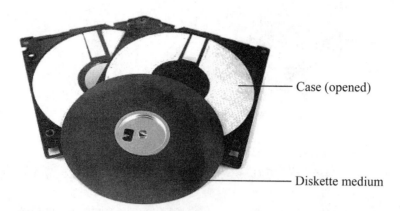

Exhibit 12-5: A diskette opened to reveal its recording medium

Floppy disks were the original storage medium for PCs. By today's standards, they hold a miniscule amount of data and are very slow to access, so they aren't used much anymore. Many modern computers don't include a floppy drive.

Form factors

The original PC floppy disks measured 5.25" in diameter and had a soft, flexible outer cover. They held relatively little data, even compared to other floppy disk technologies. A 5.25" floppy is pictured in Exhibit 12-6.

Exhibit 12-6: A 5.25" floppy disk

Later floppy disks were 3.5" in diameter and were protected by a hard outer case with a sliding metal door. Despite their hard outer case, these disks aren't "hard disks"; that term refers to the high-capacity disk drives typically installed inside a PC's case.

Even though they're physically smaller, the most popular 3.5" disks stored a lot more data than their larger predecessors. A 3.5" floppy disk is shown in Exhibit 12-7.

Exhibit 12-7: A 3.5" floppy disk

Capacities

Capacities of floppy drives vary by size and recording techniques. The two biggest factors in capacity are:

- The number of tracks
- The number of sectors in each track

Information is recorded onto the floppy disk in a series of concentric circular areas called *tracks*.

- Floppy disks use either 40 or 80 tracks.
- Each track is divided into sections, called *sectors*, in which the actual data is recorded.
- Each sector stores the same amount of data, even though sectors on inner tracks are physically smaller than those on outer tracks.

The density of a floppy disk refers to the number of sectors per track, as compared to the original floppies used in pre-PC computers. PC floppy densities vary from double density (9 sectors per track) to extra-high density (36 sectors per track).

The storage capacities of the popular PC floppy disks are listed in the following table.

Size	Tracks	Sectors per track	Density	Capacity
5.25"	40	9	Double density	360 KB
5.25"	80	15	High density	1.2 MB
3.5"	80	9	Double density	720 KB
3.5"	80	18	High density	1.44 MB
3.5"	80	36	Extra-high density	2.88 MB

Identifying a disk's storage capacity

Most modern diskettes are labeled with their maximum capacity. Some, however, lack such labeling. You can distinguish between 3.5" double-density and high-density disks by counting the holes in their corners. Double-density diskettes have a single hole (the write-protection hole described in the next section). High-density diskettes have two holes.

Write protection

You can prevent writing to floppies by engaging write protection. With 5.25" floppies, you must cover a notch in the plastic case with tape or a label designed specifically for that purpose. In the associated drives, a mechanical pin "feels" for the presence of this notch, and if it's present, writing is enabled.

With 3.5" disks, you slide open a small "door" to enable write protection. In the associated drives, if an LED light can shine through this door, then writing is disabled.

Both of these write protection devices are shown in Exhibit 12-8.

Exhibit 12-8: Floppy disks: write-protected (left) and write-enabled (right)

Disk-to-disk backups

Disk-to-disk (D2D) backups are those in which a computer's hard disk is backed up to another hard disk, instead of to another backup medium, such as tape or an optical disc. Some advantages of D2D backups include the following:

- Because the disks use file systems, multiple backup and recovery operations can access them simultaneously.
- D2D backups provide higher speed and capacity than other backup media, so backup and recovery times are shorter.
- Non-linear recovery of data is available, so you can restore a specific file faster than you can from a tape backup.

Do it!

A-1:   Comparing backup media types

Questions and answers
1 What's Hierarchical Storage Management (HSM)?
2 Where should backups be stored?
3 Tapes are accessed _____, using _____ mode.
4 What are QIC drives also known as?
5 What's the shelf life of a DDS tape?
6 What does DLT stand for? What capacities are offered by DLT?
7 What's the advantage of LTO tape?

8 What's an optical disc?

9 The speed of a CD drive is expressed in #X, where # is the number of times faster than the rate at which an audio CD spins. This power of X is accurate up to which value?

    A Two

    B Four

    C Eight

    D Twelve

    E Sixteen

    F Twenty-four

10 What is the capacity of a double-sided, double-layer (on both sides) DVD?

    A 4.7 GB

    B 8.5 GB

    C 9.4 GB

    D 17.1 GB

11 Why might you choose to back up your data on D2D media?

Managing backups

For a large-scale enterprise, you should investigate a backup technology that can automatically change tapes in a largely unattended fashion. Often large and extremely expensive, these automated tape devices are typically tape libraries that use autoloaders (see Exhibit 12-9). A tape library is a self-contained tape backup solution that is preloaded with several tapes. Most tape libraries include autoloaders to automatically load and swap tapes. A properly configured tape library takes only a fraction of the time otherwise required with a manual backup. This becomes more of an issue as more data centers operate around the clock instead of during business hours, because the available backup window grows smaller. In addition to automatically swapping tapes, these devices can automatically clean tape heads.

Exhibit 12-9: A tape library using an autoloader

At the highest level, you'll see tape libraries that can support dozens of drives and hold several hundred cartridges (see Exhibit 12-10). At that level, you probably won't configure the tape solution yourself; you'll tell vendor representatives what your objectives are and they will configure the library for you or provide guidance.

Exhibit 12-10: The StorageTek robotic tape library uses multiple SuperDLT drives for a total storage capacity of over 33 TB

Eliminating human error

Making backups can be a tedious chore fraught with misplaced tapes, unmarked or mismarked tapes, incompatible tapes, and so on. For example, if someone backed up Server_A and accidentally marked the tape Server_B, restoring Server_A data might never occur unless someone manually goes through all the tapes searching for the data. Automated backup solutions won't write a label for you, but they can lessen potential human error. Once you place the first set of tapes in the drives and properly configure the software, you can remove the human error factor from the tape backup.

Assigning backup permissions

As part of planning your backup strategy, you have to decide who will be responsible for completing backup tasks and how secure your backups need to be. The risk of human error increases with the number of people who are able to perform backups. One key consideration is determining which users should (or should not) have the ability to back up files and folders. To perform a backup, you need certain rights and permissions. In many network server operating systems, such as Windows Server 2008, members of the following groups can back up any files and folders on a member server:

- Administrators
- Backup Operators
- Server Operators

Users who are not members of administrative-level or Backup Operators groups are much more limited. The primary purpose of limiting the backup rights of a normal user is to ensure security. When users need to be able to back up files belonging to other users, they should be granted membership in a Backup Operators group, assigned at least the Read permission for the files and folders in question, or granted the appropriate rights.

Many backup utilities provide additional security by giving you the option, within each individual backup job, to allow only the owner and administrators to have access to the backup data. When this option is selected, only an administrator or the person who created the backup can restore the backup, regardless of which users have rights or permissions to restore files.

Online retention periods

Another big advantage of automated backup libraries is their extensive *online retention period (OLRP)*. OLRP is the period in which data can be restored from tape without manual intervention. Because a library can store several generations of backups at once, if you want to restore a file from, say, five weeks ago, you don't have to rummage through the storage cabinet to find the right tape. Instead, you can use the tape library software to locate and restore data from the correct tape for you.

Do it!

A-2: Exploring backup strategies and permissions

Questions and answers

1 Backups are a key means of _____ data.

2 The types of data that should be backed up include:

A Operating system files

B Configuration files

C User data

D All the above

3 Members of which of the following groups can typically back up any files and folders on a network server? (Choose all that apply.)

A Administrators

B Backup Operators

C Server Operators

D Users

4 True or false? Individual users can be granted rights that allow them to back up and restore files on a network server if necessary.

Backup software

Explanation   Most lower-cost tape drives and some disk-based devices intended for use with standalone PCs come bundled with backup software. For example, Windows Server 2008 comes with backup software, shown in Exhibit 12-11. The software tends to be quite basic, but it usually does the job it's intended for. Such software isn't capable of servicing more sophisticated backup solutions, such as automatic tape changers, remote backups, or the backing up of open files.

Most high-end tape drives and most disk-based products don't come bundled with software. Take this into consideration when comparing costs, because the software is an additional several hundred dollars per server. Software for high-end tape drives includes many more features, at a reduced cost per remote station.

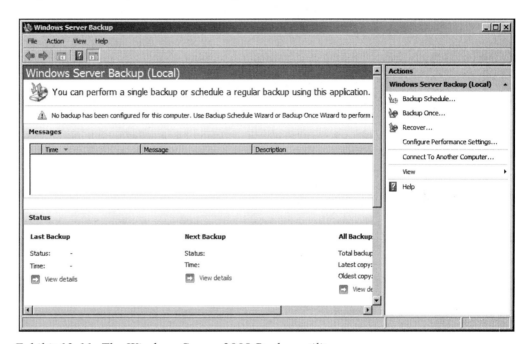

Exhibit 12-11: The Windows Server 2008 Backup utility

If you need software as part of your backup setup, there are a number of packages available, ranging from replacements for bundled software to high-end products capable of backing up a whole room full of servers onto several tape drives, sometimes simultaneously. Depending on your needs, the features to look for in backup software include the following:

- **Hard disk imaging** — The ability to restore a hard disk in its entirety without your needing to reinstall the operating system manually. This software feature creates an image of the disk and stores it on tape.

- **Virtual hard disk** — The ability to treat a backup tape as a virtual hard disk, albeit a very slow one. This capability sometimes uses the right-click menu from Windows Explorer, allowing you to perform the backup in a way similar to using the Send To item when copying a file to a floppy disk.

- **Data compression** — A built-in data compression capability you can use if your drive doesn't include its own hardware data compression capabilities.

- **Virus scan** — The ability to scan for viruses during backup or restore operations.

- **Tape management** — The ability to tell you when to replace or swap tapes. Robotic or automated media-switching devices often require proprietary drivers and administrative software to be installed.

- **Account access management** — The ability to create an account for you that has access rights to back up all data regardless of ownership. In a Windows environment, this account would belong to the Backup Operators group. The account can usually log on as a service and make backups without an administrator actually logging on.

- **Unattended backups** — The ability to perform unattended backups. The software often creates a special account that can log on by itself at scheduled times to start the backups.

- **Command-line functions** — A feature that enables you to run commands before and after the backup. This is useful for stopping services or applications that would interfere with the backup and restarting them afterward.

Backup types

Most good backup programs support a variety of backup types, including:

- Normal backup
- Incremental backup
- Differential backup
- Daily backup
- Copy backup

The following sections discuss each of these backup methods and their impact on backup procedures.

The archive bit

Backup programs use a special file attribute called an *archive bit*. A file's archive bit is set to 1 when the file needs to be backed up—that is, if it's new or if it has changed since the last backup. The bit is reset to 0 when the file is backed up, and the bit remains that way until you or an application changes the file.

Method	Archive bit
Full	Reset on all files
Incremental	Reset on any file backed up
Differential	Not reset
Daily	Not reset
Copy	Not reset

Full backups

The most common type of backup performed is known as a full backup, also referred to as a normal backup. It backs up all selected files and folders and clears their archive attribute. Clearing the archive attribute marks files as having been backed up, an important distinction when a full backup is used in conjunction with some of the other backup methods. When a file is changed, the archive attribute is reset.

Although the full backup saves all selected files and folders, it is not always the best choice for each backup job, because it ignores the state of the archive attribute. For example, if you were to do a full backup Monday, and then do another full backup of the same files on Tuesday, all of the files would be copied again, regardless of whether any changes had taken place. This would result in larger-than-necessary backups because you would be saving copies of identical files. While there is nothing wrong with this, it is inefficient.

In most situations, administrators will begin the week with a full backup of all necessary files, and then use either incremental or differential backups on subsequent days.

Incremental backups

Incremental backup only backs up those files that have changed since the last normal or incremental backup took place. An incremental backup also clears the archive attribute associated with any files and folders that it backs up.

The main purpose of an incremental backup is to reduce the overall size of backup jobs. For example, if you do a full backup on Monday and an incremental backup of these same files on Tuesday, only the files that have changed since Monday will be backed up. If another incremental backup is done Wednesday, only the files that have changed since Tuesday will be backed up, and so on. This method ensures that backups created after the initial full backup take as little time and space as possible.

Although incremental backups are the most efficient, they do result in a more involved restore process. For example, if a folder containing user data is accidentally deleted on Thursday morning, completely restoring the data will require you to first restore the full backup from Monday, and then restore the incremental backups from both Tuesday and Wednesday.

Exhibit 12-12 shows the backup and restore process for the data folder, using normal and incremental backups.

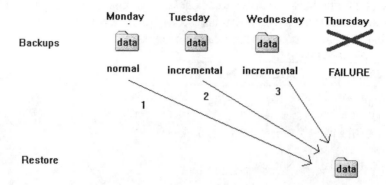

Exhibit 12-12: Incremental backup and restore operations

Differential backups

The differential backup is similar to the incremental backup with an important difference: it does not clear the archive attribute. Therefore, each time the differential backup runs, it will back up all files that have changed since the full backup, even if they've been included in a previous differential backup.

Using our previous example, if a full backup is run on Monday, all files are backed up. If a differential backup runs on Tuesday, it will back up any files that have changed. When the differential backup runs on Wednesday, it will back up all the files that have changed since Monday, including those that were backed up on Tuesday, even if they haven't changed.

The differential process makes restoration simpler because if a failure occurs on Thursday, you have to restore only Monday's and Wednesday's backups to recover all of the data. The downside is that the differential backups take longer and use more storage space.

Exhibit 12-13 shows the backup and restore processes using full and differential backups.

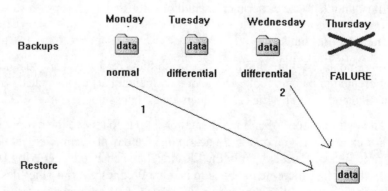

Exhibit 12-13: Differential backup and restore operations

Daily backups

A daily backup saves only the files or folders that have been created or changed on the day that the backup takes place. This method does not change the archive attribute, so it does not interfere with any other backup procedures.

Copy backups

A copy backup works just like a full backup, saving all selected files and folders, but it does not change the archive attribute. The main purpose of a copy backup is to create the equivalent of a full backup (perhaps for a backup tape to be stored off-site) without interfering with any other backup procedures.

Unique backup situations

Backups of large amounts of data can take a long time to complete. On some systems, such as a database server, users may be writing data to a database while the backup is running. If a file is being written to while it is being backed up, data can be lost or corrupted. For example, if a file is moved from a directory that hasn't been backed up into a directory that has already been backed up, that file wouldn't be included in the backup. If you have a high-availability system where you can't afford to take it offline during the backup, you can perform the backup on a snapshot. A *snapshot* is a read-only copy of the data, frozen at a point in time. With this backup method, a snapshot is made of the data, and the original data remains in use while the snapshot gets backed up.

For databases, there are two backup terms you should be aware of: cold and hot backups. For a *cold backup*, the database is closed or locked and is not available to users during the backup. A *hot backup* is a backup made with the snapshot method, while the database is still available to users.

In many backup scenarios, you are protecting just your data. However, for critical systems, you should plan for hardware failure. With a *bare-metal backup*, you include on your backup media the operating system, applications, and data files needed to rebuild or restore the critical system to an entirely separate piece of hardware. This method is referred to as bare-metal because you can restore the system to a "blank" or "bare-metal" computer without installing the operating system or applications first.

To create a bare-metal backup, you need to back up all files on the system—the operating system, application, and data files. However, some backup products can't back up files while they are in use; for example, operating system files can't be backed up while the OS is loaded. These files are referred to as open files. If your backup product can't back up open files, it might get around this limitation by scheduling a backup on the next reboot.

A-3: Exploring backup types

Questions and answers

1 Which of the following backup types will back up all selected files and folders and change their archive attribute?

  A   Full

  B   Incremental

  C   Differential

  D   Daily

2 Which of the following backup types will back up all files that have changed since the last incremental or normal backup? (Choose all that apply.)

  A   Full

  B   Incremental

  C   Differential

  D   Daily

3 Which of the following backup types will back up only the selected files and folders that have changed since the last differential or normal backup and will not change their archive attribute?

  A   Full

  B   Daily

  C   Incremental

  D   Differential

4 Which of the following backup types will back up only the selected files and folders that have changed since the last incremental or normal backup and will change their archive attribute?

  A   Full

  B   Copy

  C   Daily

  D   Incremental

5 Which of the following backup types will back up only the selected files and folders that have changed on the current day?

  A   Daily

  B   Full

  C   Copy

  D   Incremental

6 Which of the following backup types will back up all selected files and folders and will not change their archive attribute, so as not to interfere with any other backup process?

A Daily

B Copy

C Differential

D Full

Developing a backup strategy

*Explanation*Regular backups of server operating system files, application files, and user data prevent data loss resulting from disk drive failures, disk controller errors, power outages, virus infections, and other problems. Backup operations that are based on careful planning and reliable equipment make file recovery easier and less time-consuming.

There are several backup strategies you can employ. The most common is known as the *Grandfather-Father-Son (GFS)* strategy, which is described below. Backup strategies usually consist of some combination of full, incremental, and differential backups. Developing a backup strategy involves not only determining when to perform backups, but also testing the data with random and scheduled verification to make sure that tape devices and other media are functioning properly.

The Grandfather-Father-Son backup strategy

There are several generally accepted backup strategies. Many of them are based on the popular Grandfather-Father-Son (GFS) backup strategy (also known as the Child-Parent-Grandparent method), illustrated in Exhibit 12-14. This strategy uses three sets of tapes for daily, weekly, and monthly backup sets, and you implement it as follows:

1   **Back up the "Son"** — Label four tapes as "Monday" through "Thursday." These Son tapes are used for daily incremental backups during the week. For subsequent weeks, reuse these same tapes.

2   **Back up the "Father"** — Label five tapes as "Week 1" through "Week 5." These Father tapes are used for weekly full backups on Friday, the day you don't perform a Son backup. Once you make the tape, store it locally. Reuse each tape when its week arrives. Depending on your backup policy, periodically duplicate a Father tape for off-site storage. You can use another drive to perform a simultaneous backup, or use backup software that offers a tape copy feature.

3   **Back up the "Grandfather"** — No standard labeling scheme is stated, but consider labeling three tapes as "Month 1" through "Month 3." The Grandfather tapes are used for full backups performed on the last business day of the month. The tapes are valid for three months and are reused every quarter.

At a minimum, the GFS strategy requires 12 tapes, assuming that no single backup exceeds the capacity of a single cartridge.

Of course, you can modify this scheme as it suits your backup policy, but the GFS strategy is a logical, reliable place to start. For example, if you want to keep a year's data archived at all times, instead of only a quarter's, then for the Grandfather tapes you would label 12 tapes "Month 1" through "Month 12" and reuse the tapes every year.

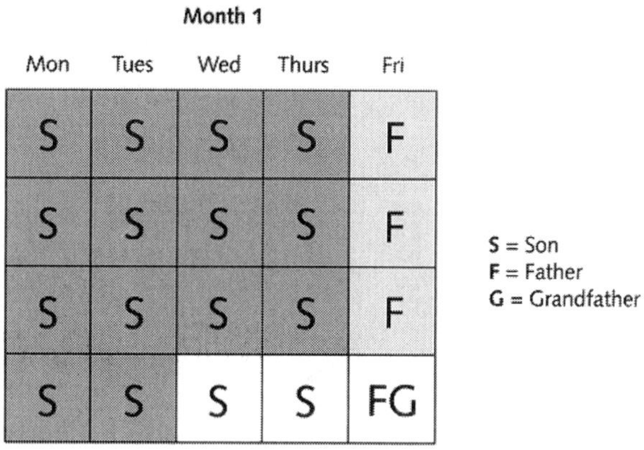

Month 1

Mon	Tues	Wed	Thurs	Fri
S	S	S	S	F
S	S	S	S	F
S	S	S	S	F
S	S	S	S	FG

S = Son
F = Father
G = Grandfather

Exhibit 12-14: The GFS tape rotation strategy

The six-cartridge backup

If you want to use fewer tapes, consider the *six-cartridge* backup strategy. This might be a better choice for smaller businesses or sites that don't generate large quantities of data. The disadvantage of the six-cartridge strategy is that you have a shorter archive history—only two weeks—whereas the GFS strategy provides a quarter's worth of history.

To perform a six-cartridge backup:

1 Label six cartridges "Friday 1," "Friday 2," "Monday," "Tuesday," "Wednesday," and "Thursday."

2 Perform the first full backup, using the "Friday 1" tape. Store the tape off-site.

3 On Monday, perform an incremental backup, using the "Monday" tape. Store the tape on site.

4 Repeat the incremental backup, using the "Tuesday," "Wednesday," and "Thursday" tapes on the corresponding days.

5 Perform the second full backup, using the "Friday 2" tape. This completes the backup cycle. Store the cartridge off-site. On each successive Friday, alternate between the "Friday 1" tape and the "Friday 2" tape.

Note that the Friday tapes are always stored off-site, as illustrated in Exhibit 12-15. This can cause a problem when you need to restore data, because you have to retrieve the tape physically, and this might not suit the timeframe necessary to restore the data. As with the GFS method, you can modify the six-cartridge method to suit your needs.

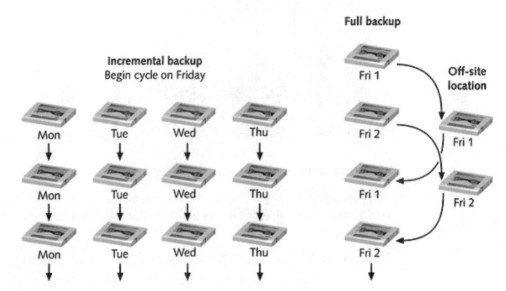

Exhibit 12-15: The six-cartridge backup strategy stores Friday tapes off-site

The Tower of Hanoi

Finally, there's the *Tower of Hanoi* backup method, borrowing from a mathematical logic game of the same name. Use five sets of media for this rotation, labeling them "A" through "E," and proceed as follows:

1 On day one, back up to "A." Reuse the "A" tape every other day.
2 On day two, back up to "B." Reuse the "B" tape every four days.
3 On day four, back up to "C." Reuse the "C" tape every eight days.
4 On day eight, back up to "D." Reuse the "D" tape every 16 days.
5 On day 16, back up to "E." Reuse the "E" tape every 32 days.

As a memory aid to the Tower of Hanoi rotation, just notice that each tape is reused in a pattern similar to binary notation. Look at the "reuse" schedule at the end of every step above. Notice that you reuse tapes every 2, 4, 8, 16, and 32 days.

An advantage of the Tower of Hanoi rotation is that you always have a daily history of data extending back 32 days. This is a flexible backup strategy requiring only five tapes (assuming that each backup requires only one tape). If you want long-term archiving, you can remove a tape and store it off-site. Label the tape with the date and replace it with another. For example, if you want to archive the "E" tape, place a date on it, send it to storage, and label a new cartridge "E" to continue the rotation. Also, you can extend the history, if you like. By adding an "F" backup every 64 days, you would have a 64-day history. Keep adding letters until you reach the history you want. The Tower of Hanoi rotation schedule is shown in Exhibit 12-16.

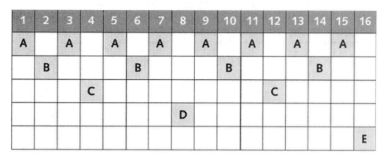

1	2	3	4	5	6	7	8	9	10	11	12	13	14	15	16
A		A		A		A		A		A		A		A	
	B				B				B				B		
			C								C				
							D								
															E

Exhibit 12-16: The Tower of Hanoi media rotation schedule

CompTIA exam objectives refer to this strategy as the *leaning tower* strategy.

Storing and securing backups

There are several steps you can take to enhance the security and operation of your backup and restore operations. You should also take steps to secure your backup cartridges.

When you develop a backup plan, consider the following recommendations:

- Secure both the storage device and the backup cartridges. Data can be retrieved from stolen cartridges and restored to another computer.
- If the software supports it, add security measures to the tape. You might be able to protect the media with a password or allow restore operations to be done by only the Administrator or Owner accounts, as with the Windows Server 2008 Backup utility.
- Back up an entire volume by using the full backup procedure. In case of a disk failure, it's more efficient to restore the entire volume in one operation than to include differential or incremental backups also.
- Archive your backups. Keep at least three current copies of backup cartridges.
  - Store one copy at an off-site location in an environmentally controlled, secure place. Check for a service bureau in your area that can provide this storage. Most service bureaus also have tape drives that can read and restore the tapes for you if necessary. In preparation for disaster recovery, know how long it takes to retrieve the tapes physically from off-site locations.
  - Store another copy in a secure, locked, fireproof cabinet, near a server that can restore from the tape.
  - The last tape can be stored wherever it suits you. Its main purpose is redundancy in case one of the other tapes becomes damaged or defective. Some organizations with a WAN infrastructure send a copy of the normal backup to another office across the WAN. That way, if the local off-site location and the local office become unavailable (as in a natural disaster), there is still the copy that was sent to the other office.

Do it!

A-4: Discussing backup software and strategies

Questions and answers

1 What's the minimum number of tapes required in a GFS tape backup strategy?

2 Which backup strategy requires fewer tapes than the GFS method?

3 What's an advantage of the Tower of Hanoi rotation strategy?

Topic B: Server redundancy and other disaster precautions

This topic covers the following CompTIA Server+ (2009 Edition) exam objectives.

#	Objective

5.2	Given a scenario, compare and contrast the different types of replication methods
	
	• Server to server
	  – Clustering
	  – Active/active
	  – Active/passive

6.2	Given a scenario, effectively troubleshoot hardware problems, selecting the appropriate tools and methods
	
	• Environmental issues
	  – Dust
	  – Humidity
	  – Temperature
	  – Power surge/failure

Clustering

Explanation

File services, print services, and client-server applications rely not only on the availability of the computers running the services, but also on the availability of network services. In an environment where there's only one computer providing a particular service (file, print, or application), an outage involving that server makes the service unavailable.

To provide both load balancing and redundancy for these services, a group, or cluster, of computers can cooperate in providing them. This cooperation is managed by clustering software that provides a service to clients in a client-server environment. For example, a public file share, a Web server, and a database application can all be managed as resources.

A cluster improves the availability of client-server applications by increasing the availability of server resources. Using a cluster, you can set up applications on two or more servers (nodes) in a cluster. Each node connects to a shared storage medium. A cluster presents a single, virtual image to clients, as illustrated in Exhibit 12-17. If one node fails, the applications on the failed node are available on the other node. Throughout this process, client communications with applications usually continue with little or no interruption. In most cases, the interruption in service is detected in about five seconds, and services can be available again in as few as 30 seconds, depending on how long it takes to restart the application.

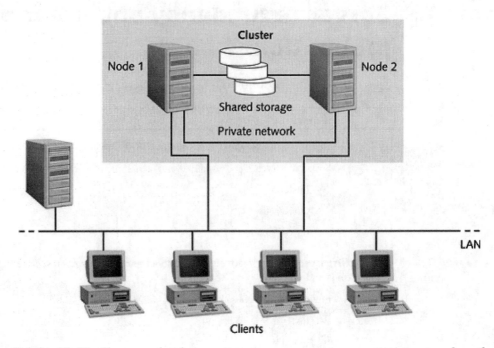

Exhibit 12-17: Cluster technology connects two or more servers to common shared storage

Clustering provides high availability and fault tolerance by keeping a backup of the primary system available. Static load balancing remains idle and unused until a failure occurs, so this is an expensive solution.

An *active cluster* is a clustering method in which all nodes perform normal, active functions and then perform additional functions for a failed member of the cluster. For example, redundant systems might have one node in the cluster servicing Web clients, while the other node provides access to a database. If either node fails, the resource (the Web server or the database server) fails over to the other node. The node that's still functioning responds to both Web and SQL requests from clients, as shown in Exhibit 12-18.

In a *passive cluster*, a server with identical services as its failover partner would remain in an idle node state until the primary node fails.

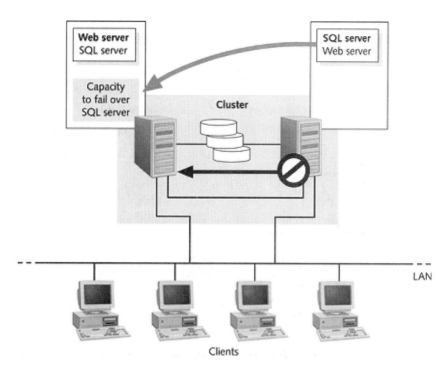

Exhibit 12-18: Active cluster redundancy

CPU, I/O, storage, and application resources can be added incrementally to expand capacity efficiently, making the solution highly scalable. This scheme provides reliable access to system resources and data, and protects your organization's investment in both hardware and software resources. Clusters are relatively affordable because they can be built with commodity hardware (high-volume components that are relatively inexpensive).

By clustering existing hardware with new computers, you protect your investment in both hardware and software: Instead of replacing an existing computer with a new one of twice the capacity, you can simply add another computer of equal capacity. For example, if performance degrades because of an increase in the number of clients using an application on a server, you can add a second server to a cluster, thereby improving performance and increasing availability.

Failover

Failover is the process of having cluster resources migrate from an unavailable node to an available node. A related process, failback, occurs when a service transfers back to the node that's been offline after it's back online. The cluster automatically initiates failover when it detects a failure on one of the cluster nodes. Because each cluster node monitors both its own processes and the other node's, the need for failover is detected without delay.

Spare parts

For hardware failure recovery, having a number of spare parts available saves you the time you'd need to order replacement parts from the original vendor. Also, as equipment ages, the availability of the parts needed to continue operation may diminish as well. All parts to be considered available as replacements for a given computer system must be compatible with both the operating system in use and other components in the system. The best strategy for mission-critical systems is to have a set of matching parts available.

Some vendors, such as Intel, sell spare-parts kits composed of the most critical system components, including:

- 12 V VRM (a voltage regulator module that helps ensure a clean power supply to the motherboard)
- Fans
- Hot-swap bay assembly with SCSI backplane
- Power supply
- CD-ROM drive
- Floppy drive
- Cables

In addition to the kit components listed above, you should also have the following spare components on hand:

- Network card
- Memory modules
- Processor
- Hard disk
- Hard disk host adapter (EIDE or SCSI)
- Motherboard
- Video card
- Sound card (optional)
- Other miscellaneous I/O boards

Spare drives

The redundancy of a RAID system wouldn't be very useful if you couldn't easily replace a failed drive. RAID controllers and associated software usually indicate when a drive fails. You can then at least shut down the system and replace the drive. This replacement drive is referred to as a *cold spare*. It's more likely, though, that the system allows hot swapping or hot spares.

Hot swapping allows you to pull the old drive and put in a new one without shutting down the system. The new drive is rebuilt automatically. You can also use a *hot spare* that's connected to the hard disk's host adapter along with the other hard disks but is dormant until another device in the drive array fails. At that time, the system automatically fails over to the hot spare, rebuilding with the data that was on the failed drive. For example, if one member of a mirrored (RAID-1) array fails, the hot spare can automatically come online and the remaining member begin to duplicate to it. You can then replace the failed drive at your convenience. The main difference between a hot-swappable disk and a hot spare is that a hot spare is on the bus at the time of the failure, whereas a hot-swap drive is manually replaced.

A hot spare is called *local* when it's dedicated to one RAID logical drive. It's also possible to have a global spare, which is available to several RAID systems.

Server management and maintenance

Server management and disaster recovery are really two balancing components in the same overall server health management scheme. You use server management software and faithful physical management of the server to prevent disaster. Then you use disaster recovery techniques to fix the inevitable problems that occur.

Server management software

There's a broad selection of server management software. In this area, third-party products can still play a role, but servers also usually include less comprehensive software that provides basic system monitoring functions. These utilities often integrate with the system BIOS or CMOS settings, and display or issue an alert when a problem occurs. For example, Exhibit 12-19 shows a very basic server monitoring utility that monitors temperature, fan speed, and voltages.

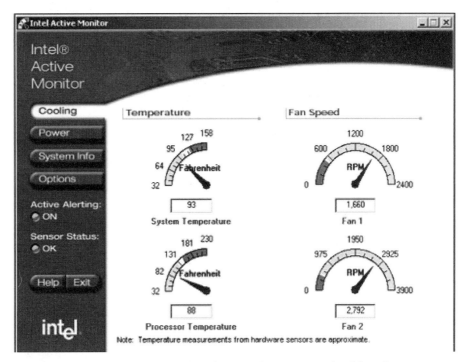

Exhibit 12-19: A monitoring utility displays basic server health indicators

Server motherboards and management software usually offer such features as the following:

- **Failure detection** — Detects temperature and voltage changes, fan speed change or failure, disk drive problems or failure, power supply failure, processor status, and ECC memory errors.

- **Software monitoring** — Detects hung applications. For serious problems, you can use management software to perform a graceful shutdown or reboot.

- **Event logging** — Stores events in NVRAM (nonvolatile RAM) so that if power is lost, the records remain.

- **Emergency Management Port** (Intel boards) — Allows you to turn on, turn off, or reset the server and view the event log, all remotely. These features require an external modem and are very useful for remotely monitoring servers over a wide geographic area from a single location.

- **Security monitoring** — Uses a jumper setting to enable chassis intrusion detection. Some systems automatically blank the video when the chassis or cabinet is open, and a password is required to resume normal video.

Most server boards include a server management utility, but if yours doesn't, download a freeware monitoring utility, such as the Motherboard Monitor, from nearly any popular download site.

Larger organizations need more than a local server management utility, so they opt for enterprise management software. A significant advantage of this type of software is that you can manage the entire network from a single seat, regardless of the physical location of any one server. For example, enterprise management software is shown being used to access an organization's California network, in Exhibit 12-20, and North American network, in Exhibit 12-21.

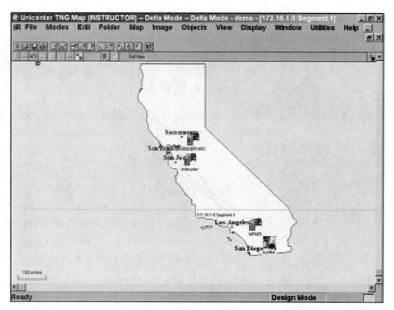

Exhibit 12-20: Unicenter TNG allows you to access your server visually

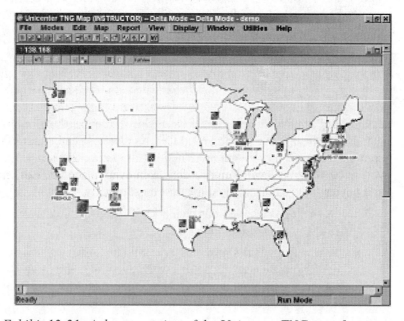

Exhibit 12-21: A demonstration of the Unicenter TNG map feature

Physical care and maintenance

Recall that two primary factors contribute to hardware device and computer peripheral failure: dirt and heat. Adequate ventilation and regular cleaning of computer equipment are necessary to maximize the lifetime of the equipment.

Hard disk drives, for example, are prone to failure in high-heat environments. Their mechanical nature causes a great deal of friction, as the platters can spin in excess of 15,000 revolutions per minute (rpm). Stack several disks inside a single computer without proper ventilation, and the combined heat of several drives can damage the electrical components, leading to drive failure. If a drive fails and data is lost before a timely backup, an expensive data recovery service bureau needs to be employed to open the disks and attempt to extract the data from the failed device.

Consider checking into a server chassis that includes *airflow guides*, which are paddles near the cooling fans that allow you to direct the airflow as desired. This is very handy when the drives or other hot components are located some distance from the actual fans or aren't in the path of the normal airflow. For example, Supermicro offers airflow guides on some of its popular models.

Related to the heat and dust that accumulate during the normal use and function of your equipment is the age of the equipment and/or the time that it has been in service. Regular monitoring of your system is necessary to note changes in I/O and other performance measures unrelated to changes in network access or activity.

If a device is performing slowly or experiencing an increase of random or unexplained errors, it may be in an early stage of failure and should be replaced as soon as possible. Some devices, such as power supplies, can't be easily monitored without server management software, but can lead to system-wide failures if performance begins to deteriorate. A power supply whose voltage is beginning to fluctuate or drop significantly can affect many components in the system, in terms of both quality and length of service. If you suspect a power supply failure, replace it immediately to avoid further damage to other system components.

Probably the most common maintenance issue for servers is planned downtime to blow out dust. The frequency of this task varies greatly depending on the environmental conditions at the site. Until you can determine the rate at which dust accumulates in the case, check accumulation weekly. Once you determine an optimum frequency for this planned downtime, be sure to schedule it regularly. When dusting, in order to avoid contaminating the environment, remember to remove the server from the server room if you're blowing out dust. Remove dust from every place you can, though the chassis fans and power supply fans accumulate dust most quickly.

Do it!

B-1: Discussing disaster precautions

Questions and answers
1 Why should spare network components be kept on site?
2 List some spare components you should have on hand.
3 Server motherboards and management software usually offer which features?

Topic C: Developing a disaster recovery plan

This topic covers the following CompTIA Server+ (2009 Edition) exam objectives.

#	Objective
5.2	Given a scenario, compare and contrast different types of replication methods • Site to site • Site types – Cold site – Warm site – Hot site – Distance requirements
5.3	Explain data retention and destruction concepts • Awareness of potential legal requirements • Awareness of potential company policy requirements
5.4	Given a scenario, carry out the following basic steps of a disaster recovery plan • Disaster recovery testing process • Follow emergency procedures (people first) • Use appropriate fire suppressants • Follow escalation procedures for emergencies • Classification of systems (prioritization during recovery)
6.5	Given a scenario, effectively troubleshoot storage problems, selecting the appropriate tools and methods • Common problems – Unsuccessful backup – Restore failure

The disaster recovery plan

Explanation

A *disaster recovery plan (DRP)* for a large enterprise can amount to hundreds of pages with thousands of contingencies. These complicated details and scenarios, if left unplanned, can go unaccomplished, leading to an unacceptable extension of system outage. When you're putting together a DRP, there are many items that need to be considered and included. Practical implementations vary from one network to another, but the most important matter is to develop a disaster recovery plan in the first place.

The DRP is critical because, in a disaster, the tendency is to hastily assemble a short list of recovery steps that come to mind. This can actually extend the time it takes to recover from disaster, because it's difficult to account for every recovery procedure. A DRP specifies what actions need to be taken, in what order, after the destructive event. Each scenario, from a single desktop computer failure to a complete outage of an entire site, should have a plan of action for those responsible.

Depending on the severity of the event, these actions can include:

- Using appropriate fire suppressants
- Evacuating the facility (people first) and notifying emergency services
- Using the appropriate notification sequence for team leaders and backups (the more severe the disaster, the higher you escalate personnel notification)
- Establishing a temporary business recovery command center
- Conducting preliminary and detailed damage assessments
- Classifying and prioritizing systems for recovery
- Getting vital records from off-site storage

In the event of a site-wide or catastrophic failure, longer-term issues must be addressed:

- Handling legal, financial, and insurance issues
- Dealing with the news media to mitigate misinformation
- Locating interim facilities to restart your business
- Recovery of PCs, LANs, and midrange systems
- Establishing voice and data communication
- Addressing human resources and accounts payable/receivable issues
- Replacing equipment, furniture, and supplies
- Notifying clients, customers, suppliers, and stockholders

Having a disaster recovery plan is a possibility only when there's actually a team to develop it. Assemble members from each major branch or function of your organization, because disasters affect all aspects of the organization, not just the IT department. The disaster recovery team needs to work well together in order to minimize downtime and loss of productivity. Preparing a disaster recovery plan can take months and, depending on the size of the organization, perhaps over a year. Your disaster recovery plan must be fully tested to ensure that it works with acceptable downtime. For an example of comprehensive disaster recovery services, see BMS Catastrophes (www.bmscat.com). For help in planning a disaster recovery solution, see Davis Logic (www.davislogic.com).

Alternate sites

In larger computing environments, it isn't practical to have enough computers in storage and configured to replace most of the equipment all at once. Larger companies, universities, and institutions can't afford to carry more than 1% or 2% of the total hardware collection in recovery-based inventory. Also, in the event of facility-, site-, or campus-wide failure, more than computers might need to be replaced. Facilities might also have to be recovered if a flood, tornado, or other natural disaster occurs.

In preparation for large-scale recovery, consider alternate sites. They can range from simple data collection and warehousing services designed to return data as needed to continue business operations, to full-scale facility duplication (*hot sites*) designed to replicate all of the hardware, software, and data infrastructure necessary to assume all business functions in the event of a primary facility failure. These hot sites are very expensive to maintain, as they have nearly a complete replica of all computers in the central facility, but if a large-scale outage will cost the company its existence, the price is worth it.

When selecting a backup site, you need to consider its location. There are no regulations governing this selection. However, a Federal Reserve Supervisory letter states that you should "maintain sufficient geographically dispersed resources to meet recovery and resumption objectives. Backup arrangements should be as far away from the primary site as necessary to avoid being subject to the same set of risks as the primary location and should not rely on the same infrastructure components used by the primary site." Specific mileage or staffing requirements for implementation are not stated.

Hot sites

Usually, a *hot site* is a facility shared with a number of subscribers from various geographic locations, each of which shares in the cost of maintaining the fully operational center. Current backups are stored at the hot site. Each subscriber usually occupies the hot site for up to six weeks after a disaster. Subscribers can also use these facilities to test their recovery plans.

Hot site recovery is appropriate for a computer operation that has more than a 24-hour outage tolerance. Data centers requiring faster service restoration must invest in redundant (spare) equipment that's immediately available to meet this need. Conversely, facilities that can afford to wait several weeks before restoring service need not engage a hot site, for they have time to order and install new equipment.

Hot sites can be set up using site-to-site mirroring. When you use a hot site, typically your organization can be up and running within hours of a disaster at your main site. However, this capacity comes at a cost. Hot sites are the most expensive type of backup site to maintain. Hot sites generally make financial sense for financial institutions, government agencies, and e-commerce providers.

Cold sites

Many service bureaus augment their hot site services with a cold site feature. This is a facility designed to receive computer equipment. The facility has in place all power lines, water lines, air conditioning, raised floors, and other items requiring a long lead time to acquire, install, and prepare for housing a computer center.

Should a company be unable to return to its home computing center within a tolerable timeframe, it would make arrangements to occupy this cold site. Computers, peripheral equipment, and related services would be ordered (purchased, leased, or rented) and prepared to assume the company's processing workload. Cold sites are used until the home site is repaired or rebuilt.

A cold site is simply available space. It doesn't include computer systems or backups. It is the least expensive backup site to maintain, but comes at a cost. The time it takes to obtain equipment, set it up, retrieve backups, and restore data so that your organization is functional again is considerably longer than that needed for a hot site.

Warm sites

A warm site is a compromise between a hot site and a cold site. A warm site typically has computer systems set up, although on a smaller scale than the original site. Warm sites have backups on hand, but they might not be complete or current, perhaps several days to a week old.

Site management

Business processes can be quite complex as you deploy remote sites, either hot, warm, or cold. Bad planning in these areas leads to confusion and delay. Several important steps are necessary to determine the activities and timeframes required for moving services and equipment between the central (or original) site and hot or cold sites, and then to the repaired or newly constructed site.

- Determine the extent of the damage and whether additional equipment, services, or supplies are needed.

- Take care to cover telecommunications issues adequately. Most medium-sized and large organizations usually have a number of telecommunications services, such as leased lines and fiber optics, connecting campuses and other facilities. This means that if a disaster occurs, such connections to other facilities may have to be abandoned, re-routed, or installed in the hot and/or cold sites in order to establish connectivity to other operational facilities. Detailed records of current operations must be carefully reviewed to be certain that your disaster recovery plan covers every conceivable technical aspect of recovering all critical services and data in the least amount of time.

- Obtain approval for expenditure of funds to bring in any needed equipment and supplies. One corporation set up an agreement with its bank so that if a catastrophic disaster occurred, the bank would supply a mobile branch staffed with at least two tellers who would dispense the finances and keep all necessary records.

- Notify local vendor marketing and/or service representatives if there's a need for immediate delivery of components to bring the computer systems to an operational level, even in a degraded mode.

If an alternate site is necessary, the following additional major tasks must be undertaken:

- Obtain governmental permissions and assistance, as necessary. For example, you are likely to need building permits to construct even a temporary site.

- Coordinate the moving of equipment and support personnel into the alternate site. Be sure to hire the services of a dependable security firm to protect company assets, because looting is to be expected.

- Bring the tape backups from off-site storage to the alternate site.

- As soon as the hardware is up to specifications to run the operating system, load software and run necessary tests. One of the best solutions is to record recent images of server hard drives for a fast restore.

- Prepare backup materials and return these to the off-site storage area.

- Coordinate client activities to ensure that the most critical jobs are being supported as needed.

- Be sensitive to the employees involved in the relocation. For example, in a natural disaster, employees might be suffering from the death of friends or loved ones, or they might be without a home.

- As production begins, ensure that periodic backup procedures are being followed and materials are being placed in off-site storage periodically.

- Keep administration and clients informed of the status, progress, and problems.

Troubleshooting backup and restore

As part of your disaster recovery plan, you should be verifying that your backups were completed successfully and periodically testing those backups by completing a restore of the latest backup in a test environment. If you run into any problems, you should check the following:

- The most common cause of backup or restore problems is user error. Verify that the backup application software has been configured correctly.
- Verify that the program is running with appropriate permissions. If the backup or restore is being run from a remote computer, verify permissions on both the computer where the program is being run and the computer where the backup will be stored or where the restore file resides.
- Apply any updates or patches that the manufacturer of the backup application has supplied for that application.
- Check device drivers for the backup device in the operating system (use Device Manager in Windows). Update drivers if necessary.
- Verify that the backup device is enabled in the BIOS.
- If the backup device is a SCSI device, check its SCSI ID and the ID of all other devices in the chain to verify that there isn't a conflict.
- Physically check the backup device hardware, including the device itself, its connection to the computer, and the controller. Verify compatibility between device and controller.

Do it!

C-1:   Discussing disaster recovery plans

Questions and answers
1 What's a hot site?
2 What's a cold site?
3 For recovery from a primary facility failure with less than 24-hour downtime tolerance, what alternate site strategy is most appropriate?

Unit summary: Preparing for disaster

Topic A
In this topic, you learned about factors to consider when purchasing a backup unit. You learned that, for a large-scale enterprise, you should probably investigate an **automated backup technology**, such as tape libraries that use autoloaders. You learned about the various tape media standards and other types of backup media (such as optical drives and USB flash drives). You also learned about the various **types of backups** (full, incremental, differential, daily, and copy) and about various backup strategies, such as the GFS and Tower of Hanoi strategies.

Topic B
In this topic, you learned that to provide load balancing and redundancy, a group of computers, or a **cluster**, can cooperate in providing services. A cluster improves the availability of client-server applications by increasing the availability of server resources. You also learned that, for hardware failure recovery, it's helpful to have a number of spare parts available, including spare drives for RAID systems. You then learned that some **system monitoring software** can detect problems, such as failing hard drives, fans, and power supplies, and high temperatures.

Topic C
In this topic, you learned that it's essential to assemble a disaster recovery team and develop a **disaster recovery plan**. You learned about the typical components of such a plan, and about the options for alternate work sites: hot sites, cold sites, and warm sites. You also learned about the importance of careful planning for handling the logistics involved in keeping the business running after a disaster.

Review questions

1 What is the minimum number of tapes required in a GFS tape backup strategy?

   A 12

   B 24

   C 48

   D 60

2 You want to back up all of the files on a hard disk in your computer. You have just replaced your old, single-medium tape device with a new, 12-tape automated tape library system. When you attempt to initiate the backup, the process fails. What should you do?

   A Install the driver for the new device.

   B Restore the catalog from the old device; then retry the backup.

   C Make sure that you use only new, blank tapes for the backup.

   D Reboot the computer.

3 Your company's Internet servers are becoming overloaded due to an increase in commerce traffic to your Web site. You decide to implement a clustering solution. What kind of clustering model should you implement to provide the desired load balancing?

   A Active

   B Passive

   C Disruptive

   D Peanut

4 Which of the following are necessary for disaster recovery?

 A Hot site

 B Hot swap implementation

 C Data backup

 D Fire drills

5 You want to have a separate location prepared to which you can transfer all data management services immediately upon the failure of your network operations center. What type of site do you set up?

 A Alternate site

 B Backup storage site

 C Hot site

 D Cold site

6 Why should one or more backups be stored off-site?

 A For security reasons

 B Because backup data is not usually needed immediately

 C So it is available to a remote site

 D So that primary site disasters will not affect the data

7 Which of the following are not part of a disaster recovery plan?

 A Handling legal, financial, and insurance issues

 B Performing a tape backup immediately after disaster strikes

 C Locating interim facilities in which to restart or continue your business

 D Recovery of PCs, LANs, and midrange systems

8 Which backup strategy provides the fastest backup time?

 A Grandfather-Father-Son

 B Six-cartridge

 C Tower of Hanoi

 D Incremental backup

9 Which of the following methods backs up data and clears the archive bit?

 A Normal backup

 B Differential backup

 C Copy backup

 D Daily backup

10 Which backup strategy provides the least expensive media allocation?

 A Grandfather-Father-Son

 B Tower of Hanoi

 C Normal daily backup

 D Mirroring

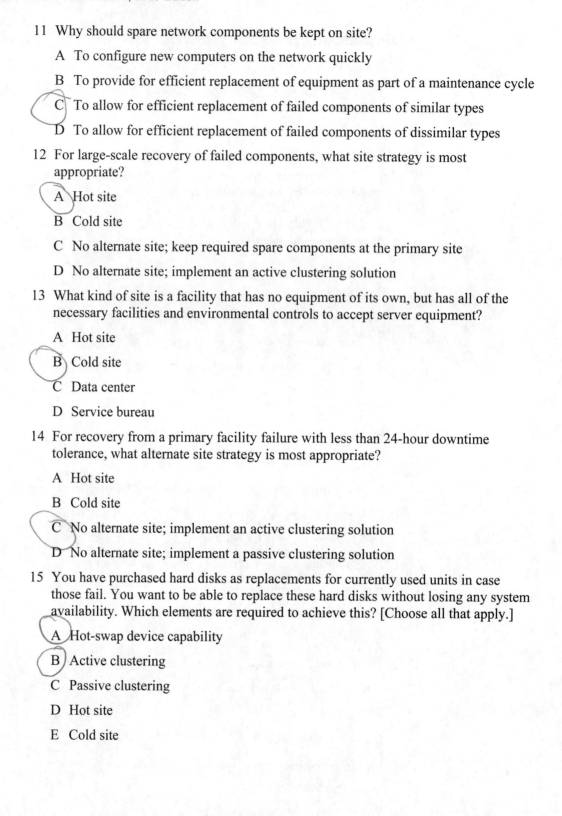

11 Why should spare network components be kept on site?

    A To configure new computers on the network quickly

    B To provide for efficient replacement of equipment as part of a maintenance cycle

    C To allow for efficient replacement of failed components of similar types

    D To allow for efficient replacement of failed components of dissimilar types

12 For large-scale recovery of failed components, what site strategy is most appropriate?

    A Hot site

    B Cold site

    C No alternate site; keep required spare components at the primary site

    D No alternate site; implement an active clustering solution

13 What kind of site is a facility that has no equipment of its own, but has all of the necessary facilities and environmental controls to accept server equipment?

    A Hot site

    B Cold site

    C Data center

    D Service bureau

14 For recovery from a primary facility failure with less than 24-hour downtime tolerance, what alternate site strategy is most appropriate?

    A Hot site

    B Cold site

    C No alternate site; implement an active clustering solution

    D No alternate site; implement a passive clustering solution

15 You have purchased hard disks as replacements for currently used units in case those fail. You want to be able to replace these hard disks without losing any system availability. Which elements are required to achieve this? [Choose all that apply.]

    A Hot-swap device capability

    B Active clustering

    C Passive clustering

    D Hot site

    E Cold site

Independent practice activity

In this activity, you'll learn more about disaster recovery.

1 In your Web browser, go to **www.davislogic.com**. Davis Logic specializes in contingency planning and disaster recovery.

2 On the left side of the Davis Logic Web page, click the **Disaster Recovery** link. Notice several publications that would be excellent research guides in planning for disaster recovery.

3 On the Disaster Recovery page, scroll down and look for a bulleted list of possible disaster events. In this text, we've specified only a few types of disasters, such as natural ones, that could make your site unavailable. Write down some other types of events that could constitute a disaster.

4 Close the browser.

Appendix A
Certification exam objectives map

This appendix covers these additional topics:

A CompTIA Server+ Certification (2009 Edition) exam objectives with references to corresponding coverage in this course manual.

Topic A: **Comprehensive exam objectives**

Explanation   This section lists all CompTIA Server+ Certification (2009 Edition) exam objectives and indicates where each objective is covered in conceptual explanations, activities, or both.

1.0 System Hardware

Objective	Conceptual information	Supporting activities
1.1 — Differentiate between system board types, features, components, and their purposes		
• Dip switches / jumpers	Unit 2, Topic C Unit 3, Topic A	C-1 A-2
• Processor (single and multi)	Unit 2, Topic C	C-1
• Bus types and bus speeds	Unit 6, Topic A Unit 6, Topic B Unit 6, Topic C	A-1–A-6 B-1 C-1
• Onboard components	Unit 2, Topic C	C-1
– NICs	Unit 2, Topic C	C-1
– Video	Unit 2, Topic C	C-1
– Audio	Unit 2, Topic C	C-1
– USB	Unit 2, Topic C	C-1
– HID	Unit 2, Topic C	C-1
– Serial	Unit 2, Topic C	C-1
– Parallel	Unit 2, Topic C	C-1
• Expansion slots	Unit 6, Topic A Unit 6, Topic C	A-1, A-6
– PCI	Unit 6, Topic A Unit 6, Topic C	A-1, A-6 C-1
– PCIe	Unit 6, Topic A Unit 6, Topic C	A-1, A-6 C-1
– PCIx	Unit 6, Topic A	A-1, A-6
– AGP	Unit 6, Topic C	C-1
– ISA	Unit 6, Topic A	A-1, A-6
• BIOS	Unit 3, Topic A Unit 3, Topic B	A-1, A-2 B-1
• Riser card / backplane	Unit 2, Topic C Unit 4, Topic A Unit 4, Topic B	C-1 IPA IPA

Objective	Conceptual information	Supporting activities
• Storage connectors	Unit 6, Topic B Unit 7, Topic A	B-1 A-1
– SCSI	Unit 6, Topic B Unit 7, Topic A	B-1 A-1
– SATA	Unit 6, Topic B Unit 7, Topic A	B-1 A-1
– IDE	Unit 6, Topic B Unit 7, Topic A	B-1 A-1
– Floppy	Unit 6, Topic B Unit 7, Topic A	B-1

1.2 — Deploy different chassis types and the appropriate components

Objective	Conceptual information	Supporting activities
• Cooling	Unit 1, Topic C	C-1
– Fans	Unit 1, Topic C	C-1, C-2
– Water cooled	Unit 1, Topic C	C-1, C-2
– Passive	Unit 1, Topic C	C-1
– Active	Unit 1, Topic C	C-1
– Shroud	Unit 1, Topic C	C-1
– Ducts	Unit 1, Topic C	C-1
– Redundant cooling	Unit 1, Topic C	C-1, C-2
– Hot swappable	Unit 1, Topic C	C-1, C-2
– Ventilation	Unit 1, Topic C	C-1, C-2
• Form factor	Unit 1, Topic A	A-1
– Space utilization (U size, height, width, depth)	Unit 1, Topic A	A-1
• Power	Unit 1, Topic B Unit 7, Topic A	B-1 A-1
– Connectors	Unit 1, Topic B Unit 7, Topic A	B-1 A-1
– Voltages	Unit 1, Topic B	B-1
– Phase	Unit 1, Topic B	B-1
• Redundant power	Unit 1, Topic A	A-2
• Shutoff switches – chassis intrusion	Unit 1, Topic A	A-2
• Power buttons	Unit 1, Topic A	A-2
• Reset buttons	Unit 1, Topic A	A-2
• Diagnostic LEDs	Unit 1, Topic A	A-2
• Expansion bays	Unit 1, Topic A Unit 7, Topic A	A-2 A-1

Objective	Conceptual information	Supporting activities
1.3 — Differentiate between memory features/types, and given a scenario, select an appropriate processor		
• Memory pairing	Unit 4, Topic A	A-1
• ECC vs. non ECC	Unit 4, Topic A Unit 4, Topic B	A-1 B-1
• Registered vs. non-registered	Unit 4, Topic A	A-1
• RAID and hot spares	Unit 7, Topic B	B-1
• Types	Unit 4, Topic A	A-1
– DDR	Unit 4, Topic A Unit 4, Topic B	A-1 B-1
– Fully buffered	Unit 4, Topic A	A-1
– DIMM	Unit 4, Topic A Unit 4, Topic B	A-1 B-1
– DDR2	Unit 4, Topic A Unit 4, Topic B	A-1 B-1
– SDRAM	Unit 4, Topic A	A-1
– DDR3	Unit 4, Topic A Unit 4, Topic B	A-1 B-1
• Memory compatibility	Unit 4, Topic A	A-1
– Speed	Unit 4, Topic A	A-1
– Size	Unit 4, Topic A Unit 4, Topic B	A-1 B-1
– Pins	Unit 4, Topic A Unit 4, Topic B	A-1 B-1
– CAS latency	Unit 4, Topic A	A-1
– Timing	Unit 4, Topic A	A-1
– Vendor specific memory	Unit 4, Topic A Unit 4, Topic B	A-1 B-1
• On board vs. riser card	Unit 4, Topic A Unit 4, Topic B	A-1 B-1
1.4 — Explain the importance of a Hardware Compatibility List (HCL)		
• Vendor standards for hardware	Unit 6, Topic D	D-2
• Memory and processor compatibility	Unit 9, Topic D	D-1
• Expansion cards compatibility	Unit 6, Topic D	D-2
• Virtualization requirements	Unit 8, Topic B	B-1

Objective	Conceptual information	Supporting activities
1.5 — Differentiate between processor features/types, and given a scenario, select an appropriate processor		
• Multicore	Unit 2, Topic A	A-1
• Multiprocessor	Unit 2, Topic A	A-1
• Cache levels	Unit 2, Topic A	A-1
• Stepping	Unit 2, Topic A	A-1
• Speed	Unit 2, Topic A	A-1
• VRMs	Unit 1, Topic B Unit 2, Topic C	B-1 C-1
• Execute disable (XD) or not execute (NX)	Unit 2, Topic A	A-1
• Hyperthreading	Unit 2, Topic A	A-1
• VT or AMD-V	Unit 2, Topic A	A-1
• AMD vs. Intel (non-compatible CPUs)	Unit 2, Topic A	A-1
• Processor architecture (RISC, CISC)	Unit 2, Topic A	A-1
• Vendor slot types	Unit 2, Topic B	B-1
• 64 bit vs. 32 bit	Unit 2, Topic A	A-1
• Heat dissipation (heat sinks, fans, liquid cooling)	Unit 1, Topic C	C-1
1.6 — Given a scenario, install appropriate expansion cards into a server while taking fault tolerance into consideration		
• Manufacturer specific	Unit 6, Topic B Unit 6, Topic C Unit 6	B-2 C-3 IPA
– Fax cards	Unit 6, Topic B Unit 6, Topic C	B-2 C-3, IPA
– PBX cards	Unit 6, Topic B Unit 6, Topic C	B-2 C-3, IPA
– Camera cards	Unit 6, Topic B Unit 6, Topic C	B-2 C-3, IPA
– VoIP	Unit 6, Topic B Unit 6, Topic C	B-2 C-3, IPA
• HBAs	Unit 6, Topic B	B-1, B-2, IPA
• NICs	Unit 6, Topic B	B-2, IPA
• Video	Unit 6, Topic B Unit 6, Topic C	B-2 C-1, IPA
• Audio	Unit 6, Topic B Unit 6, Topic C	B-2 C-2, IPA

Objective	Conceptual information	Supporting activities
• Storage controller (SCSI, SATA, RAID)	Unit 6, Topic B Unit 6	B-1, B-2 IPA
— SCSI low voltage / high voltage (LVD/HVD)	Unit 6, Topic B Unit 6	B-1, B-2 IPA
— SCSI IDs	Unit 6, Topic B Unit 6	B-1, B-2 IPA
— Cables and connectors	Unit 6, Topic B Unit 6	B-1, B-2 IPA
— Active vs. passive termination	Unit 6, Topic B Unit 6	B-1, B-2 IPA
• Port expansion cards	Unit 6, Topic B Unit 6, Topic C Unit 6	B-2 C-2 IPA
— USB	Unit 6, Topic B Unit 6, Topic C Unit 6	B-2 C-2 IPA
— FireWire	Unit 6, Topic B Unit 6, Topic C Unit 6	B-2 C-2 IPA
— Serial	Unit 6, Topic B Unit 6, Topic C Unit 6	B-2 C-2 IPA
— Parallel	Unit 6, Topic B Unit 6, Topic C Unit 6	B-2 C-2 IPA
1.7 — Install, update, and configure appropriate firmware		
• Driver / hardware compatibility	Unit 3, Topic A Unit 3, Topic B	A-2 B-2
• Implications of a failed firmware upgrade (redundant BIOS)	Unit 3, Topic A	A-2
• Follow manufacturer instructions and documentation	Unit 3, Topic A	A-1, A-2, A-3

2.0 Software

Objective	Conceptual information	Supporting activities
2.1 — Install, deploy, configure, and update the NOS (Windows / *nix)		
• Installation methods (optical media, USB, network share, PXE)	Unit 8, Topic C Unit 8, Topic D	C-2 D-1
• Imaging – system cloning and deployment (Ghost, RIS/WDS, Altiris, virtualization templates)	Unit 8, Topic B Unit 8, Topic D	B-1 D-1
• Bootloader	Unit 8, Topic C	C-2
• File systems		
– FAT	Unit 7, Topic A	A-2
	Unit 8, Topic C Unit 8, Topic D	 D-1
– FAT32	Unit 7, Topic A	A-2
	Unit 8, Topic C Unit 8, Topic D	 D-1
– NTFS	Unit 7, Topic A	A-2
	Unit 8, Topic C Unit 8, Topic D	 D-1
– VMFS	Unit 8, Topic C	
– ZFS	Unit 8, Topic C	
– EXT3	Unit 7, Topic A	
	Unit 8, Topic C	
• Driver installation		
– Driver acquisition	Unit 8, Topic D	D-2
– Installation methods	Unit 8, Topic D	D-2
– Require media	Unit 8, Topic D	D-2
• Configure the NOS		
– Initial network	Unit 8, Topic C	
	Unit 8, Topic D	D-2
– User	Unit 8, Topic C	C-2
	Unit 8, Topic D	D-1
– Device	Unit 8, Topic C	
	Unit 8, Topic D	D-2
– Roles	Unit 8, Topic A Unit 8, Topic D	A-3 D-5
– OS environmental settings	Unit 8, Topic D	D-1–D-5, D-7
– Applications and tools	Unit 8, Topic D	D-5
• Patch management	Unit 8, Topic D	D-3, D-4, IPA

Objective	Conceptual information	Supporting activities
2.2 — Explain NOS security software and its features		
• Software firewall		
– Port blocking	Unit 8, Topic D	D-5
– Application exception	Unit 8, Topic D	D-5
– ACL	Unit 8, Topic D	D-5
• Malware protection software		
– Antivirus	Unit 8, Topic D	D-6
– Antispyware	Unit 8, Topic D	D-6
• Basics of file level permissions vs. share permissions	Unit 10, Topic A	A-8
2.3 — Given a scenario, implement and administer NOS management features based on procedures and guidelines		
• User management		
– Add and remove users	Unit 10, Topic A	A-3, A-4, A-5
– Setting permissions	Unit 10, Topic A	A-7
– Group memberships	Unit 10, Topic A	A-6
– Policies	Unit 10, Topic A	A-8
– Logon scripts	Unit 10, Topic A	A-9
• Resource management		
– ACLs	Unit 10, Topic A	A-7
– Quotas	Unit 10, Topic B	B-3
– Shadow volumes	Unit 10, Topic B	B-2
– Disk management	Unit 10, Topic B	B-1
– Performance monitoring	Unit 10, Topic C	C-1
– Baselining	Unit 10, Topic C	C-1
• Monitoring (tools and agents)		
– SNMP (MIBs)	Unit 10, Topic C	C-2
– WBEM (WMI)	Unit 10, Topic C	C-3, C-4
2.4 — Explain different server roles, their purposes, and how they interact		
• File and print server	Unit 8, Topic A	A-3
• Database server	Unit 8, Topic A	A-3
• Web server	Unit 8, Topic A	A-3
• Messaging server	Unit 8, Topic A	A-3

Objective	Conceptual information	Supporting activities
• DHCP server	Unit 8, Topic A	A-3
• Directory services server	Unit 8, Topic A	A-3
• DNS server	Unit 8, Topic A	A-3
• Application server	Unit 8, Topic A	A-3
– Update server and proxy server	Unit 8, Topic A	A-3
– Filtering server	Unit 8, Topic A	A-3
– Monitoring server	Unit 8, Topic A	A-3
– Dedicated	Unit 8, Topic A	A-3
– Distributed	Unit 8, Topic A	A-3
– Peer to peer	Unit 8, Topic A	A-3
• Remote access server	Unit 8, Topic A	A-3
• Virtualized services	Unit 8, Topic A	A-3
• NTP server	Unit 8, Topic A	A-3
• Explain the different between a workstation, desktop and a server	Unit 8, Topic A	A-2
• Server shutdown and startup sequence (one server vs. multiple servers vs. attached components)	Unit 8, Topic A	A-3

2.5 — Summarize server virtualization concepts, features, and considerations

Objective	Conceptual information	Supporting activities
• Resource utilization	Unit 8, Topic B	B-1, B-2
• Configuration	Unit 8, Topic B	B-1, B-2, B-4
• Interconnectivity	Unit 8, Topic B	B-1
• Management server	Unit 8, Topic B	B-1
• Reasons for virtualization	Unit 8, Topic B	B-1
– Cost benefits	Unit 8, Topic B	B-1
– Redundancy	Unit 8, Topic B	B-1
– Green initiative	Unit 8, Topic B	B-1
– Disaster recovery	Unit 8, Topic B	B-4
– Testing environment	Unit 8, Topic B	B-1
– Ease of deployment	Unit 8, Topic B	B-1

Objective	Conceptual information	Supporting activities
2.6 — Describe common elements of networking essentials		
• TCP/IP	Unit 9, Topic A	A-4
– Subnetting	Unit 9, Topic A	A-5
– DNS	Unit 9, Topic A	A-5
– DHCP	Unit 9, Topic A	A-5
– Classes	Unit 9, Topic A	A-5
– Gateways	Unit 9, Topic A	A-5
– Static vs. dynamic	Unit 9, Topic A	A-5
– IP stack	Unit 9, Topic A	A-4
– Ports	Unit 9, Topic A	A-5
• Ethernet	Unit 9, Topic A	A-1, A-2, A-3
– Types	Unit 9, Topic A	A-1, A-2
– Speeds	Unit 9, Topic A	A-3
– Cables	Unit 9, Topic A	A-1, A-2
• VPN	Unit 9, Topic A	A-6
• VLAN	Unit 9, Topic A	A-6
• DMZ	Unit 9, Topic A	A-6

3.0 Storage

Objective	Conceptual information	Supporting activities
3.1 — Describe RAID technologies and its features and benefits		
• Hot spare	Unit 7, Topic B	B-1
• Software vs. hardware	Unit 7, Topic B	B-1
• Cache read/write levels (data loss potential)	Unit 7, Topic B	B-1
• Performance benefits and tradeoffs	Unit 7, Topic B	B-1
3.2 — Given a scenario, select the appropriate RAID level		
• 0, 1, 3, 5, 6, 10, 50	Unit 7, Topic B	B-1
• Performance benefits and tradeoffs	Unit 7, Topic B	B-1

Objective	Conceptual information	Supporting activities
3.3 — Install and configure different internal storage technologies		
• Hot swappable vs. non-hot swappable	Unit 7, Topic A	A-3
• SCSI, Ultra SCSI, Ultra320 (termination), LUNs	Unit 7, Topic A	A-1, A-2
• SAS, SATA	Unit 7, Topic A	A-1, A-2
• Tape	Unit 7, Topic A	A-1, A-2
• Optical	Unit 7, Topic A	A-3
– DVD	Unit 7, Topic A	A-3
– DVD-R	Unit 7, Topic A	A-3
– CD-ROM	Unit 7, Topic A	A-3
– CD-R	Unit 7, Topic A	A-3
– CD-RW	Unit 7, Topic A	A-3
– Blu-Ray	Unit 7, Topic A	A-3
• Flash	Unit 7, Topic A	A-3
• Floppy (USB)	Unit 7, Topic A	A-3
• Controller (firmware levels)	Unit 7, Topic A	A-1
• Hard drive (firmware, JBOD)	Unit 7, Topic A	A-1
3.4 — Summarize the purpose of external storage technologies		
• Network attached storage	Unit 7, Topic A	A-4
• Storage area network	Unit 7, Topic A	A-4
• Tape library	Unit 7, Topic A	A-4
• WORM	Unit 7, Topic A	A-4
• Optical jukebox	Unit 7, Topic A	A-4
• Transport media	Unit 7, Topic A	A-4
– iSCSI	Unit 7, Topic A	A-4
– SATA	Unit 7, Topic A	A-4
– SAS	Unit 7, Topic A	A-4
– SCSI	Unit 7, Topic A	A-4
– Fiber Channel	Unit 7, Topic A	A-4

4.0 IT Environment

Objective	Conceptual information	Supporting activities
4.1 — Write, utilize, and maintain documentation, diagrams, and procedures		
• Follow pre-installation plan when building or upgrading servers	Unit 11, Topic A	A-1
• Labeling	Unit 11, Topic A	A-1
• Diagram server racks and environment topologies	Unit 11, Topic A	A-1
• Hardware and software upgrade, installation, configuration, server roles, and repair logs	Unit 11, Topic A Unit 11, Topic B	A-1 B-1
• Document server baseline (before and after service)	Unit 11, Topic A Unit 11, Topic B	A-1 B-1
• Original hardware configuration, service tags, asset management, and warranty	Unit 11, Topic A	A-1
• Vendor-specific documentation	Unit 11, Topic A	A-1
– Reference proper manuals	Unit 11, Topic A	A-1
– Websites	Unit 11, Topic A	A-1
– Support channels (list of vendors)	Unit 11, Topic A	A-1
4.2 — Given a scenario, explain the purpose of the following industry best practices		
• Follow vendor-specific server best practices	Unit 11, Topic A	A-1
– Documentation	Unit 11, Topic A	A-1
– Tools	Unit 11, Topic A	A-2
– Websites	Unit 11, Topic A	A-1
• Explore ramifications before implementing change – determine organizational impact	Unit 11, Topic B	B-1
• Communicate with stakeholders before taking action and upon completion of action	Unit 11, Topic B	B-1
• Comply with all local laws/regulations, and industry and corporate regulations	Unit 11, Topic A Unit 11, Topic B	A-1 B-1
• Purpose of Service Level Agreements (SLAs)	Unit 11, Topic A	A-1
• Follow change control procedures	Unit 11, Topic B	B-1
• Equipment disposal	Unit 11, Topic B	B-2

Objective	Conceptual information	Supporting activities
4.3 — Determine an appropriate physical environment for the server location		
• Check for adequate and dedicated power, proper amperage and voltage	Unit 11, Topic B	B-1
– UPS systems (check load, document service, periodic testing)	Unit 11, Topic B	B-1
– UPS specifications (run time, max load, bypass procedures, server communication and shutdown, proper monitoring)	Unit 11, Topic B	B-1
• Server cooling considerations – HVAC	Unit 11, Topic B	B-1
– Adequate cooling in room	Unit 11, Topic B	B-1
– Adequate cooling in server rack	Unit 11, Topic B	B-1
– Temperature and humidity monitors	Unit 11, Topic B	B-1
4.4 — Implement and configure different methods of server access		
• KVM (local and IP based)	Unit 8, Topic D	D-7
• Direct connect	Unit 8, Topic C	C-3
	Unit 8, Topic D	D-2– D-5
• Remote management		
– Remote control	Unit 8, Topic D	D-7
– Administration	Unit 8, Topic D	D-7
– Software deployment	Unit 8, Topic D	
– Dedicated management port	Unit 8, Topic D	
4.5 — Given a scenario, classify physical security measures for a server location		
• Physical server security	Unit 11, Topic C	C-1
– Locked doors	Unit 11, Topic C	C-1, IPA
– Rack doors	Unit 11, Topic C	C-1
– CCTV	Unit 11, Topic C	C-2, IPA
– Mantraps	Unit 11, Topic C	C-2
– Security personnel	Unit 11, Topic C	C-2, IPA
• Access control devices (RFID, keypads, pinpads)	Unit 11, Topic C	C-1, C-3
• Biometric devices (fingerprint scanner, retina scanner)	Unit 11, Topic C	C-3

Objective	Conceptual information	Supporting activities
4.5 — Given a scenario, classify physical security measures for a server location (continued)		
• Security procedures	Unit 11, Topic C	C-1
– Limited access	Unit 11, Topic C	C-1
– Access logs	Unit 11, Topic C	C-1, C-2
– Limited hours	Unit 11, Topic C	C-1
• Defense in-depth – multiple layers of defense	Unit 11, Topic C	C-1, IPA
• Reasons for physical security	Unit 11, Topic C	C-1
– Theft	Unit 11, Topic C	C-1
– Data loss	Unit 11, Topic C	C-1
– Hacking	Unit 11, Topic C	C-1
• Secure documentation related to servers	Unit 11, Topic A Unit 11, Topic C	A-1 C-1
– Passwords	Unit 11, Topic A Unit 11, Topic C	A-1 C-1
– System configurations	Unit 11, Topic A Unit 11, Topic C	A-1 C-1
– Logs	Unit 11, Topic A Unit 11, Topic C	A-1 C-2

5.0 Disaster Recovery

Objective	Conceptual information	Supporting activities
5.1 — Compare and contrast backup and restoration methodologies, media types, and concepts		
• Methodologies (full, incremental, differential)	Unit 12, Topic A	A-3
– Snapshot	Unit 12, Topic A	A-3
– Copy	Unit 12, Topic A	A-3
– Bare metal	Unit 12, Topic A	A-3
– Open file	Unit 12, Topic A	A-3
– Databases	Unit 12, Topic A	A-3
– Data vs. OS restore	Unit 12, Topic A	A-3
– Rotation and retention (grandfather, father, and son; leaning tower)	Unit 12, Topic A	A-4

Objective	Conceptual information	Supporting activities
• Media types	Unit 12, Topic A	A-1
– Tape	Unit 12, Topic A	A-1
– Disk	Unit 12, Topic A	A-1
– Worm	Unit 12, Topic A	A-1
– Optical	Unit 12, Topic A	A-1
– Flash	Unit 12, Topic A	A-1
• Backup security and off-site storage	Unit 12, Topic A	A-2, A-4
• Importance of testing the backup and restoration process	Unit 12, Topic A	

5.2 — Given a scenario, compare and contrast the different types of replication methods		
• Disk to disk	Unit 12, Topic A	A-1
• Server to server	Unit 12, Topic B	B-1
– Clustering	Unit 12, Topic B	B-1
– Active/active	Unit 12, Topic B	B-1
– Active/passive	Unit 12, Topic B	B-1
• Site to site	Unit 12, Topic C	C-1
• Site types	Unit 12, Topic C	C-1
– Cold site	Unit 12, Topic C	C-1
– Hot site	Unit 12, Topic C	C-1
– Warm site	Unit 12, Topic C	C-1
– Distance requirements	Unit 12, Topic C	C-1

5.3 — Explain data retention and destruction concepts		
• Awareness of potential legal requirements	Unit 12, Topic C	C-1
• Awareness of potential company policy requirements	Unit 12, Topic C	C-1
• Differentiate between archiving and backup	Unit 12, Topic A	

5.4 — Given a scenario, carry out the following basic steps of a disaster recovery plan		
• Disaster recovery testing process	Unit 12, Topic C	C-1
• Follow emergency procedures (people first)	Unit 12, Topic C	C-1
• Use appropriate fire suppressants	Unit 12, Topic C	C-1
• Follow escalation procedures for emergencies	Unit 12, Topic C	C-1
• Classification of systems (prioritization during recovery)	Unit 12, Topic C	C-1

6.0 Troubleshooting

Objective	Conceptual information	Supporting activities
6.1 — Explain troubleshooting theory and methodologies		
• Identify the problem and determine the scope	Unit 5, Topic A	A-1
– Question users/stakeholders and identify changes to the server/environment	Unit 5, Topic A	A-1
– Collect additional documentation/logs	Unit 5, Topic A	A-1, A-3, A-4, A-5
– If possible, replicate the problem as appropriate	Unit 5, Topic A	A-1
– If possible, perform backups before making changes	Unit 5, Topic A	A-1
• Establish a theory of probable cause (question the obvious)	Unit 5, Topic A	A-1–A-5
– Determine whether there is a common element of symptom causing multiple problems	Unit 5, Topic A	A-1–A-5
• Test the theory to determine the cause	Unit 5, Topic A	A-1
– Once theory is confirmed, determine next steps to resolve problem	Unit 5, Topic A	A-1, A-4, A-5
– If theory is not confirmed, establish new theory or escalate	Unit 5, Topic A	A-1
• Establish a plan of action to resolve the problem and notify impacted users	Unit 5, Topic A	A-1, A-2
• Implement the solution or escalate as appropriate	Unit 5, Topic A	A-1
– Make one change at a time and test/confirm that the change has resolved the problem	Unit 5, Topic A	A-1
– If the problem is not resolved, reverse the change if appropriate and implement a new change	Unit 5, Topic A	A-1
• Verify full system functionality and, if applicable, preventative measures	Unit 5, Topic A	A-1
• Root cause analysis	Unit 5, Topic A	A-1, A-2
• Document findings, actions, and outcomes throughout the process	Unit 5, Topic A	A-1

Objective	Conceptual information	Supporting activities
6.2 — Given a scenario, effectively troubleshoot hardware problems, selecting the appropriate tools and methods		
• Common problems		
– Failed POST	Unit 3, Topic B Unit 5, Topic C	B-1 C-1, C-2, C-3
– Overheating	Unit 5, Topic C	C-2
– Memory failure	Unit 3, Topic B Unit 5, Topic C	B-1 C-2, C-5, C-7
– Onboard component failure	Unit 3, Topic B Unit 5, Topic C Unit 6, Topic D	B-1 C-2 D-1, D-2, D-3
– Processor failure	Unit 3, Topic B Unit 5, Topic C	B-1 C-2
– Incorrect boot sequence	Unit 3, Topic B Unit 5, Topic C	B-2 C-2, C-3
– Expansion card failure	Unit 6, Topic D	D-1, D-2, D-3
– Operating system not found	Unit 5, Topic C	C-3
– Drive failure	Unit 6, Topic D	D-1, D-2, D-3
– Power supply failure	Unit 5, Topic C	C-1
– I/O failure	Unit 5, Topic C Unit 7, Topic C	C-3 C-5
• Causes of common problems		
– Third-party components or incompatible components	Unit 5, Topic C	C-3
– Incompatible or incorrect BIOS	Unit 3, Topic B Unit 5, Topic C	B-1 C-3
– Cooling failure	Unit 5, Topic C	C-2
– Mismatched components	Unit 5, Topic C	C-3
– Backplane failure	Unit 5, Topic C	C-2, C-3
• Environmental issues	Unit 12, Topic B	B-1
– Dust	Unit 12, Topic B	B-1
– Humidity	Unit 12, Topic B	B-1
– Temperature	Unit 12, Topic B	B-1
– Power surge / failure	Unit 12, Topic B	B-1
• Hardware tools	Unit 5, Topic B	B-1
– Power supply tester (multimeter)	Unit 5, Topic B	B-1
– System board tester	Unit 5, Topic B	B-1
– Compressed air	Unit 5, Topic B	B-1
– ESD equipment	Unit 5, Topic B	B-1

Objective	Conceptual information	Supporting activities
6.3 — Given a scenario, effectively troubleshoot software problems, selecting the appropriate tools and methods		
• Common problems		
– User unable to logon	Unit 10, Topic A	A-2, A-3
– User can't access resources	Unit 7, Topic C	C-5
	Unit 10, Topic A	A-7, A-8
– Memory leak	Unit 5, Topic C	C-6
– BSOD / stop	Unit 5, Topic C	C-2
– OS boot failure	Unit 5, Topic C	C-3
– Driver issues	Unit 5, Topic C	C-3
– Runaway process	Unit 5, Topic C	C-7
– Cannot mount drive	Unit 7, Topic C	C-5
– Cannot write to system log	Unit 7, Topic C	C-4
– Slow OS performance	Unit 7, Topic C	C-5
– Patch update failure	Unit 9, Topic D	D-3
– Service failure	Unit 5, Topic C	C-3
– Hangs; no shut down	Unit 5, Topic C	C-5
– Users cannot print	Unit 10, Topic B	B-4
• Cause of common problems		
– Malware	Unit 8, Topic D	D-6
	Unit 5, Topic C	C-7
– Unauthorized software	Unit 5, Topic C	C-7
– Software firewall	Unit 8, Topic D	D-5
	Unit 9, Topic C	C-1, C-2
– User account control (UAC/SUDO)	Unit 10, Topic A	A-7
– Improper permissions	Unit 7, Topic C	
	Unit 10, Topic A	A-7, A-8
– Corrupted files	Unit 5, Topic C	C-3
– Lack of hard drive space	Unit 7, Topic C	C-4, IPA
– Lack of system resources	Unit 7, Topic C	C-5
– Virtual memory (misconfigured, corrupt)	Unit 5, Topic C	C-7
– Fragmentation	Unit 7, Topic C	C-3
– Encryption	Unit 7, Topic C	C-5

Objective	Conceptual information	Supporting activities
– Print server drivers/services	Unit 10, Topic B	B-4
– Print spooler	Unit 10, Topic B	B-4
• Software tools		
– System logs	Unit 7, Topic C	C-4
– Monitoring tools (Resource Monitor, Performance Monitor)	Unit 7, Topic C	C-4
	Unit 10, Topic C	C-1
– Defragmentation tools	Unit 7, Topic C	C-3

Objective	Conceptual information	Supporting activities
6.4 — Given a scenario, effectively diagnose network problems, selecting the appropriate tools and methods		
• Common problems		
– Internet connectivity failure	Unit 9, Topic C	C-1, C-2
– Email failure	Unit 9, Topic C	C-1, C-2
– Resource unavailable	Unit 9, Topic C	C-1, C-2
– DHCP server misconfigured	Unit 9, Topic C	C-1, C-2
– Non-functional or unreachable	Unit 9, Topic C	C-1, C-2
– Destination host unreachable	Unit 9, Topic C	C-1, C-2
– Unknown host	Unit 9, Topic C	C-1, C-2
– Default gateway misconfigured	Unit 9, Topic C	C-1, C-2
– Failure of service provider	Unit 9, Topic C	C-1, C-2
– Can reach by IP, not by host name	Unit 9, Topic C	C-1, C-2
• Causes of common problems	Unit 9, Topic C	C-1, C-2
– Improper IP configuration	Unit 9, Topic C	C-1, C-2
– VLAN configuration	Unit 9, Topic C	C-1, C-2
– Port security	Unit 9, Topic C	C-1, C-2
– Improper subnetting	Unit 9, Topic C	C-1, C-2
– Component failure	Unit 9, Topic C	C-1, C-2
– Incorrect OS route tables	Unit 9, Topic C	C-1, C-2
– Bad cables	Unit 9, Topic C	C-1, C-2
– Firewall (misconfiguration, hardware failure, software failure)	Unit 9, Topic C	C-1, C-2
– Misconfigured NIC, routing/switch issues	Unit 9, Topic C	C-1, C-2
– DNS and/or DHCP failure	Unit 9, Topic C	C-1, C-2
– Misconfigured hosts file	Unit 9, Topic C	C-1, C-2

Objective	Conceptual information	Supporting activities
• Networking tools	Unit 9, Topic B	B-1
– ping	Unit 9, Topic B	B-3
– tracert / traceroute	Unit 9, Topic B	B-4
– ipconfig / ifconfig	Unit 9, Topic B	B-2, B-3
– nslookup	Unit 9, Topic B	B-4
– net use / mount	Unit 9, Topic B	B-5
– route	Unit 9, Topic B	B-2
– nbtstat	Unit 9, Topic B	B-6
– netstat	Unit 9, Topic B	B-6

6.5 — Given a scenario, effectively troubleshoot storage problems, selecting the appropriate tools and methods

Objective	Conceptual information	Supporting activities
• Common problems		
– Slow file access	Unit 7, Topic C	C-5
– OS not found	Unit 5, Topic C	C-3
– Data not available	Unit 7, Topic C	C-5
– Unsuccessful backup	Unit 12, Topic C	C-5
– Error lights	Unit 7, Topic C	C-5
– Unable to mount the device	Unit 7, Topic C	C-5
– Drive not available	Unit 7, Topic C	C-5
– Cannot access logical drive	Unit 7, Topic C	C-5
– Data corruption	Unit 7, Topic C	C-5
– Slow I/O performance	Unit 7, Topic C	C-5
– Restore failure	Unit 12, Topic C	C-7
– Cache failure	Unit 7, Topic C	C-5
– Multiple drive failure	Unit 7, Topic C	C-5
• Causes of common problems		
– Media failure	Unit 5, Topic C	C-1, C-2, C-3
– Drive failure	Unit 5, Topic C	C-1
– Controller failure	Unit 5, Topic C	C-1
	Unit 6, Topic D	D-1, D-2, D-3
– HBA failure	Unit 6, Topic D	D-1, D-2, D-3
– Loose connectors	Unit 5, Topic C	C-4
– Cable problems	Unit 7, Topic C	C-5

Objective	Conceptual information	Supporting activities
– Misconfiguration	Unit 5, Topic C	C-3
– Improper termination	Unit 6, Topic D	D-1
– Corrupt boot sector	Unit 5, Topic C	C-3
– Corrupt file system table	Unit 5, Topic C	C-3
– Array rebuild	Unit 7, Topic C	C-5
– Improper disk partition	Unit 5, Topic C	C-3
– Bad sectors	Unit 5, Topic C	C-3
– Cache battery failure	Unit 5, Topic C	C-5
– Cache turned off	Unit 5, Topic C	C-5
– Insufficient space	Unit 5, Topic C	C-5
– Improper RAID configuration	Unit 5, Topic C	C-5
– Mismatched drives	Unit 5, Topic C	C-5
– Backplane failure	Unit 5, Topic C	C-2, C-3
• Storage tools		
– Portioning tools	Unit 7, Topic A	A-5
– Disk management	Unit 7, Topic A	A-2, A-3
	Unit 7, Topic C	
	Unit 10, Topic B	B-1
– RAID array management	Unit 7, Topic B	B-1
	Unit 7, Topic C	C-5
– Array management	Unit 7, Topic B	B-1
	Unit 7, Topic C	C-5
– System logs	Unit 7, Topic C	C-4
– Net use / mount command	Unit 7, Topic C	C-5
– Monitoring tools	Unit 7, Topic C	C-4

Appendix B

CompTIA Server+ acronyms

This appendix covers these additional topics:

A Acronyms appearing on the CompTIA Server+ exams covering 2009 objectives.

Topic A: Acronym list

Explanation   The following is a list of acronyms and abbreviations that appear on the CompTIA Server+ Certification exam (2009 Edition). Candidates are encouraged to review the complete list and attain a working knowledge of all listed abbreviations as a part of a comprehensive exam preparation program.

Acronym	Spelled out
*nix	Unix/Linux/Solaris/OS X/BSD
AD	Active Directory
AGP	Advanced Graphics Port
AMD-V	AMD Virtualization
BIOS	Basic Input/Output System
BSOD	Blue Screen of Death
CPU	Central Processing Unit
CRU	Customer Replaceable Unit
DC	Domain Controller
DHCP	Dynamic Host Configuration Protocol
DMZ	Demilitarized Zone
DNS	Domain Name Service
DSRM	Directory Services Restore Mode
EISA	Extended Industry Standard Architecture
FAT	File Allocation Table
FRU	Field Replaceable Unit
FTP	File Transfer Protocol
HBA	Host Bus Adapter
HCL	Hardware Compatibility List
HID	Human Interface Device
HTTP	Hyper Text Transport Protocol
HTTPS	Secure Hyper Text Transfer Protocol
HVAC	Heating, Ventilating and Air Conditioning
IMAP4	Internet Mail Access Protocol

Acronym	Spelled out
ISA	Industry Standard Architecture
iSCSI	Internetworking Small Computer Serial Interface
JBOD	Just a bunch of disks
LAN	Local Area Network
LDAP	Lightweight Directory Access Protocol
LKGC	Last Known Good Configuration
LUN	Logical Unit Number
NOS	Network Operating System
NTFS	New Technology File System
NTP	Network Time Protocol
NX	No Execute
OS	Operating System
OSPF	Open Shortest Path First
PCI	Peripheral Component Interconnect
POP3	Post Office Protocol
RAID	Redundant Array of Inexpensive/Integrated Disks/Drives
RAM	Random Access Memory
SAS	Serial Attached SCSI
SATA	Serial ATA
SCSI	Small Computer Serial Interface
SLA	Service Level Agreement
SMTP	Simple Mail Transport Protocol
SNMP	Simple Network Management Protocol
TCP/IP	Transmission Control Protocol / Internet Protocol
USB	Universal Serial Bus
VLAN	Virtual Local Area Network
VM	Virtual Machine

Acronym	Spelled out
VMFS	VMWare File System
VoIP	Voice over IP
VPN	Virtual Private Network
VT	Virtualization Technology
WBEM	Web-based Enterprise Management
WMI	Windows Management Instrumentation
WORM	Write Once Read Many
XD	Execute Disable

Course summary

This summary contains information to help you bring the course to a successful conclusion. Using this information, you will be able to:

A Use the summary text to reinforce what you've learned in class.

B Determine the next courses in this series (if any), as well as any other resources that might help you continue to learn about server management.

Topic A: Course summary

Use the following summary text to reinforce what you've learned in class.

Unit summaries

Unit 1

In this unit, you learned that **system cases** come in a wide variety of sizes and shapes, and you identified the characteristics and common features of various chassis styles. You also learned about **power supplies** and **cooling mechanisms** for removing the heat generated by servers and related components, in both standalone and rack-mounted server configurations.

Unit 2

In this unit, you learned about **CPUs** and the features that determine their performance characteristics. You then examined the various CPU packages and the corresponding slots and sockets into which they're inserted. Next, you learned about **motherboards** and the various form factors for them.

Unit 3

In this unit, you learned about the **BIOS**. You learned that hardware configuration data used by the BIOS is stored in CMOS, which is powered by a battery installed on the motherboard. You then learned how to use the BIOS setup utility to change the **CMOS configuration data**, how to flash the BIOS, and how to recover from a failed BIOS update attempt. You also learned that the BIOS tests a computer's hardware at boot time by following the **POST** process, and you learned about various beep and numeric error codes that might be reported during the POST if the BIOS detects a hardware failure.

Unit 4

In this unit, you learned that **RAM** is the hardware component that stores active data and applications. You also learned about the various characteristics of memory—such as whether it's volatile or non-volatile and synchronous or asynchronous—and about the technology by which it's accessed. Finally, you learned about the various **memory modules**, including SIMMs, DIMMs, and SODIMMs. You also learned that errors in memory can be detected and corrected through **parity** or **ECC**.

Unit 5

In this unit, you learned that there are various methods you can use to troubleshoot problems: the CompTIA Server+, CompTIA Network+, Novell, and ASID **troubleshooting models**. You also learned that problem and resolution tracking is important to long-term success. Then, you learned about the hardware and software tools in a typical technician's **toolkit**, identifying the function of each tool and its use in troubleshooting. Next, you learned about the **common symptoms, causes, and resolutions** of problems with power supplies, motherboards, CPUs, memory, BIOS, and CMOS. Lastly, you learned how to diagnose and resolve problems with **system startup**, including boot errors, startup errors, and operating system load errors.

Unit 6

In this unit, you learned that a **bus** is a communication pathway, and you learned how a computer's hardware communicates by using interrupts, IRQ lines, I/O addresses, DMA channels, and base memory addresses. You learned that the **PCI bus**, which is currently the most popular expansion bus, supports PnP and shared system resources and is considerably faster than previous bus technologies. Next, you learned that **drive controllers** are the adapter boards that plug into a PC's expansion slots, and you learned about the various **interface standards**, including IDE/ATA, SCSI, USB, and IEEE 1394. You learned about **video bus standards**, such as AGP, and you learned that you can use PCI and PCIe buses to add video adapters to your systems. You also learned about **display standards** and **sound cards**, and you identified common **symptoms** of hardware-related problems.

Unit 7

In this unit, you installed a **hard drive** and prepared it for use by the operating system. You also examined **external storage technologies**, such as NAS, SANs, and tape libraries. Then you learned about RAID storage technologies and explored the various **RAID levels** so that you're prepared to select the correct level for a given scenario. Lastly, you identified common symptoms of **hardware-related problems** and identified possible resolutions to those problems.

Unit 8

In this unit, you learned about **basic networking models** and **server roles**. Then you learned that **server virtualization** enables you to implement the functionality of multiple servers via software running on one physical host. You also learned about the benefits and drawbacks of virtualization. Next, you installed **Linux** and signed onto the new Linux server, and you installed **Windows Server 2008** and customized the installation.

Unit 9

In this unit, you learned about **network cabling** types, features, and specifications, and you examined the **TCP/IP protocol stack**. Then, you learned how MAC addresses, IP addresses, character-based names, and port addresses are used to **identify computers** on a network. You learned how the **DNS service** resolves character-based host names to IP addresses. Next, you learned about testing the functionality of a TCP/IP network connection by using tools such as **ping**, **nslookup**, and **tracert**. Finally, you learned about common networking problems.

Unit 10

In this unit, you learned how to implement and manage **user accounts** and **groups** on a network operating system using **Active Directory** in Windows Server 2008. You then used those accounts to secure a network resource, and you learned how to control user accounts by using **group policies** and **scripts**. Next, you learned how to implement and manage **disk resources** on a network operating system by determining the status of your server's disks and volumes, creating shadow volumes, and implementing disk quotas. Finally, you learned how to **monitor** the server and network by using Performance Monitor, SNMP, and system management scripts, using WBEM and WMI.

Unit 11

In this unit, you learned that **network documentation** typically contains descriptions of systems and their components, network diagrams and maps, contact information, and vendor-specific information. You also learned about the various tools used to create the documentation, including logs and dedicated inventory software. Next, you learned about the **disposal** and **destruction** of computers and components, and you learned about **environmentally appropriate** ways to dispose of decommissioned hardware. You learned how to establish **physical access security**, and you examined how logs can be used to increase physical security and surveillance methods. Finally, you identified **biometric authentication systems**, such as fingerprint scanners, hand geometry scanners, retina scanners, iris scanners, voice analyzers, and signature verification.

Unit 12

In this unit, you learned about the factors to consider when you purchase a **backup unit**, and you learned about different **backup types**. Then you learned about **load balancing** and **clustering**, and you learned that **system monitoring software** can detect problems such as high temperatures and failing hard drives, fans, and power supplies. Finally, you learned that it's essential to have a **disaster recovery plan**.

Topic B: Continued learning after class

It is impossible to learn server management in a single day or even a week. To get the most out of this class, you should begin working with servers and network operating systems as soon as possible. We also offer resources for continued learning.

Next courses in this series

This is the only course in this series.

Other resources

For more information, visit www.axzopress.com.

Glossary

AC (alternating current)
Current that flows repeatedly back and forth through the circuit at a constantly varying voltage level.

Access time
Overall amount of time between when a request is made and when the data is available on the bus.

Accounting
The system security stage that involves tracking the user's actions.

ACL (access control List)
A list of access control entries (ACEs), each of which specifies a "who" and a permission. Most resources will be able to access your NDS database and use the user and group accounts as the "who."

Agent
SNMP software running on a managed device.

APIPA (Automatic Private IP Addressing)
A Microsoft proprietary, though widely implemented, technique for assigning IP addresses when a DHCP server is unavailable and no static address has been manually assigned. APIPA was standardized by the IETF in RFC 3927.

Authentication
The positive identification of the entity, either a person or a system, that wants to access information or services that have been secured.

Authorization
A predetermined level of access granted to an entity so that it can access a resource.

Backbone
A primary segment of the network that connects other network segments. The bandwidth of a backbone is typically greater than that of any of the networks it interconnects.

BIOS (Basic Input/Output System)
The computer's firmware—a set of software instructions that are stored on a chip on the motherboard and that enable basic computer functions, such as getting input from the keyboard and mouse.

Bus
A communication pathway within a computer.

CAS latency
A delay between when an address of the data being requested arrives on the bus and when the memory is ready to return that data.

Chassis intrusion switch
A switch that is triggered when you open the system case. Such switches either prevent you from booting your PC or activate an alert or alarm.

CIM (Common Information Model)
A model that describes how IT resources, including applications, servers, and hardware devices, are represented as programming objects.

Client/server authentication
An authentication system in which user accounts are created centrally and stored on a server.

CMOS
An area of memory that stores BIOS configuration information.

Conductor
A material that permits the flow of electricity.

Core
An execution unit within a CPU. Modern CPUs often have two or more cores.

Data bus
The bus that transfers data between the CPU and RAM.

DC (direct current)
Current that flows in a single direction at a constant voltage through a circuit.

Disaster recovery plan (DRP)
An enterprise-level planning document that describes how the organization will return to normal operations after a disaster.

Disk quota
A setting that specifies the maximum amount of space allocated to network users.

Distribution group
A group that has no security functions and is used with e-mail applications.

DNS (Domain Name System)
The service that correlates computer names with IP addresses and vice versa.

Drive controller

The adapter board that plugs into a PC's expansion slot.

Drive interface

The communications standard that defines how data flows to and from the disk drive.

ESD (electrostatic discharge)

A phenomenon that occurs when the charges on separate objects are unequal and the charge imbalance creates an electrical field that can cause objects to attract or repel each other.

Expansion bus

The bus to which add-on adapter cards are connected to enhance the functionality of a PC.

File system

The scheme that defines how data is stored on a drive. The file system includes the tables and structures that describe where files are stored on the volume and the size of the various volumes on the computer.

Firmware

Software written permanently or semi-permanently to a computer chip.

Grandfather-Father-Son (GFS)

A backup strategy that uses three sets of tapes for daily, weekly, and monthly backup sets. You rotate through these tape sets according to a specific scheme.

Heat pipes

Small tubes, typically built into cooling fins, filled with a small amount of fluid.

Heat sink

A cooling mechanism that absorbs and transfers heat better than its surroundings.

Hibernate mode

An ACPI-defined power state in which the computer takes all current applications running in RAM, saves them to the system's swap file on the hard disk, and then turns the system's power off.

Host

The physical computer than enables one or more virtual machines to run on it. Also, a computer on a network.

Hybrid RAID

RAID implementations that combine two or more standard RAID levels.

Interrupt

A signal sent by a device to the CPU to gain its attention.

IPv4

Version 4 of the TCP/IP specification; it defines 32-bit addresses composed of four 8-bit numbers, written in decimal notation separated by periods.

IPv6

Version 6 of the TCP/IP specification; it defines 128-bit addresses composed of eight 16-bit numbers, written in hexadecimal notation separated by colons.

iSCSI

A standard that implements SCSI commands and protocols over an Ethernet network.

Journaling

A file system technique in which data changes are written to a log file before being committed to disk, making such file systems less likely to become corrupt in the event of a system crash.

MAC address

Media Access Control address, a unique and permanent identifier embedded in a network adapter at the time of manufacturing.

MIB (Management Information Base)

A database of information maintained by an SNMP agent.

Multi-mode fiber optic cabling

Fiber optic cabling that supports multiple transmission paths.

NAS (network attached storage)

A self-contained storage device connected to the network. In essence, a NAS device is a standalone file server.

NX (no execution)

A CPU feature than enables the system to separate data and executable code into distinct areas of memory.

One-factor authentication

Authentication requiring only one type of input, which is usually something you know—for example, your user name and password.

PCIe

PCI Express bus specification. Sometimes called PCI-E.

PCIx

PCI Extended bus specification. Sometimes called PCI-X.

Port

A numeric address between 0 and 65,535 that identifies an application.

POST (power-on self test)
A series of basic checks that the computer runs at startup to make sure the system components are in working order.

Private IP addresses
IP addresses that are valid on the local network but invalid for use on the Internet.

Public IP addresses
IP addresses that are valid on and visible to devices on the Internet.

Rack cooling
Cooling and conditioning applied to a single computer and networking equipment rack. Rack cooling can either augment room cooling or replace it.

Rack unit
A standard height within a computer rack. One rack unit (1U) is 1.75".

Registers
Small, yet very fast memory locations within the CPU.

RG-58
The type of coaxial cable used for Ethernet networking.

Room cooling
Cooling and conditioning applied to an entire room used to house computer and networking equipment.

Row cooling
Cooling and conditioning applied to a row of connected computer and networking equipment racks. Row cooling can either augment room cooling or replace it.

SAN (storage area network)
A storage system that's connected to a network and provides block-level storage facilities. A SAN can replace a server's primary hard drive or provide supplemental storage.

Security group
A group that can be used to grant permissions to network resources.

Shadow volume
A read-only copy of files, including open files, on a selected volume at a particular point in time.

Single-mode fiber optic cabling
Fiber optic cabling that supports a single transmission path.

Single-phase electricity
Electricity delivered over three wires. An AC voltage is delivered on two conductors that vary in unison (though opposite in polarity), with the third conductor acting as a ground connection. See *Three-phase electricity*.

Six-cartridge backup strategy
A backup strategy that uses fewer tapes than other systems, but is unsuitable for large backup sets. It uses six tapes or sets of tapes in a specific rotation.

SLA (service-level agreement)
A document specifying how clients and support personnel are to interact, what they can expect from each other, and what timeframes are acceptable for the resolution of problems.

SNMP (Simple Network Management Protocol)
A standard technology for managing devices connected to a network.

Stepping
A version indicator within a CPU line. A stepping is a combination of letters and numbers, such as A0. A change in the number, such as to A1, indicates a minor design change. A change in the letter indicates a more substantial change.

STP
Shielded twisted-pair, a type of network cabling.

Three-factor authentication
An authentication system that requires three types of input: something you know, something you have, and something you are.

Three-phase electricity
Electricity delivered over three conductors, with AC power being provided on all three (sometimes a fourth conductor provides a ground connection). The peak of the AC signal in one conductor is delayed by one-third of a cycle from the next conductor. See *Single-phase electricity*.

Tower of Hanoi
A backup strategy that uses five sets of tapes rotated in a specific scheme based on the mathematical game of the same name.

Trap
A condition that will cause an SNMP agent to contact the network management system rather than waiting to be polled.

Troubleshooting
The process of determining the cause of, and ultimately the solution to, a problem.

Two-factor authentication
An authentication system that requires two types of input: something you know, plus either something you have or something you are.

User account
A collection of information that pertains to a user, such as the person's user name, password, access rights, and permissions.

User name
A name that uniquely identifies the user to a computer or network system when he or she logs in.

UTP
Unshielded twisted-pair, a type of network cabling.

Virtualization
A technology through which one or more simulated computers run within a physical computer.

VM (virtual machine)
A simulated computer running on a host in a virtualized environment.

Voltage
The force of electricity caused by a difference in charge, or electrical potential, at two locations; measured in volts.

Volume
A logical drive.

WBEM (Web-based Enterprise Management)
A standards-based architecture for application and systems management.

WMI (Windows Management Instrumentation)
Microsoft's implementation of WBEM.

Index